Latin America

History and Culture

An Encyclopedia for Students

Barbara A. Tenenbaum, *Editor in Chief*

Volume 4

CHARLES SCRIBNER'S SONS
An Imprint of The Gale Group
New York

Copyright © 1999 Charles Scribner's Sons

All rights reserved. No part of this book may be reproduced in any form without the permission of Charles Scribner's Sons.

Developed for Charles Scribner's Sons by Visual Education Corporation, Princeton, N.J.

Library of Congress Cataloging-in-Publication Data

Tenenbaum, Barbara A.
    Latin America, history and culture : an encyclopedia for students /
  Barbara A. Tenenbaum, editor in chief.
      p. cm.
    Includes bibliographical references (v. 4, p.   ) and indexes.
    Contents: v. 1. Acapulco — Climate and vegetation. Index — v. 2. Clothing —
Immigration and emigration. Index—v. 3. Imperialism—Platt Amendment. Index —
v. 4. Political parties — Zimmerman telegram. Bibliography. Index.
    ISBN 0-684-80576-6 (set : alk. paper). — ISBN 0-684-80572-3 (v. 1 : alk. paper). — ISBN
0-684-80573-1 (v. 2 : alk. paper) — ISBN 0-684-80574-X (v. 3 : alk. paper) —
ISBN 0-684-80575-8 (v. 4 : alk. paper)
    1. Latin America Encyclopedias.   I. Title.
F1406.T46   1999
980´.003 — dc21
                                                                                   99-23057
                                                                                    CIP

1 2 3 4 5 6 7 8 9 10

PRINTED IN THE UNITED STATES OF AMERICA

A Time Line of Latin America

ca. 9000 B.C.	*Humans establish settlements in Latin America.*
ca. 4000 B.C.	*Agricultural settlements develop in Amazon region.*
ca. 3500 B.C.	*Llamas are domesticated in Peru.*
1400–400 B.C.	*Chavin culture develops in South America.*
ca. 1000 B.C.	*Olmec culture flourishes in Mexico.*
ca. A.D. 100–900	*Moche, Tiwanaku, and Huari cultures develop in South America.*
	Teotihuacán and Maya cities develop in Mexico.
ca. 950	*Toltec civilization emerges in Mexico.*
ca. 1100–1474	*Chimu kingdom develops in northern Peru.*
ca. 1200	*Inca civilization emerges in Peru.*
ca. 1300	*Aztec civilization develops near Mexico City.*
1434–1519	*Aztec-dominated Triple Alliance gains control over Valley of Mexico and builds an empire.*
1460–1470	*Inca conquer the Chimu.*
1469	*Isabella of Castile marries Ferdinand of Aragon, uniting the kingdoms of Spain.*
1492	*Christopher Columbus reaches Caribbean islands.*
1493	*Columbus settles Hispaniola.*
1494	*Spain and Portugal sign Treaty of Tordesillas.*
1498	*Vasco da Gama sails around Africa to India.*
1500	*Pedro Álvares Cabral lands on the Brazilian coast.*
ca. 1500–1860s	*Approximately 12 million Africans are brought to Latin America as slaves.*
1507	*First world map showing "America" is published.*
1511	*First Spanish settlement is established in Cuba.*
	First audiencia in Spanish America is established on Hispaniola.
1512	*First Roman Catholic bishop arrives in America.*
1513	*Juan Ponce de León claims Florida for Spain.*
	Vasco Núñez de Balboa sees the Pacific Ocean from Panama.

Pachacuti *(ca. 1391–1473)*
Prince Henry the Navigator *(1394–1460)*
Christopher Columbus *(ca. 1451–1506)*
Amerigo Vespucci *(1454–1512)*
Moctezuma II *(ca. 1466–ca.1520)*
Bartolomé de Las Casas *(1474–1566)*
Diego de Almagro *(ca. 1475–1538)*
Vasco Núñez de Balboa *(ca. 1475–1519)*
Ferdinand Magellan *(ca. 1480–1521)*
Hernán Cortés *(ca. 1484–1547)*
Pedro de Alvarado y Mesía *(ca. 1485–ca.1541)*
Atahualpa *(ca. 1498–1533)*
Pedro de Valdivia *(1500–1553)*

Francisco de Orellana *(1511–1546)*

1519	Hernán Cortés founds first Spanish city in Mexico.	
	Charles I is crowned in Spain.	
1519–1522	Ferdinand Magellan circumnavigates the globe.	
1521	Cortés conquers Aztec empire.	
1522–1524	Franciscan missionaries arrive in Mexico.	
1524	Council of the Indies is formed to oversee Spanish colonies in the Americas.	
1527	Civil war erupts in Inca empire between Huascar and Atahualpa.	**Philip II of Spain** *(1527–1598)*
1531	According to legend, the Virgin of Guadalupe appears in Mexico.	**John Hawkins** *(1532–1595)*
1535	Viceroyalty of New Spain is created.	**Alonso de Ercilla y Zúñiga** *(1533–1594)*
1536	Francisco Pizarro and Diego de Almagro conquer Inca empire.	**Garcilaso de la Vega El Inca** *(1539–1616)*
1541	Spanish settlement of Chile begins.	
	Pizarro is assassinated.	
	Francisco de Orellana leads the first expedition down the Amazon.	
1542	Bartolomé de Las Casas speaks out against mistreatment of the Indians.	
	Spain revokes its grants to conquistadors' heirs.	**Francis Drake** *(1545–1596)*
1549	Tomé de Sousa builds Brazilian capital at Salvador.	
ca. 1555	*Popul Vuh* manuscript is created by the Maya.	
1556	Philip II becomes king of Spain.	
1565	City of St. Augustine is founded in Florida.	
	Jesuit missionaries arrive in Spanish America.	
1570–1571	Holy Office of the Inquisition is established in Lima and Mexico City.	
1571	Manila galleon trade route is established between Mexico and the Philippines.	
1572	Viceroy Francisco de Toledo of Peru captures Tupac Amaru I and destroys last Inca settlement at Vilcabamba.	
1580–1640	Portuguese and Spanish monarchies are united.	**Santa Rosa de Lima** *(1586–1617)*
1598	Juan de Oñate establishes a settlement at San Juan de los Caballeros in New Mexico.	**John Maurits** *(1604–1679)*
ca. 1609	Santa Fe is founded in New Mexico.	
1621	Dutch West India Company is founded to establish plantations in South America.	
1630–1654	Dutch govern northeast region of Brazil.	
1637–1639	Brazil's boundary expands to include the entire Amazon basin.	**Sor Juana Inés de la Cruz**
1654	Dutch are ousted from Brazil.	*(ca. 1651–1695)*

1680–1692	*Pueblo Rebellion temporarily ends Spanish control of New Mexico.*	
1700–1713	*War of Spanish Succession brings Bourbon monarch to the Spanish throne.*	Junípero Serra *(1713–1784)*
		Charles III of Spain *(1716–1788)*
1719	*Viceroyalty of New Granada is established.*	
1730–1735	*Comunero Revolt erupts in Paraguay over Jesuit land.*	
		Aleijadinho *(ca. 1738–1814)*
1739	*Viceroyalty of New Granada is reestablished.*	Tupac Amaru *(1738–1781)*
1756–1763	*Seven Years' War in Europe gives Britain ownership of French colonies in the Americas.*	Toussaint L'Ouverture *(1743–1803)*
		Francisco de Miranda *(1750–1816)*
		Tupac Catari *(1750–1781)*
1767	*Jesuits are expelled from Spanish America.*	Miguel Hidalgo y Costilla *(1753–1811)*
1769	*Spaniards establish settlements in California.*	Jean Jacques Dessalines *(1758–1806)*
		José Bonifácio de Andrada *(1763–1838)*
1776	*Viceroyalty of Río de la Plata is established.*	Henri Christophe *(1767–1820)*
1777	*Portugal and Spain sign the Treaty of San Ildefonso.*	Josefa Ortiz de Domínguez *(1768–1829)*
		Bernardo O'Higgins *(1778–1842)*
1780–1783	*Tupac Amaru II leads Great Andean Rebellion.*	Simón Bolívar *(1783–1830)*
1781	*Comunero Revolt erupts in Colombia.*	
1791–1804	*Haitian Revolution ends French colonial rule and abolishes slavery there.*	Antonio López de Santa Anna *(1794–1876)*
		Antonio José de Sucre Alcalá *(1795–1830)*
1803	*United States purchases the Louisiana Territory from France.*	Pedro I of Brazil *(1798–1834)*
1807–1808	*Napoleon invades Iberian Peninsula; Portuguese court flees to Brazil.*	Benito Juárez *(1806–1872)*
1810	*Simón Bolívar joins revolutionary movement in Venezuela.*	Juan Bautista Alberdi *(1810–1884)*
1811	*Paraguay declares its independence from Spain.*	
		Juan Pablo Duarte *(1813–1876)*
1816	*Argentina declares its independence from Spain.*	
1818	*Chile wins its independence from Spain.*	
1819	*Adams-Onís Treaty gives Spanish Florida to the United States. Gran Colombia is formed.*	
1821	*Mexico becomes independent.*	Gabriel García Moreno *(1821–1875)*
1822	*Brazil declares its independence from Portugal.*	
1823	*Monroe Doctrine prohibits colonization of the Americas.*	
1823–1824	*United Provinces of Central America is formed.*	
1824	*Battle of Ayacucho liberates South America from Spanish colonial rule.*	William Walker *(1824–1860)*
1825	*Bolivia becomes an independent nation.*	Pedro II of Brazil *(1825–1891)*
1828	*Uruguay wins its independence.*	Antonio Leocadio Guzmán Blanco *(1829–1899)*
1835–1836	*Battle of the Alamo spurs the movement for Texas independence; battle of San Jacinto results in Texas independence.*	Porfirio Díaz *(1830–1915)*

1836–1839	War erupts between the Peru-Bolivia Confederation and Chile.	
1838	Honduras and Costa Rica withdraw from the United Provinces of Central America.	Joaquím Maria Machado de Assis *(1839–1908)*
1846–1848	Mexican-American War is fought over the territory of present-day Texas.	Antonio Maceo *(1845–1896)*
1847–1848	Caste War of Yucatán threatens the Creole government there.	Princess Isabel of Brazil *(1846–1921)*
1848	Treaty of Guadalupe Hidalgo ends the Mexican-American War and establishes the boundary between the two nations.	
1853	Gadsden Purchase transfers 30 million acres of Mexican land to the United States.	Hipólito Yrigoyen *(1852–1933)* José Julián Martí y Pérez *(1853–1895)*
1856	El Salvador becomes an independent republic.	José Batlle y Ordóñez *(1856–1929)*
1856–1857	Central American nations unite to defeat William Walker.	Juan Vicente Gómez *(1857–1935)*
1863	French troops invade Mexico; Maximilian becomes emperor of Mexico.	
1864–1870	War of the Triple Alliance is fought between Paraguay and the allied forces of Argentina, Brazil, and Uruguay.	
1865	Dominican Republic becomes independent.	
1866–1867	Napoleon withdraws troops from Mexico; Maximilian is executed.	
1868–1878	Ten Years' War for Cuban independence is fought.	Francisco Indalecio Madero *(1873–1913)*
1870–1930	Waves of European immigration transform Brazil, Uruguay, and Argentina.	Francisco "Pancho" Villa *(1878–1923)* Emiliano Zapata *(ca. 1879–1919)*
1879–1884	War of the Pacific pits Chile against Bolivia and Peru.	Mario Vargas Llosa *(1883–1954)*
1886	Slavery is abolished in Cuba.	Diego Rivera *(1886–1957)*
1888	Slavery is abolished in Brazil.	
1889	First Pan-American Conference is held in Washington, D.C. Brazilian empire falls.	Gabriela Mistral *(1889–1957)* Rafael Leónidas Trujillo Molina *(1891–1961)*
1895	Cuba begins a second struggle for independence from Spain.	Juan Domingo Perón *(1895–1974)*
1898	USS Maine *blows up in Havana harbor; Spanish-American War begins. Cuba and Puerto Rico win their independence from Spain.*	
1899–1902	U.S. Army occupies Cuba. War of the Thousand Days brings violence to Colombia.	Miguel Ángel Asturias *(1899–1974)* Fulgencio Batista y Zaldívar *(1901–1973)*
1903	Panama becomes independent of Colombia. United States passes the Platt Amendment protecting its interests in Cuba and limiting the island's sovereignty.	
1904	Construction begins on the Panama Canal.	Pablo Neruda *(1904–1973)*
1910–1920	Mexican Revolution is fought to oust President Porfirio Díaz and to demand land reform.	Salvador Allende Gossens *(1908–1973)*

1913	*United States ambassador plots with counterrevolutionary forces in Mexico; President Madero is assassinated.*	Jorge Amado *(born 1912)* Alfredo Stroessner *(born 1912)*
1914	*Panama Canal opens.*	
1915	*United States invades Mexican port of Veracruz.*	Augusto Pinochet Ugarte *(born 1915)*
1916–1924	*United States occupies the Dominican Republic.*	
1917	*New Mexican constitution is adopted.*	Oscar Arnulfo Romero *(1917–1980)*
1922	*Modern Art Week is celebrated in São Paulo, Brazil.*	María Eva Duarte de Perón *(1919–1952)*
1926–1929	*Cristero Rebellion erupts in Mexico as Catholics rebel against anticlerical measures.*	Fidel Castro Ruz *(born 1926)* Gabriel García Márquez *(born 1927)*
1929	*World is hit by a severe economic depression.*	Ernesto "Che" Guevara *(1928–1967)* Carlos Fuentes *(born 1928)*
1930	*Getúlio Vargas takes power in Brazil.*	Carlos Saúl Menem *(born 1930)*
1932–1935	*Chaco War breaks out between Bolivia and Paraguay.*	Derek Walcott *(born 1930)* Mario Vargas Llosa *(born 1936)*
1939–1945	*Latin Americans support Allied forces during World War II.*	Alberto Keinya Fujimori *(born 1938)*
1940s–1960s	*La Violencia claims 100,000 to 250,000 lives in Colombia.*	Oscar Arias Sánchez *(1940)* Pelé *(born 1940)*
1945	*Gabriela Mistral is the first Latin American woman to win the Nobel Prize for literature.*	Isabel Allende *(born 1942)* Daniel Ortega Saavedra *(born 1945)*
1947	*Nations of Western Hemisphere accept responsibility for their mutual defense in Rio Treaty.*	
1948	*Organization of American States (OAS) is formed.*	Carlos Salinas de Gortari *(born 1948)*
1952–1986	*Bolivian Revolution brings political and economic change to the country.*	Jean-Bertrand Aristide *(born 1953)*
1954	*Guatemalan coup, backed by the United States, forces President Arbenz to resign.*	
1959	*Cuban Revolution, led by Fidel Castro, ousts Fulgencio Batista.*	Rigoberta Menchú Tum *(born 1959)*
ca. 1960	*Civil war begins in Guatemala.*	
1960	*Brasília replaces Rio de Janeiro as the capital of Brazil.*	
1961	*Bay of Pigs Invasion by Cuban exiles is defeated.* *United States launches the Alliance for Progress.*	
1962	*Cuban missile crisis threatens the balance of world power.* *Jamaica becomes independent.* *OAS imposes sanctions against Cuba.*	
1963	*Pan-American highway is completed, linking the Americas from Alaska to Chile.*	
1964–1985	*Brazil is under military rule.*	
1968	*Student protest in Mexico City ends in bloodshed.*	
1969	*Football War between El Salvador and Honduras erupts in a soccer stadium.*	

1973	*Military coup ousts Chilean president Salvador Allende.*
1974–1983	*Argentina's Dirty War leaves thousands of political opponents dead or "disappeared."*
1977	*Panama Canal Treaty is signed, keeping the canal open to all nations, even during wartime.*
1979	*Sandinistas overthrow dictator Anastasio Somoza in Nicaragua.*
1980	*Mariel boatlift allows Cubans to leave for the United States.*
1981–1995	*Ecuador and Peru go to war over border dispute.*
1982	*Argentine military seizes British-owned Falkland Islands; Britain defeats Argentina in Falklands/Malvinas War.*
1983	*United States troops invade Grenada.*
1988	*Contras and Sandinistas sign cease-fire in Nicaragua.*
1989	*United States troops invade Panama and seize Manuel Noriega.* *Chile forces Augusto Pinochet to leave presidency.* *Paraguay ousts dictator Alfredo Stroessner.*
1990	*Alberto Fujimori is elected president of Peru.* *Violeta Barrios de Chamorro is elected president of Nicaragua.*
1992	*El Salvador's 12-year civil war ends.*
1993	*Changes to Argentina's constitution enable President Carlos Saúl Menem to run for re-election.* *Colombian army kills Pablo Escobar, boss of the Medellín drug cartel.*
1994	*North American Free Trade Agreement (NAFTA) goes into effect, sparking revolutionary activity in Chiapas, Mexico.* *United States troops return Jean-Bertrand Aristide to power in Haiti.* *Fernando Henrique Cardoso wins presidential election in Brazil.*
1995	*United States provides economic aid to Mexico.*
1996	*Guatemala's 35-year armed conflict ends.* *Tupac Amaru guerrillas seize hostages in Peru.*
1997	*Mexico's Institutional Revolutionary Party (PRI) loses its majority in congress for first time in 68 years.* *Peruvian troops kill Tupac Amaru rebels and free hostages.*
1998	*Hurricane Mitch devastates Central America.* *Ecuador and Peru end their border dispute.*
1999	*Panama takes possession of the Panama Canal.*

Political Parties

The political parties that emerged in most Latin American countries after independence in the early 1800s were organized around two opposing approaches to government, the liberal and the conservative. This division continues to define most political organizations in the region, although their basic definitions have changed.

In the 1800s, liberal was the equivalent of what conservative is today. At that time, the liberals were in favor of freeing the individual from the constraints placed by the church and the military. Consequently, liberals were intent on selling property held by the church. The conservatives, skeptical of change, supported the church and the military and considered them two important forces that promised continuity. Both groups had one common concern, however: the nonwhite population. The liberals were unsure of what to do with nonwhites, and the conservatives looked to the church for guidance. Neither group wanted to see the nonwhite population gain political, social, or economic influence.

In the 1900s, many countries, such as Cuba, Bolivia, Mexico, Peru, and Nicaragua, experienced revolutions. During this period, many political parties throughout Latin America included the term *revolution* in their names—such as Panama's Democratic Revolutionary Party (PRD), Bolivia's National Revolutionary Movement (MNR), and Peru's American Popular Revolutionary Alliance (APRA)—even when their programs may have been far from revolutionary. A single organization, currently known as the Institutional Revolutionary Party (PRI), has dominated Mexico's political life for decades after the country's president founded it in 1929. Although the PRI claimed to embody the ideals of the Mexican Revolution, it became corrupt and undemocratic. People also blamed the PRI for Mexico's economic downturn and a bloody rebellion in the southern province of Chiapas. By the late 1990s, the PRI faced serious challenges to its long supremacy in Mexican politics.

In some countries, anarchist*, socialist*, and Communist* parties emerged, primarily in Brazil, Uruguay, and Argentina, where there was heavy immigration from Europe. Another key feature of Latin American politics is that most countries have many parties, some with unique agendas, making for very lively, and often volatile, politics. Frequently, no single party is able to win a majority of votes, so it is common for several parties to unite in support of a candidate who is acceptable to the majority. These temporary unions are called coalitions, fronts, or alliances.

When a popularly elected government is considered too radical*, the military often intervenes and uses force to take over the government. The most notable example of this occurred in Chile, which had the longest running democratic tradition in Latin America until 1973, when President Salvador ALLENDE was ousted by the military and General Augusto PINOCHET came to power. Pinochet ruled with an iron hand until 1989 and remained a powerful force for another decade.

Each political party active in Latin America represents the interests of particular groups, such as organized labor or the military. Many parties exist to promote a particular program of political, social, or economic

* **anarchist** referring to anarchism, a political theory that promotes the idea that all governmental forms are unnecessary and undesirable
* **socialist** relating to socialism, a system in which the means of production and distribution of goods in a society are owned and controlled by the state
* **Communist** referring to a social system in which land, goods, and the means of production are owned by the state or community rather than by individuals
* **radical** favoring extreme change or reforms

change. One of Brazil's largest political organizations, the Brazilian Democratic Movement Party (PMDB) was founded to promote resistance to military government. The Brazilian Workers Party (PT), another important political organization, was founded by factory workers seeking the right to strike for better working conditions. By the late 1980s, the PT was also working for improved social and economic conditions for the rural and urban poor.

Pombaline Reforms

The Pombaline reforms were a series of laws that changed the administrative organization of BRAZIL and the economic, social, and cultural policies of the Portuguese empire. Enacted in the mid-1700s, these reforms were designed to increase the flow of wealth into the royal treasury of Portugal, weaken the influence of foreign merchants on Portuguese trade and commerce, and strengthen the Portuguese empire.

Reforming Portugal and Its Empire.
By the mid-1700s, the Portuguese empire had begun to decline in importance, and Portugal had become dependent, both militarily and economically, on England. When José I ascended the Portuguese throne in 1750, he appointed the Marquês de Pombal, a prominent statesman, as his prime minister. Pombal soon dominated Portuguese politics.

Shortly after his appointment, Pombal instituted a series of reforms to strengthen and reorganize Portugal and its empire. To limit the power of the CATHOLIC CHURCH, Pombal curbed the Holy Office of the INQUISITION by placing it under royal authority. He also changed Portuguese inheritance and property laws to prevent the church from accumulating more wealth. He expelled the Jesuits* from Portugal and its colonies to prevent them from gaining power in the empire.

Pombal also directed his reforms at cultural and economic life in Portugal and its colonies. He reorganized Portugal's educational and military systems and banned African slavery in Portugal and Indian slavery in Brazil. He encouraged the development of agriculture and industry by regulating the flow of imports and exports and by establishing monopolies* for certain products. To stimulate commerce overseas, Pombal founded TRADING COMPANIES and gave them exclusive rights to engage in trade activities.

Reforms in Brazil.
Because Pombal believed that Brazil was the key to restoring Portugal's power and prosperity, he appointed colonial administrators to implement and monitor his reforms there. In response to growing concern about foreign interests and claims in South America, Pombal decided to promote Portuguese settlement in the unoccupied areas of northern and western Brazil. He ordered the massive resettlement of more than 1,900 farmers from the Azores and Madeira islands—Portuguese possessions in the eastern Atlantic Ocean—to Brazil.

* **Jesuit** popular name for the Roman Catholic religious order officially known as the Society of Jesus; also, a member of that order

* **monopoly** exclusive control or domination of a particular type of business

Population and Population Growth

Pombal also instituted reforms to change the administrative organization of Brazil. He created new administrative districts and placed these and other formerly privately held districts under the authority of the Portuguese crown. He moved the capital of the viceroyalty* from BAHIA to RIO DE JANEIRO in 1763 and created new governing institutions, including the Junta do Comércio (Board of Trade) and the Erário Régio (Royal Treasury).

Pombal also instituted economic reforms in Brazil, including the creation of a Junta da Fazenda (Board of Treasury) in each captaincy. Accountable only to the Royal Treasury in Portugal, these local boards were responsible for collecting and distributing royal income. Pombal also created specialized economic institutions, such as the Mesas de Inspeção de Açúcar e Tabaco (Boards for the Inspection of Sugar and Tobacco), and established policies designed to encourage the expansion of agriculture, mining, and trade.

Judicial reforms included the creation of a Relação (High Court) in Rio de Janeiro and localized Juntas de Justiça (Boards of Justice) throughout Brazil. Local magistrates* were no longer allowed to base their decisions on church law or Roman law. Instead, they followed the laws of the country, along with local customs and well-established practices.

Military reorganization was less successful in Brazil than in Portugal. Although Pombal was able to reinforce Brazil's southern frontiers, the northern and western frontiers remained somewhat vulnerable. To ensure enrollment in the military, Pombal ordered a census* in the captaincies, making it difficult for males to avoid military service.

In social and cultural matters, Pombal encouraged intermarriage between whites and Indians, and he attempted to integrate Indians into white society. To reform Brazil's educational system, he severed the ties between the church and education and contributed to the formation of a Brazilian-born elite.

The Pombaline reforms had mixed results in Brazil. Pombal succeeded in reorganizing the administrative institutions of Brazil and in changing the colony's cultural and social policies. The economic reforms, on the other hand, had only limited success. However, Pombal's economic policies set the stage for a surge of economic growth in the late 1700s and early 1800s. (*See also* **Captaincy System; Portugal and the Portuguese Empire.**)

> ### Slavery Continues
> Although the Pombaline reforms abolished Indian slavery, the practice continued in Brazil for some time. The expansion of agriculture and development of export crops, encouraged by Pombal's new economic policies, created an increased demand for labor. Brazilian colonists met this demand by enslaving local Indians. Indian slavery was very common in the Amazon region, which had an economy based in part on agricultural exports. Slavery in this and other areas of Brazil persisted well into the 1800s.

* **viceroyalty** region governed by a viceroy, a royally appointed official
* **magistrate** official with administrative and often judicial functions
* **census** an official count of the population

See color plate 6, vol. 2.

Popul Vuh

See *Manuscripts and Writing, Pre-Columbian.*

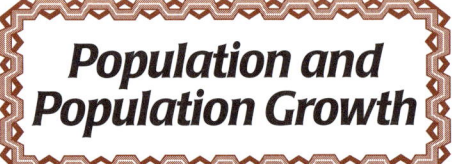

Population and Population Growth

In the last 30,000 years, Latin America has experienced dramatic fluctuations in the size and growth rate of its population, mostly as a result of colonization, disease, nutrition, slavery, intermarriage, immigration, and warfare. The turning points in the region's demography* are marked by six distinct stages: initial immigration from Asia, growth of agriculture and urban centers, European

Population and Population Growth

Most of the population of Latin America is concentrated in a few areas, as this map shows. The region's most densely populated areas are found on the Caribbean islands and in the highlands of Mexico and western South America. South America's interior regions remain sparsely populated.

* **demography** characteristics of human populations, such as density, birthrates, death rates, and growth
* **pre-Columbian** before the arrival of Christopher Columbus and other Europeans in the Americas in the 1490s
* **indigenous** referring to the original inhabitants of a region
* **domesticate** to adapt an animal or plant for use by humans

* **archaeological** relating to archaeology, or the science of studying past human cultures, usually by excavating ruins
* **famine** extreme and general scarcity of food

conquest, stabilization and recovery, growth of national populations, and transitions in the 1900s.

Population in Spanish America. In pre-Columbian* times, the region that later became Spanish America was populated by indigenous* peoples who had originally migrated to the Americas from Asia. Although they were initially hunters and gatherers, these Native Americans eventually domesticated* animals, developed irrigation systems, and established thriving agricultural economies. In some areas, the development of agriculture was accompanied by population increases and the emergence of sophisticated urban cultures. By 1500, large Indian populations inhabited central Mexico and the Andean highlands. Cities had more than 100,000 inhabitants, while the tropical rain forests and desert regions remained sparsely populated. Archaeological* evidence suggests that these pre-Columbian civilizations had high population densities but that their mortality, or death, rates were also high because of dietary deficiencies, ritual human sacrifice, famines*, and illnesses, such as tuberculosis, anemia, and sexually transmitted diseases.

When the Spaniards came to the "New World" in 1492, they unwittingly brought European diseases (smallpox, measles, influenza,

Population and Population Growth

and later, malaria and yellow fever) to which the Indians lacked resistance. During the resulting catastrophe, experts estimate, between 20 and 90 percent of indigenous populations were wiped out. Warfare, economic exploitation, and enslavement further reduced the Indian population.

By the 1600s, the Indian population began to recover and to stabilize. In some areas, Spanish colonists provided Indians with better, more nutritious foods, which aided in their recovery. The population also grew because of rising birthrates, immigration, and intermarriage. Spanish immigration during the colonial* period averaged 3,000 to 4,000 annually. Most of these immigrants were males, who because of the lack of Spanish women, married indigenous women. This resulted in a large mestizo* population, which by the early 1800s, accounted for about one-third of the population in some regions.

During this period, the Spaniards brought more than 2 million African slaves to Spanish America. Although their numbers were significant, these slaves had little impact on the population. Many suffered and died because of mistreatment or disease. Some intermarried with Indians and mestizos, contributing to the racial mixture in Spanish America. Despite these increases, disease, famine, and political conflict continued to affect the population, contributing to high mortality rates until well after the colonial period.

In the early 1800s, population growth in Spanish America began to accelerate because of improved health, education, sanitation, and an abundant food supply. At the same time, the population patterns changed as Latin America fragmented into individual nations after independence. Until the 1970s, many of the new nations operated under Argentine theorist Juan Bautista ALBERDI's slogan "to govern is to populate."

Between 1880 and 1935, more than 5 million European immigrants flocked to Spanish America, drawn by the promise of economic opportunity. Immigrants were attracted to those nations where the wages were higher than in their homelands and jobs and economic opportunities were abundant. Most went to Argentina, Uruguay, and Cuba, while Mexico, Central America, the Andean republics*, and Chile received barely any immigrants. Meanwhile, the nonimmigrant population also increased rapidly during this period, primarily as a result of lower mortality rates.

After about 1930, population growth rates in Latin America began to skyrocket. This was primarily due to continued high birthrates, lower death rates, and longer life expectancy, facilitated by improved nutrition, education, and medical care. In the 1950s, the population growth rate in Latin America was the highest in the world. In recent years, governmental efforts to slow the rate of population growth have had limited success. The region continues to experience significant annual increases in population. Cities have grown as a result of both natural increase and the migration of people from the countryside. Simultaneously, political and economic instabilities have generated a flood of emigration, with people crossing national borders or migrating to Europe and the United States.

---

* **colonial** referring to the period between the European conquest and independence, generally from the early 1500s to the early 1800s

* **mestizo** person of mixed European and Indian ancestry

* **republic** government in which citizens elect officials to represent them and govern according to law

Population and Population Growth

The future of population growth in Latin America is uncertain. If the population continues to expand rapidly, this may cause a breakdown of the political and economic systems as nations try to cope with enormous numbers of people. Even if growth rates fall, the region will probably reach a population of more than half a billion by the mid-2000s, more than ten times the population in 1900.

Population in Brazil.

Brazil has experienced many of the same trends in population and population growth as Spanish America. The history of Brazilian population in colonial times was shaped by several factors: the arrival of Portuguese settlers, the reduction of indigenous peoples, and the importation of African slaves.

In 1500, scattered Indian tribes numbering about 2.5 million people inhabited the Atlantic coast of Brazil. Many of these Indians were killed during Portuguese military campaigns in the 1560s and 1570s, and some died of European diseases. Whole tribes disappeared. Those who survived, especially in the interior and in the Amazon region, were enslaved by the Portuguese and forced to work in mines and on plantations. By 1585, the Portuguese had replaced Indian slaves with Africans. An estimated 2.5 million to 4.3 million black slaves had been brought to Brazil. In some areas, Africans outnumbered whites and Indians, making up about 70 percent of the population. Despite their large numbers, the African population grew very slowly because of a low fertility rate.

In early colonial times, the European population grew slowly, increasing from about 20,000 in 1570 to 100,000 in 1700. Then it increased more rapidly, reaching about 2 million by 1798. Population growth continued to accelerate in the 1800s, partly because of increased immigration from Europe; about one-third of the population growth in the late 1800s was a result of immigration.

The ethnic and racial composition of Brazil's population changed significantly in the 1800s and 1900s. In the 1800s, the number of free blacks grew dramatically, and they soon came to dominate some regions. Simultaneously, when the slave population declined and the need for laborers encouraged immigration, the foreign-born population of Brazil increased from 4 percent in 1872 to 7 percent in 1900. The country's racially mixed population had expanded to about 39 percent by 1980.

Another dominant characteristic of population growth in Brazil is internal migration, the movement of people from one part of the country to another. Before 1950, internal migration occurred when people moved from rural areas to new frontier areas. Since 1960, internal migration has referred to the movement of people from rural to urban areas or from one city to another. As a result, many of Brazil's cities have grown dramatically. Although internal migration has involved people of all social and economic classes, most people moving into the cities have been from lower-income groups. Today urban poverty is one of Brazil's most pressing problems. (*See also* **Africans in Latin America; Asians in Latin America; Class Structure, Colonial and Modern; Immigration and Emigration; Race and Ethnicity.**)

Death Among the Indians

Although the population density in many pre-Columbian civilizations was high, the death rates among these peoples were very high as well. A severe famine in ancient Mexico killed thousands and probably contributed to the fall of the Maya civilization. Central and South American Indians suffered from vitamin and protein deficiencies, which resulted in sickness, crippling disorders, and early death. Archaeological evidence shows that the average person lived to be about 35 years old, about the same as in Western Europe at the time. The acceptance of this short life span was reflected in Aztec, Maya, and Inca cultural traditions, which had several gods, ceremonies, and rituals devoted to sickness and death.

See color plate 2, vol. 2.

Port-au-Prince

The capital of HAITI, Port-au-Prince is also the nation's chief port and commercial center. Situated on a magnificent bay in southern Haiti, the city has a population of more than 1.2 million. Most of these people live in squalid slums and terrible poverty.

Founded by French sugar planters in 1749, Port-au-Prince quickly grew into a leading port because of its well-protected, deep harbor. In 1770, the city replaced Cap Haitien as the capital of the French colony of Saint Domingue (as Haiti was known then). Soon after Haiti gained independence from France in 1804, Port-au-Prince came to dominate the political life of the new nation, serving as the stronghold of the mulatto* elite who controlled Haiti's political, economic, and cultural life.

* **mulatto** person of mixed black and white ancestry

During the 1800s and early 1900s, Port-au-Prince grew politically, but it remained economically backward, suffering from earthquakes, fires, and internal strife. In the 1940s and early 1950s, the government attempted to improve the quality of life in the city, but these efforts were largely unsuccessful. Under the DUVALIERS, who ruled Haiti from 1957 to 1986, Port-au-Prince continued to grow as a political center. Although François Duvalier implemented some public works projects and removed some slums during his regime, the city continued to deteriorate.

See color plate 10, vol. 4.

Today Port-au-Prince is the center of Haiti's commercial and intellectual life. The city is home to the State University of Haiti, the National Library, and the National Archives. Other landmarks include the National Palace, the Cathedral of Notre Dame, the National Museum, and the Iron Market—a magnificent building that houses the local market. (*See also* **Caribbean Antilles; Cities and Urbanization.**)

Portales Palazuelos, Diego José Pedro Víctor

1793–1837
Chilean political leader

* **assayer** person who appraises or analyzes the worth of items
* **conservative** inclined to maintain existing political and social views, conditions, and institutions
* **liberal** person who supports greater participation in government for individuals; one who is not bound by political and social traditions
* **hacienda** large rural estate, usually devoted to agriculture

Diego Portales brought order and stability to CHILE after the chaos that struck the nation following its independence from Spain. Born into a large family of more than 23 children, Portales graduated from the University of San Felipe and became an assayer* at the mint. In 1821, he moved to Peru, where he established a business. However, the unsettled political situation there forced him to close the business at great personal cost.

Returning to Chile in 1824, Portales purchased from the government an exclusive right to sell tobacco, playing cards, and liquor. However, domestic turmoil made it impossible for him to make a profit, and again he lost most of his investment. These experiences convinced him of the need for political order and stability.

Portales became involved in a political group called the *estanqueros,* which advocated the creation of a strong central government. He allied himself with conservative* forces who gained control of Chile in 1830, and he worked to remove political opposition, depriving liberals* of their power and, sometimes, their lives. He removed army officers who posed a threat to the government and created a national guard to suppress revolts. Yet despite his growing power, Portales worked to establish a government of laws rather than a personal dictatorship.

In 1833, Portales retired to his hacienda* but remained in touch with the government. Two years later, he reentered public life when political

turmoil threatened to erupt. Over the next few years, Portales served in various government positions. During this time, he developed VALPARAÍSO into a major seaport and forged new foreign policy goals aimed at keeping Chile out of regional disputes.

In 1836, when Peru and Bolivia formed a confederation*, Portales believed it would threaten Chile's domination of the Pacific coast. Fearing that the confederation would turn against Chile, Portales launched the WAR OF THE PERU-BOLIVIA CONFEDERATION. However, the war threatened to destroy Chile's government. Political opponents hoped to take advantage of popular discontent and overthrow the ruling administration. Portales responded with a wave of political repression, but this tactic had only limited success. In 1837, a rebellious army unit captured and murdered Portales.

The political system that Portales established in Chile survived his death. Although harsh, the system brought the order necessary for economic development and progress. While other Latin American nations suffered from political and economic turmoil, Chile prospered largely because of Portales's vision.

* **confederation** group of states joined together for a purpose; an alliance

Portinari, Cândido Torquato

1903–1962
Brazilian painter

Cândido Torquato Portinari was born in Bródosqui, in the Brazilian state of SÃO PAULO. The son of Italian immigrants, he grew up in a poor, working-class environment. He became interested in painting when he was helping decorate a local church. At age 15, he began study at the National School of Fine Arts in Rio de Janeiro. In 1928, Portinari received an award that enabled him to travel and study in Europe, where he was influenced by the works of European painters, including the Spanish artist and sculptor Pablo Picasso.

In the 1930s, Portinari became involved in a movement that rejected European art forms and focused on Latin American social themes.

As a social realist, Cândido Portinari often depicted the daily life of workers in his paintings. His art was also inspired by his harsh experiences as a youth on coffee and cotton plantations. In this 1935 painting titled *Coffee*, Portinari captures the strenuous work of immigrant laborers on Brazilian coffee plantations harvesting, sorting, and carrying coffee beans.

Portugal and the Portuguese Empire

His work reflects his early exposure to the harsh working conditions on Brazil's coffee and cotton plantations. Painting both large murals and smaller works, Portinari concentrated on depicting the arduous labor and poverty of plantation workers and miners. In 1935, he gained international recognition with a painting titled *Coffee*.

See color plate 7, vol. 1.

Portinari's paintings combined traditional ideas, a realistic style, and nationalist themes. His portraits of Brazilians of all social classes reflect a keen awareness of the ethnic diversity of Brazilian society. Among his prominent works is a series of four large murals titled *Discovery of the New World,* which he completed for the Library of Congress in Washington, D.C. Portinari died in 1961. (*See also* **Art, Colonial to Modern.**)

Portugal and the Portuguese Empire

Portugal, the westernmost country on the European continent, shares the Iberian Peninsula with Spain. The nation's location on the edge of Europe near the Atlantic Ocean has played an important role in its history. Since ancient times, Portuguese sailors have braved the waters of the Atlantic in search of markets and trade routes to Africa, Asia, and the Americas. Their pivotal role during the Age of Exploration helped make Portugal the center of a vast and wealthy empire.

Growth of the Nation. The modern nation of Portugal has its roots in the Middle Ages*. In the A.D. 700s, the Muslims from North Africa conquered most of the Iberian Peninsula. Over the next several hundred years, Christian forces struggled to reconquer the region, establishing independent kingdoms where they succeeded. In 1139, a Christian nobleman named Alfonso Henriques defeated the Muslims near Coimbra in Portugal. Four years later, he established an independent kingdom and took the title Alfonso I, king of Portugal. Alfonso and his successors continued to fight the Muslims, eventually completing the reconquest in 1249.

* **Middle Ages** period between ancient and modern times in western Europe, generally considered to be from the A.D. 500s to the 1500s

During the 1200s and 1300s, Portuguese monarchs rebuilt their country. Although frequent wars with Spain threatened the kingdom, Portugal remained independent. In the early 1400s, Portugal entered a period of maritime* expansion, leading to the creation of Europe's first global empire.

* **maritime** related to the sea or shipping

Exploration in the Atlantic. Encouraged by Prince HENRY THE NAVIGATOR, son of King João I, the Portuguese ventured forth from their kingdom for economic gain and to open new markets for trade. They also hoped to spread the Christian faith and to satisfy their curiosity about strange lands. In 1415, Portugal captured the north African port of Ceuta from the Muslims. Ceuta linked the Portuguese to markets throughout the Muslim world and encouraged them to pursue further exploration and conquest. They captured several other outposts along Africa's northern and northwestern coasts and continued to sail into the Atlantic and along the western coast of Africa.

Portugal and the Portuguese Empire

During the mid-1400s, they established fortified trading posts in Angola, Congo, Mozambique, and São Tomé, along the western coast of Africa. These outposts became the source of ivory, pepper, gold, and other exotic and valuable goods. The Portuguese also imported several thousand slaves from Africa, initiating the slave trade, an important economic activity in the decades that followed. During that time, Portugal also colonized the Atlantic islands of the Madeiras, the Azores, and Cape Verde, which gave the Portuguese many valuable products, including woods, sugar, and wine.

Expanding the Empire. Successful trade with their Atlantic island colonies and African coastal outposts encouraged the Portuguese to set their sights on more distant lands. They became determined to find a direct water route to Asia. In 1488, King João II commissioned the voyage of explorer Bartholomeu Dias that completed the first successful expedition around the tip of Africa to the Indian Ocean. In 1497, during the reign of Manuel I, explorer Vasco da Gama successfully sailed from Portugal to southwestern India, opening a direct trade route with Asia.

During the next 100 years, Portugal became the dominant European power in Asia. The monarchy maintained several outposts along the shores of the Indian Ocean, in the East Indies, and in China and Japan. Portugal's eastern empire, centered on India with its capital at Goa, brought immense riches to Portugal through trade in spices, silks, and other exotic goods.

In 1500, Portuguese commander Pedro Álvares CABRAL reached Brazil during the second Portuguese expedition to India. This discovery established Portugal's first territorial claim in the Americas, and it opened another continent to Portuguese expansion. With the colonization of Brazil, Portugal's empire stretched more than halfway around the world.

Managing Overseas Activities. In the 1400s, the Portuguese monarchy established special agencies to supervise the empire's trading activities in its African colonies. As the empire expanded, new agencies were added to oversee new colonies. By the 1500s, the Casa da India (House of India) administered most overseas activity. It served as a private trading agency for the monarchy, as a customhouse that collected tariffs* on trade goods, and as a supply house for outfitting overseas expeditions.

In 1509, the Portuguese monarchy reorganized the agencies that supervised its colonial activity and established new rules to centralize its authority and unify its administrative responsibilities. During the 1500s, the monarchy instituted several financial and administrative reforms in its colonies. In 1604, many overseas responsibilities were transferred from the Casa da India to the Conselho da India (Council of India). This new council was given broad powers to govern Portugal's overseas empire.

Glory and Decline. The wealth that flowed from its overseas colonies made Portugal one of the richest nations in Europe. A great seafaring

---

Portugal's Last Outpost in Asia

For several centuries, Portugal maintained a small trading outpost in China called Macao. Located on two small islands on a rocky peninsula on the coast of southern China, Macao was founded by Portugal in 1557. It is the oldest permanent European settlement in East Asia. For many years, Macao was reputed to be a haven for smugglers, especially after it lost its trade dominance to Hong Kong, the neighboring British colony. Today Macao is mostly Chinese, although some historic architecture reflects its Portuguese heritage. In 1987, China and Portugal signed an agreement by which Macao was transferred to Chinese control in 1999.

° **tariff** tax on imported or exported goods

Portugal and the Portuguese Empire

power, Portugal stood at the forefront of advances in shipbuilding and navigation. Its capital, Lisbon, became a busy commercial center, and the nation's wealth stimulated great artistic and cultural achievements. However, Portugal dominance was short-lived. By the 1570s, the nation had entered a period of decline, largely as a result of the enormous costs of maintaining the empire. Portugal also faced increasing economic competition from other European powers, especially from Britain and the Netherlands. Political threats from its neighbor Spain loomed as well.

In 1580, King PHILIP II OF SPAIN claimed the Portuguese throne and took control of the empire. The Spanish ruled there until 1640, when the Portuguese revolted against the Spaniards and reestablished their independence. However, during the 60 years of Spanish rule, the empire had declined considerably. During that time, the Dutch had captured many of Portugal's Asian outposts, established colonies there, and taken over the trade routes. The Dutch also seized portions of northeastern Brazil, but the Portuguese eventually drove them out of that region in 1654.

Remains of Empire. In 1642, Portugal created the Conselho Ultramarino (Overseas Council) to administer all its overseas possessions except North Africa and the Atlantic islands of the Madeiras and the Azores. Portugal then began to focus its attention on Brazil. By the 1690s, the colonists had discovered gold and diamonds in Brazil, which they imported to Portugal. This wealth refilled the empire's treasury and contributed greatly to Portuguese affluence. When mining declined in the 1700s, it was replaced by the export of Brazilian agricultural products, such as cotton and cacao*, and the continued sale of sugar. By the mid-1700s, Brazil became the key to Portugal's prosperity. To strengthen its remaining empire, the Portuguese monarchy instituted the POMBALINE REFORMS, which changed its administrative, economic, social, and cultural policies in Brazil and elsewhere.

* **cacao** bean from which chocolate is made

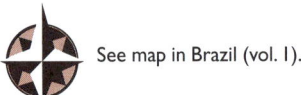
See map in Brazil (vol. I).

In the early 1800s, Portugal faced the threat of a French invasion. When French forces invaded Portugal in 1807, the royal family fled to Brazil and made RIO DE JANEIRO their temporary capital. Portuguese forces regained control of Portugal in 1811, but the monarchy did not return there until 1821. The following year, Brazil declared its independence, becoming the first colony to break away from the Portuguese empire.

Torn by civil wars in the 1800s, Portugal was preoccupied with internal problems. Nevertheless, exploration into the interior of Africa strengthened the nation's hold on its colonies of Angola and Mozambique. Portugal's political problems ended in 1910, when the monarchy was overthrown and a republic* was established. During the 1900s, the once-great Portuguese empire continued to crumble. It lost many Indian outposts in 1961, and a revolution in 1974 ended with the loss of Mozambique, Angola, and other African colonies. Today the last remaining overseas Portuguese possessions are the islands of the Madeiras and the Azores in the Atlantic. (*See also* **Dutch in Latin America; Explorers and Exploration; Portuguese in Latin America.**)

* **republic** government in which citizens elect officials to represent them and govern according to law

Portuguese in Latin America

Since the 1500s, thousands of people have migrated from Portugal to Latin America, including thousands from the Azores and the Madeiras, Portuguese islands in the Atlantic. Most of these immigrants settled in BRAZIL, although since the mid-1900s, many have migrated to the West Indies, VENEZUELA, and other Latin American nations.

In the early 1800s, most Portuguese immigrants were young, single males, who were leaving Portugal in search of better economic opportunities or to escape military service there. Although these individuals worked in a variety of occupations, most became commercial clerks and merchants in the port cities.

By the mid-1800s, as the slave trade ended, the Brazilian government encouraged immigration to meet its labor needs. During that time, there was a substantial increase in the number of Portuguese immigrants, especially agricultural workers. Most of these Portuguese migrants settled in the states of Bahia, Pernambuco, Rio de Janeiro, and São Paulo, where they worked on coffee or sugar plantations.

Throughout the late 1800s, Portuguese immigrants continued to flow into Brazil. Although they initially worked in agriculture, many soon took up work as artisans* and merchants. Unlike other Europeans, who migrated almost exclusively to southern Brazil, Portuguese immigrants settled throughout the country.

During the 1800s, male Portuguese immigrants outnumbered females. Not until the end of the 1800s did the number of female immigrants begin to increase, largely as a result of new job opportunities in major cities such as Rio de Janeiro and São Paulo. Portuguese immigration to other Latin American countries remained minimal until the 1940s. Since then, Venezuela has attracted the greatest number of Portuguese. (*See also* **Immigration and Emigration; Portugal and the Portuguese Empire.**)

* **artisan** skilled crafts worker

Portuguese Monarchs

Two dynasties* ruled PORTUGAL AND THE PORTUGUESE EMPIRE during the colonial period: the House of Aviz and the House of Bragança. Monarchs from these dynasties played a major role in Portugal's conquest and colonization of BRAZIL and other overseas colonies. Under their leadership, Portugal and Brazil experienced great political, economic, and social changes.

The Aviz dynasty, founded in 1385 by João I, promoted overseas exploration to stimulate Portugal's economic growth. During his reign—from 1385 to 1433—João centralized power and established close relations with England. His son, Henrique, later known as Prince HENRY THE NAVIGATOR, attempted to establish a direct sea trade route between Portugal and Asia.

Portugal reached the height of its power in the late 1400s, during the reign of João II, the grandson of João I. Like his predecessor, João II made overseas exploration a vital part of Portugal's economic expansion. During this time, Portugal colonized the Madeira islands and the Azores in the Atlantic Ocean and commissioned the voyage of explorer

* **dynasty** succession of rulers from the same family or group

Bartholomeu Dias that completed the first successful expedition around the tip of Africa. João II also negotiated the Treaty of TORDESILLAS with Spain, which divided the administration of the two countries' overseas territories.

João's successor, his cousin Manuel, ruled from 1495 to 1521. Manuel I is best known for the overseas discoveries he sponsored. In 1497, he sent explorer Vasco da Gama on the voyage that found a direct sea route to India. Manuel also sponsored expeditions to explore the coast of Brazil, instituted economic and administrative reforms, and updated Portuguese law.

João III, the son of Manuel I, ruled Portugal from 1521 to 1557. Under his rule, Portuguese colonization of Brazil intensified. He divided the Brazilian coastline into administrative units called captaincies; established a government in BAHIA under a royal governor, Tomé de SOUSA; and sent Jesuits* to convert Indians to Christianity. Yet Portugal declined under João's reign because of French and British challenges to Portuguese trade and the enormous costs of maintaining an overseas empire.

In 1580, the Portuguese throne passed to PHILIP II OF SPAIN, bringing an end to rule by the Aviz dynasty. Spain ruled Portugal until 1640, when a revolt returned power to the Portuguese. The new ruler, João IV, founded the Bragança dynasty. Although João lost much of Portugal's eastern empire to the Dutch, he supported uprisings against Dutch colonists in Brazil and strengthened Portuguese control there.

Portugal experienced a golden age under João V, grandson of João IV, who ruled from 1706 to 1750. Gold and diamonds from Brazilian mines were shipped to Portugal, bringing great riches to the empire. João used this wealth to build huge public works and to support various cultural activities.

João V was succeeded by José I, who ruled until 1777. During this time, Portugal and Brazil underwent enormous changes, especially because of the reforms enacted by the king's adviser and chief minister, Marquês de Pombal. Designed to increase Portugal's wealth and to strengthen its empire, the POMBALINE REFORMS changed the administrative organization of Brazil and the economic, social, and cultural policies of the entire Portuguese empire. When João V died in 1777, his daughter Maria succeeded him as ruler of Portugal. During her reign, Maria reversed many of Pombal's reforms. Although it is unclear when Maria began to show signs of mental illness, her son JOÃO VI took over the government in 1792. In 1799, he was officially given the title of regent*.

In 1807, during João VI's reign, the Portuguese royal court fled to Brazil to escape French invasions of Portugal and remained there until 1821. When João VI and the royal court sailed back to Portugal, his oldest son, PEDRO I, stayed in South America and was crowned emperor of an independent Brazil in 1822. Pedro I ruled Brazil until 1831, when he abdicated the Brazilian throne in favor of his son, PEDRO II. The last Portuguese emperor of Brazil, Pedro II, ruled until the monarchy was overthrown during an uprising in 1889. A succession of monarchs continued to rule Portugal until a republic* was established in 1910.

---

* **Jesuit** popular name for the Roman Catholic religious order officially known as the Society of Jesus; also, a member of that order

* **regent** person appointed to govern while the rightful monarch is too young or unable to rule

* **republic** government in which citizens elect officials to represent them and govern according to law

Positivism

The philosophy known as positivism emerged in France in the mid-1800s. Proposed by Auguste Comte, positivism emphasizes that all knowledge should be based on reason and experience. In Latin America, positivism became a major intellectual force in the late 1800s, and it played an important role in attempts to modernize Latin American society.

Comte identified three stages of human thought. The first two focus on religious belief and abstract ideas about existence and reality. The third stage, according to Comte, is the positive, in which the reliance on supernatural explanations for certain phenomena and events is replaced by an explanation based on observable data, experiment, and science.

Beginning in the 1870s, Latin Americans expressed an interest in positivism. Eager to overcome the social legacy of the colonial period, they believed that this philosophy and its acceptance would stimulate progress similar to that underway in western Europe and North America at the time. However, the philosophy was not adopted throughout Latin America. Despite its acceptance among many respected intellectuals, positivism did not take firm root in Latin America outside Brazil, Mexico, and Chile.

In Mexico, positivist thought played an important role in educational reforms, especially during the presidency of Benito Juárez in the 1860s. During the rule of Porfirio Díaz in the late 1800s and early 1900s, a group of advisers known as the *científicos* were accused of supporting positivist ideas about Indian racial inferiority. In Chile, positivist thinkers played an important role in supporting democracy.

Positivism had its greatest impact in Brazil. In the 1880s, positivist thinkers were at the forefront of the movement to overthrow Dom Pedro II. They played a brief but influential role in the creation of the new republic*. The Brazilian national flag (designed by a positivist) bore the motto "Order and Progress," which clearly reflected positivist ideals.

By the early 1900s, positivism largely disappeared as an intellectual force in Latin America, except in Brazil, where a few positivist churches exist today. Although still functioning in the 1990s, the Positivist Church commands little influence over the intellectual and cultural life of Brazil.

* **republic** government in which citizens elect officials to represent them and govern according to law

Potato

A major food crop in the world today, the potato originated in the ANDES region of South America. For centuries before the arrival of Europeans, the pre-Columbian* peoples of the Andes relied heavily on the potato as a food staple. After its introduction in Europe in the 1500s, the potato gradually became an important food crop there as well.

The potato is a member of the *Solanaceae* family, which includes several other plants that originated in the "New World," including tomatoes, tobacco, and CHILE peppers. Thousands of distinct types of potato are grown in the Andes region, each distinguishable by its color, shape,

* **pre-Columbian** before the arrival of Christopher Columbus and other Europeans in the Americas in the 1490s

and other characteristics. More than 3,600 of these varieties are on display at the International Potato Center in Lima, Peru.

The earliest plant remains of potatoes in the Andes region date from around 5000 B.C. Artistic depictions of potatoes appear on ancient Peruvian ceramics* from the Nasca culture, dating as early as A.D. 1. However, there is no evidence that potatoes were grown outside the Andes region before 1500. Potatoes were particularly important to the INCA, who used a form of freeze-dried potatoes to feed their armies as they expanded their empire.

The potato first arrived in Europe in the 1500s, brought to Spain in 1570 and then to England in 1588. Initially, potatoes grew best in southern Europe, but they were soon adapted to cultivation in other regions as well. Although the potato was slow to become established in Europe, it soon revolutionized European agriculture. For almost 200 years, the potato was primarily a curiosity in Europe. Some countries even prohibited its cultivation because it resembled certain deadly plants and because some Europeans believed that the plant could cause diseases such as leprosy and tuberculosis. It was only after 1785, following efforts by the king of France to promote the crop, that the potato gained general acceptance in Europe.

Potatoes played a major role in increasing the productivity of land in northern Europe, and they eventually replaced wheat and rye in importance. Potatoes were especially important in Ireland, where they became the major source of food.

Today potatoes are produced under many different farming conditions and for various uses—from a source of food to an ingredient in certain types of alcohol. Farmers in the Andes region, especially in Peru and Bolivia, cultivate several varieties of potato that are frost resistant and can be grown at altitudes greater than 13,000 feet. In this and other regions of the world, the potato remains a major food crop, and is especially important in the less developed regions of the world. (*See also* **Agriculture**.)

This drawing by Guamán Poma de Ayala shows Inca people planting potatoes, a staple crop cultivated in the valleys of the Andes since 5000 B.C. Instead of using wheat flour to bake bread, the Inca used chuño, a pasty substance made from dried potatoes. Many Europeans favored potato cultivation because potatoes provided a greater yield than grain on the same amount of land.

* **ceramics** pottery, earthenware, or porcelain objects; the manufacture of such objects

Potosí

* **colonial** referring to the period between the European conquest and independence, generally from the early 1500s to the early 1800s
* **imperial** relating to an emperor or empire

A city and region in southern BOLIVIA, Potosí became a famous silver-mining center during the Spanish colonial* era. Located on a cold, barren plateau high in the ANDES, at an elevation of about 13,000 feet, the silver-rich imperial* city of Potosí was the envy of Spain's rivals.

Potosí was founded in 1545, when the Spanish discovered silver on the upper reaches of a mountain they called Cerro Rico (Rich Hill). Cerro Rico became the largest source of silver the world had ever known, yielding roughly half of Spanish America's silver output in the mid-1600s. Located in the shadow of Cerro Rico, Potosí grew rapidly as the MINING industry developed.

By 1600, much of the easily accessible ore in Cerro Rico had been mined, and silver production leveled off. As other regions of Spanish America began to dominate the silver-mining industry, Potosí experienced a long period of economic decline. In the early 1800s, during the

wars of independence, Potosí's mines were neglected and destroyed, and the city suffered greatly. Silver mining in Potosí recovered somewhat in the mid-1800s, due largely to new technologies that facilitated the recovery of less accessible ore deposits.

In the late 1890s, the region of Potosí became an important source of tin, which contributed to a new period of growth and prosperity. Although huge deposits of silver ore remain in Cerro Rico, they are difficult and expensive to mine. The TIN INDUSTRY remains important to the city of Potosí, which today is a leading industrial center. Present-day Potosí still reflects its colonial heritage. Its narrow, winding streets and colonial buildings are home primarily to Indians, many of whom are descendants of colonial mine workers. The city is the capital of the department* of Potosí, which forms the southwestern border of Bolivia, bordering on Argentina to the south and on Chile to the west. (*See also* **Gold and Silver**.)

* **department** province or administrative district of the government

Pre-Columbian Art

See *Art, Pre-Columbian*.

Pregnancy and Birth

See *Women*.

Presidios

The term *presidio* refers to a military post—such as a fort—in Spanish America. Established throughout Latin America from the mid-1500s, the presidios were the basic institutions of Spanish colonization. Established from Chile in the south to the SPANISH BORDERLANDS in the north, these fortified settlements defended Spanish America.

Coastal presidios, such as those in Havana, Cuba, were often heavily armed fortifications that protected the monarchy's maritime* trade routes against pirates and foreign invaders. They often housed more than one hundred men. Most presidios, however, were located in frontier regions and consisted only of a small walled fort with towers. They guarded mines and defended frontier settlements from attacks by hostile Indians. The earliest frontier presidios consisted of just a handful of armed men under the command of a low-ranking officer. In time, however, they grew in size and complexity as Indian attacks and foreign invasions became more serious threats.

Located wherever they were needed, some presidios contained no permanent structures. Instead, soldiers were assigned to the posts in times of extreme danger, and additional men from local communities were added to the force. Spanish authorities frequently gave land grants to the soldiers of presidios and encouraged them to settle permanently in the area with their families. This policy stimulated colonization and led to the establishment of self-sufficient frontier communities that helped consolidate Spanish control. (*See also* **Forts and Fortifications**.)

* **maritime** related to the sea or shipping

Prison

See *Crime and Punishment*.

Property

See *Land, Ownership of*.

Protestantism

Protestantism has traditionally played a small role in Latin America because the two major colonial powers—Spain and Portugal—were Catholic. As a result, Latin Americans were generally Catholic. More recently, however, Protestantism has begun to play a more important role in Latin America.

During the colonial period, Protestants in Latin America—known as *evangélicos*, or evangelicals—were prosecuted by the Spanish INQUISITION. Thus, the few Protestants who came to the region largely downplayed their religious faith. Long after the Inquisition ended in 1820, Latin Americans continued to think of Protestantism as a foreign religion that was hostile to their own religious beliefs and culture.

After independence in the 1800s, many Latin American governments legalized the practice of other religions. Most nations, however, retained Catholicism as the official state religion. Despite greater religious freedom, Protestantism remained largely confined to the foreign population. The Anglican* Church, for example, established strongholds in parts of Central America and in Argentina, Chile, and Brazil, but it served only British subjects who were engaged in commercial and diplomatic* activities in the region. Similarly, German evangelical churches were established in Brazil and Chile to serve German immigrants there. Neither church tried to convert Latin American Catholics.

Beginning in the 1820s, British Methodists* sold Bibles in Latin America and worked to convert the indigenous* peoples to their faith. Visiting missionaries from other European Protestant groups also worked to convert the Indians to Protestantism. However, neither had much impact on the Indians, and in some regions, they were expelled from the country because of their missionary activities.

Protestant missionaries began immigrating to Latin America permanently in the late 1800s, when European and North American groups—including the Methodists and Presbyterians*—arrived to work among the Spanish-speaking Catholics and non-Spanish-speaking Indians. They were soon joined by nondenominational* mission agencies such as the Central American Mission and the Christian Missionary Alliance. Together they established churches, schools, hospitals, and vocational training institutes. They also translated the Bible and other religious works into indigenous languages. Their efforts met with great success, especially in countries where the missionaries had the approval of government leaders, as in Guatemala, Chile, and Brazil.

The liberal* governments that came to power in the mid-1800s greatly approved of the work of the Protestant missions. Some leaders

* **Anglican** relating to the Church of England
* **diplomatic** demonstrating tact and skill at conducting negotiations among nations
* **Methodist** member of an English Protestant church that was founded on the teachings of John and Charles Wesley
* **indigenous** referring to the original inhabitants of a region
* **Presbyterian** follower of Calvinism, or member of the Presbyterian Church
* **nondenominational** not restricted to a particular religious denomination, or group
* **liberal** supporting greater participation in government for individuals; not bound by political and social traditions

The Moravian Missionaries

The Moravian Church is a Protestant denomination that originated in Germany. In the mid-1800s, the Moravians established missions and schools for the Mosquito Indians and British Protestants living on Nicaragua's Atlantic coast (then a British protectorate). When the British abandoned their claim to the coast in 1850, the Moravians continued to work with the Mosquito Indians, encouraging them to maintain a separate identity from other Nicaraguans. For this reason, they have periodically come into conflict with the Nicaraguan government.

supported the missions in the hope that they would encourage hard work among the people and inspire economic development. Others hoped that they would counter the power of the CATHOLIC CHURCH, which frequently opposed liberal reforms. This link between the missionaries and the liberals was especially strong in Mexico during the rule of Benito JUÁREZ.

In spite of government support, Protestantism remained on the fringes of Latin American society until the 1960s. However, Latin Americans gradually embraced Protestantism, and increasing numbers converted. The change stemmed from the emergence of national Protestant groups who had no ties to the old mission system, changes within the Catholic Church, the decline of traditional rural society, and the breakdown of family networks.

In recent years, the greatest trend in Protestant growth has been the rise of Pentecostal groups, which emphasize an emotional religious experience, including faith healing, prophecy, and speaking in tongues. In countries with a large Protestant population, most churches are Pentecostal; these churches are especially popular among the urban and rural poor. Between 1960 and 1990, the Protestant population in many countries doubled, tripled, or grew even more dramatically.

Provincias Internas

* **New Spain** Spanish colony in Mexico

* **jurisdiction** area of authority

The Provincias Internas, or Internal Provinces, were an administrative district created for northern New Spain*. Organized in the 1770s as part of the BOURBON REFORMS, the Provincias Internas were intended to strengthen Spain's military and economic control of its North American colonies.

In the late 1700s, the defense of the northern frontiers of its North American empire became a vital concern to the Spanish monarchy, especially after Britain defeated France in the Seven Years' War and the United States gained its independence. Spain sought to protect this frontier region from these potential rivals, as well as from hostile Indians, by reorganizing its administration and economy there.

The idea of the Provincias Internas was proposed by a colonial official, José de GÁLVEZ, during his visit to the region from 1768 to 1770. Formed in 1776, the region was organized into a single administrative district, including California, Arizona, New Mexico, Texas, and several provinces in northern Mexico, and its governor reported directly to the king of Spain. Between 1776 and 1823, the district was reorganized on several occasions—at times divided into parts and at other times reunited into a single district. These changes, as well as shifts in policy and overlapping military and civil jurisdictions* within the province, contributed to administrative turmoil.

Colonial officials formulated bold policies to establish peace and security in the Provincias Internas. They hoped to reduce administrative and defense costs by bringing frontier groups—both colonists and Indians—under Spanish control and by using them as buffers, or protective barriers, against foreign invasions. The resulting peace, it was hoped, would attract more settlers and promote economic growth and prosperity.

During the period of the Provincias Internas, the colonial population of the region more than doubled. Mining and agriculture expanded modestly in the more settled areas, and trade played an increasingly important role in the province. The presence of the Provincias Internas also helped stem European advances into the region. However, administrative turmoil ultimately undermined Spain's overall goals for the region. When Mexico gained independence from Spain in 1821, the Provincias Internas were incorporated into the new nation as a series of distinct provinces. (*See also* **Spain and the Spanish Empire.**)

Public Health

See *Medicine*.

Public Sector

The public sector is the portion of a nation's economy that involves any type of government activity that is funded by taxes, such as national defense, law enforcement, education, social security, and public health. The public sector also includes any economic activity in which the government is directly involved, from the purchase of goods and services necessary for the functioning of the government to government ownership and operation of businesses. In the years since independence, many Latin American countries have struggled to define the role of the public sector in their national economies.

Colonial Roots. The European colonial powers viewed Latin America as a source of wealth and raw materials. They sent military forces to protect their colonies from attacks by rivals and built public buildings and roads necessary for the colonial administration. During the colonial period, basic services such as schools and hospitals were run by religious groups, Indians, Spaniards, and private individuals and were open only to members of each particular group.

Independence and Liberalism. After independence, Latin American leaders inherited nations whose economic development had been restricted by colonial policies for almost 300 years. Several newly independent governments dramatically increased public spending, particularly for secular* education. During the 1850s, Brazil invested public money in science, and the Chilean government used government funds to build warehouses and dock facilities for overseas trade. However, just as in colonial times, most of these services benefited only the wealthy and those in the cities and had little impact on the poor and others on the margins of society, who were just as happy to fend for themselves.

Even after independence, colonial policies continued to curb the growth of an effective public sector. Since colonial rulers discouraged the growth of industry or manufacturing, the new governments depended greatly on income from tariffs*. However, the demand for the region's exports, which consisted almost exclusively of agricultural and

* **secular** nonreligious; connected with everyday life

* **tariff** tax on imported or exported goods

Public Sector

mineral products, fluctuated greatly. As a result, governments often went from periods of prosperity to periods when they lacked money to cover their expenses.

From about 1860 to 1930, Latin American nations experienced an export boom that provided taxes to finance many public works projects. Governments financed the construction of roads, RAILROADS, and ports to facilitate the speedy and cost-efficient transport of goods locally and overseas. Several nations instituted social security and welfare services, especially for government employees. However, when people began to retire early to live off their pensions, governments found themselves burdened with the added expense of supporting these former workers. This era of prosperity ended with World War I and the Great Depression*. As the world economy collapsed, countries could no longer afford to import as many goods. Many Latin American countries raised tariffs on imports to help local businesses survive. Gradually, the money from tariffs that had supported most public spending dried up, leaving governments looking for other sources of revenue.

Great Depression period in the 1930s marked by low economic activity and high unemployment

Government Activism.

By the 1930s, governments throughout the world became aggressively involved in economic planning. They formed state-run corporations to stabilize national economies and to stimulate economic growth. For example, Argentina created a state petroleum company; Brazil set up corporations for water, power, electricity, steel, and oil; and Mexico nationalized* its petroleum industry. During the 1950s, Bolivia nationalized its TIN INDUSTRY, Chile's government began its takeover of the COPPER INDUSTRY, and in Cuba, the Communist* government of Fidel Castro took over the country's economy entirely. During the 1960s and 1970s, governments also nationalized many foreign-owned enterprises. By the mid-1980s, Latin American governments owned thousands of factories, banks, utility companies, hotels, and farms and controlled the region's natural resources.

nationalize to bring land, industries, or public works under state control or ownership

Communist referring to a social system in which land, goods, and the means of production are owned by the state or community rather than by individuals

Initially, these corporations produced enough income to support and expand Latin America's public services. By the 1980s, however, they were in trouble because of inefficiency, mismanagement, and outright corruption. Many were deeply in debt, and governments were forced to print money to keep the companies in business. This caused massive inflation, severe economic crises, and a sharp drop in the quantity and quality of public services. By the late 1980s, the governments in some countries gradually reduced their foreign debts, and economic conditions began to improve. Again in the late 1990s, Mexico and Brazil were in serious debt crises. The U.S. Congress voted to aid the two nations by issuing new loans to pay off their old ones. The United States undertook this drastic step to prevent the two largest Latin American economies from collapsing and to help its own economy, which earns billions of dollars from trade with the region.

Dollars from the United States

In recent decades, Latin Americans in the United States have been sending a portion of their monthly earnings to relatives back home. These payments, known as remittances, amount to enormous sums of money when added together. The government of El Salvador estimates that Salvadorans working in the United States remit as much as $1 billion annually. The Mexican government readily acknowledges five times as much in remittances to relatives. These payments provide relief to recipients who might otherwise be forced to rely on already heavily burdened treasuries at home.

The Public Sector Today.

Faced with the need to control spending, Latin American countries began to reduce the size of their public sectors. In 1973, Chile became the first to sell many of its state-owned

companies to private investors. Mexico and Argentina followed suit, but countries such as Brazil and Peru have been slower. Some governments have attempted to cut spending on salaries and pensions, albeit reluctantly, because of the political risks involved. Brazil in particular was unwilling to take such action until the late 1990s. In the 1990s, Chile established privately run pension companies, and Peru and Colombia also turned to such systems. Most governments have also tried to improve tax collection to raise more money, but many people are still too poor to provide much tax revenue, and tax evasion by the wealthy is as widespread as elsewhere.

Meanwhile, the quality of public services and publicly funded infrastructure, such as roads, power, and other utilities, remains poor. Economists agree that for the situation to improve, Latin American nations must reduce unnecessary public spending, improve tax collection, and reduce the wide gap between rich and poor. The challenge for the public sector lies in improving services for everyone.

Pueblo Rebellion

* **indigenous** referring to the original inhabitants of a region
* **missionary** person who works to convert nonbelievers to his or her faith
* **tribute** payment made to a dominant power
* **encomienda** right granted to a conqueror that enabled him to control the labor of and collect payment from an Indian community

The Pueblo Rebellion, in the late 1600s, was the single most important event in the history of the Spanish colony of NEW MEXICO. An indigenous* uprising against Spanish rule, it helped preserve the religious and cultural identity of New Mexico's Pueblo Indians and redefined the social relations between the Indians and the Spaniards.

In the mid-1600s, tensions erupted between the Pueblo Indians and the Spanish, largely because the Indians were frustrated and angered by persistent Spanish attempts to convert them to Christianity. Spanish missionaries* destroyed Indian shrines and religious objects and punished those who practiced their traditional religious beliefs. The Indians also resented the economic burden of tribute* and forced labor required of them under the *encomienda*ystem.

By the 1660s, the Pueblo Indians began to restore some of their native ceremonies, and many Pueblo leaders spoke out against Spanish occupation of their land and cultural domination by Spanish missionaries. However, the Spanish continued to dominate the Indians and forced them to accept Christianity and Spanish culture.

Tired of the repression, the Pueblo Indians, led by a Tewa Indian named Popé, planned to retaliate against the Spaniards and to restore Indian rule. Popé and others leaders traveled to several Pueblo villages and gained a large following that was ready to revolt by the summer of 1680. Although the Spaniards learned of the impending uprising from their Indian allies, it was too late to avert disaster.

The Pueblo Rebellion erupted on August 10, 1680, when Indians throughout New Mexico attacked Spanish settlements. The fury of the uprising overwhelmed missionaries and settlers. Within a few days, the Indians had killed 21 missionaries and more than 380 colonists. Survivors fled to Santa Fe, the colonial capital, but the Indians laid siege to the town, forcing its inhabitants to flee to El Paso, Texas. News of the

* **mission** settlement started by Catholic priests whose purpose was to convert local people to Christianity

success of the Pueblo Rebellion spread quickly to other Indian groups in the Southwest, leading to uprisings there as well.

Following the rebellion, the Pueblo Indians destroyed Spanish missions* and property and reestablished their own religious and cultural traditions. Although the Spaniards reconquered New Mexico in 1692, they did not regain control of the Indian villages. The monarchy's attempts to replace the Pueblo religion met with firm resistance from the Indians and a lack of cooperation from colonial officials and settlers. Pueblo Indians still firmly believe that they owe their survival as a people to the Pueblo Rebellion. (*See also* **Missions and Missionaries; Spanish Borderlands**.)

Puerto Rico is the smallest and easternmost island of the Greater Antilles, a chain of islands in the West Indies that also includes Cuba and Hispaniola. Although officially known as the Commonwealth of Puerto Rico, the island is a self-governing territory of the United States.

Spanish Rule

Before the arrival of Europeans, Puerto Rico was inhabited by the Taino Indians, the last of several indigenous* peoples who inhabited the island over the course of more than a thousand years. The Taino called the island Boriquén (Land of the Brave Lord).

Discovery and Early Settlement. In 1493, Christopher COLUMBUS became the first European to visit Boriquén, when he landed on the island during his second voyage to the "New World." He claimed the island for Spain, named it San Juan Bautista, and left for the neighboring island of Hispaniola.

Spanish settlement of the island began in 1508, when explorer Juan Ponce de León arrived there with 42 settlers. Soon after, the Spaniards founded the town of Caparra on the island's northeast coast. The town had an excellent harbor, which the Spaniards named Puerto Rico (Rich Port). In time, this name was applied to the entire island. In 1521, they established another settlement nearby. Named San Juan, it developed into the island's most important settlement and eventually became its capital.

When disagreements arose over control of Puerto Rico, the Spanish authorities intervened and granted the right to govern the island to Christopher Columbus's brother Diego. Diego Columbus governed the colony until 1536, when he sold his rights to the Spanish crown. In 1564, the crown incorporated the island into the Spanish captaincy* system and appointed a captain-general to administer its affairs.

Development of the Colony. During the early years, settlers focused their attention on mining for gold. When the gold deposits were exhausted, the colonists shifted their attention to agriculture. They

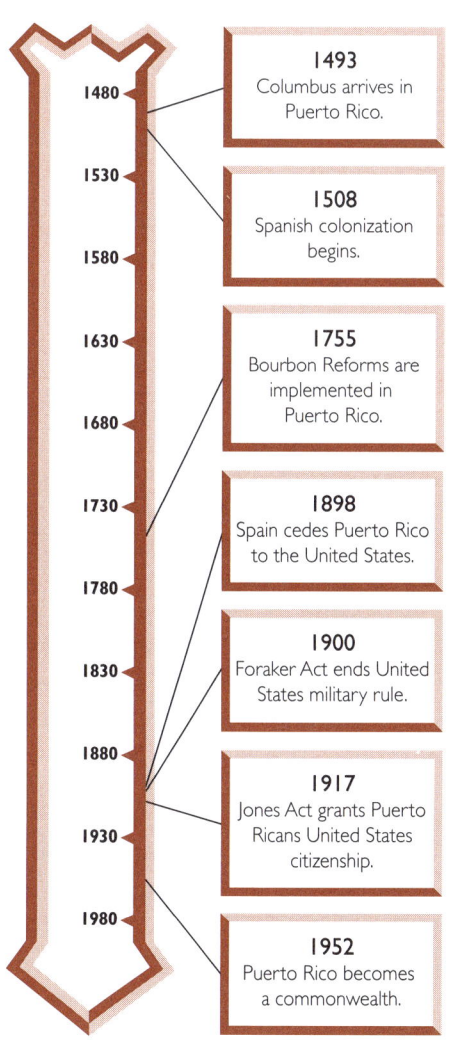

- **indigenous** referring to the original inhabitants of a region
- **captaincy** governmental system established by the Portuguese monarchy for the settlement and colonization of Brazil
- **cacao** bean from which chocolate is made
- **galleon** large sailing ship used for war and trade, especially by the Spanish
- **buccaneer** maritime adventurer who roamed the Caribbean between 1630 and 1700, attacking Spanish settlements and trade and terrifying Spanish colonists
- **Creole** person of European ancestry born in the Americas
- **autonomy** ability to make decisions and take action on one's own
- **conservative** inclined to maintain existing political and social views, conditions, and institutions
- **liberal** supporting greater participation in government for individuals; not bound by political and social traditions
- **republic** government in which citizens elect officials to represent them and govern according to law

See map in Caribbean Antilles (vol. 1).

introduced sugar in 1512, tobacco and cacao* by the 1600s, and coffee in the 1700s.

Early Spanish colonization had a disastrous effect on the Taino, most of whom died of European diseases, rebellions, and the harsh treatment they received working as slaves in mines and on plantations. By the early 1500s, the Spaniards had begun to import black slaves from Africa to replace the dwindling number of Indians. By the late 1500s, San Juan had become an important outpost of the Spanish empire. Treasure-filled galleons* stopped at San Juan during their voyage from the Americas to Spain, making the port an attractive target for Spain's European rivals. In the late 1500s and early 1600s, San Juan suffered attacks by French, English, and Dutch buccaneers*. To protect the city, the Spaniards strengthened their defenses and built several forts, such as the one at El Morro, which still guards San Juan.

An Era of Change. During the 1700s, the Spanish monarchy initiated a series of economic and political reforms, known as the BOURBON REFORMS, in its American colonies. However, they did not implement these reforms in Puerto Rico until 1755, when the monarchy permitted a trading company—the Compañía de Barcelona—to control the flow of goods between Spain and the island. However, the company was disbanded in 1784, partly because its officials had abandoned the legal system to join in the lucrative smuggling activities that took place between Puerto Rico and Spain's other colonies. Nevertheless, the reforms stimulated agricultural production and integrated Puerto Rico into Spain's system of colonial defense.

During the early 1800s, a time when many Spanish colonies began pushing for independence, Puerto Rico's Creole* population demanded greater power and autonomy*. Their demands led to new tax and trade policies and some self-sufficiency. As independence movements raged in other parts of Spanish America, many Spanish loyalists escaped to Puerto Rico. As supporters of Spain, these immigrants bolstered conservative* groups on the island who opposed independence. The colonial officials put down several uprisings in the 1820s and enforced loyalty to the crown. When they uncovered plots for revolts, they executed the rebel leaders. Many reforms were reversed, and liberal* Creoles were denied a voice in island affairs.

Still, the hope for independence remained alive. In 1868, a group of rebels captured the town of Lares, declared Puerto Rico a republic*, and set up a provisional government. However, the rebels were quickly defeated by the Spanish opposition. The rebels' proclamation, the Grito de Lares (Cry of Lares), became the symbol for Puerto Rico's independence from Spain and the United States.

Despite these setbacks, a movement for self-government remained alive. Liberal reformers worked within the existing political system to gain autonomy, and their efforts paid off in 1898, when Spain granted the island limited self-government. However, before the islanders had a chance to begin their new government, Spain and the United States went to war, and Puerto Ricans were again denied the right to control their own affairs.

Puerto Rico

From Farms to Factories

During the early 1940s, Puerto Rico faced high unemployment and widespread poverty. To improve living conditions on the island, the United States government created a program called Operation Bootstrap. This program improved education, reduced illiteracy, and built better housing for the poor. Operation Bootstrap's main purpose, however, was to change the basis of the economy from agriculture to manufacturing. The program provided incentives, such as low-wage labor and tax exemptions, to United States companies willing to establish factories in Puerto Rico. Between 1952 and 1992, the number of factories operating on the island increased from 83 to 2,000. Today manufacturing is the single most valuable industry in Puerto Rico.

° **cede** to yield or surrender, usually by treaty

° **draft** compulsory enlistment in the military

° **tariff** tax on imported or exported goods

United States Rule

Early in 1898, the SPANISH-AMERICAN WAR erupted between Spain and the United States. United States troops invaded Puerto Rico in July and captured the island with little resistance. Spain ceded* Puerto Rico to the United States, beginning a new era in the history of the island nation.

Early Years of United States Rule.

The United States took control of Puerto Rico and installed a military government. The military policed the island, constructed highways and other public works, established a system of public education, and organized the island's finances. However, there was little indication that any form of self-government was possible in the foreseeable future.

In 1900, after repeated calls for self-government by Puerto Ricans, the U.S. Congress passed the FORAKER ACT, which ended direct military rule and established a civil government. According to the law, all high government officials would be appointed by the United States president, but the government would also include a house of delegates elected by the islanders. The U.S. Congress reserved the right to review and approve or deny all legislation.

The United States officials ruling the island understood little about Puerto Rican culture or values. Instead, they tried to "Americanize" the people, for example, by requiring that all education be conducted in English although the local language was Spanish. (After years of dispute, Puerto Ricans settled the issue in 1991, when they voted to make Spanish their official language.) These policies caused Puerto Ricans to oppose United States officials and caused disputes. In 1917, the U.S. Congress passed the Jones Act, granting United States citizenship to Puerto Ricans and making males eligible for the military draft*.

Economic Impact of United States Rule.

The early years of United States rule provided few economic benefits for Puerto Rico. The island's wealth remained concentrated in the hands of large corporations and a small number of wealthy individuals. Tariffs* on Puerto Rican exports made it difficult to compete with United States–made products on the local and world markets. On the other hand, free trade policies with the United States provided a ready market for Puerto Rican goods.

Eventually, United States policies and investments in Puerto Rico began to benefit the island. During the 1940s, the United States initiated Operation Bootstrap, a program that helped reform agriculture and stimulate industrial expansion. Other job programs promoted Puerto Rican employment in industries in the United States, leading to increased migration between Puerto Rico and the North American mainland. Puerto Ricans also became eligible for various economic assistance programs offered in the United States.

Political Uncertainty.

In 1950, the U.S. Congress passed a law that required Puerto Ricans to choose between continuing as a dependent territory of the United States or creating a self-governing commonwealth.

The islanders chose to form a commonwealth, and in 1952, the Puerto Rican government, with the approval of the U.S. Congress, declared Puerto Rico an Associated Free State. As a commonwealth, Puerto Rico enjoys autonomy in its internal affairs. However, its foreign affairs are handled by the United States, with whom it shares a common currency, a defense system, citizenship rights, and an economic market.

Today Puerto Rico remains a commonwealth attached to the United States. Periodically, some groups on the island have urged complete independence from the United States, while others support the idea of statehood, urging that the island join the United States as a full-fledged state. Given an opportunity to vote on their status in 1967, 1993, and 1998, Puerto Ricans chose to continue their status as a commonwealth. However, the movement for statehood is strong, and there is an active independence movement as well. Thus, the political future of the island remains uncertain. (*See also* **Caribbean Antilles; Imperialism; Nationalism; Spain and the Spanish Empire; United States–Latin American Relations.**)

Puig, Manuel

1932–1990
Argentine novelist and screenwriter

Manuel Puig is best known as the author of *El beso de la mujer araña (Kiss of the Spider Woman)*, a 1976 novel that was made into a successful play and movie in the United States. Puig's novels have been translated into many languages, and he has received awards and gained international acclaim for his screenplays.

Born in General Villegas, a town in the province of Buenos Aires, Puig was educated at a United States boarding school in the city of Buenos Aires. As a child, he had such a passionate interest in movies made in the United States that he learned English so that he could enjoy them more. Puig became interested in French and Italian movies too, and he studied filmmaking in Italy in the mid-1950s. He also lived for a time in Sweden and England.

On returning to Argentina in 1960, Puig wrote screenplays and worked as an assistant director in the Argentine film industry. When his screenplays failed to generate interest, he moved to New York City to devote himself to writing novels. His first novel was published in 1968. *La traición de Rita Hayworth (Betrayed by Rita Hayworth)* is the story of a boy who escapes his unexciting life in rural Argentina by fantasizing about the lives of famous movie stars. Puig's next novel, *Boquitas pintadas (Heartbreak Tango),* also examines the world of frustrated individuals who find escape in movies and television soap operas.

Puig's novels, including *El beso de la mujer araña,* deal with themes of sexual and political repression, alienation*, and criticism of conventional lifestyles. Puig published eight novels, two plays, and two movie screenplays before his death in 1990. (*See also* **Cinema; Literature.**)

* **alienation** feeling of being apart from or not belonging to society

Punishment

See *Crime and Punishment*.

Queirós Law

See *Slave Trade*.

Quetzalcoatl

- **Mesoamerican** referring to Mesoamerica, a culture region that includes central and southern Mexico, Guatemala, Belize, El Salvador, and parts of Honduras, Nicaragua, and Costa Rica

Quetzalcoatl was one of the most important Mesoamerican* deities. To distinguish him from the TOLTEC ruler of the same name, his followers called him Ehecatl, meaning "wind" or "life-giving breath," and the ruler was called Topiltzín. By the time of the conquest, the two Quetzalcoatls—god and legendary ruler—were largely viewed as a single being.

The Nahuatl word *quetzalcoatl* literally means "quetzal-feather snake." Thus, Indians depicted the god as a rattlesnake with scales covered by the long green feathers of the quetzal, a brightly colored bird found in parts of Central America. These features also represented the union of the sky and the earth because the Indians believed that Quetzalcoatl was instrumental in the creation of the universe.

The symbol of the feathered serpent appeared in Mesoamerican art as early as A.D. 1, in the temple at TEOTIHUACÁN in central Mexico. The Toltecs, and later the Aztecs, used the image of Quetzalcoatl extensively in their stone sculptures, depicting the god with a mask projecting from his lower face through which he blew the wind.

- **cult** system of religious beliefs and rituals not officially approved by mainstream faiths; group following these beliefs

Topiltzín (Our Esteemed Lord) Quetzalcoatl of Tollán ruled the Toltecs during one of their most prosperous periods and was a follower of the cult* of Ehecatl Quetzalcoatl. According to legend, Topiltzín left Tollán, promising to return. When he died, his soul went to heaven, where it was transformed into the planet Venus. During his rule, Topiltzín was believed to have established the basis for legitimate political power in Mesoamerica. Nearly all rulers after him claimed political legitimacy

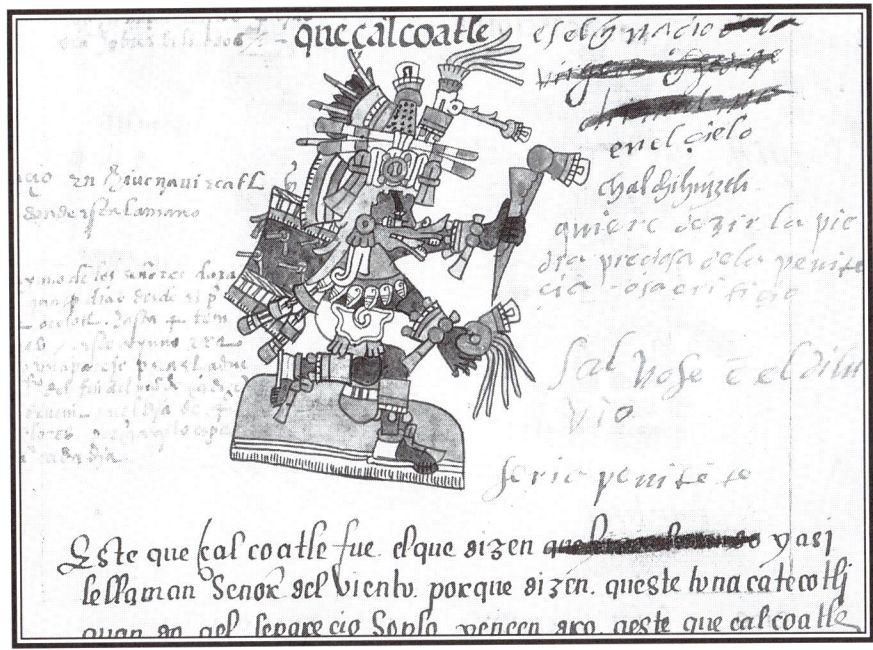

This 16th-century illustration from the *Codex Telleriano Remensis* shows the Mesoamerican deity Quetzalcoatl, who was often depicted in art as a feathered serpent. Several versions of the legend of Quetzalcoatl have been preserved in colonial writings.

through their links to the royal house of Tollán. In fact, Aztec chief MOCTEZUMA II claimed that he was a direct descendant of Topiltzín Quetzalcoatl. Moctezuma also initially believed that conquistador* Hernán CORTÉS was the returning Topiltzín. (*See also* **Art, Pre-Columbian; Coins and Coinage; Divinities.**)

* **conquistador** Spanish explorer and conqueror

Quilombo

Runaway slaves in colonial Brazil sought refuge in war camps called *quilombos* and in hideouts, or *mocambos*. These communities for runaways represented a vital means of slave resistance and were a persistent feature of slave societies. In Brazil, *quilombos* appeared in the late 1500s and remained until slavery was abolished in 1888.

Quilombos ranged from small hideouts for a handful of runaways to vast, organized communities that housed and protected thousands. The most famous of these was PALMARES. Although some *quilombos* were located in isolated and inaccessible places, they usually existed at the edges of plantations and towns. Here the runaways relied on barter, on the occasional theft of food or weapons, and on help from people sympathetic to their plight.

The presence of *quilombos* served as a reminder of the brutality of slavery, and they were therefore a constant source of irritation to colonial authorities, who incessantly tried to find and destroy them. While many *quilombos* fell to military attack, some survived for decades and others were never destroyed. Using guerrilla* tactics and spy networks, runaway slaves transformed the *quilombos* into sophisticated fortresses that could protect them, their crops, and their livestock.

* **guerrilla** referring to a group that uses surprise raids to obstruct or harass an enemy or overthrow the government

The success of a *quilombo* depended largely on cooperation among its members, who usually represented a variety of cultural backgrounds. Many were from various nations in Africa, and others were Brazilian-born slaves of African parents or of African-European descent. Occasionally, there were free people, including whites and Indians. As a result, a rich blend of cultures developed within the *quilombos* as elsewhere in Brazilian society. (*See also* **Slavery.**)

Quipu

In the absence of any form of writing, the people of ancient Peru developed the *quipu*, a device used for record keeping that consisted of a series of colored strings, knots, and twists. Developed by the HUARI sometime before A.D. 1000, the *quipu* was also adopted by the INCA.

The *quipu* consisted of a long main cord to which shorter strings were tied. In each of the shorter strings, the record keepers tied different types of knots at various intervals to indicate different transaction amounts. Sometimes they attached secondary strings to the main strings. The strings were also distinguished by their color and by the manner in which they were twisted. In addition to recording state transactions and

° **liturgy** form of a religious service, including spoken words, songs, and actions

statistics, *quipus* were also used as a memory aid for reciting long stories and liturgies*.

The Inca *quipu* was made and read by professional specialists called *quipucamayoq*. The major limitation of the device was that it could be read only by someone who knew to what the recorded information referred.

Quiroga, Horatio

1878–1937
Uruguayan writer

Horatio Quiroga, one of Spanish America's greatest storytellers, is famous for his powerful short fiction. He attended the University of Montevideo and, in 1903, went to live in rural Argentina. Many of his stories are set in the spectacular Argentine wilderness—the jungle, the plantations, and the mighty Paraná River.

Quiroga suffered many violent personal tragedies in his life. His father died in a hunting accident when he was only three months old, his first wife and his stepfather committed suicide, and Quiroga killed one of his best friends in a shooting accident. Many of his early stories are filled with monstrous and extraordinary images of death. In the years following the suicide of his wife in 1915, Quiroga wrote some of his best stories—*Cuentos de amor, de locura y de muerte* (Stories of Love, Madness, and Death), the haunting *Cuentos de la selva (South American Jungle Tales),* and *Los desterrados (The Exiles).*

Quiroga spent much of his life in Argentina as a representative of the Uruguayan government in San Ignacio, Misiones. In 1927, he remarried and had a family, and his later works drew on his own rich experiences with people. Some of his best writings translated into English include *The Exiles and Other Stories* and *The Decapitated Chicken and Other Stories.* Suffering from chronic disease and cancer, he committed suicide in 1937.

Quito

° **sierra** rugged mountains

° **conquistador** Spanish explorer and conqueror

° **hacienda** large rural estate, usually devoted to agriculture

° **audiencia** highest regional court in a Spanish colony; also, the district under its jurisdiction

Quito is the capital of Ecuador. With a population of more than 1 million, it is one of the country's largest cities, second only to GUAYAQUIL. Located in the interior of Ecuador, Quito lies in the northern sierra*, more than 9,000 feet above sea level, and at the foot of the dormant volcano Pichincha.

Quito served as a capital of the northern INCA empire during the rule of Huayna Capac and his son, ATAHUALPA. When the Spanish conquistador* Sebastián de Belalcázar approached the city in 1534, Atahualpa's general destroyed it. The Spanish then took control of the region and forced the large Indian population to work on their haciendas* in the surrounding valleys. As wealthy Spanish landowners placed their large estates in trusted hands and came to live in Quito, the city became an important center of Spanish government and law; in 1563, it became the seat of the *audiencia* of Quito.

Following the initial arrival of the Spanish, Quito's population was devastated by epidemics* of European diseases. The population fell from

Quito, an important artistic center during the colonial era, is known for its religious paintings and sculpture. This photograph shows a Quito street with a view of Cerro Panecillo in the distance. A statue of the Virgin Mary rests atop this famous hill.

* **epidemic** outbreak of a disease that affects a large number of people
* **colonial** referring to the period between the European conquest and independence, generally from the early 1500s to the early 1800s

between 750,000 and 1,000,000 in 1534, to about 95,000 in 1590, a loss of about 90 percent. Nevertheless, by the 1600s, the region was beginning to recover. Aided by the rich grazing lands of the Andes, which were stocked with Spanish merino sheep, and a rapidly growing workforce, Quito soon developed a successful TEXTILE INDUSTRY. Using forced labor, Quito produced the region's famous *paño azul* (blue cloth) as well as woolen ponchos and blankets, which were exported to the silver-mining districts of Peru. However, a series of epidemics in the late 1600s again greatly reduced the population, which fell from about 50,000 in the mid-1600s to 20,000 by 1830. The loss of workers combined with the introduction of cheap, high-quality European cloth crippled the region's textile production. Quito's population and its economy continued to lag until the 1900s.

During the colonial* period, Quito also gained a reputation as a city with a special devotion to Catholicism. The city was the home of many monasteries and convents, which became major centers of religious art production in South America. Some of the best representations of Spanish colonial sculpture and painting came out of the Quito School of the Art, which was founded in 1552.

Ecuador, divided in half by the towering Andes, developed striking regional differences in culture and politics. Quito became the political center of Ecuador, while Guayaquil, on the Pacific coast, became the country's commercial center. A deep rivalry developed between the two cities. Most of the nation's income—from import and export taxes—that came through the port of Guayaquil was controlled by the national government in Quito. The two cities clashed over this and other issues and their rivalry continued into the 1900s. After World War II, the coastal region gained political advantage as Guayaquil developed into a modern urban center and came to dominate the banana industry. However, in the late 1900s, oil found in the eastern slopes of the Andes helped create a prosperous PETROLEUM INDUSTRY in Quito. Since then, Quito has enjoyed increased wealth and political advantage, and oil from this region is now Ecuador's leading export. (*See also* **Art, Colonial to Modern; Quito Revolt of 1765.**)

Quito, Audiencia of

See *Ecuador; Quito.*

Quito Revolt of 1765

* **viceroyalty** region governed by a viceroy, a royally appointed official

Sparked by economic reforms in the viceroyalty* of New Granada, the Quito Revolt of 1765 was of the most serious threats to Spanish colonial authority. The reforms threatened to raise taxes at a time when the region was entering a period of economic depression* caused by the decline of the TEXTILE INDUSTRY.

To compensate for the declining profits from textiles, wealthy landowners around Quito began growing sugarcane and processing it into *aguardiente*—cane liquor. The middle and lower classes who became unemployed because of the closure of the city's textile mills sought jobs

Race and Ethnicity

° **depression** period of little economic activity during which many people become unemployed

° **bootleg** produced or distributed illegally

in Quito's growing underground economy. They raised crops on small plots of land around the city, operated small grocery stores or butcher shops, or sold bootleg* liquor. When the viceroy implemented economic reforms that transferred control of the *aguardiente* monopoly and the *alcabala* (sales tax) from local farmers to the Spanish treasury and threatened to raise taxes on rural haciendas and small farms, the public erupted in anger.

Revolts broke out in the spring of 1765. With popular support, rebel leaders disbanded the royal government, drove European-born residents from the city, and took control of Quito and the surrounding countryside. However, political differences soon emerged among the revolutionaries*, especially when those in the middle and lower classes sought greater political participation. Over the next year, ethnic, class, and political differences further weakened the revolution. In 1766, the viceroy's army entered the city and the citizens of Quito, now divided, offered little resistance. (*See also* **Ecuador; Quito**.)

° **revolutionary** person engaged in a war to bring about change

Since the time of the Spanish and Portuguese conquests, the population of Latin America has been composed of many racial and ethnic groups. Consequently, the region's history has been profoundly affected by the social, cultural, political, and economic interactions among these groups.

Race and Ethnicity in Colonial Latin America

From the beginning of the colonial period, white Europeans dominated Latin American society, while the Indians, African slaves, and free blacks generally had fewer rights and less access to economic opportunities. Despite their superior attitude and social position, many Europeans had children with, and even married, Africans and Indians. Their offspring represented the creation of new ethnic groups—one of the most important consequences of the European conquest.

European Attitudes and the Conquest. The roots of interethnic relations in Latin America can be traced to attitudes that prevailed in Iberia (Spain and Portugal) during the late Middle Ages*. During that time, the Iberian Peninsula was home to the Spaniards, Portuguese, Jews, and Moors*. Although these groups had lived side by side for hundreds of years, the Spaniards and the Portuguese gradually began to consider the others members of impure races and therefore unworthy of equal treatment. By the late 1400s, the Spanish monarchy had passed laws that discriminated against Jews and Muslims, and by the early 1600s, these laws applied to blacks and mulattos (persons of mixed European and African descent) as well.

° **Middle Ages** period between ancient and modern times in western Europe, generally considered to be from the A.D. 500s to the 1500s

° **Moors** North African Muslims who conquered Spain in the A.D. 700s

When the conquistadors* arrived in the Americas, they adopted similar attitudes toward the region's indigenous* peoples. They considered the Indians weak and irresponsible and in need of protection, especially

° **conquistador** Spanish explorer and conqueror

° **indigenous** referring to the original inhabitants of a region

30

Race and Ethnicity

* **missionary** person who works to convert nonbelievers to his or her faith
* **assimilate** to adopt the beliefs or customs of a society
* **tribute** payment made to a dominant power
* **pre-Columbian** before the arrival of Christopher Columbus and other Europeans in the Americas in the 1490s

when they lived in frontier regions. There the conquerors forced the Indians to live in missions or in towns where they were supervised by the Catholic Church and its missionaries*, converted to Christianity, and assimilated* into European culture. Most Indians, however, continued to live in their homes and only came together for the purpose of religious instruction. Europeans also considered it their right to exploit the labor of the Indians and claim tribute* from them just as pre-Columbian* Indian empires had done. By the mid-1500s in Spanish America and 200 years later in Brazil, Indians were legally free, but they were at the bottom of the social and economic pyramids in Latin America.

The Mestizos.

During the conquest, the Spaniards and Portuguese claimed Indian women as prizes. Sometimes the women were offered to them as gifts by CACIQUES, or local chiefs. Although few Europeans married the Indian women they took in these ways, they fathered many children with them. Their offspring, called *castizos* or MESTIZOS, could be accepted as Spanish or Portuguese, depending on their physical appearance, dress, occupation, residence, and income. The term *castizo* referred to a person with one-quarter Indian and three-quarters Spanish ancestry. However, accurate genealogical investigations were rare, and researchers have discovered that records were often altered to make a person whiter than judged at birth. People of mixed Hispanic and Indian ancestry who appeared darker, or were placed lower in the social or economic order, were called mestizos. Although mestizos were at first considered equal to Europeans, they eventually came to be seen as second-class citizens, especially when they were not recognized by their fathers. By the 1570s, mestizos were supposedly barred from receiving land grants or entering the priesthood, but the rules were never rigidly enforced. This allowed individuals with talent or connections to rise even faster than whites who had neither.

This detail, called *Fusion of the Races*, is from a mural by Jorge González Camarena titled *Presencia de la América Latina*. This section of the mural shows the many races and ethnicities that merged to create present-day Latin America. The large face stands for all indigenous races, and the woman at the lower left represents Latin America.

Race and Ethnicity

East Meets West

During the 1800s, the Asian population in Latin America increased significantly because of the influx of a large number of contract laborers. In fact, between 1849 and 1874, an estimated 80,000 Chinese laborers came to Peru to work on sugar plantations and to extract guano. Around the same time, another 114,000 Chinese arrived in Cuba, stayed long after their contracts ended, and married local women. In the late 1800s, a number of Japanese arrived in Brazil, primarily seeking agricultural employment. Today there are more than a million individuals of Asian descent in Latin America, including Peru's president, Alberto Fujimori.

° **Creole** person of European ancestry born in the Americas

° **hacendado** owner of a hacienda, or large estate

Mulattos and Zambos. Africans of many backgrounds formed the third-largest racial group in Latin America, after Indians and Iberians. In the 1530s, the Portuguese were the first to bring African slaves to Brazil. Some Spaniards (and later the Dutch, French, and English) also engaged in the SLAVE TRADE, primarily to supplement the workforce on their PLANTATIONS and in the GOLD AND SILVER mines. Soon the colonists began to have relations with the African female slaves, and a mulatto population arose.

During the colonial period, some blacks from Spain and Portugal came to the Americas as slaves or free servants. These blacks occupied a position superior to that of the Indians by virtue of their association with their masters. They married Indian women and produced offspring known as *zambos*. Although the blacks, mulattos, and *zambos* together formed a large racial group, they had fewer rights than the mestizos. In areas where blacks constituted a significant part of the population, mulattos (called *pardos* in Venezuela and Brazil) came to represent a racial and social intermediate group between whites and blacks but were discouraged from marrying white Europeans and excluded from all positions of power.

Independence and Change

After the WARS OF INDEPENDENCE, the legal framework of the system of social class was abolished, and those in privileged positions (whites and Creoles*) in Latin American society began to change their attitudes toward some groups in Latin America. This was largely due to the prominent role played in the wars of independence by several mestizos and Indians, such as José Antonio PÁEZ of Venezuela and José MORELOS Y PAVÓN of Mexico. Blacks, mulattos, and *zambos* also made significant contributions to the independence movements, but they saw less improvement in their legal and economic status and in the treatment they received.

Independence but Little Freedom. Although independence ended most legal forms of discrimination against Indians, it also ended many of the legal protections they had enjoyed under colonialism. The payment of tribute, which had been abolished by the Spaniards, was revived in several countries. Moreover, Indian lands in some places were divided into small private lots, enabling hacendados* and other whites to claim the property. These and other abuses resulted in Indian uprisings during the 1800s, most of which were usually put down with violence and bloodshed. Nevertheless, some Indians, such as Mexico's Benito JUÁREZ, rose to prominent positions in society because of their wealth, education, or military status. Blacks, particularly slaves, did not fare much better than Indians, but as the strict boundaries blurred, conditions generally improved for free blacks and mulattos. Although the Latin American nations had gained political freedom from Europe, many blacks remained enslaved. Mexico and Central America abolished slavery in the 1820s, but other countries, such as Brazil and Cuba, did not outlaw the practice until the late 1800s.

Race and Ethnicity

During the late 1800s, new social theories from Europe argued that Indians and blacks were inferior to whites. The idea of inferior blood gained influence in Latin America and elsewhere. Many Latin American leaders, as well as ordinary citizens, began to consider the people of color in their countries a threat to their economic, technological, and social advancement. Consequently, many governments began to encourage large-scale immigration from Europe. They hoped that the immigrants would help "whiten" a population that they believed had been weakened by the mixing of races. However, the Indians and newly freed slaves became alarmed at this development because the new immigrants were lured to Latin America with the promise of land and jobs some of which were generally performed by black laborers and Indians. Thousands of blacks and Indians were adversely affected by the wave of immigration.

The Rise of Indigenismo and Black Consciousness.

After World War I, the spread of socialist* and Communist* ideas had a major effect on Latin American society. Artists and intellectuals together with some Indians embraced a movement known as INDIGENISMO, which celebrated the indigenous cultural heritage and demanded equal treatment for Indians. The movement found expression in literature and art, and such painters as Diego RIVERA, José Orozco, and David Siqueiros and the writers Miguel Ángel ASTURIAS and Ciro Alegría, documented the contributions that Indians had made to Latin American culture, history, and society.

During the 1930s, blacks from the Caribbean and Africa developed a similar movement that championed a new appreciation for the social and cultural contributions of Africans to humanity—NÉGRITUDE. Brazilian painter Cândido PORTINARI (born to Italian parents) featured blacks in his art. Blacks were also at the center of historical accounts that reevaluated the contributions of blacks to Latin American history. Although the movement addressed the long-standing prejudice against blacks, it was less successful in achieving equal treatment than was *indigenismo*.

Race and Ethnicity in Modern Latin America.

Since the mid-1900s, Indians have had major successes in their struggle for equal rights. Latin American governments have begun to recognize the rights of indigenous people, and Indians have been appointed to positions in government. They have also organized themselves to increase their political strength.

Blacks, again, have been less successful in their struggle for equality. This is particularly true in Brazil, where they comprise the poorest segments of society and suffer the highest rates of disease and crime. In recent years, however, Brazil has become more interested in its Afro-Brazilian citizens and has taken steps to address some of their problems. (*See also* **Africans in Latin America; Asians in Latin America; Germans in Latin America; Immigration and Emigration; Indian Policy; Middle Easterners in Latin America; Slave Revolts; Slavery; Slavery, Abolition of.**)

---

* **socialist** relating to socialism, a system in which the means of production and distribution of goods in a society are owned and controlled by the state

* **Communist** referring to a social system in which land, goods, and the means of production are owned by the state or community rather than by individuals

Radio and Television

Radio and Television

* **literacy** the ability to read and write; illiteracy is the inability to read and write

* **indigenous** referring to the original inhabitants of a region

In Latin America as elsewhere, the electronic media—radio and television—dispense information to more people than the print media. Newspapers and magazines, the reading of which requires more than minimal literacy* and purchasing power, have largely remained available only to the middle and upper classes. Except in countries where the literacy rate is high, such as Argentina and Uruguay, poor and working-class people in Latin America largely rely on radio and television for their information and entertainment.

In contrast to many developing countries where the radio and television stations are exclusively owned and operated by the state, the electronic media in Latin America are largely privately owned, used mostly for entertainment, and supported primarily by advertising. This pattern has developed in part from Latin America's economic relationship with manufacturers and advertisers in the United States. As part of their overall development plan, many Latin American governments use radio and television to attract more citizens into a developing consumer economy.

Radio. Except for a few indigenous* groups and isolated rural dwellers, almost everyone in Latin America listens to the radio. Radio programs are inexpensive to produce, and they cater to diverse interests. Most regions in Latin American have several AM and FM stations that broadcast music as well as informational and political programs.

From the 1930s, when radio began, through the 1960s, radio programs consisted of variety shows, sports, news, and *radionovelas*—serial dramas similar to soap operas in the United States. Since then, some of these programs have moved to television. Today radio programs concentrate on news, music, talk shows, and sports. The AM stations carry news, talk shows, and music that cater to the interests of people outside the Spanish and Portuguese mainstream. The AM stations in Lima, Peru, for example, broadcast programs in the Quechua and Aymara languages. The FM stations usually feature music programming that focuses on national and international popular music.

Although television is beginning to take over the role of broadcasting national news, the radio remains the primary medium for local news, political discussions, and educational programs. Most radio stations are locally programmed, although network radio has become important in some countries, particularly in the Andean highlands.

Television. In the years that followed the introduction of television in Latin America in the 1950s, this medium was restricted to urban, middle-class audiences. Since the 1960s, television has truly become a mass medium. In Brazil and Mexico, about 90 percent of the population watches television regularly. About 80 percent of urban households have television sets, and in rural areas, people watch television at friends' homes or in public places. Television became commonplace in the 1980s, when satellite dishes brought television programs to outlying small towns and United States cable stations to those who could afford it.

TV Globo

Established in 1962, TV Globo is Brazil's largest television network. During its early years, the network received government aid—money for advertising and the use of government satellites. By 1968, TV Globo had become the most watched network in Brazil. It began to produce its own daily programs, including *telenovelas*, comedies, and talk shows. In recent years, subsidiaries of TV Globo have expanded into the record industry, magazine publishing, and direct satellite broadcasting. They have also begun to influence election campaigns.

Because of the high cost of producing television programs, the industry remains more centralized than radio. Most countries have two or three commercial television networks and often a government or educational channel as well. Several new networks and independent stations emerged in the 1980s and 1990s, when the cost of production technology fell and the number of trained personnel increased.

Television programming in Latin America has gone through several phases. In the 1950s, when television was transmitted live, programs were produced locally. In the 1960s, videotape technology made it possible to import programs. In the 1970s and 1980s, television stations in Brazil, Colombia, Mexico, and Venezuela began to produce their own programs. By the 1990s, Bolivia, Chile, and the Dominican Republic were also producing television programs. During that same period, some Latin American countries became regional exporters. Today imported television programs in the Dominican Republic are as likely to come from Mexico or Venezuela as from the United States. Latin American programs are also popular in the United States, especially in cities with large Hispanic populations, such as Los Angeles.

One of the most popular types of television programs is the *telenovela,* a prime-time serial drama. Variety shows, usually televised live, are also popular. They feature games, music, amateur performances, contests, or discussions, and they are presented by a host—*animador*—who interacts with the audience. Some variety shows, such as *Siempre en domingo* (Always on Sunday) in Mexico, run for several hours, from the afternoon into the evening. Children's shows, such as Brazil's *Xuxa Show,* hosted by actress-singer Xuxa, are also popular. The *Xuxa Show* was the highest-rated daytime program in Brazil in the 1990s. Broadcast in 16 countries worldwide, it combines imaginative stories and games with serious topics, such as ways to protect the environment. (*See also* **Technology.**)

Railroads

Since the 1800s, railroads have helped unify Latin America. They have linked interior regions to the coast, played an important role in Latin America politics and progress, and made transportation faster and cheaper. Railroads also facilitated the growth of the fruit industry in Central America, the lumber industry in the Andean highlands, the coffee industry in Brazil, and the meat industry in Argentina. Latin American leaders of the 1800s who were committed to modernization encouraged the development and expansion of railroads. With this vast new industry, however, these leaders also faced challenges of financing, management, development, and labor relations.

The railroad era in Latin America began in Mexico in 1837 with the start of a rail line between Mexico City and the port of Veracruz, a distance of about 200 miles. Only short segments totaling about 90 miles of track were laid between 1837 and 1860, but by 1873, the line—renamed the Ferrocarril Mexicano—had begun to operate. Other lines followed rapidly. By 1911, with help from British and United States investors, Mexico had more than 15,000 miles of track.

Remember: Words in small capital letters have separate entries, and the index at the end of this volume will guide you to more information on many topics.

Railroad construction in other Latin American nations began in the 1850s. Argentina's first railroad was built in 1854, and by 1914, its rail network had grown to more than 20,000 miles. About 70 percent of the network was owned by the British. Brazil's early railroads were also constructed with the help of British investment and engineers. The country's first major railway line, begun in 1854, was completed in the 1860s near São Paulo to facilitate the transportation of coffee for export. By 1900, Brazil had almost 10,000 miles of track.

Meanwhile, in Chile, the railroads were owned by the state. The Ferrocarril de Santiago a Valparaíso, located in the heavily populated northern Central Valley, was completed in 1863. In 1869, Peru began railroad construction to link the coast with the interior. The railroad was a joint venture between North American businessman Henry Meiggs and the Peruvian government. By 1920, Peru had 1,700 miles of track. The railroad industry in this region developed slowly because of the mountainous terrain.

One of the largest employers of industrial workers in Latin America, the railroads strictly controlled the workers much like landowners controlled rural laborers. That is, the railroad owners offered benefits to the workers in exchange for their loyalty to the particular rail line. By the 1880s, workers had begun to organize themselves into independent labor unions and to demand changes in labor policies. Over time, railroads owned or regulated by Latin American governments amended their policies to satisfy the workers' requests, and by the 1940s, Brazil, Argentina, and Mexico had gained the support of their rail workers.

In the 1900s, in a movement toward nationalization, foreign-owned and managed railroads were placed under state control. As the management became more streamlined, the industry grew. Regional railroads merged, resulting in lower costs and expanded service with new branch lines and better station facilities. Today Latin America has about 90,000 miles of rail track. Argentina, with almost one-third of the total, has an extensive network running from Buenos Aires to its other cities. Freight and passengers move along Brazil's 23,000 miles of track lines, which are located mostly in the heavily populated southeast. Mexico, Chile, and Cuba have smaller networks. (*See also* **Coffee Industry; Labor and Labor Movements.**)

Rain Forests

Rain forests—called *selva* in Ecuador and Peru—are found in regions that receive more than 80 inches of rainfall spread evenly throughout the year. Trees grow so abundantly in rain forests that the treetops form a dense covering, or canopy, which can reach as high as 150 feet. Climbing plants, called lianas, wind upward around tree trunks and branches, while orchids and ferns grow out from the tree branches. The vegetation is so thick that little light reaches the forest floor. In places where sunlight penetrates, such as in clearings, jungles—forests with dense undergrowth—form.

Rain Forests

Many people believe that treatments to relieve the symptoms of some diseases may exist in the diverse plant life of the world's rain forests. This belief, among others, has inspired activists and environmentalists to work toward halting the destruction of the rain forests.

See map in Agriculture (vol. 1).

° **dyewood** wood from which dyes are extracted
° **cacao** bean from which chocolate is made

Saving the Forest

Part of the once vast rain forest belt of Central America, the Lacandon forest is Mexico's largest surviving tropical wilderness area. In 1875, it covered an area of more than 520,000 square miles. Despite heavy lumbering, the Lacandon forest remained largely intact until 1950. Then a combination of mechanized lumbering, road construction, settlement, extensive cattle ranching, uncontrolled burning, and large-scale energy projects destroyed much of the forest. By 1990, about 70 percent was lost. However, in the 1990s, the Mexican government passed regulations to ensure that the remaining forest area is preserved.

Most rain forests are found in the tropics, the region around the equator. The largest rain forests in the world are found in the AMAZON REGION of South America. About 60 percent of these forests lie in Brazil and the rest in French Guiana, Suriname, Guyana, Venezuela, Colombia, Ecuador, Peru, and Bolivia. There are also other, smaller rain forests throughout Latin America—along the Pacific coast of Ecuador and the eastern shores of Brazil and on several islands in the Caribbean. Central America has pockets of rain forests stretching from southern Mexico to Panama. In fact, Argentina, Chile, Paraguay, and Uruguay are the only Latin American countries with no rain forests. Although rain forests are predominantly found in lowland areas, some, called montane forests, exist at higher altitudes. Mangroves, such as those on Brazil's northeastern coast, are a special type of rain forest and are found where rivers open into the sea.

The tropical rain forests of Central and South America have the greatest diversity of plant life in the world—more than 20,000 known species. These forests have furnished the world with many natural products, including timber, dyewoods*, rubber, spices, tropical fruits, nuts, cacao*, spices, and MEDICINAL PLANTS. Wildlife abounds in these rain forests. There is a tremendous variety of insects, fish, snakes, reptiles, brightly colored birds, amphibians, monkeys, primates, and other mammals. Many of these creatures spend most of their lives in the trees, rarely descending to the forest floor. Some are peculiar to Central and South America and

Ranching

- **arable** suitable for producing crops
- **indigenous** referring to the original inhabitants of a region

are found nowhere else in the world. The region is also rich in minerals. Its soil, however, is poor, and only a very small percentage of the area is arable*.

The rain forests are the home of many indigenous* tribes, although their populations have declined since Europeans arrived in the Americas. The Amazonian Indians, for example, estimated at between 2 million and 5 million in 1500, today number about 150,000 to 200,000. These peoples live by hunting and gathering or by using agricultural methods suited to these forests. However, modern methods of reclaiming forestland are quickly destroying much of the South American rain forests. For example, to harvest one specific tree, 50 to 100 trees of lesser value may be destroyed.

Cattle ranching, oil exploration, the clearing of land for the cultivation of cash crops, and the migration of people from densely populated areas are just some reasons rain forests are being destroyed. However, since the 1970s and 1980s, awareness of the scientific, tourist, and economic values of the forests has grown. Latin American governments have strengthened their environmental laws, and they pay better attention to the conservationist practices of the native peoples and forest dwellers. As a result, more people are beginning to understand the global importance of protecting the rain forests. (*See also* **Climate and Vegetation; Environmental Movements; Forests; Geography; Lumber Industry; Medicine.**)

Ranching

See *Hacienda; Land, Ownership of; Livestock.*

Recife

Recife is the capital of the state of PERNAMBUCO and the economic, cultural, and political center of northeastern BRAZIL. Once Brazil's largest city and the center of the international sugar industry, Recife is now the seventh-largest city, with a population of well over 1 million.

Strategically located on Brazil's sugar coast, where the Capibaribe and Beberibe rivers flow together, Recife was attacked by the French in 1561, by English pirates in 1578, and by the Dutch, who occupied the city from 1630 to 1654. The SUGAR INDUSTRY briefly lost its primacy to the southern state of Bahia, although Recife's wealthy and foreign-oriented business class eventually overshadowed the traditional planters there. After independence, the city emerged as the provincial* capital in 1823. Recife grew steadily as rural laborers moved to the city and the sugar industry became centralized. By 1872, Recife's population had reached some 100,000.

- **provincial** having to do with the provinces, outlying districts, administrative divisions, or conquered territories of a country or empire

With its long-standing contact with foreign ideas and its location away from the hub of Brazil, Recife developed into a center with great regional pride. However, several revolts erupted there in the 1800s and again briefly in 1911 and 1930. During the 1900s, Recife's experiments

Reducciones

See *Missions and Missionaries; Religious Orders.*

Refugees

See *Asylum.*

Religions, African–Latin American

When the Spaniards and Portuguese forcibly brought slaves from Africa to Latin America, the slaves brought the cultural traditions and religious beliefs of their homelands with them. Over time they preserved and adapted their culture and religion to suit life in the cities and on PLANTATIONS in the Americas. Soon new religious institutions that reflected the combination of African and Latin American influences developed.

Transforming and Adapting Traditional Religions. The strongest religious groups came from the forest and coastal regions of West Africa. Depending on the conditions that the members of these groups encountered in the Americas, they were able to preserve many of the complex patterns of their spiritual beliefs. Still, their traditions were influenced by the agricultural and trade practices, opportunities for manumission*, and the established European religion.

Because Spain, Portugal, and France generally adopted Roman Catholicism as their official religion, slaveholders in their colonies were legally required to baptize their slaves. However, the CATHOLIC CHURCH actively supported slave rights, encouraged masters to free their slaves, and allowed Africans to convert and participate in Catholic services. Consequently, the African slaves and their descendants developed religions that were separate from, but related to, Christianity, such as CANDOMBLÉ in Brazil, VOODOO in Haiti, and SANTERÍA in Cuba.

By contrast, Protestant churches in the British and Dutch colonies did not enforce the baptism of slaves. Therefore, African slaves and free blacks in British and Dutch territories came to accept Christianity by joining Baptist and Methodist churches. Since these churches emphasized local leadership and personal conversion, people were also able to develop alternative forms of Protestant Christianity, such as Rastafarianism* in Jamaica.

* **manumission** formal or voluntary act of freeing from slavery

* **Rastafarianism** Jamaican religion whose members worship Haile Selassie and believe that Africa, especially Ethiopia, is the Promised Land

Religions, African–Latin American

° **assimilate** to adopt the beliefs or customs of a society

Syncretism. Africans adapted their traditional religions to Christian beliefs through syncretism, the practice of assimilating* different religious beliefs, such as by associating a traditional African deity with a saint or holy figure from the Catholic faith. For example, in some areas of Brazil, Africans worshiped Ogum, a god of the Yoruba people from present-day Nigeria on the feast of Saint George. Ogum was the Yoruba's god of fire and the protector of blacksmiths who made iron weapons and farm tools. Saint George, the subject of many works of Catholic art, was typically pictured as an armored figure on a white horse, slaying a dragon with a long iron sword. The Yoruba ORIXÁS (deities) and the Catholic saints were intermediaries between God and their followers. The cultural elements of the iron weapons linked the two deities. Moreover, the iron weapons may have served as important symbols for the African slaves during their struggles with their masters.

Important African–Latin American Religious Traditions. During the 1700s and 1800s, African–Latin American religious traditions were especially strong in areas where sugarcane was cultivated—Haiti, Cuba, and northeastern Brazil. African religions shaped the culture and society in those countries, and emigrants from there carried these traditions to other countries throughout the Western Hemisphere.

Perhaps the most famous of these religions is voodoo (vodou, or vodun). Translated as "spirit" in the Fon language of the African nation of Dahomey (present-day Benin), voodoo focuses on appealing to the spirits for protection and inspiration to survive the harsh life of the Africans in Haiti. It was the main religion of the slaves who overthrew the French colonists on Saint Domingue (present-day Haiti) and established the "black republic" of Haiti in the early 1800s. Exiled Haitians then introduced voodoo in New Orleans, Louisiana.

In northeastern Brazil—a region with many African slaves—several houses of worship based on African traditions were established during the late 1700s and early 1800s. While some maintained very pure versions of African beliefs, others incorporated European and Indian ideas to produce thousands of new forms of worship that are collectively known as Umbanda. Early leaders of Umbanda—middle-class European Brazilians—adopted the curing rituals of African and Indian spirits. However, some rejected the animal sacrifices, drinking, and drumming and dancing, because they associated these practices with more primitive forms of Umbanda.

Candomblé, another African religion, has become popular throughout Brazil. Each Candomblé center is led by a *mãe de santo* (mother of saint) or a *pai de santo* (father of saint) and observes an annual cycle during which it celebrates each of the religion's deities. Possession by spirits is an important part of Candomblé, and some members of each house enter trances in which they attempt to learn the wishes or follow the instructions of particular deities. Others serve in administrative and supportive roles for their house in return for protection by the deities.

In Cuba, the most widespread African religious tradition is Santería, named for the association between Catholic saints and Yoruba spirits.

The Way of the Saints

The African-Cuban religion Santería, or "the way of the saints," resembles the Catholic belief in which patron saints watch over those named after them or those born on their feast day. In Santería, however, the relationship is much deeper than in traditional Catholicism. A person's problems are seen as signs that he or she is neglecting the patron saint, or *orixá*. The solution often lies in rituals and sacrifice that mark the beginning of a lifelong relationship that passes through several stages. It sometimes results in a "marriage" in which the human becomes an *iyawo* (bride) to the spirit. The spirit then permanently inhabits the person, who becomes a priest.

Other traditions include Palo or Mayombe, a form of worship brought from the Congo region of central Africa, and a secret religious society known as Abakua. These religions have not had as strong an impact on Cuban society as Santería, but they have influenced festivals and popular music.

Although several African religious traditions exist in Latin America, only those practiced in Cuba, Haiti, and Brazil have been adopted in other countries, including Argentina, Colombia, the Dominican Republic, Mexico, Puerto Rico, Venezuela, and the United States. The religions serve not only as forms of belief but also as models for a renewed consciousness of African heritage. (*See also* **Protestantism**; **Slavery**; **Spiritism**.)

Religions, Indian

* **indigenous** referring to the original inhabitants of a region

* **archaeologist** scientist who studies past human cultures, usually by excavating ruins

* **cult** system of religious beliefs and rituals not officially approved by mainstream faiths; group following these beliefs

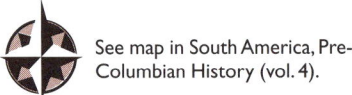
See map in South America, Pre-Columbian History (vol. 4).

Long before Europeans reached the Americas and began to spread Catholicism, the indigenous* peoples of the region had developed rich religious traditions of their own. Much like other religions, theirs sought to explain humanity's place in the world. Moreover, since nature played such an important role in their lives, Indian religions also focused on understanding and respecting the forces of nature.

Mesoamerican Religions. Most of the religions of MESOAMERICA (Mexico and Central America) were based on the patterns established by the OLMECS, who built a dominant culture in the region beginning sometime around 1200 B.C. From the remains at Olmec sites such as San Lorenzo and LA VENTA, archaeologists* believe that a small but powerful class of priests may have risen to become leaders of Olmec society. They oversaw the construction of religious centers that featured temples, altars, pyramids, and sculptures dedicated to gods who represented the forces of nature. To the Olmecs, as well as to later Mesoamerican peoples, those forces were alive and personal, and understanding them was the key to preserving the universe.

As the Olmecs, and later the MAYA, AZTECS, and INCA, shifted from hunting and gathering to agriculture-based societies, they found themselves at the even greater mercy of natural forces such as sun, rain, heat, and cold. Thus, they associated their most important gods and cults* with these forces. For instance, the largest structure in the ancient temple complex at TEOTIHUACÁN was the Pyramid of the Sun. Burn marks at key locations and the remains of a drainage system within the temple complex suggest that rituals involving water and fire took place there.

One of the ways the Olmecs sought to understand nature was through an interpretation of time. They developed a calendar to determine the most favorable times for religious ceremonies and rituals and to predict the changing seasons, which was not only a matter of religious importance but also crucial to their survival because it marked the proper planting and harvesting times for different crops. The Olmecs also felt that it was crucial for human activities to be in harmony with

Religions, Indian

Death rituals are very important to many Mesoamerican and South American religions. This photograph shows the Yawalapiti Indians of Brazil participating in a flute dance, which is part of a sacred ceremony called *kuarup* to honor the dead.

* **hereditary** passed on from one's ancestors

* **shaman** priest who uses magic or spiritual powers to heal the sick

* **hallucinogenic** capable of distorting senses and feelings or altering one's awareness

the movements of the heavenly bodies, particularly the sun and the moon. The importance that the Olmecs placed on understanding and predicting the passage of time was shared by later Mesoamerican societies, many of whom developed their own calendars and ideas about the nature of time.

One aspect of Mesoamerican religions that particularly struck the first European explorers was human sacrifice. The Olmecs, Maya, and Aztecs practiced human sacrifice, believing that the world was inherently unstable and that it became stable only when the gods were appeased with human blood. Therefore, they maintained that human sacrifice was necessary to maintain the stability of creation. Their victims included captured Spaniards, other prisoners of war, and ordinary Indians. Thus, the practice of human sacrifice among the Aztecs was motivated both by religion and by politics. As another way to ensure the stability of the universe, Aztec religious leaders sought the favors of their gods with offerings of human hearts.

South American Traditions. The forces of nature were also central to the religious traditions of South America. The major gods of the Inca, for example, represented the most important natural forces. Their principal deity, Viracocha, was associated with creation; Inti was the sun god; Illapa controlled the weather; and Pachacamac and his wife, Pachamama, ruled the earth and the sea. The Inca were a highly centralized and settled agricultural society, which like many Mesoamerican societies, was run by a hereditary* priestly class. The Inca were aggressive empire builders who conquered many of their neighbors. In doing so, they often incorporated the gods of conquered people into their system of belief to tie the defeated people more closely to the empire. Thus, like the religion of the Aztecs, aspects of Inca religion had a strongly political character that suited the needs of the Inca's priestly leaders.

Instead of a single, large empire dependent upon large-scale agriculture, the rain forests of the Amazon region featured many small chiefdoms that were typically hunting and gathering societies that also practiced some agriculture. Since they did not concentrate on conquering other peoples, they were less concerned with the political uses of religion. Rather than a dominant class of priests, individual shamans*, were their most important religious figures. Although some families were long known for producing shamans, anyone who aspired to be a shaman could do so by working as an apprentice under a living shaman. The role of the shaman was to ensure that the tribe was living in harmony with the wishes of the gods. This often involved communicating with the spirits by entering a trance, which they achieved with hallucinogenic* drugs. Shamans were also responsible for all aspects of the tribe's spiritual well-being. This included curing the sick and maintaining good relations with the animal spirits so that game would be plentiful. Earthly fortune or misfortune was also directly linked to the community's harmony with the spiritual world. Shamans in other Indian societies used similar processes. (*See also* **Calendars, Pre-Columbian; Divinities; Spiritism; Syncretism.**)

Religious Groups

See *Catholic Church; Islam; Jews in Latin America; Protestantism; Religions, African–Latin American; Religions, Indian.*

Religious Orders

° **indigenous** referring to the original inhabitants of a region

° **conquistador** Spanish explorer and conqueror

° **mission** settlement started by Catholic priests whose purpose was to convert local people to Christianity

° **evangelize** to preach Christian beliefs; to convert to Christianity

° **clergy** priests and other church officials qualified to perform church ceremonies

° **persecute** to harass someone, usually because of his or her beliefs, race, or ethnic origin

° **encyclical** letter sent by the pope to all bishops of the Roman Catholic Church

° **heresy** religious belief that conflicts with the teachings of the Catholic Church

From the beginning, the conversion of the indigenous* peoples to Christianity was the only legitimate reason for the conquest of the Americas. Therefore, members of prominent Roman Catholic religious orders accompanied the Spanish and Portuguese conquistadors* to the "New World." These European religious orders had a significant impact on Latin America's culture and civilization under colonial rule and after independence.

The Franciscans. The Franciscans, members of the Order of Friars Minor, a religious brotherhood founded by Saint Francis of Assisi in 1209, were the first to arrive in the Americas. In 1493, some Franciscans accompanied Christopher COLUMBUS on his second voyage to the Caribbean and established the first Franciscan mission* in the Caribbean Antilles. From there, the Franciscans made their way to the Latin American mainland and to areas of the present-day United States. Junípero SERRA, founder of many California missions, was a Franciscan.

In 1522, at the request of conquistador Hernán CORTÉS, the Spanish monarchy sent Franciscans to Mexico to evangelize* the Indians. They were very successful, largely because they learned Indian languages and because they instructed the Indians on new techniques in art, crafts, and agriculture. By 1532, Franciscans had arrived in Peru and eventually established missions throughout central and southern South America. In the mid-1600s, a branch of the Franciscan order, known as the Capuchins, established settlements in present-day Colombia, Guyana, Trinidad, and Venezuela. The Capuchins also founded missions in the Amazon region and conducted valuable studies of the indigenous peoples and their languages.

In the mid 1700s, the Spanish crown decided to exercise greater control over the church and seized most of its property or turned it over to clergy* not affiliated with a religious order. By the time the WARS OF INDEPENDENCE erupted in the early 1800s, the number of Franciscans in Latin America had declined sharply. During and after the wars, when leaders who were suspicious of the influence of the church came to power, Franciscans were persecuted*. Several fled to safety in Europe, and the order did not significantly reappear until after 1891, when the pope issued an encyclical* calling for social action among the clergy.

The Dominicans. The Dominican order (Order of Preachers) was founded in 1215 to wipe out heresy*. In the eyes of the Catholic Church and the Spanish crown, their antiheretical focus made them ideally suited to missionary work in Latin America. Members of the order arrived in the Americas in 1510 in response to rumors of an outbreak of heresy on the island of HISPANIOLA. They made an immediate impact on Spanish society there by preaching that all human beings

Religious Orders

are equal in the eyes of God and by criticizing the system of forced Indian labor. Their sermons moved one colonist, Bartolomé de LAS CASAS, to join the order and work to improve the Spaniards' treatment of the Indians.

Within 20 years of their arrival, the Dominicans sent friars to Mexico and Peru. In Mexico, they concentrated their greatest efforts in the south, where they had nearly complete autonomy*. They built some of the most impressive churches in the region, including the spectacular cathedral of Santo Domingo in Oaxaca. The Dominicans were among the first religious orders to arrive in Peru. Six Dominican friars accompanied conquistador Francisco PIZARRO during his conquest of Peru. As a reward, Pizarro named the only surviving friar bishop of Lima. Besides their missionary work, the Dominicans also played an important role in studying Indian languages. In Mexico, friar Diego Durán produced a detailed study of Aztec history and culture, and in Peru, friar Domingo de Santo Tomás published the first grammar and a dictionary of the Quechua language. Other prominent Catholics including Saint Martín de Porres, Saint Rosa de Lima, and Saint Mariana de Jesús Paredes, were also members of this order.

autonomy independent self-government

The Jesuits.

The Society of Jesus, whose members are known as the Jesuits, was founded in 1534 by Saint Ignatius Loyola and six companions. From their earliest days, the Jesuits made foreign missionary work and education their highest priorities. They founded colleges throughout Europe and gained a reputation for their intellect and extensive knowledge of theology*.

theology study of religious faith

The Jesuits arrived in Portuguese Brazil in 1549, but much later in Spanish America because King PHILIP II feared rivalries between the Jesuits and the orders that were already in that region. Moreover, the Jesuits, who were based in Rome, had a greater degree of independence, which did not sit well with the Spanish crown. Still, because the Jesuits were trained and well organized, Philip permitted them to establish missions in the Americas, the first of which was built in 1565 in Florida. This settlement was generally unsuccessful, but it taught the Jesuits the value of learning local languages and customs and of creating an economic base for their missions that was independent of the crown and the conquistadors.

In 1571, the Jesuits left Florida for Mexico, and by the end of the century, they had established the largest mission system in Latin America, stretching from Mexico to Argentina and Chile. Their success was attributed to the colleges they established. The colleges charged no tuition because each was supported by income from farms and estates owned by the Jesuits. The colleges survived even when the colonial economy declined. By 1767, there were 35 Jesuit colleges throughout Latin America. The order also ran eight universities, the most famous of which were in Lima, Mexico City, and Córdoba. In the missions, universities, and colleges, the Jesuits taught classical subjects, but their main goal was to convert local Indians.

The most famous Jesuit missions were the Indian *reducciones* in northern Argentina and Paraguay. To prevent the Indian converts from being corrupted by the merchants and settlers, only the missionaries

were allowed entry into the *reducciones*. These missions also served to protect the Indians from settlers who raided the frontier for slaves.

By the mid-1700s, the Jesuits, like other religious orders, were targeted by the Spanish crown, which considered their network of colleges and economic assets too powerful. In 1759, the Marqués of POMBAL convinced the Portuguese king that the Jesuits were weakening royal authority in Latin America. Consequently, 600 Jesuits were expelled from their colleges and missions in Brazil, freeing the Indians under their control. By 1767, the Jesuits were expelled from Spanish territories as well, and the Franciscans took control of their missions.

Although the Jesuits returned to Latin America in the mid-1800s, they never regained the status they had previously enjoyed. By the 1960s, the Jesuits associated themselves with the poor and supported LIBERATION THEOLOGY, a movement that saw religion as a way to achieve political and social equality. Today Jesuits are leaders in Latin America's struggle for human rights, economic justice, and the eradication of poverty.

Other Religious Orders. Several other prominent religious orders worked throughout Latin America. The Augustinians (members of the Order of Hermit Friars of Saint Augustine), named after the fifth-century bishop and saint Augustine of Hippo, were especially active in Mexico. They arrived in 1533 and established a large church in Mexico City. By the late 1500s, there were more than 600 Augustinians in 72 missions in Mexico. The order also established a significant presence in Peru in the late 1500s. Noteworthy Augustinians include Alonzo de la Vera Cruz, founder of the University of Mexico in 1553; Andrés de Urdaneta, a former sailor who is credited with discovering the sea route from the Philippines to Acapulco; and Agustín Farfán, a physician who wrote Mexico's first medical handbook.

The Santa Casa da Misericórdia, founded in Lisbon in 1498 as a charitable organization, was the most prestigious religious brotherhood in the Portuguese world. Its members—known as Misericórdian—helped prisoners, widows, sailors, slaves, orphans, and the poor. Racial purity was a precondition to membership in this organization, and applicants with Jewish, Moorish, or African blood were usually rejected. The Santa Casa is best known for the hospitals the Misericórdians built in Brazil, which served the poor of all races. The Misericórdians also did charity work in prisons, feeding the inmates and providing legal assistance.

The Mercedarian order (Order of Our Lady of Mercy for the Ransom of Captives) was founded in 1218 for ransoming Christians captured by Muslims. Although a Mercedarian monk sailed to the Americas on Columbus's second voyage, the Mercedarians' first mission was not founded until 1514 (in Santo Domingo). The order did not have a large presence in Latin America. By 1600, there were about 250 members, and by 1750, there were about 1,200, most of whom lived in Central America. Still, they played an important role in colonial education, establishing schools for the elite and occupying important positions in the universities.

The Salesians, members of the Society of Saint Francis de Sales, founded in Italy in 1859, arrived in Argentina in 1875 to do charitable work. The order worked mainly in southern Argentina and Chile. In

---

Big Order, Small Impact

Although the Order of Saint Benedict is one of the most important religious orders in Europe, the Benedictines played a minor role in Latin America. This was largely because Benedictine friars were devoted to a life of self-reflection rather than to conducting missionary work. During the 1500s, the Benedictines eventually founded missions in Brazil, but by 1894, only 10 monks remained in the country. Unlike many other orders, this one has revived in recent years. By 1985, it had seven abbeys and 170 monks in Brazil alone. The Benedictine women had 30 monasteries and more than 500 nuns throughout the region.

addition to missionary and charitable work, Salesians established industrial and agricultural schools, teacher-training schools, and business colleges, many of which are still in operation.

The order of the Carmelites (Discalced) was founded in Jerusalem during the Crusades of the 1100s. The Carmelites had arrived in the Americas by 1527 and established their first mission in New Spain by 1585. By the 1600s, they had set up monasteries in Colombia, Argentina, Peru, Bolivia, and Chile, and by 1720, in Brazil. The first community of Carmelite nuns was founded in Puebla, Mexico, in 1604. Spanish nuns established communities in Argentina, Bolivia, Chile, Colombia, Ecuador, Peru, and Cuba, while Portuguese nuns founded communities in Brazil. Today there are nearly 100 Carmelite houses in 15 countries of Latin America.(*See also* **Christian Base Communities; Penitentes.**)

Retablos and Ex-Votos

* **baroque** art style developed in Europe between 1550 and 1700 and marked by elaborate and detailed decoration

Retablos and ex-votos are religious paintings that were produced mainly in Mexico both during and after the colonial period. Derived from the Latin *retro tabula,* or "behind the altar," the term *retablo* originally referred to the carved and painted screens that appeared behind the altars of churches. After 1800, the term also referred to small paintings or images hung on altars in private homes. Retablos picture events in the life of Christ, the saints, or other holy figures in the Catholic Church. Retablo painters were usually self-taught artists who copied the paintings they saw in churches. As a result, the retablos preserve the baroque* style of these older paintings.

Ex-votos (from the Latin *votum,* or "vow") are a type of retablo that depict miracles—recovery from accident, illness, or other misfortune. They often contain a text that locates, dates, and explains the event. Because they were based on real events, ex-votos are typically more creative than other retablos. Moreover, they serve as a record of the clothing, architecture, occupations, religious beliefs, and occurrences in the lives of the people of Mexico. These works were also hung in churches, next to an image of Christ or the saint responsible for the miracle. After a time, these images were removed to make room for new ones, thus becoming "ex-votos."

The demand for retablos and ex-votos declined after the development of mechanically produced images. However, they had a great impact on the work of later Mexican artists, including Frida Kahlo and Diego Rivera. (*See also* **Art, Colonial to Modern.**)

Rice Industry

Rice is basic to the Latin American diet. It is grown in nearly every country in the region as well as under a variety of conditions. "Upland," or "dryland," rice is cultivated in areas where the rainfall is adequate or where artificial irrigation exists. "Wet rice" is grown in river deltas, interior swamps, in low-lying areas along the coasts. Although some local varieties of rice exist, most of the rice grown in Latin America is the common white rice of Asian origin.

* **Middle Ages** period between ancient and modern times in western Europe, generally considered to be from the A.D. 500s to the 1500s

* **cash crop** crop grown primarily for profit rather than for local consumption
* **monopoly** exclusive control or domination of a particular type of business

Originally introduced in Europe and Africa by Arabs during the Middle Ages*, rice was being grown in Spain and Portugal by the 1500s. Soon settlers from these countries brought rice to Latin America. Rice plants from settlements in the Cape Verde Islands, off the coast of Africa, were brought to the Brazilian town of Salvador by Portuguese colonists. African slaves, particularly those from the northwest African coast, brought techniques of rice cultivation to the Americas. By the mid-1600s, several plantations in Brazil were growing rice in their outlying fields, and Spanish landowners in Peru were exporting surplus rice to Panama.

By the 1700s, rice was valued as an easily produced, nutritious food for Latin America's growing population. After the British demonstrated that rice could be successfully grown as a cash crop*, the Portuguese invested money to develop the rice industry in Brazil. They created a monopoly* to produce rice and to sell it overseas in the hope of reducing their trade deficits with other countries. However, the Napoleonic Wars in Europe in the early 1800s and the wars of independence in Latin America soon after disrupted trade, and the industry's government funding declined.

Today three-fourths of the rice-growing land in Latin America lies in Brazil. Most of the rice grown here is of the "upland" type and is produced by large-scale commercial agricultural firms. In Argentina, Colombia, Ecuador, Peru, and Uruguay, rice is grown on the frontier by farmers on small plots of land that have been cleared and burned. In the 1990s, Latin American governments attempted to expand rice production by developing hybrid varieties of rice (produced by crossbreeding different types) and increasing the use of machines and chemical fertilizers. (*See also* **Agriculture; Food and Drink**.)

Rio de Janeiro

Rio de Janeiro is the second-largest city in BRAZIL and one of the world's most celebrated cities. A popular vacation spot, Rio is famed for its hotels, cafés, and beautiful beaches.

Founded in 1565, Rio de Janeiro was a small and insignificant town, overshadowed by Recife, Olinda, and Salvador—cities in the sugar-rich provinces of northeastern Brazil. In the 1690s, with the discovery of gold and diamonds in the nearby province of MINAS GERAIS, Rio gained importance as a port. It also became a key political center when conflicts erupted between Spain and Portugal over control of the RÍO DE LA PLATA.

In 1763, Rio replaced Salvador as the capital of Brazil, but it was considered small and backward by European standards. Its population was only 43,000, and one-third of the people were slaves. However, when the French invaded Portugal in 1807 and the Portuguese court fled to Rio, the city officially became the political and economic center of the empire. Earlier restrictions on trade, industry, and education were lifted, and the city prospered and became more sophisticated. By 1821, Rio's population had grown to about 112,000, half of whom were slaves.

Brazil broke away from Portuguese control in 1822, and Rio emerged as the leading city of the newly independent nation. Profits from the COFFEE INDUSTRY, introduced in the late 1700s, transformed Rio into a city

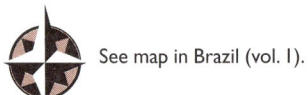
See map in Brazil (vol. 1).

Río de la Plata

Rio de Janeiro is one of the best-known vacation spots in the world. A popular tourist attraction in Rio is the Corcovado peak, which overlooks the city. At the summit stands a 93-foot-high, illuminated statue of Christ the Redeemer. With arms outstretched, he blesses the people below.

of wealth and European-style luxury. By 1870, the population had increased to 235,000, and the city had added many improvements, including public transportation, new docks, and a rail line. Growth also brought problems: disease, inadequate housing, and by the 1890s, the first hillside slums, or favelas.

Despite its problems, Rio was the undisputed center of Brazilian politics, high society, literature, and art. In the early 1900s, Brazil's leaders implemented reforms to encourage manufacturing and to improve local agriculture. By 1920, Rio boasted a population of about 1.2 million, but its position as the country's leading city was being challenged by SÃO PAULO.

By 1900, coffee from São Paulo dominated the world market, and the wealth that once poured into Rio now went to São Paulo's treasury. With less income, Rio's leaders found it difficult to meet the growing demands for housing and basic services, such as water and sewage control. Still, the city continued to grow, reaching a population of 2.3 million by 1945. Construction of highways and buildings continued through the 1950s, but the city was rapidly deteriorating. The construction of a new capital at Brasília in 1960 worsened Rio's problems as federal funding and employment shifted to the new city. In the late 1990s, with a population of nearly 10 million, the city experienced a revitalization as inflation* and crime declined. Today Rio de Janeiro is the center of Brazilian music, art, and science. With its dramatic seaside location, it is one of the world's most fascinating cities. (*See also* **Cities and Urbanization**.)

* **inflation** sharp increase in prices due to an increase in the amount of money or credit relative to available goods and services

Río de la Plata

The Río de la Plata is the estuary* of the Paraná and Uruguay rivers that forms the north-south border between URUGUAY and ARGENTINA. The estuary drains more than 1.5 million square miles in Paraguay, Uruguay, Argentina, Bolivia, and Brazil. However, it is only 10 to 13 feet deep and must be dredged* frequently for the safe navigation of ships.

Río de la Plata, Viceroyalty of

° **estuary** wide part of a river where it nears the sea

° **dredge** to deepen with the use of machines

When Spaniard Juan Díaz de Solís sailed the Río de la Plata in 1516, he believed it to be a passage to a western sea leading to the East Indies. At first, the Spaniards and Portuguese called the region Mar Dulce (Sweet Sea), but they soon renamed it after hearing legends of the King of the Mountains of Silver (*plata* in Spanish), who supposedly lived in the region.

Nations regularly fought for control of the territory. When disputes arose between Spaniards in Buenos Aires and Asunción, the Portuguese took advantage of the situation to establish a settlement there in 1680. The Spaniards responded by founding a military base at Montevideo in 1724. Although the Treaty of San Ildefonso of 1777 recognized the area as Spanish territory, the British attempted to establish an outpost there in the early 1800s. In 1814, after Argentina became independent, Montevideo separated from Buenos Aires and established itself as an independent province that later became Uruguay. Brazilians invaded the province and stayed until 1828, when they were forced out by Uruguayan and Argentine militias*. (*See also* **Geography**; **Río de la Plata, Viceroyalty of**; **San Ildefonso, Treaty of**.)

° **militia** army of citizens who may be called into action in a time of emergency

Río de la Plata, Viceroyalty of

° **viceroy** one who governs a country or province as a monarch's representative; royally appointed official

° ***audiencia*** highest regional court in a Spanish colony; also, the district under its jurisdiction

° ***intendant*** supervisor of an administrative district in Spanish America

° **bureaucrat** administrative official

The Viceroyalty of Río de la Plata, established by the Spanish crown, consisted of present-day Argentina, Paraguay, Uruguay, and Bolivia. It was the last viceroyalty to be established by the Spanish and the first to break from the empire. The viceroyalty was established in 1776, when King CHARLES III separated the region from the Viceroyalty of Peru, which was so distant from its capital at Lima that smuggling and tax evasion had become a drain on the empire. Charles appointed a new viceroy* and gave him extensive powers over the region's tax collection, the military, and religious matters in the hope that the viceroy would help generate wealth for Spain.

In 1778, the monarchy declared free trade, and merchants in the region were allowed to trade directly with Spain. A rich trade in hides and salted beef supplied the needs of slaveholders in Cuba and Brazil, and industries in the interior grew rapidly. Soon, BUENOS AIRES became the capital of the viceroyalty and the region's main port and center of trade.

In 1783, the local *audiencia** was given control over the viceroyalty's courts because of complaints regarding delays in settling legal matters. The monarchy also appointed intendants* to oversee the viceroyalty's seven provinces. Following this division of power, bitter struggles ensued between the viceroy, the *audiencia,* and the intendants, frustrating the monarchy's attempts at financial reform. Meanwhile, the bureaucrats* who performed the daily tasks in the viceroyalty were growing resentful of the crown because they were overworked, underpaid, and disrespected. Despite these problems, the viceroyalty prospered. The potential for trade brought foreign merchants and investment to the region, and a growing class of wealthy merchants rose to become the main source of tax revenues for the viceroyaly's government. Still, Buenos Aires remained a marginal outpost of the

empire, and the monarchy sent few qualified officials to the region. The royal officials who were sent often had little understanding of, or sensitivity to, the needs of the merchants. Their actions, such as the 1799 law forbidding the transportation of goods in non-Spanish ships, angered the merchants and the citizens. In 1810, frustrations erupted; the merchants, citizens, and governmental bureaucrats of Buenos Aires declared a revolt, and the viceroyalty became independent. (*See also* **Intendancy System; Spain and the Spanish Empire; Wars of Independence.**)

Rio Grande

* **annex** to add a territory to an existing state

See map in Spanish Borderlands (vol. 4).

The Rio Grande forms the boundary between Mexico and Texas. It rises from the San Juan mountains in Colorado, flows through New Mexico, and empties into the Gulf of Mexico after a course of 1,885 miles. In 1845, when the United States annexed* Texas, the river became the focus of a boundary dispute between the United States and Mexico. The United States claimed that the river formed the southern border of Texas, whereas Mexicans maintained that the Nueces River, farther north, was the border. In 1846, the two nations clashed at the town of Carricitos on the Rio Grande, a battle that convinced the U.S. Congress to declare war on Mexico.

Today the river, known to Mexicans as Río Bravo, is almost completely dry in places. This is due in part to the demands of the growing population in cities along its banks and to the manufacturing plants, or MAQUILADORAS, that have emerged to take advantage of inexpensive Mexican labor and proximity to markets in the United States. (*See also* **Mexican-American War; Spanish Borderlands; United States–Mexico Border; United States–Latin American Relations.**)

Rio Treaty

* **republic** government in which citizens elect officials to represent them and govern according to law
* **minister** state official appointed to manage specific government activities

The Rio Treaty of 1947, also called the Inter-American Treaty of Reciprocal Assistance, was a mutual defense agreement among the republics* in the Western Hemisphere. The nations that signed the treaty, which was based on the Act of Chapultepec of 1945, agreed to provide assistance to any nation among them that was the target of aggression or if the security of the Western Hemisphere was threatened. They also agreed that an attack against any member state would be considered an attack against them all. Under the treaty, a special committee of ministers*—the Organ of Consultation—was vested with the authority to decide policy and to agree on the type of action that the member states should take in case of an emergency. The committee was authorized to use military force if two-thirds of the ministers present agreed. The Rio Treaty became the basis on which the ORGANIZATION OF AMERICAN STATES (OAS) was founded, as well as a model for the North Atlantic Alliance of 1949. (*See also* **Inter-American Relations.**)

Rivadavia, Bernardino

1780–1845
Argentine statesman

* **liberal** person who supports greater participation in government for individuals; one who is not bound by political and social traditions
* **diplomatic** demonstrating tact and skill at conducting negotiations among nations
* **vagrant** person without a fixed home or steady job

Bernardino Rivadavia played a leading role in Argentine politics during the nation's independence movement. The son of a wealthy Spanish merchant, Rivadavia served as an officer in the army and fought against the British invasion of Buenos Aires in 1806. In 1810, Rivadavia supported Argentina's revolution against Spain and served as secretary of the First Triumvirate from 1811 to 1812. Rivadavia allied himself with the liberals*, who supported public education, civil rights, and the abolition of slave trade. He urged the creation of a strong central government but faced opposition from those who wanted power to remain in the hands of provincial leaders.

In 1812, after the triumvirate was overthrown, Rivadavia left on a diplomatic* mission to Europe until 1821, when he returned to Argentina as the new chief minister. He established the University of Buenos Aires, reduced the power of the Catholic Church, and promoted economic development. Because his economic plans depended greatly on British investment, trade, and markets, Rivadavia offered his British partners generous terms in Argentina. However, he ignored average Argentines and rounded up vagrants* and forced them into the army or into labor gangs. In 1826, Rivadavia became president of the United Provinces of the Río de la Plata and attempted to create a united and centralized Argentina. However, his opponents, led by dictator Juan Manuel de Rosas, forced him to resign in 1827. Two years later, he retired to Spain, where he died in 1845.

Rivera, Diego

1886–1957
Mexican artist

* **cubism** artistic style that emerged in Europe in the early 1900s and that features the subject of a painting, sculpture, or drawing as geometric forms
* **martyr** someone who suffers or dies for the sake of a cause or principle

Diego Rivera, one of Mexico's most famous artists, is known primarily for the murals he painted both in Mexico and in the United States. However, he also produced paintings, drawings, watercolors, book illustrations, and designs for theatrical productions. His artistic genius combined with his political activism made him one of the most fascinating people of the 1900s.

Rivera was born in the city of Guanajuato and studied art in Paris from 1911 to 1921. During this time, he became an admirer of such artists as Paul Cézanne, El Greco, and Diego Velázquez, whose techniques he adapted for his own work. Rivera also experimented with different styles, especially cubism*, which influenced much of his later mural work.

In 1921, Rivera returned to Mexico to begin his career as a muralist, and during the 1920s, he produced some of his most celebrated murals, including *The Deliverance of the Peon,* which he painted at the Ministry of Education in Mexico City in 1926. In this mural, Rivera used the theme of Christ's descent from the cross to represent the martyrs* of the Mexican Revolution.

Rivera's belief in the power of technology to improve people's lives is reflected in his mural *Detroit Industry,* painted at the Detroit Institute of Arts. In one panel of this work, *Production of Automobile Bodies and Final Assembly,* Rivera merges North American technology and Mexican mythology. He portrays the Aztec earth goddess Coatlicue as a fender-stamping machine, and he includes images of the origins of human life alongside images that show the various industries of Detroit.

Roa Bastos, Augusto

Mexican artist Diego Rivera was as famous for his political and personal controversies as he was for the outstanding murals he painted. Rivera is seen here painting a mural titled *Market at Tlatelolco* on the walls of the Palacio Nacional in Mexico City.

See color plate 13, vol. 1.

Rivera was not only an artist but also a controversial political activist, lecturer, and writer. He often found himself in conflict with other artists, art critics, and the Communist* Party (of which he was a member and from which he was expelled several times). Like the most famous of his four wives, the artist Frida KAHLO, Rivera was a champion of the Mexican Indian. He believed that Mexico must honor its pre-Columbian* past before it could develop its own art and identity. His controversies as well as his paintings and murals have ensured him a prominent place in the history of modern art. (*See also* **Art, Colonial to Modern**.)

* **Communist** referring to a social system in which land, goods, and the means of production are owned by the state or community rather than by individuals
* **pre-Columbian** before the arrival of Christopher Columbus and other Europeans in the Americas in the 1490s

Roa Bastos, Augusto

born 1917
Paraguayan novelist

Novelist Augusto Roa Bastos is renowned for his portrayal of the culture and history of PARAGUAY. Raised by his uncle, a bishop in Paraguay's jungle region, Roa Bastos wrote his first play and short story while still in his early teens.

Between 1932 and 1935, Roa Bastos fought against Bolivia in the CHACO WAR, an experience that greatly influenced his writing. After the war, he worked as a crime reporter for the newspaper *El País* in Asunción. In 1937 he wrote his first novel, *Fulgencio Miranda* (unpublished), which won the Ateneo Paraguayo Prize. He also won the National Prize

for Poetry in 1942 for *El ruiseñor de la aurora*. In 1944, Roa Bastos went to Europe to cover the events of World War II for *El País*. He returned to Paraguay in 1945 but was exiled for political reasons. He moved to Brazil and then to Buenos Aires, where he taught literature at the Argentine Writers' Society.

In Argentina, Roa Bastos published several novels and collections of short stories and developed a long-term association with the Argentine film industry. His 1960 novel, *Hijo de hombre (Son of Man),* set during the Chaco War, won an international literary competition. In 1974, he published his masterpiece, *Yo el Supremo (I the Supreme),* based on the life of Paraguayan dictator José Gaspar Rodríguez de FRANCIA. From 1976 to 1985, Augusto Roa Bastos taught at the University of Toulouse in France. He continues to live in Toulouse, although he has spent more time in Paraguay since the overthrow of dictator Alfredo STROESSNER in 1989. (*See also* **Literature**.)

Roads

See *Highways and Roads*.

Roca, Julio Argentino

1843–1914
President of Argentina

* **caudillo** authoritarian leader or dictator, often from the military

Julio Argentino Roca, nicknamed "the Fox," was a clever politician who dominated ARGENTINA from 1880 to 1904. During that time, he twice served as president, and between the two terms, he effectively controlled the government of the country. His presidency was a time of political order and tremendous economic growth for Argentina.

Roca's rise to power began in the army. He conducted successful military campaigns against the Ranqueles Indians in the PAMPAS. By transferring land from the Indians to the local caudillos*, he gained the support of landowners and politicians in the interior. In 1880, he was elected president, and under his rule, the Argentine economy boomed. The country became the world's leading exporter of corn and the world's second-largest exporter of wheat. Roca presided over the best railroad system in Latin America, and foreign investment—especially British—poured into Argentina. Although Roca championed the interests of the provinces over those of the merchants in the capital, BUENOS AIRES boasted fine shops and an impressive opera house and became known as the Paris of the Americas.

From 1886 to 1898, Roca controlled the government by choosing his presidential successors. He was reelected in 1898, but his second term was less successful than his first. He nearly went to war with Chile, and his policies met with strong opposition from the working class. The economy continued to grow, but foreign debt was high. After his second term ended and his chosen successor died, Roca lost his influence in Argentine politics. He spent his later years in Europe but died in Buenos Aires in 1914.

Roman Catholic Church

See *Catholic Church*.

Romero, Oscar Arnulfo

1917–1980
Archbishop of El Salvador

* **seminary** religious school where priests are trained
* **monsignor** title given to a high-ranking official, such as a bishop, of the Roman Catholic Church

Oscar Arnulfo Romero served as archbishop of EL SALVADOR from 1977 to 1980. During that time, he became an advocate of HUMAN RIGHTS, using his sermons to preach the equality and dignity of all peoples. As a youth, Romero was a carpenter's apprentice, but in 1931, he entered the seminary*. He went to Rome to continue his education and was ordained a priest in 1942. When World War II forced an end to his studies, Romero returned to El Salvador where he served as a parish priest until 1967, when he became a monsignor*. In 1974, he was appointed bishop of Santiago de María. During this time, Romero, a moderate, rejected the principles of LIBERATION THEOLOGY, a movement that was gaining popularity in Latin America. He warned priests against becoming involved in politics and encouraged them to follow their traditional roles, among them promoting brotherhood, faith, and charity.

In 1977, Romero was elected archbishop of El Salvador. Shortly afterward, his friend Father Rutilio Grande was murdered. When the government failed to investigate the crime and instead stepped up its attacks on the church, Romero withdrew his support for the government and gave up his moderate views. He began to preach against violations of human rights and set up a commission to record abuses of power by the government. For his efforts, the British Parliament nominated him for the Nobel Peace Prize. In February 1980, Romero angered the Vatican by protesting United States military aid to El Salvador, and

Although Oscar Arnulfo Romero initially opposed liberation theology, he became a leader in the movement after his appointment as archbishop of El Salvador. Romero soon gained the respect of his people, as well as the world, for his crusades against human rights violations in El Salvador. The despair of Romero's followers after his assassination can be seen in this photograph, which was taken at his funeral in 1980.

on March 24, he was assassinated while conducting mass. Romero remains a powerful symbol of the new direction of the CATHOLIC CHURCH toward preserving human rights.

Roosevelt Corollary

Issued by President Theodore Roosevelt of the United States in 1904, the Roosevelt Corollary stated that if any Latin American government was involved in "chronic wrongdoing," the United States would intervene to uphold the MONROE DOCTRINE. When European nations threatened to use force to collect their debts from Latin American countries, the United States saw a threat to hemispheric security. The United States proposed to police the region on behalf of Europe, ensuring that it would be the only power to use force in Latin America. The Roosevelt Corollary allowed the United States to expand its influence in Latin America. The United States intervened in the Dominican Republic in 1905, occupied CUBA in 1906, interfered in the politics of Central America from 1906 to 1933, and backed military governments in Haiti and the Dominican Republic. (*See also* **Imperialism; United States–Latin American Relations.**)

Rosa de Lima, Santa

1586–1617
First American saint

* **canonize** to declare a saint

Santa Rosa de Lima, (shown on page 56) a member of the Dominican order, was the first person born in the Americas to become a saint of the Catholic Church. One of 12 children born to Puerto Rican and Peruvian parents, Rosa had deep religious convictions as a young girl. However, her parents discouraged her from entering church service because they needed her at home. Nevertheless, at age 20, Rosa became a nun and spent the rest of her life serving the church and her fellow Peruvians. She set up a hospital next to her house and provided a Christian education to local children. Rosa often entered a state of religious ecstasy—reaching a close union with God—and is believed to be responsible for several small miracles related to nature. Her religious devotion included acting out the passion of Christ, for which she made and wore a crown of thorns and a cross. She was named patroness of Lima in 1669 and canonized* in 1671.

Rosas, Juan Manuel de

1793–1877
Argentine dictator

Juan Manuel de Rosas was an *estanciero* (large landowner) and a military commander who ruled ARGENTINA for more than 20 years in the mid-1800s. As a dictator, Rosas used a combination of political terror and support from other *estancieros* to control the nation.

Rosas formed his political principles while managing his cattle ranch south of BUENOS AIRES. He used strict disciplinary methods to ensure the obedience and loyalty of the peasants, gauchos, and Indians who worked for him. In 1820, he turned these workers into a cavalry*,

Rubber Industry

- **cavalry** soldiers who fight on horseback
- **militia** army of citizens who may be called into action in a time of emergency
- **guerrilla** referring to a group that uses surprise raids to obstruct or harass an enemy or overthrow a government
- **federalism** distribution of power between a central government and the member states
- **autonomy** independent self-government

which he used to put down an uprising in Buenos Aires. In 1828, after a coup led by General Juan Lavalle overthrew Manuel Dorrego, the governor of Buenos Aires, Rosas stepped in to oppose Lavalle. The following year, Rosas led a militia* composed of *estancieros* and friendly Indians, and successfully waged a guerrilla* war against Lavalle and captured Buenos Aires. That same year, he was elected governor and given absolute power to rule.

His political policies were guided by two aims: to guarantee that the *estancieros* dominated Argentina's economy and to ensure that he controlled all power from Buenos Aires. To fulfill the first goal, he seized and settled Indian land on the frontier, rewarded his supporters with land, sold public land, or gave it away. Eventually, property became concentrated in the hands of a few wealthy *estancieros*. In this way, Rosas gained the total support of the *estancieros*, who then came to his aid during the rural uprisings of 1829 and 1835.

Despite his support of landowners in the provinces, Rosas did not believe in federalism*; he wanted power concentrated in his hands alone. He used political pressure to ensure that the Argentine people dressed, spoke, and acted only in ways approved by his government. He also retained a large army to discourage interference by foreign powers and from within Argentina. He employed a unique political police force, the Mazorca, to terrorize his enemies. Despite his policies and brutal measures, Rosas appealed to the Argentine people because he offered peace and stability, which they paid for with absolute obedience to his regime.

Rosas faced opposition several times, most notably in 1839, when a group of reformers from MONTEVIDEO rose in revolt. At the same time, a French blockade caused serious financial damage to several large landowners in southern Argentina, who then blamed Rosas for their troubles. However, since the two groups did not coordinate their activities, Rosas successfully crushed both. He also brought the interior provinces under his control, but those near URUGUAY and BRAZIL challenged his authority, demanding greater trading rights, a share of customs revenues, and local autonomy*. In 1851, a powerful *estanciero*, Justo José de URQUIZA, led the allied forces of Brazil, Montevideo, and the province of Entre Ríos and invaded Buenos Aires province. In the ensuing war, the Argentine people and the *estancieros* refused to support Rosas. In 1852 he was defeated at the battle of Monte Caseros. After the battle, Rosas rode to the house of the British minister, boarded a British ship, and fled to England, where he lived in exile for the rest of his life. (*See also* **Federalism**.)

The much admired Santa Rosa de Lima is shown here in an 18th-century painting. Canonized only 50 years after her death, Rosa's remains lie next to those of another Latin American saint—Martin de Porres— in a chapel of the Dominican church in Lima. Her house and garden nearby have remained popular sites for pilgrims visiting Lima.

Rubber Industry

Latin America was once the source of most of the world's natural rubber, which was gathered from several latex-bearing plants that are native to the Amazon region. Indians living there have known of the elastic properties of latex for many centuries. They gathered the latex and smoked it over an open fire to turn it into a solid mass

from which they made numerous objects. By the 1700s, Portuguese colonists had learned of the value of latex, and they ordered waterproof boots and other latex items for their armies. The demand for rubber remained small, however, until the late 1830s, when scientists in Great Britain and the United States developed vulcanization, a process that helped retain the elasticity of rubber. Suddenly, many uses were found for vulcanized rubber, and with the invention of the bicycle and the automobile, demand for it grew dramatically.

To keep up with the demand, colonial authorities, financed by Belém in Brazil and by Great Britain, encouraged the speedy gathering of rubber. The boom that followed brought men and money to the Amazon region, and several new towns and cities, such as MANAUS, were founded in the interior. Unfortunately, in their haste to make profits, the colonists' gathering efforts took them deep into the region's rain forests, where they damaged many trees.

In 1876, England's Royal Botanic Gardens sent a shipment of young rubber plants to Ceylon (Sri Lanka) and Malaya (Malaysia), where they were planted. By 1913, the rubber industry in Brazil had largely collapsed because of competition from Southeast Asia. Brazil and the Guianas attempted to plant new rubber trees, but their efforts failed because the Pará rubber tree had become vulnerable to a leaf blight found in the region.

When the Japanese seized Southeast Asia during World War II, the United States tried to promote rubber gathering in the Western Hemisphere to replace the lost supplies, but this attempt failed as well. By the early 1960s, synthetic rubber factories were established in Brazil, Argentina, and Mexico. Today about two-thirds of the rubber used in Latin America is synthetic. Although Brazil is trying to revive its rubber industry by planting trees where the leaf blight may not appear, it is too early to tell if this effort will succeed on a large scale. (*See also* **Amazon Region; Brazil; Rain Forests.**)

Rurales

The Rurales were Mexico's rural police force from the mid-1860s to the early 1900s. Founded by President Benito JUÁREZ in 1861, the force initially included bandits whom Juárez had recruited to buy their loyalty. Dictator Porfirio DÍAZ later weeded out most of the bandits. The Rurales patrolled major transportation routes and went to potential trouble spots, especially those of interest to foreign investors. Dressed in fancy jackets, tight pants with silver buttons, and large sombreros, they gained fame as one of the world's finest police forces. However, few were good horsemen or decent marksmen, and they often failed to catch the people they pursued. Still, they became romantic, even mythical, figures in Mexico. When the Mexican Revolution erupted in 1910, the Rurales were loyal to Díaz. His successors, Francisco Madero and Victoriano Huerta, supported the force until it was disbanded in 1913. (*See also* **Banditry; Crime and Punishment.**)

Sá e Benavides, Salvador Correia de

1602–1681

Portuguese royal administrator

° **captain-general** title of provincial rulers in colonial Latin America whose main duty was the military defense of a territory

Salvador Correia de Sá e Benavides was one of the most important figures in the Portuguese empire of the 1600s. During his lifetime, he journeyed across the Atlantic Ocean many times to serve and defend the crown's possessions in Africa and the Americas.

Born in Spain, Sá first traveled to Brazil at the age of 12 or 13 with his father, who twice served as the royal governor of RIO DE JANEIRO. As a young man, Salvador helped defend Brazil against the Dutch, and in 1627, he received the title of admiral of the Southern Coast and Río de la Plata. He became governor of Rio de Janeiro in 1637 and then administrator of the mines of SÃO PAULO. In 1644, he was appointed to the Overseas Council, a body that reported to the king on Portugal's overseas territories.

In 1647, Sá was named governor and military defender of the west central African colony of Angola and was given the task of driving the Dutch from the region. Within a month of his arrival, the Dutch forces surrendered to him. Sá's contemporaries regarded his successes in Angola as his greatest achievement.

In 1658, he was named governor and captain-general* of the Repartição do Sul (Rio de Janeiro and lands to the south), as well as Espírito Santo to the north. However, he lost his governorship in 1662 because of the harsh manner in which he put down a revolt in the region. He returned to Portugal, where his reputation and popularity at court were eventually restored. (*See also* **Portugal and the Portuguese Empire**.)

Saavedra Lamas, Carlos

1878–1959

Argentine diplomat and statesman

° **tariff** tax on imported or exported goods

° **conservative** inclined to maintain existing political and social views, conditions, and institutions

° **nationalist** relating to devotion to the nation's interests

° **rector** head of a university or school

Carlos Saavedra Lamas was one of Argentina's leading statesmen and diplomats. His efforts to negotiate a peaceful settlement to the CHACO WAR between Bolivia and Paraguay earned him the Nobel Peace Prize.

Born in Buenos Aires, Saavedra Lamas received a law degree from the University of Buenos Aires in 1903 and began a career as a professor of law and economics. Later, however, he turned to politics. As a congressional deputy, he wrote the tariff* law protecting Argentina's SUGAR INDUSTRY. He also served briefly as minister of the interior and minister of justice and public education.

Saavedra Lamas achieved international prominence during the five years he served as minister of foreign affairs under President Agustín Justo. As Argentina's conservative* and nationalist* representative at numerous international conferences, he challenged attempts to make the United States the dominant authority in the Western Hemisphere. In 1933, he drafted an antiwar pact that was signed by the United States, Italy, and more than a dozen Latin American nations. The culmination of his diplomatic career came in 1936, when he was awarded the Nobel Peace Prize for helping end the Chaco War.

Retiring from public service after 1938, Saavedra Lamas remained active in national affairs. He wrote several books on law, peacekeeping, economics, and education. He also returned to teaching and became rector* of the University of Buenos Aires in 1941.

Sábato, Ernesto

born 1911
Argentine writer and thinker

* **communism** system in which land, goods, and the means of production are owned by the state or community rather than by individuals
* **surrealist** relating to a style of art, literature, or theater that creates fantastic images by placing or combining objects in an unnatural way
* **metaphysics** branch of philosophy concerned with the fundamental nature of reality

Ernesto Sábato, who had planned a career in science, became one of Argentina's most respected authors. As a young man, he attended the University of La Plata, where he received a Ph.D. in physics. During this time, Argentina was undergoing a period of political upheaval. Sábato's great concern for the social problems of his country led him to support communism*. Five years, however, he broke with the party. In the late 1930s, he traveled to Paris to further his scientific studies. There he met artists who were involved in the surrealist* movement and discovered his own love of and talent for writing. In 1945, he was fired from his position as a university professor in Argentina for publicly declaring his opposition to the dictatorship of Juan PERÓN. He then turned to writing as a career.

In his novels and essays, Sábato combines his creative imagination with his interest in philosophy and metaphysics*. Many of his works deal with ideas about human existence. His three novels are *El túnel (The Tunnel); Sobre héroes y tumbas (On Heroes and Tombs);* and *Abaddón, el Exterminador (The Angel of Darkness)*. In addition, he has written five books of essays that help explain the ideas and philosophy behind his works. In 1984, he helped investigate the disappearance of political opponents who had been arrested by the Argentine government. His report, *Nunca más,* tells the tragic story of *los desaparecidos* (the "disappeared" ones). Sábato has received numerous international awards and honors, including Argentina's Prize of National Consecration for his contribution to the nation's cultural heritage. (*See also* **Human Rights; Literature.**)

Sabinada Revolt

* **siege** prolonged effort by armed troops to force the surrender of a town or fort by surrounding it and cutting it off from aid

* **mulatto** person of mixed black and white ancestry

The Sabinada Revolt was a rebellion that broke out in the province of BAHIA in northeastern Brazil during the late 1830s. Although the revolt was started by soldiers, many of its leaders were civilians. The most famous of these leaders was a doctor named Francisco Sabino Álvares da Rocha Vieira (or Sabino), who gave the rebellion its name.

Rebel forces occupied the city of SALVADOR—then Brazil's second-largest city—in 1837 and declared it to be independent from the central government. However, wealthy merchants, large property owners, and troops loyal to the king laid siege* to the city and cut off its food supply. Hundreds of rebels and innocent bystanders were massacred when the loyalist forces captured Salvador in 1838. Sabino was captured, tried, and exiled, and thousands of other rebels were condemned to hard labor.

Historians have interpreted the Sabinada Revolt in several ways. Some see it as a battle between liberals, who supported greater regional authority, and conservatives, who supported the centralized power of the king. Others view the revolt as the reaction of soldiers to a series of unpopular military reforms. Most recently, historians have explored the idea that the rebellion was a revolt against race and class divisions in Brazilian society. As the revolt ran its course, poor mulattos* and blacks who joined the fight sought more extreme changes than the men who had started the rebellion. Those of the lower classes, some of whom had

St. Augustine

burned the houses of their enemies during the revolt, suffered the harshest punishments once the rebellion was over. (*See also* **Brazil; Pedro II of Brazil**.)

St. Augustine

St. Augustine is the oldest existing city of European origin in the United States. It was the capital of Spanish FLORIDA until 1763, and marked the northernmost outpost of Spain's empire in the Americas.

The city was founded in 1565 by Pedro MENÉNDEZ DE AVILÉS, who was sent by PHILLIP II OF SPAIN with orders to clear the French from Florida. Menéndez seized and fortified an Indian village along the coast and named the camp St. Augustine in honor of the patron saint of Avilés, Spain. In 1586, English captain Sir Francis DRAKE burned and looted the city. In 1599, the city was again devastated, this time by fire and a hurricane. Although flooding was a recurring problem, the Spanish rebuilt their city on the same site.

As the only Spanish city in Florida, St. Augustine was the seat of all branches of government. Two officials of the royal treasury served as the *regidores* (governors) of the CABILDO (city council), and the royal governor doubled as captain-general*. Florida served as a military outpost to protect mission settlements and had officers, warehouses, and quarters for convicts and slaves. St. Augustine was a religious center and the headquarters of the Franciscan* order in the region, which included Cuba.

In the 1670s, the city's defenses were improved to protect against piracy and the English. The Castillo de San Marcos, a huge fortress that still stands today, was completed in 1695. A seawall was also constructed

* **captain-general** provincial rulers in colonial Latin America whose main duty was the military defense of a territory

* **Franciscan** member of the Order of Friars Minor, a religious brotherhood

Although St. Augustine was founded by the Spaniards, by the time East Florida was annexed by the United States in 1821, the city was made up of several racial and ethnic groups, including Irish, English, Scots, Africans, Americans, and Cubans.

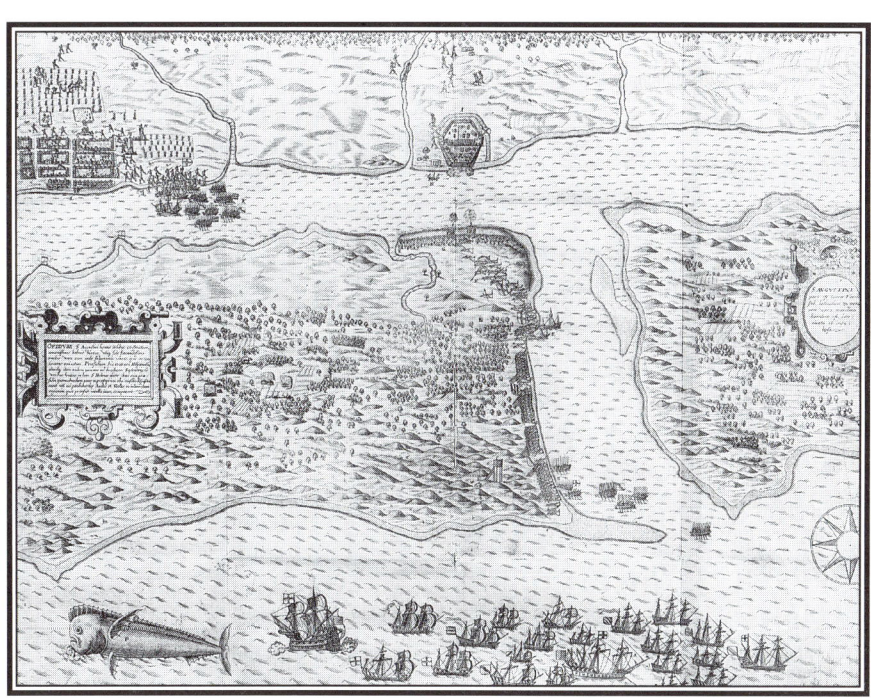

to protect the city from tropical storms. Twice during the 1700s, English invaders laid siege* to the city without success. However, in 1702, the English destroyed the city. This time its inhabitants rebuilt St. Augustine as a walled city. In 1740, it withstood yet another English invasion. In 1763, after the SEVEN YEARS' WAR, Spain exchanged Florida for British-held Havana, Cuba.

In 1783, the British returned Florida to Spain, and St. Augustine became the capital of the Spanish territory of East Florida. A distinctive style of architecture developed in the city. Two-story houses made of coquina (a type of limestone formed from broken shells and coral) were constructed with open courts and balconies facing the street. Some of these buildings still stand. The colony became a mixture of people from the islands off the coast of Spain along with Europeans, Scots, Irish, English, North Americans, Cubans, and Africans. By the time East Florida became part of the United States in 1821, St. Augustine was Spanish chiefly in name.

* **siege** prolonged effort by armed troops to force the surrender of a town or fort by surrounding it and cutting it off from aid

St. Christopher (St. Kitts)

See *British West Indies.*

St. Lucia

See *British West Indies.*

St. Vincent

See *British West Indies.*

Salesians

See *Religious Orders.*

Salgado, Sebastião

born 1944
Brazilian photographer

* **Sahel** region in Africa that lies just south of the Sahara

Sebastião Salgado is recognized as one of the world's leading photographers and photojournalists. He was born in southeastern Brazil, where his parents owned a large cattle farm. As a young man, he obtained a doctorate in agricultural economy from the Sorbonne in Paris. His first job, with the International Coffee Organization, took him to Africa. There, in 1973, he changed careers and became a photojournalist, documenting the drought in the Sahel* region. He went on to work for several prominent photography agencies, covering news stories in Africa, Europe, and Latin America.

Salgado began gathering material for *Other Americas,* his book about the peasants he had encountered in his travels. In 1982, he received an award from the French government to continue his work in Latin America. Meanwhile, working with a French humanitarian aid group, he returned to the Sahel in 1984 to photograph the effects of another disastrous famine. His book *Sahel: L'homme en détresse* (Sahel: Man in

Distress) brought him international fame. In 1992, he completed *Workers: An Archeology of the Industrial Age,* an ambitious project about workers and manual labor. A more recent work, *Terra: Struggle of the Landless,* tells the story of Brazil's rural and urban poor through photographs.

Salgado's publications have been internationally praised and called "quiet monuments to the dignity of the poorest of the poor." In an attempt to define his work, some have labeled it documentary photography. (*See also* **Photography** [with picture].)

Salinas de Gortari, Carlos

born 1948
President of Mexico

° **doctorate** highest academic degree given by a university or college

° **denationalize** to end government control or ownership of land, industries, or public works

° **fraud** trickery or misrepresentation

Carlos Salinas de Gortari was elected president of Mexico by the smallest margin in the nation's presidential campaign history. He was the candidate of the Institutional Revolutionary Party (PRI), the political party that has won every national election in Mexico since 1929. After completing his six-year term in office, Salinas left Mexico.

Salinas was born in Mexico City. The son of a former Mexican senator, he began his political career with the PRI at the age of 18. After earning a doctorate* in political economy and government from Harvard University, he served under president Miguel de la Madrid as secretary of budgeting and planning. Salinas was nominated the PRI's presidential candidate in 1987.

During his presidency, Salinas reduced the role of the state in the Mexican economy. His administration sold off state-owned companies and significantly denationalized* the banking industry. He proposed the NORTH AMERICAN FREE TRADE AGREEMENT, a treaty that reduced trade barriers between Mexico, the United States, and Canada. He also tried to lower his country's debt, keep up its loan payments, and attract foreign investment to Mexico. However, by the end of his term, Salinas' policies had failed to bring economic benefits to the working and lower-middle classes.

Salinas also adopted a controversial policy toward the Catholic Church. He reestablished relations with the Vatican and welcomed Pope John Paul II to Mexico in 1990. Salinas's administration was marked by an increase in human rights violations and abuses, however, and he was severely criticized by human rights groups, such as Amnesty International.

When he took office, Salinas promised to reform Mexican politics. Although the government did make some changes, elections continued to be influenced by fraud* and violence. Failed political reform was one of the reasons for the emergence of a revolutionary peasant movement known as the Zapatista Army of National Liberation, in the southeastern Mexican state of Chiapas. That uprising, together with the assassination of the PRI's presidential candidate, Luis Donaldo Colosio, dominated the end of Salinas's term. Economic collapse in 1994 and the conviction of Salinas's brother, Raúl, in a political murder case prompted Salinas to leave Mexico with his reputation severely damaged. (*See also* **Political Parties; United States–Latin American Relations.**)

Salt Trade

- **pre-Columbian** before the arrival of Christopher Columbus and other Europeans in the Americas in the 1490s
- **rock salt** hard layers of salt beneath the ground formed by evaporation of seawater millions of years ago

Salt has been a highly valued substance in Latin America since pre-Columbian* times. It is essential to the diet of both humans and domesticated animals. In addition, salt has been used in preserving meat, tanning hides, mining silver, and other Latin American industries.

Long before the European conquest, Indians recognized salt as a vital part of their diets and obtained it in a variety of ways. Peoples of the Andes mountains ate salt loaves, processed from salt springs. These loaves helped maintain good health because they contained iodine, an element essential to the body. Salt was also gathered from rock salt* and from dried salt lake beds. A third source was sea salt. This was produced by allowing the sun to evaporate seawater, leaving the salt behind. Today most table salt is produced by this method at large solar saltworks next to the ocean.

Tribes that controlled the production and trade of salt gained economic power. In places where salt was relatively scarce, it was traded for gold, emeralds, cotton, and dried fish. In Central America, the salt trade was a prominent part of the Maya economy. During colonial times, Spaniards took control over much of the salt production. In the late 1770s, dried beef and hide production in Buenos Aires, Argentina, increased the demand for salt. Large caravans made annual trips of about 250 miles to the Salinas Grandes (large salt flats) located in the pampas. In Brazil, the Portuguese king kept salt as a royal monopoly*. Salt was shipped to Brazil from Portugal, and colonists were forbidden to produce or sell it.

- **monopoly** exclusive control or domination of a particular type of business

Salvador

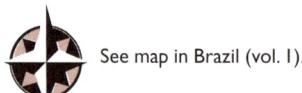
See map in Brazil (vol. I).

Salvador is the capital of the Brazilian state of Bahia. Located on the Atlantic coast, the city sits on a cliff overlooking a large harbor known as the Bay of All Saints. Founded in 1549 by Portuguese colonists, Salvador is one of Brazil's oldest cities. It served as Brazil's capital for more than 200 years, before Rio de Janeiro was named the new capital in 1763. During the colonial period, Salvador became a wealthy city and was home to several important churches and the colony's first high court.

Salvador's wealth came from the Recôncavo—a region of fertile land surrounding the city, where slave labor was used to produce sugar and tobacco for export. The demand for slaves for this region's farms made Salvador a major port in the transatlantic SLAVE TRADE. The city's wealth also made it a target of pirates and the enemies of Portugal. Captured by Dutch forces in the 1624, Salvador was retaken by Portugal the following year.

During the 1800s, Salvador experienced a series of setbacks that reduced its wealth and power. The city suffered a nine-month siege during Brazil's war for independence, and it experienced several SLAVE REVOLTS. Between 1837 and 1838, Salvador also experienced a bloody federalist rebellion known as the SABINADA REVOLT. During this uprising, hundreds of rebels and city dwellers were massacred by forces loyal to the government.

San Agustín

° **cacao** bean from which chocolate is made

Salvador continued to decline until the 1960s, when petroleum production enabled the city once again to become a major export center. In addition to petroleum, Salvador exports cacao*, sugar, tobacco, vegetable oils, diamonds, aluminum, and hardwood. Because of the city's history as a slave port, people of African descent comprise a large segment of the population, and the city has a strong Afro-Brazilian heritage. Salvador is also a major tourist destination. (*See also* **Brazil**.)

San Agustín

° **archaeological** relating to archaeology, or the science of studying past human cultures, usually by excavating ruins

° **artifact** in archaeology, a human-made object such as a tool, household utensil, or work of art

° **archaeologist** scientist who studies past human cultures, usually by excavating ruins

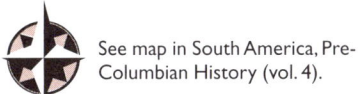
See map in South America, Pre-Columbian History (vol. 4).

San Agustín is an important archaeological* site that contains Indian monuments and artifacts*. Located in southern Colombia, the region has been the focus of research by archaeologists* since the discovery of artificial mounds and giant stone sculptures. Humans are believed to have lived in the area since before 1000 B.C. Monuments and artifacts found at the site have enabled researchers to trace San Agustín's development, which they divide into three periods: Early, Middle, and Late.

During the Early Period (1000 B.C.–A.D. 1), most of the population of San Agustín lived in areas where fertile soil enabled farmers to grow crops without the benefit of advanced tools or sophisticated knowledge. Researchers have learned very little about the social organization or trading activities of the people living in the area during that period.

By the Middle Period (A.D. 1–A.D. 850), San Agustín's population had doubled. Concentrations of people in certain areas suggest that political control had grown more centralized. By studying pollen samples, scientists have concluded that the people of the region may have cultivated corn, potatoes, and beans. Gold ornaments have been found there, which suggests that a small gold trade existed. The Middle Period also marked the peak of sculpture in San Agustín.

The population of the San Agustín region continued to grow during the Late Period (850–1530). However, the tombs, sculpture, pottery, and goldwork created during this period are simpler than those created during the Middle Period. By the time of the Spanish conquest, centralized power had weakened, and the people of the region were probably living in small chiefdoms. (*See also* **Archaeology**.)

San Ildefonso, Treaty of

The Treaty of San Ildefonso, signed in 1777, was one in a series of agreements aimed at settling territorial disputes between Portugal and Spain in South America. In 1776, Spanish forces claimed a portion of the Rio Grande do Sul, now the southernmost territory of BRAZIL. A year later they also claimed the region of Santa Catarina to the north.

The Treaty of San Ildefonso ended the fighting between the Spanish and Portuguese. In exchange for the return of the captured areas, Portugal acknowledged Spanish control of Colônia do Sacramento, an important trading center on the Río de la Plata. Spain also gained the Banda Oriental (present-day Uruguay) as well as territory occupied by several

° **Jesuit** popular name for the Roman Catholic religious order officially known as the Society of Jesus; also, a member of that order

Jesuit* missions in present-day Paraguay. The treaty was important because it carried out principles agreed upon in the Treaty of MADRID in 1750, which recognized that possession of land was the legal basis for settlement. (*See also* **Portugal and the Portuguese Empire; Spain and the Spanish Empire.**)

San Jacinto, Battle of

The battle of San Jacinto, fought in 1836, was the final battle in the war for TEXAS independence from MEXICO. The Mexican army was defeated, and Texas gained its independence and nearly a million square miles of territory.

After their defeat at the battle of the Alamo, Texas forces began a month-long retreat from the Mexican army. Under the command of General Sam Houston, the Texas rebels gathered reinforcements and then turned to engage the enemy. The Mexican army, led by President Antonio López de SANTA ANNA, was encamped on the plains between Buffalo Bayou and San Jacinto Bay, near the present-day city of Houston, Texas. On April 21, after Mexican reinforcements arrived, General Houston destroyed a bridge to prevent further reinforcement or retreat of either army. That afternoon, while the Mexicans were taking their siesta*, the Texans attacked. In a battle that lasted only 18 minutes, Texas forces soundly defeated the Mexican army and captured Santa Anna. While being held prisoner, Santa Anna signed a treaty granting Texas its independence and ending the war. (*See also* **Alamo, Battle of the.**)

° **siesta** afternoon nap or rest

San José, Costa Rica

San José is the capital of COSTA RICA and the country's largest city. Located in a valley of the *meseta central* (central plateau), San José is the nation's center of government, trade, education, banking, and manufacturing. Coffee, one of Costa Rica's most important exports, is grown on the slopes of volcanoes that overlook the city. One of these volcanoes, Irazú, badly damaged the city when it erupted in 1963 and 1964.

The Spanish first settled San José during the mid-1700s and named it for Saint Joseph, the patron saint of the first Catholic church in the valley. The city prospered as a trading center for tobacco as well as a center of contraband*. By the end of the 1700s, San José rivaled the colonial capital of Cartago in importance. After Costa Rica gained independence in 1823, a struggle erupted over whether it would become part of the Mexican empire or join a federation called the United Provinces of Central America. The people of San José supported the federation. In 1835, the city strengthened its position by fighting and defeating the united forces of three rival cities.

Since the 1940s, the region surrounding San José has grown rapidly. Today more than a million Costa Ricans (about one-half of the nation's population) live in the valley, where San José and its neighboring cities have begun to resemble one great megalopolis*. San José is a major transportation center with an international airport, links to the

° **contraband** smuggling; illegal traffic in goods

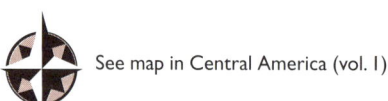
See map in Central America (vol. I).

° **megalopolis** densely populated region containing one or more large cities and their suburbs

San Juan, Puerto Rico

Pan-American Highway system, and railroads to ports on both the Pacific Ocean and Caribbean Sea.

San Juan, Puerto Rico

° **convent** house of a religious order

See map in Caribbean Antilles (vol. 1).

° **metropolitan** referring to a large city and its surrounding suburbs

San Juan is the capital and largest city of PUERTO RICO. Explorer Juan Ponce de León established the first permanent Spanish settlement near the present-day city of San Juan in 1509, and the city was moved to its present location in 1521. Situated on a large bay on the island's northern coast, the city was originally called Puerto Rico, meaning "rich port," the name later given to the island itself.

In 1536, the island came under the control of Spain's colonial system, and San Juan was chosen as the seat of one of the island's two CABILDOS (city councils). A strong Catholic community developed in the city, and several RELIGIOUS ORDERS established convents*, schools, and hospitals there.

For two centuries, San Juan functioned as Puerto Rico's only legal port. (Trade with the non-Hispanic world was forbidden by the crown.) During the colonial period, Spain built fortifications to protect the city from attacks by the French and British. In 1797, the city's fortifications helped it withstand a massive, two-week assault by 60 British ships. El Morro, a fortress with 20-foot-thick walls, still stands at the city's harbor entrance.

During the SPANISH-AMERICAN WAR in 1898, the United States landed troops in Puerto Rico. San Juan initially resisted this invasion, but within months the Americans had achieved a peaceful transfer of power. In the decades that followed, the United States invested large sums of money in Puerto Rico.

Today the population of San Juan's metropolitan* area is more than a million, with 430,000 in the city alone. The city is a manufacturing center as well as home to many of Puerto Rico's universities and museums. It is divided into two sections. Old San Juan is located on an island just off the coast and contains buildings from the city's colonial past. New San Juan, located on the mainland, has residential areas, restaurants, offices, and modern hotels along the city's beautiful beaches. (*See also* **Catholic Church**.)

San Martín, José Francisco de

1778–1850
South American
independence leader

° **Iberian Peninsula** territory in Europe occupied by Spain and Portugal

José Francisco de San Martín led troops against Spanish rule in ARGENTINA, CHILE, and PERU during the WARS OF INDEPENDENCE in the 1800s. Although San Martín failed in his attempt to create the United States of South America, to the people of Argentina, he is a national hero.

Early Career. San Martín was born in Argentina to Spanish parents. When he was a child, his family took him to Spain to be educated. As a young man, he joined the Spanish army and fought in Africa, the Iberian Peninsula*, and France. He retired from the Spanish army while in his early 30s and soon afterward, joined an organization that was seeking South American independence from Spain.

San Martín, José Francisco de

A Modest Hero

After liberating Santiago, Chile, from Spanish rule, San Martín received 10,000 gold pesos as a reward from the grateful city. San Martín accepted the gift but donated it for the establishment of a national library. Later, during a trip to his native city of Buenos Aires, Argentina, he disguised himself because he wanted to avoid a public congratulation. He was discovered, however, and the people of that city honored him with a ceremony.

---

* **coup** sudden, often violent overthrow of a ruler or government
* **royalist** supporter of the king or queen, especially in times of civil war or rebellion
* **captain-general** title of provincial rulers in colonial Latin America whose main duty was the military defense of a territory
* **propaganda** material intended to turn readers toward or away from a particular cause
* **diplomacy** art of conducting negotiations among or between nations

As the "protector of a free Peru," José Francisco de San Martín, shown here, implemented various social and political reforms. San Martín fought gambling; ended torture in judicial proceedings; abolished slavery, tribute, and *encomienda*; and established a free press.

Returning to Argentina, San Martín became a member of the elite of Buenos Aires. Impressed by his experience as a former lieutenant colonel, Argentine revolutionaries gave him command of an army regiment. San Martín's well-trained troops soon became a model for other regiments.

Liberation Begins.

In 1812, San Martín led an overthrow of the Argentine government. This coup* helped to strengthen the Argentinian independence movement. A year later, his army defeated a larger force of royalists*. The region, however, continued to be threatened by the Spanish colonial power of Peru. San Martín realized that South American independence would never be secure as long as Spanish forces held Lima, the Peruvian capital.

San Martín was soon appointed commander of a force to liberate Upper Peru (present-day Bolivia). Instead of advancing toward Lima by way of Bolivia, where revolutionary troops had already suffered heavy losses, however, he proposed a bold, new strategy to defeat the Spanish. He planned to cross the Andes and attack Chile. From Chile, he planned to advance northward by sea and attack Lima, the heart of Spanish colonial power in South America.

In 1816, he informed the revolutionary regime that he needed an army of 4,000 men to accomplish his plan. They appointed him captain-general* of the Army of the Andes, and sent him more men, weapons, and supplies.

The Army of the Andes.

San Martín began preparing his army to free Chile from Spanish rule. In addition to teaching basic military maneuvers, he placed spies in enemy camps, spread false rumors, and encouraged local uprisings. He also provided his army with a printing press with which to spread propaganda* and inform the public of the army's progress.

San Martín's army, mounted on mules, moved out of western Argentina. By way of hazardous mountain passes—some 10,000 or 12,000 feet above sea level—they crossed the Andes, defeating royalist forces as they went. After defeating the royalists at the battle of Chacabuco, with the help of Chilean General Bernardo O'Higgins, San Martín entered the city of Santiago, Chile. He declined the title of governor of Chile, and O'Higgins was chosen instead. In 1818, San Martín and O'Higgins proclaimed Chile's independence. Two months later, the patriots defeated the remaining royalists at the battle of Maipú. Meanwhile, San Martín tried diplomacy* to end the war, asking Great Britain to help persuade Spain to grant independence to South America.

Liberation of Peru.

In 1820, a united Argentine and Chilean army sailed for Peru. Because his forces were outnumbered, San Martín avoided battles and chose instead to provoke rebellions among the people and desertions in the Spanish ranks by spreading revolutionary propaganda. After the royalist forces retreated, San Martín entered Lima and declared Peru's independence. He then assumed political and military command of the new nation as "protector of a free Peru."

- **constitutional monarchy** government in which the power of the monarch, or ruler, is limited by laws and a constitution
- **republic** government in which citizens elect officials to represent them and govern according to law
- **federation** political union of separate states with a central government

Two years after liberating Peru, San Martín met with Simón Bolívar, the liberator of the northern provinces of South America. What occurred at these meetings is still disputed, but the two men are thought to have discussed the form of government that the new nations should adopt. San Martín favored a constitutional monarchy*, while Bolívar favored a republic*. Both men sought to form a federation* called the United States of South America. However, Bolívar refused to help San Martín defeat the Spanish troops who still controlled Peru's highlands. San Martín offered to serve under Bolívar but was again refused. Failing to reach an agreement with Bolívar, San Martín resigned as protector of Peru. He spent the remainder of his life in Europe in voluntary exile. In 1880, his remains were moved from France to Argentina and buried in the cathedral in Buenos Aires.

San Salvador

San Salvador is the capital and largest city of El Salvador. Surrounded by volcanic mountains, the city lies in a valley about 20 miles north of the Pacific Ocean. San Salvador is also the name of one of the nation's 14 departments, or subdivisions.

The Spanish founded the city of San Salvador in 1525. Originally, the name San Salvador was given to both the city and the territory in which it was located. The city's elite helped lead the movement for Central American independence from Spain during the early 1800s. Following the end of Spanish rule, the city briefly served as the capital of the United Provinces of Central America, a federation of Central American states.

San Salvador was the scene of dramatic events during the country's 13-year civil war, including the murder of Archbishop Oscar Arnulfo Romero in 1980 and the celebration of the end of the civil war in 1992. During the second half of the 1900s, the city's population grew as rural people migrated to the city looking for work and seeking to escape the war's destruction.

San Salvador is linked to the other major capitals of Central America by the Pan-American Highway. Because of its central location, good communication systems, and government and financial services, San Salvador and its metropolitan* area have become the heart of El Salvador's industry. The city, however, has been devastated repeatedly by earthquakes throughout its history. An earthquake in 1986 seriously damaged buildings and killed about 1,000 people. (*See also* **Central America, United Provinces of.**)

- **metropolitan** referring to a large city and its surrounding suburbs

San Xavier del Bac is one of the most beautiful and best preserved Catholic missions* in North America. Begun in 1700 by Jesuit* priest Eusebio Kino, the mission is located on the Santa Cruz River near Tucson, Arizona.

At the time of Kino's arrival in the region in 1692, the village of Bac (a Pima Indian word meaning "where the water emerges") had about

° **mission** settlement started by Catholic priests whose purpose was to convert local people to Christianity

° **Jesuit** popular name for the Roman Catholic religious order officially known as the Society of Jesus; also, a member of that order

° **mortar** cement or other substance used between bricks or stones in building

° **adobe** sun-dried clay

° **mesquite** spiny tree or shrub that grows in the southwestern United States

° **Franciscan** member of the Order of Friars Minor, a religious brotherhood

800 inhabitants. Believing that they were eager for religious instruction, Kino baptized the Indians and made preparations to establish a mission there. He brought cattle, sheep, goats, and horses from neighboring ranches and planted wheat and maize to ensure that the mission was self-supporting. In early 1700, Kino laid the foundation for the first church, which he dedicated to his patron saint, Saint Francis Xavier. The church was built using of local stone and mortar*, but it is not known whether it was ever completed. In 1751, following a series of Indian uprisings against Spanish rule, the mission was destroyed. In the late 1750s, despite Indian resistance, the church was rebuilt with adobe* walls and sturdy beams of mesquite* under the direction of another Jesuit priest, Alonso Espinosa.

When the Franciscan* missionaries arrived in the region in 1767, they found the mission in disrepair and under frequent attack by the local Apache Indians. In 1772, Franciscan priest Francisco Garcés began the task of reviving the mission. Around 1780, the old church was dismantled and construction of a new church was begun by Fray Juan Bautista Velderrain. Some of the original beams had been saved and were used in the new mission, which was completed around 1800. By 1828, however, the Franciscans had abandoned the mission and returned to Spain. The mission remained vacant until priests returned in 1859, five years after southern Arizona was purchased by the United States. Today the mission is an operating parish* that serves the Tohono O'odham Indians of the San Xavier Reservation.

The church's frescoes*, sculptures, RETABLOS, and elaborate altar decorated in gold and silver are fine examples of Mexican folk and baroque* art. In 1991, an extensive project was begun to restore the church, popularly known as the White Dove of the Desert, to its original beauty. (*See also* **Architecture; Art, Colonial to Modern**.)

° **parish** within a diocese, an area with its own church and pastor

° **fresco** type of painting in which color is applied to moist plaster and becomes chemically bonded to the plaster as it dries

° **baroque** art style developed in Europe between 1550 and 1700 and marked by elaborate and detailed decoration

Sandinistas

The Sandinista National Liberation Front (Frente Sandinista de Liberación Nacional, or FSLN) was the revolutionary group that overthrew the government of dictator Anastasio Somoza Debayle, ending a 40-year dynastic* rule. Named after guerrilla* leader Augusto César SANDINO, the FSLN was founded in 1961 by Carlos Fonseca, Tomás Borge, and Silvio Mayorga to oppose the Somoza regime. The FSLN's initial military efforts against Luis Somoza Debayle, president of NICARAGUA from 1956 until 1963, and his brother, Anastasio, who commanded the National Guard at the time, were unsuccessful. By 1967, Anastasio had become president, and most FSLN leaders had been killed or imprisoned. The FSLN regrouped in the northern hills. By 1978, the Sandinistas emerged as a major guerrilla force with about 3,000 members.

In 1978, the FSLN occupied the National Palace and forced Anastasio Somoza to release FSLN prisoners, including its future leader, Daniel ORTEGA SAAVEDRA. The raid publicized the FSLN's cause and established the organization as the largest and best-organized opposition group in

° **dynastic** related to a dynasty, a succession of rulers from the same family or group

° **guerrilla** referring to a group that uses surprise raids to obstruct or harass an enemy or overthrow a government

See map in Central America (vol. I).

69

Sandinistas

Sandinista National Liberation Front (FSLN) rebels are shown here in 1979 celebrating their victory over the Somoza government. The early years of FSLN rule were marked by successful literacy and public health campaigns. The FSLN also implemented agrarian reforms to redistribute land and promoted economic growth. The party gained its ultimate victory when it won the presidency in 1984. Since 1990, it has become a minority party.

° **Marxism** social, political, and economic principles advocated by philosopher Karl Marx, involving theory and practice of socialism

° **literacy** ability to read and write; illiteracy is the inability to read and write

° **agrarian** referring to farmland, its use, or its ownership

° **embargo** official order prohibiting the movement of merchant ships in or out of certain ports or countries

the country. In 1979, the FSLN finally removed Somoza from power and took control of Nicaragua.

The FSLN controlled power through the nine-member National Directorate. The group was influenced by Marxism* and established close ties with Cuba and the Soviet Union. The FSLN implemented successful literacy* and public health campaigns as well as agrarian* reforms. In 1984, it won the elections, and Ortega Saavedra became president.

Soon after the FSLN came to power, the United States imposed an embargo* and tried to overthrow the government. Relations with the United States deteriorated even further when President Ronald Reagan blocked United States financial assistance to Nicaragua and began a secret war against the FSLN. He authorized the CENTRAL INTELLIGENCE AGENCY (CIA) to create an anti-Sandinista force known as the CONTRAS to conduct military operations against the FSLN. When the U.S. Congress prohibited such support for the contras, the Reagan administration continued to secretly fund them through the illegal sale of arms to Iran. In 1985, President Reagan imposed an embargo on trade with Nicaragua, which continued until 1990.

In 1989, Costa Rican president Oscar ARIAS SÁNCHEZ proposed a peace plan that brought an end to the fighting and set up elections in 1990. The FSLN lost the elections but won enough seats in the National Assembly to remain Nicaragua's largest single political party. It also retained control of the army until the early 1990s. The Sandinistas have accepted their role as an opposition party and remain the best-organized political group in Nicaragua. (*See also* **Communism; United States– Latin American Relations.**)

Sandino, Augusto César

1895–1934
Guerrilla general and Nicaraguan hero

* **illegitimate** referring to a child born of parents who are not married to each other
* **socialist** relating to socialism, a system in which the means of production and distribution of goods in a society are owned and controlled by the state
* **Marxist** relating to social, political, and economic principles advocated by philosopher Karl Marx, involving theory and practice of socialism
* **anarchist** referring to anarchism, a political theory that believes that all governmental forms are unnecessary and undesirable
* **liberal** supporting greater participation in government for individuals; not bound by political and social traditions
* **conservative** inclined to maintain existing political and social views, conditions, and institutions

Augusto César Sandino, the illegitimate* son of a small businessman and a coffee picker, led the armed resistance against United States–backed Nicaraguan governments during the 1920s and 1930s. Sandino became a national hero and an inspiration for the SANDINISTA liberation movement.

Early Life and Political Activity.

Sandino had a difficult childhood, toiling in the coffee fields with his mother. At age ten, he witnessed his mother's miscarriage while she was in prison for unpaid debts. In 1906, he went to live with his father. However, he was treated poorly, while his half brother Socrates received all of his father's attention. In 1916, Sandino left for Costa Rica but returned three years later to start his own business. Forced to abandon the business after shooting a man during an argument, Sandino moved to Mexico to work in the oil fields. There he was exposed to socialist*, Marxist*, and anarchist* political ideas.

In 1926, Sandino returned to Nicaragua, supposedly to join the army of liberal* General José María Moncada. That same year, Emiliano Chamorro turned over the presidency to Adolfo Díaz, a conservative* colleague, while Moncada formed a provisional government in the north. Sandino urged Moncada to take action against Díaz, but Moncada rejected his ideas, and Sandino headed for the northern mountains to form his own army. In 1927, the United States arranged a truce between Moncada and Díaz, who agreed to step down from the presidency. The U.S. Marines took over the National Guard, and Moncada disbanded his army, asking Sandino to do the same. Sandino refused.

Instead, Sandino began to launch attacks against the Nicaraguan government, retreating after each attack to his base in the village of El Chipote. The marines searched for the village for months but were unable to find it. When they finally discovered Sandino's camp, they bombed the village. However, when the marines entered El Chipote, they found stuffed dummies, not Sandino's actual troops. By then, Sandino had acquired a mystical reputation because of his ability to avoid capture.

Truce and Betrayal.

In 1932, President Franklin D. Roosevelt of the United States implemented the GOOD NEIGHBOR POLICY, by which the United States reduced its interference in Latin American political affairs. The same year, liberal Juan Bautista Sacasa was elected president of Nicaragua, and Anastasio Somoza García was appointed chief of the National Guard. Sacasa sent a peace delegation to the northern hills to negotiate a truce with Sandino. In early 1933, they reached an agreement that accelerated the marines' departure from Nicaragua, and shortly thereafter, Sandino disarmed his army.

From this point, Sandino's life took a severe downward turn. His wife died giving birth to their daughter, and the National Guard attacked his supporters, prompting Sandino to ask Sacasa to declare the guard unconstitutional. Sacasa then invited Sandino to a meeting with Somoza in MANAGUA. The meeting seemed to go well for Sandino, but when he left the president's house with his half brother Socrates and two Sandinista

generals, they were kidnapped and murdered by the National Guard. Sandino's remains were never found. (*See also* **Nicaragua**.)

Sanguinetti, Julio María

born 1936
President of Uruguay

* **coup** sudden, often violent overthrow of a ruler or government
* **regime** prevailing political system or rule
* **amnesty** official pardon granted to individuals for past offenses against the government

In 1985, Julio María Sanguinetti became the first popularly elected president of URUGUAY following the military coup* of 1973. At that time, Sanguinetti had had 30 years of experience in politics. He was elected to the Chamber of Deputies in 1962 and re-elected in 1966 and 1971. He was the minister of education and culture under President Juan María Bordaberry in 1972 but resigned in 1973 to protest the influence of the military in politics.

Building on the success of his newspaper, *Correo de los Viernes,* Sanguinetti ran a skillful campaign for president and won the election in 1985. He took over a country that was in recession and suffering from the effects of repression and torture under previous military regimes*. He released all political prisoners, restored constitutional rights, and implemented an economic policy based on foreign trade. The economy recovered, but Sanguinetti's government lost popularity when it was forced to grant amnesty* to former military leaders after they refused to participate in trials concerning their violations of human rights during previous years.

According to Uruguay's constitution, Sanguinetti was ineligible for reelection in 1989. However, he won the presidency again in 1994. During this term, he presided over Uruguay's entry into the MERCOSUR trading bloc. (*See also* **Dictatorships, Military**.)

Santa Anna, Antonio López de

1794–1876
President of Mexico

* **liberal** person who supports greater participation in government for individuals; one who is not bound by political and social traditions

Antonio López de Santa Anna was the most important political figure in MEXICO between 1821 and 1855. He served as president nine times during those years, often giving up power soon after gaining office. As a general in the Mexican army, he led many important military campaigns against foreign powers, including Spain, France, and the United States.

Early Military Career. Born in Jalapa in the state of Veracruz, Santa Anna began his military career in 1810. He initially joined the forces loyal to the king of Spain during Mexico's struggle for independence, but by 1821, he had switched sides to support General Agustín de ITURBIDE. When Iturbide won, he awarded Santa Anna a political-military position in Veracruz. Two years later, however, Santa Anna overthrew Iturbide and was intermittently involved in national politics for the rest of the 1820s. In 1829, when Spain tried to reconquer Mexico, Santa Anna defeated the invading army at Tampico, establishing his reputation as a hero and military strategist.

In 1833, supported by the liberals*, Santa Anna was elected president for the first time, but he turned power over to his vice president, Valentín Gómez Farías. However, Mexico's conservatives* opposed the anticlerical reforms proposed by Gómez Farías and convinced Santa

- **conservative** one who is opposed to sudden change, especially in existing political and social institutions
- **oust** to remove from office

Anna to oust* him and retake control. In 1834, supported by the conservatives, Santa Anna began his second term as president. His political career remained uneventful until 1836, when he was elected to lead the Mexican army to put down the Texas Revolution. After several early victories, including the battle at the Alamo, Santa Anna was captured. He secured his release by granting independence to Texas, a move that angered many Mexicans.

Political Comeback and Final Defeat.
In 1838, when French troops invaded Mexico, Santa Anna returned to the battlefield, where he lost a leg. In 1839, he was declared president, and during the next five years, he took office three times, only to give up power shortly afterward. He was out of the country when the MEXICAN-AMERICAN WAR began in 1846, but he returned to Mexico by slipping through a United Stated naval blockade*. In Mexico, his opponents accused him of making a deal with the United States government that allowed him to return to Mexico. Nevertheless, Santa Anna was once again appointed president, and he was in and out of office in 1847. He led the Mexican troops in several unsuccessful battles, including those of Buena Vista, Cerro Gordo, and Chapultepec.

- **blockade** barrier set up to impede the advance of an enemy

Mexico was in political turmoil after the war. Finally, in 1853, a conservative alliance brought Santa Anna back and gave him extraordinary powers in the hope that he could hold the nation together. From 1853 to 1855, Santa Anna ruled harshly as a military dictator until the alliance that brought him to power disintegrated, and his role in politics declined.

Mexican history portrays Santa Anna as a greedy and fickle dictator who caused much of Mexico's instability. Yet he was able to defeat two foreign invasions and fought unsuccessfully against a third. His ability to lead troops helped Mexico survive a difficult period in its history. (*See also* **Dictatorships, Military; Mexican War of Independence**.)

Santa Cruz, Andrés de

1792–1865
President of Peru, Bolivia, and the Peru-Bolivia Confederation

- **royalist** supporter of the king or queen, especially in times of civil war or rebellion
- **tribute** payment made to a dominant power

Andrés de Santa Cruz, a royalist* officer, switched sides in 1820 and fought for Bolivian independence. He later became one of the most able presidents of BOLIVIA. Santa Cruz was born in La Paz to a Spanish colonial official and the heiress of a wealthy Indian chieftainship. He left school in 1811 to join his father's regiment and fought against the Argentine armies that invaded Bolivia in 1817. After being captured twice, he took up the cause of South American independence from Spain and fought under the Venezuelan commander Antonio José de SUCRE. In 1827, after PERU and Bolivia became independent, Santa Cruz was appointed president of Bolivia by Simón Bolívar but was soon voted out in favor of Sucre. When Peru invaded Bolivia in 1829, Sucre resigned, and Santa Cruz again became president.

An able leader, Santa Cruz developed Bolivia's textile industry, encouraged exports, and established a government based on tribute* from the local Indians. His main goal, however, was to unite Peru and Bolivia; in 1835, he invaded Peru and defeated his opponents there. He

successfully united the two countries and reorganized them into three units. Each unit elected its own president, and Santa Cruz named himself the protector of the new Peru-Bolivia Confederation. However, Chile and Argentina feared the power of the confederation, and Chile invaded Peru in 1838. The following year, the Chileans won a major battle near Lima, and Santa Cruz was forced to flee to Ecuador. He was never able to return to Bolivia and died in exile in France. (*See also* **War of the Peru-Bolivia Confederation**.)

Santander, Francisco de Paula

1792–1840
Vice President of Gran Colombia
and President of New Granada

* **republic** government in which citizens elect officials to represent them and govern according to law
* **cacao** bean from which chocolate is made
* **federalist** supporting the distribution of power between a central government and the member states
* **royalist** supporter of the king or queen, especially in times of civil war or rebellion

Francisco de Paula Santander led the armies of Simón BOLÍVAR, defeated the Spanish forces, and helped unite the states that later formed the Republic* of NEW GRANADA (present-day Colombia and Panama). Born to a wealthy cacao* planter, Santander joined the armed forces of the revolution in the early 1800s and supported those who wanted to create a federalist* state in New Granada. In 1816, the federalists lost the battle of Cachirí, and Santander was forced to flee to VENEZUELA. There, he defended Venezuela against the royalists*, and in 1819, Bolívar appointed him to lead the invasion of New Granada.

After defeating the royalists there, Bolívar united Venezuela and New Granada, formed the state of GRAN COLOMBIA, and named Santander vice president. While Bolívar continued to fight the royalists, Santander organized and ran the country. However, when Bolívar returned in 1828, he and Santander disagreed on several issues, and Bolívar removed Santander from office. Santander's supporters then tried to assassinate Bolívar, and despite the lack of proof against him, Santander was exiled.

By 1832, Gran Colombia had separated into several countries, and Santander returned from exile to become the first elected president of the Republic of New Granada. As president, he promoted public order, balanced the budget, and expanded public education. Santander's commitment to constitutional government earned him the nicknames "Man of Laws" and "Civil Founder of the Republic." Santander is held in high esteem as one of the founders of the Colombian nation. (*See also* **Wars of Independence**.)

Santería

See *Religions, African–Latin American*.

Santiago

Santiago is the capital of CHILE and the country's largest city. It lies in an enclosed valley between a coastal mountain range and the towering Andes mountains. The city was founded on the site of a small Indian settlement in 1541 by conquistador* Pedro de VALDIVIA. Throughout the colonial period, other cities threatened to overshadow Santiago, especially the outpost of Concepción, where the Spanish military forces

Santiago

In the heart of downtown Santiago lies the city's central square—the Plaza de Armas. A statue of Pedro de Valdivia, the city's founder, stands in the foreground. City Hall, the Cathedral of Santiago (dating from 1780), and several shops line the plaza. Various government and other public buildings are located near this central plaza.

* **conquistador** Spanish explorer and conqueror

* **diplomat** person authorized by his or her government to conduct international relations

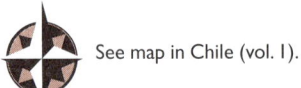
See map in Chile (vol. 1).

were concentrated, and La Serena, which was the center of commerce. Ultimately, the elite of Santiago succeeded in making the city the nation's center of government and culture.

The original site of Santiago forms the core of the city and is the location of most government offices, foreign embassies, theaters, and cultural institutions. The Casa de la Moneda, which was a mint in colonial times and today serves as the presidential palace, and the Barrio Cívico, a complex of ministries dating from the 1930s, are also located there.

The eastern section of the city, an area known the Barrio Alto, is well ventilated by mountain winds. With wide avenues and many parks, it is the preferred residential area of the wealthy. The Barrio Alto also has large malls, residences of foreign diplomats*, a military academy, and a medical school. The northern and western sections of the city are dominated by suburbs. An international airport is located north of the city, and to the west lie several industrial parks and factories. South of the city, but within easy reach by subway or highway, stretch many large residential neighborhoods—some middle class, others inhabited by the poor. In the southwest are slums. In one of these neighborhoods, called La Florida, protestors, known locally as *pobladores,* clashed with the forces of General Augusto PINOCHET when he was in power from 1973 to 1989.

Santiago is Chile's major transportation hub and is connected by railway lines to the port of Valparaíso (70 miles to the west) and the southern regions of the country. The city is also the connecting point for the northern and southern stretches of the Pan-American Highway, a roadway that runs the length of South America. The capital is also an industrial center composed of manufacturing plants whose output accounts for more than half of Chile's total industrial production.

Santiago's financial, cultural, and educational institutions include the stock exchange, the country's leading newspapers, television stations, three major universities, the Air Force Academy, and the Officers

° **metropolitan** referring to a large city and its surrounding suburbs

School of Carabineros (the national police). Despite these assets and its superb natural setting, Santiago has problems common to most growing cities. The heavy use of cars and trucks and the concentration of industries in the region have caused serious air pollution, and the Mapocho River, which flows through Santiago, has been polluted by dangerous chemical discharges. As the urban problems increase, Santiago's wealthier citizens are moving toward the slopes of the Andes. As a result, the class and economic differences within Santiago's metropolitan* area are becoming more pronounced. (*See also* **Highways and Roads**.)

Santo Domingo is the capital of the DOMINICAN REPUBLIC. During the early colonial period, the city was the center of Spanish power in the Caribbean and served as the starting point for expeditions of exploration and conquest to the Americas, but it fell into disrepair shortly afterward.

Santo Domingo was founded by Bartholomew Columbus, brother of Christopher Columbus, on August 4, 1496. Six years later, a violent hurricane destroyed many of the settlement's original wooden buildings, and the Spaniards rebuilt the city using stone. Santo Domingo had the first cathedral, university, hospital, and paved street in the Americas. However, in 1586, the city was looted and partially destroyed by English privateer* Francis Drake. Moreover, with the expansion of colonial rule in the Americas and the discovery of gold in Mexico and Peru, Santo Domingo became the backwater of the colonial empire.

° **privateer** privately owned ship authorized by the government to attack and capture enemy vessels; also, the ship's master

See map in Caribbean Antilles (vol. I).

For about 300 years, natural disasters, civil wars, and foreign invasions kept the city from flourishing. Even after independence, Santo Domingo grew slowly, its population reaching only about 19,000 by 1908. In 1930, a hurricane destroyed most of the capital, except the colonial stone buildings. Dictator Rafael Leónidas TRUJILLO MOLINA, who was then in power, organized a public building program. The city's impressive Presidential Palace, the Palace of Fine Arts, and the buildings at "La Feria" (The Fair) were built as part of this program. Today the city has more than 2 million inhabitants and serves as the seat of the nation's politics and government.

The Audiencia of Santo Domingo was one of the first Spanish institutions founded in the Americas. The *audiencia*, or high court, heard legal cases, handled the government and administration of Spain's colonial territories, heard appeals from civil and criminal courts in the Spanish Caribbean, and was responsible for matters involving the royal treasury.

In 1511, the Spanish monarchy established the *audiencia* in SANTO DOMINGO on the island of HISPANIOLA. The *audiencia* was installed with the intention of saving people the expense and time of traveling to

Spain for their legal needs and to curb the powers that the crown had reluctantly awarded to Diego Colón, son of Christopher Columbus.

During the first 30 years, the *audiencia* and its three judges reduced Colón's power in the region and helped settle territorial disputes between conquistadors*. The *audiencia* also helped formulate and implement policies with Colón and the region's treasury officials. However, the *audiencia* was not active in protecting the rights of the colony's Indians, partly because its early judges were involved in the slave trade and benefited from *encomienda** and forced Indian labor. The judges also enriched themselves by seizing smuggled goods and by requiring the local colonists pay a fee for a judicial visit to a district. In 1523, when Colón returned to Spain, the *audiencia* assumed the responsibility for governing the island. In 1529, a fourth official, the president of the *audiencia*, arrived from Spain. Although the four officials were expected to govern jointly, the judges and the president often disagreed over who had the greater power to dispense justice and administer the colony.

As Spain expanded into more profitable colonies, such as Mexico and Peru, Santo Domingo declined in importance. The *audiencia*'s jurisdiction* changed many times over the years, growing larger with the addition of newly claimed territories (such as Florida), then smaller as the new regions acquired *audiencias* of their own. By the late 1500s, the Audiencia of Santo Domingo was considered the lowest-ranking *audiencia* in Spanish America. (*See also* **Audiencia**.)

* **conquistador** Spanish explorer and conqueror

* **encomienda** right granted to a conqueror that enabled him to control the labor of and to collect payment from an Indian community

* **jurisdiction** area of authority

Santos-Dumont, Alberto

1873–1932
Brazilian inventor
and pioneer of flight

* **dirigible** lighter-than-air aircraft with a rigid framework covered by a thin shell and filled with gas; can be steered, unlike a balloon

Alberto Santos-Dumont is known internationally as the "father of aviation." He achieved many milestones in the history of flight but was driven to despair by ways in which his inventions were used. Born in Brazil's Minas Gerais province, Santos-Dumont was interested in mechanics and aviation from an early age. In 1891, the young Santos-Dumont moved to Paris to join a group of inventors who were experimenting with flight. Six years later, he became the first person to use an internal combustion engine for flying, and in 1901, he flew a dirigible* of his own design over Paris.

These early achievements had involved lighter-than-air craft, but Santos-Dumont next turned his attention to heavier-than-air machines: airplanes. In 1906, he won an award flying the *14-Bis,* a plane he had designed. The European press proclaimed him conqueror of the air—a title disputed by the Wright brothers, who were then secretly experimenting with flight in the United States. In 1908, Santos-Dumont created a water plane (precursor of the hydroplane), and the following year, he produced the world's first successful monoplane (single-winged aircraft like modern planes).

Although Santos-Dumont had many interests—he designed the first wristwatch and wrote three books—flying was his passion. When World War I broke out in 1914, he spoke out against the use of aircraft in war. During an uprising in Brazil in 1932, when the federal government sent planes to bomb the city of São Paulo, Santos-Dumont was so horrified

that Brazilians were dropping bombs on their fellow citizens that he committed suicide. The town of his birth, Palmira, was renamed Santos Dumont in his honor.

São Paulo

* **Jesuit** popular name for the Roman Catholic religious order officially known as the Society of Jesus; also, a member of that order

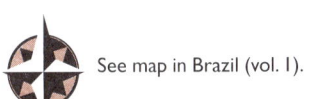
See map in Brazil (vol. I).

São Paulo, one of the world's most populous urban centers, is a state in south-central BRAZIL as well as a city in that state. Since the late 1800s, the state and the city have dominated the nation's political life, and remain the driving force behind the modern economy of Brazil.

In 1532, explorer Martim Afonso de Sousa founded the first Portuguese settlement at the coastal island of São Vicente, part of the present-day state of São Paulo. The Portuguese continued to establish settlements along the coast until 1554, when Jesuit* priests traveled about 30 miles inland to spread Christianity among the Indians. This inland settlement marked the beginning of the city of São Paulo. During most of the colonial period, São Paulo was an isolated, poor town with a few thousand inhabitants.

In the 1600s, the city served as the base from which *bandeiras* departed on expeditions in search of slaves or treasure in the interior regions of southern and central Brazil. In the early 1700s, the city enjoyed a spurt of prosperity when gold was discovered in the nearby province of MINAS GERAIS. However, after the gold rush ended, São Paulo returned to the staples of its earlier trade: sugar, mules, and cotton.

By the early 1800s, São Paulo had a population of about 20,000 and exported tea, which was grown with great effort on the infertile land surrounding the city. By the mid-1800s, São Paulo had become a modest city with a population of about 25,000, a prominent law school, and several colleges. The state experienced a rapid and dramatic change in the 1860s, when Brazilians began growing coffee in the northwestern regions. The city flourished as the center of Brazil's fast-growing coffee industry, and by the 1880s, Brazil was exporting more coffee than sugar and cotton. Newly built railroads carried the coffee crop from the rural districts to the city of São Paulo and then on to the port of Santos. The city's importance also grew in other ways. The law school became the center of intellectual and political thought, and many of its graduates entered national politics. São Paulo was the center of Brazil's abolitionist, or antislavery, movement, and the city's leaders were the first to call for the end of monarchy rule in Brazil.

Brazil overthrew Emperor Pedro II in 1889, and the city's population grew from 65,000 in 1890 to 600,000 by 1920, mainly because of immigration from Italy, Portugal, Spain, Japan, and the Middle East. The city also experienced a growth in industry, which created an urban working class. By 1940, São Paulo had almost 2 million inhabitants, and the region's economy continued to grow. Industry, not coffee production, fueled the growth. The city became Brazil's leader in modern industries, such as textiles, chemicals, pharmaceuticals, automobiles, and electrical equipment. In recent years, São Paulo's population has continued to increase, primarily because of the migration of rural Brazilians to the city.

° **metropolitan** referring to a large city and its surrounding suburbs

By the late 1990s, the metropolitan* area had a population approaching 18 million.

Sarmiento, Domingo Faustino

1811–1888
Argentine educator and president

° **progressive** inclined to support social improvement and political change by governmental action

Domingo Faustino Sarmiento successfully combined education and politics in his career. Born in the city of San Juan, Argentina, Sarmiento studied languages, literature, and the Bible and taught elementary school as a teenager. Convinced of the need for an orderly government, he fought against Argentine dictator Juan Manuel de ROSAS, who dominated politics from 1829 to 1852. In the 1830s, Sarmiento started *El Zonda,* a newspaper that expressed his progressive* views on agriculture, modernization, and education, including that of women. In 1839, he founded a secondary school for girls. In 1840, he was forced to flee to Chile because of his outspoken criticism of Rosas.

Sarmiento did not return to Argentina for 15 years. Meanwhile, he expanded and modernized Chile's educational system and traveled in Europe and the United States to study teaching methods. In 1845, he published *Civilización i barbarie: Vida de Juan Facundo Quiroga (Life in the Argentina Republic in the Days of the Tyrants; or, Civilization and Barbarism).* The book was an insightful examination of Argentine politics and was highly critical of Rosas. Sarmiento wrote many other works as well, including a volume on his travels in the United States.

° **envoy** person representing a government abroad

In 1855, three years after Rosas fell from power, Sarmiento returned to Argentina, setting in Buenos Aires, where he served as the director of education. Later, as a senator and then governor of San Juan Province, Sarmiento continued to promote educational reform. During the 1860s, he served as Argentina's envoy* to Peru and the United States. Elected president in 1868, Sarmiento was finally in a position to realize his lifelong goals of modernizing Argentina. He promoted cultural, economic, and educational development, and he encouraged immigration. Sarmiento brought more than 80 teachers from Europe and the United States to Argentina. His efforts, and those of his followers, made Argentina's schools the best in Latin America. Sarmiento also expanded the country's road and railway systems, founded public libraries, and modernized and beautified the city of Buenos Aires. Despite his opposition to the methods of the caudillos*, he was known to be dictatorial when it came to crushing political opposition.

° **caudillo** authoritarian leader or dictator, often from the military

Sarmiento later served in the Senate and held several other posts. He founded *La educación común,* (Public Education), an educational journal, and *El Censor,* a newspaper, before his death in 1888 in Asunción, Paraguay. His complete writings were published in 53 volumes the same year. (*See also* **Education**.)

Schools

See *Education*.

Science

From the earliest days of exploration, the Americas were a source of scientific information for the European powers. In fact, Christopher COLUMBUS and other explorers documented the natural history of the region during their expeditions. By doing so, they began a tradition in which scientific research in the Americas was sponsored by, and closely tied to, the interests of the European powers. After independence, however, that support of scientific achievement in the Americas disappeared, and little scientific activity was renewed until the late 1800s.

The Colonial Era. The European powers were eager to benefit from the natural products, especially minerals and plants, that they discovered in the Americas. Therefore, explorers were encouraged to gather scientific information that eventually played a key role in reshaping European ideas about the natural world. Many of these observations overturned the scientific beliefs that the Europeans had accepted for centuries.

By the 1700s, science was considered a prestigious activity and a pursuit that promised economic benefits. The European powers devoted a relatively large percentage of their annual budgets to scientific activities. Moreover, since military activities were also considered scientific, even more money was being spent on science than was reflected in the budgets. At the time, most scientists took up military careers that enabled them to pursue projects that had military and scientific usefulness, such as mapping coastlines and establishing boundary lines. However, placing science in the hands of the military limited the spread of scientific knowledge because the military considered all scientific results as state secrets and they remained hidden from the public.

The area of greatest interest to Latin American scientists during the colonial period was botany*. In the mid-1700s, Sweden's Carl Linnaeus had developed a system of classifying plants and animals, and many naturalists traveled to the Americas to collect new species. Soon scientific institutions were established throughout Latin America. By the end of the 1700s, New Granada had an astronomical observatory, and Mexico City had two first-class technical institutions—the Colegio de Minería trained mining engineers, and the Casa de Moneda (mint) became a center for innovative TECHNOLOGY, particularly in the area of mechanics.

The Independence Period. As the colonial period ended, it appeared that a strong foundation for scientific studies had been laid in Latin America. However, with political independence, Latin America lost funding and direction from Europe. Moreover, the leaders of the newly independent nations focused on building political power rather than on the advancement of science. Still, some professionals, such as doctors and engineers, continued to pursue scientific research.

By the late 1800s, a scientific revival had begun, and several new institutions were founded in Latin America. Many of these had a practical focus, such as the Mining School of Ouro Prêto in Brazil, which was established to take advantage of the country's mineral resources.

* **botany** branch of biology that deals with the study of plants

Scientists debated Darwin's theory of evolution and the ideas of Louis Pasteur, who developed the germ theory of disease. Medical research institutes were founded throughout the region. Researchers at the Oswaldo Cruz Institute in Brazil solved the mystery behind American sleeping sickness. In 1881, Cuban researcher Carlos Finlay identified the mosquito that carried the yellow fever virus. His theory was confirmed after the Spanish-American War, when the U.S. Public Health Service successfully wiped out the disease in Cuba and Panama. In the late 1800s, many countries, most notably Brazil, adopted POSITIVISM, a belief that scientific principles and objective knowledge should be used to govern nations.

Many foreigners, particularly those from the United States, were involved in Latin American scientific activity at this time. Latin American scientists sought training in Europe, the United States, and elsewhere. United States–based organizations such as the Rockefeller Foundation promoted Latin American sciences, encouraged scientists to engage in field and laboratory work, and pushed to make teaching and research full-time positions so that scientists did not have to support themselves by holding multiple jobs. In fact, Latin America's first two Nobel Prize winners, Bernardo HOUSSAY (1947) and Luis LELOIR (1970), were supported by research grants from the Rockefeller Foundation.

In 1909, the Argentine government founded a physics institute at the University of La Plata for research. Albert Einstein's visit to Argentina, Uruguay, and Brazil in 1925 sparked an explosion of interest and research in modern physics. Brazil became a leader in experimental physics during the 1930s, and in 1947, researchers at the astrophysical laboratory in Chacaltaya, Bolivia, discovered a new subatomic particle called the pi-meson. After World War II, Brazil, Argentina, and Mexico became centers of research in nuclear physics.

Laws of the Hurricanes

Spaniard Benito Viñes y Martorell (1837–1893), arrived in Havana, Cuba, in the mid-1800s to take charge of the Belén Observatory. There he devoted his life to finding a way to detect the signs of approaching hurricanes. Viñes studied the movement of the clouds, the changes in barometric pressure, and the paths of hurricanes in previous years. Soon he was able to predict, within reasonable limits, the path a hurricane would follow. In 1875, he made the first accurate hurricane forecast in history. Although Viñes did not have the sophisticated tools used by weather forecasters today, his "laws of the hurricanes" remain valid, and his work is considered a historical landmark in hurricane forecasting.

The Post–World War II Period. During the 1940s and 1950s, there was a strong push to establish national scientific research councils to stimulate public and governmental interest in science. Despite the creation of such organizations, Latin America suffered the loss of scientific talent from the 1950s through the 1970s as scientists and researchers migrated to the United States and Europe. This was due in large part to the unstable political conditions in the region and dictatorial leaders who wanted to control science for political purposes.

In the 1960s, Latin American scientists began to debate whether scientific investment should concentrate on practical projects that focus on the immediate economic and social needs of the people. Some argued that one cannot effectively pursue applied science projects without conducting research in basic, or pure, science, which provides the foundation for applied knowledge. There has also been a recognition that science is international and cannot be restricted to one nation. Despite these debates, the quality of the region's scientific institutions continues to improve. As educational and economic standards rise, Latin American scientists will likely make even more significant contributions to international scientific knowledge. (*See also* **Astronomy; Education; Medicine.**)

Sculpture

See *Art, Colonial to Modern; Art, Pre-Columbian.*

Selk'nams

* **anthropologist** scientist who studies human beings, especially in relation to origins and cultural characteristics

* **guanaco** animal related to the camel and llama

The Selk'nams (also called the Onas) were an Indian group that lived on TIERRA DEL FUEGO, the cold, rugged island off the southern tip of South America. Anthropologists* believe the Selk'nams settled the island before rising sea levels separated it from the continent about 11,000 years ago.

The Selk'nams are descended from hunters and gatherers who migrated into PATAGONIA around 9000 B.C. As these early Indians drifted apart and settled in areas with different environments, they formed distinct tribes. By about A.D. 1000, the Selk'nams had developed their own culture, one different from that of the Indians of the Patagonian mainland and from the Indians living on the smaller islands in the region.

In northern Tierra del Fuego, the Selk'nams specialized in hunting guanaco* and rodents. They built shelters of posts and skins around their fires. In the south, Selk'nams also hunted guanaco, while those in the southeast hunted sea mammals, such as seals, living along the coast. In this region, the Selk'nams lived in cone-shaped huts with walls made from dried mud to protect them from the freezing winds. Despite the cold, early European explorers noted that the Selk'nams wore little protective clothing apart from occasional cloaks made from animal skins.

There were about 4,000 Selk'nams on Tierra del Fuego when Europeans began colonizing the island in the late 1800s. By the 1990s, fewer than 50 of their descendants remained on the island. (*See also* **Indians**.)

Selva

See *Forests; Rain Forests.*

Senado da Câmara

* **alderman** elected municipal official who serves on the governing council of a city or town
* **procurator** agent or official who manages the affairs of other people

The *senado da câmara,* or town council, was the smallest and most independent body of self-government in colonial BRAZIL. The council enforced local laws, settled land disputes, imposed and collected taxes, and communicated citizens' complaints to the higher authorities. Within the councils, Portuguese-born royal officials often struggled with local elites for control of these affairs.

Each council had eight members: three aldermen*, two justices of the peace, a procurator*, a president or a presiding judge, and an ordinary judge. Local property owners elected most of these officials, but some councils had a crown judge who was appointed by the royal government. Crown judges tried to control the membership of the council by declaring who was eligible for local office.

Overtime, town councils grew more powerful and independent. In some cities, such as Rio de Janeiro and SALVADOR, councils succeeded in having

governors removed from office. The *senado da câmara* remained vigorous throughout the colonial period, often challenging Portuguese officials.

Sendero Luminoso

- **guerrilla** referring to a group that uses surprise raids to obstruct or harass an enemy or overthrow a government
- **militant** aggressive, willing to use force
- **communism** system in which land, goods, and the means of production are owned by the state or community rather than by individuals

The Sendero Luminoso (Shining Path) is a revolutionary movement that formed in PERU during the early 1960s. In 1980, it launched a campaign of terrorism and guerrilla* warfare against the Peruvian government. The government struck back at Shining Path in the early 1990s, seriously reducing the group's power. The group remained active in the late 1990s, however, especially in the remote highland regions of Peru.

Shining Path was started by Abimael Guzmán Reynoso, a professor of education at a university in the highland region of Ayacucho. Guzmán was a member of the Communist party who believed in a militant* form of communism*. He acquired a loyal following at the university, and some of his supporters returned to their peasant communities to teach in local schools. Under Guzmán's leadership, Shining Path prepared for what he called a "people's war" against the Peruvian government.

The war began in 1980, just before Peru's first national elections in 17 years. At first, most of the fighting occurred in Ayacucho, but gradually Shining Path became active throughout Peru. The organization attacked, threatened, and assassinated political leaders in order to weaken Peru's government. Shining Path seized weapons during its attacks on the police and the military, obtained dynamite by raiding mining operations, and acquired money through the illegal DRUG TRADE.

The government struck back at Shining Path with military campaigns that often violated the civil rights of civilians. The conflict in the countryside forced more than 250,000 peasants to flee to the cities. By 1992, it had caused the deaths or disappearances of more than 26,000

This photograph shows dozens of Shining Path guerrillas participating in a 1992 surrender ceremony at the Tarapoto barracks near Lima, Peru. At the ceremony, these rebel soldiers surrendered their weapons and accepted amnesty from President Alberto Fujimori. According to the terms of the amnesty agreement, the men were allowed to return to civilian life after serving for two years in the Peruvian army.

people. Property damage and economic losses were huge. Peru's tourist industry sharply declined because travelers feared being kidnapped or murdered.

In 1992, government forces captured Guzmán and arrested more than 1,200 members of Shining Path. By 1994, violence inspired by Shining Path had greatly declined. Peru's government predicted that the group would soon disappear entirely. However, a new leader, Oscar Ramírez Duran, emerged in the mid-1990s and rallied Shining Path followers. In the late 1990s, the group carried out a series of terrorist and guerrilla actions, including bombings, the murder of antidrug police, and the kidnapping of oil company workers. (*See also* **Communism in Latin America; Guerrilla Movements.**)

Serra, Junípero

1713–1784
Missionary in New Spain

* **missionary** person who works to convert nonbelievers to his or her faith

* **presidio** Spanish fort built to protect mission settlements

Junípero Serra was a Franciscan missionary* who played a key role in the Spanish colonization of California (then part of the SPANISH BORDERLANDS). He founded several missions that strengthened Spain's control of the area and served as centers for future settlement.

Born on the Spanish Mediterranean island of Mallorca, Serra's original name was Miguel José Serra. In 1730, when he joined the Franciscans, a Roman Catholic religious brotherhood, he took the name Junípero. After advanced study and service as a professor of philosophy, Serra traveled to the Americas in 1749 and became a missionary among the Indians.

In 1768, Serra took charge of missions in Lower California (located on the Baja Peninsula on Mexico's northwest coast). From there, he helped plan the Spanish settlement of Alta (Upper) California. He accompanied a military expedition traveling north and established Alta California's first mission, in 1769, near present-day San Diego. The following year, he traveled farther north up the California coast and established the mission of San Carlos Borromeo at Monterey. This mission and the presidio* built nearby became the capital of Spanish California.

Over the next 14 years, Serra and the Franciscans founded nine more missions. The missionaries there converted Indians to Christianity and taught them new farming methods and how to weave and make pottery. After his death, Serra became known as "the Apostle of California" because of his work converting Indians to the Catholic faith.

The Roman Catholic Church honored Serra for his accomplishments in Christianizing the California Indians. In 1988, Serra was beatified, which means that the church granted him blessed status and authorized public honor of him. The church also announced that it was considering making Serra a saint—a move that aroused some protests. Although Serra's admirers point to his success in spreading the Catholic faith, some Indians claim that Serra and other missionaries enslaved their ancestors, forced them to give up their traditional ways of life, and punished them with whippings if they resisted. Whatever the church's final decision about Serra's religious status, he will be remembered as a leading figure in the settlement of Spanish California. (*See also* **California; Missions and Missionaries; Religious Orders.**)

Service Industry

The service industry is one of the three major sectors of any country's or region's economy, along with agriculture and manufacturing. Unlike agriculture and manufacturing, however, the service industry does not produce material goods. Instead, it provides services that meet people's needs. The many ways in which people earn money by doing things for one another, from waiting on tables in restaurants to teaching in schools, make up the service sector of an economy.

Trends and Developments. Personal services, such as those provided by domestic servants, hotel and restaurant workers, travel guides, and barbers, are part of the service economy. Other important segments of the service economy include banking and finance, trade and commerce (including retail sales), education, health and social work, transportation, communications, and government and administration.

The percentage of Latin America's population working in the service industry grew during the second half of the 1900s. Between 1960 and 1978, for example, the percentage of working people employed in the service industry rose from 44 to 57 percent in Argentina, from 40 to 54 percent in Chile, and from 25 to 35 percent in Mexico. These changes indicate trends in the region's economic development. A greater number of people working in the service industry means that fewer people are earning their living by farming, while more opportunities are available in business and in professions such as teaching and health care.

However, not all service sector jobs are secure professional positions. The majority of jobs in the service industry are poorly paid. Many people working in this industry are occasional or part-time employees. Others, such as street vendors and shoe shiners, are self-employed.

Domestic Service. Domestic service—working in someone else's home—has always been an important part of the Latin American economy, especially as an area of employment for women. During the 1500s, many domestic servants, perhaps as many as half of them, were men. By the 1700s, however, most were women. With few other opportunities available to them, women relied on domestic service as a way to earn money. Although Latin American society did not accept the idea of women in other jobs, many people felt that private homes offered suitable, protected places for women to work.

Between the 1940s and the 1970s, improved economic conditions throughout Latin America and the growth of the service sector created new job opportunities for women. Upper- and middle-class women entered the labor force in greater numbers, creating a demand for domestic servants to do the work that remained at home. Women's employment in domestic service increased in Latin America during this time. In the 1980s and 1990s, however, the demand for full-time, live-in servants shrank in Latin America as a result of improved day care for children, a greater concern for privacy, and wider use of labor-saving devices, such as washing machines. More people began hiring domestic services on a part-time or occasional basis.

Shortened Lunch Break

In 1999, the centuries-old tradition of the afternoon siesta came to an abrupt end for government workers in Mexico. Under a new law, federal employees are prohibited from taking more than one hour for lunch. Before the 1999 legislation, government workers had been able to take a two- or three-hour midday break and then return to work until nine or ten o'clock at night. The Mexican government said it expected to save millions of dollars by cutting down on the electricity used by late-working employees. However, critics pointed out that many Mexicans used the afternoon break to work a second job to supplement their income from low-paying government jobs.

Service Industry

Other Aspects of the Service Industry. Transportation is another part of the service sector in Latin America. However, the nature of transportation work has changed over time. During the colonial period, most transport was by water, requiring sailors and others to haul, load, and unload cargo. The development of new forms of transportation for rail, highway, and air travel created new service jobs. The jobs that became available ranged from those of laborers building railways through forests and over mountains to those of pilots flying airplanes.

Unlike transportation, tourism is a fairly new segment of the Latin American economy. There have always been travelers, but only after trains, steamships, and other modern modes of transportation made travel comfortable did large-scale tourism develop. In the early 1900s, people seeking a warm place to spend their leisure time began visiting the Caribbean. By the end of the 1900s, Latin America accounted for a tenth of all the money spent on tourism in the world.

Tourism exemplifies the interconnectedness of the service industry. Tourism involves a variety of related service jobs, including those of travel agents, transport workers, hotel and restaurant workers, travel guides, and the people who develop advertising for resorts. The increasing economic importance of tourism is another factor in the rise of the

Many economists believe that a large service industry indicates a well-developed economy. This table shows the percentage of people working in the service industry in several Latin American nations. Venezuela, which has a large service industry, also has an average yearly income of $9,000 per person (1996 estimate). By contrast, Guatemala, which has a smaller service industry, has an average yearly income of $3,460 per person (1996 estimate).

Percentage of Labor Force in the Service Industry, 1998

Latin American Nation	Percentage of Labor Force
Argentina	57
Bolivia	Data unavailable
Brazil	56
Chile	38
Colombia	46
Costa Rica	54
Cuba	Data unavailable
Dominican Republic	32
Ecuador	38
El Salvador	16
Guatemala	14
Haiti	Data unavailable
Honduras	20
Jamaica	26
Mexico	32
Nicaragua	43
Panama	32
Paraguay	Data unavailable
Peru	44
Uruguay	33
Venezuela	64

Source: The World Almanac and Book of Facts, 1999.

Seven Cities of Cíbola

The Spaniards who conquered and colonized Mexico during the 1500s believed that somewhere north of Mexico there existed a wealthy civilization known as the Seven Cities of Cíbola. The search for these mythical cities led to several explorations of what is now the United States Southwest.

According to a medieval legend, seven bishops left Spain and founded the golden cities of Cíbola. Prompted by the hope of finding another rich civilization, such as that of the AZTEC in Mexico or the INCA in Peru, the Spaniards searched for Cíbola in the territories north of Mexico. In 1539, Friar Marcos de Niza left Mexico City to search for the cities. After his return, he described a vast, rich empire in the Spanish Borderlands*. A follow-up expedition led by explorer Francisco Vázquez de Coronado failed to find this empire, however, because it did not exist. The searchers found only the Indian villages of New Mexico, which Friar Marcos had exaggerated in his reports.

* **Spanish Borderlands** northern frontier of New Spain, consisting of present-day Florida, Texas, Arizona, New Mexico, and California

Seven Years' War

The conflict that was known in Europe as the Seven Years' War (1756–1763) was called the French and Indian War in North America. Because Spain fought on the losing side of the war, it gave up some of its territories in the Americas when it signed a peace settlement to end the hostilities.

The war in Europe pitted Prussia (part of present-day Germany) and Great Britain against France, Austria, and Russia. In North America, the French fought the British. Spain entered the war on the side of France in 1761. The following year, Great Britain captured the port of Havana, Cuba, one of Spain's oldest Caribbean colonies. The British returned the port to Spain in 1763. The peace settlement signed that year favored Great Britain, whose powerful navy had dominated the fighting. Britain acquired Canada and some Caribbean islands from France and gained Florida in exchange for the return of Cuba. The war had revealed the weakness of Spain's power in the Americas. In response, King CHARLES III strengthened Spain's ties with the colonies and improved their defenses.

Shining Path

See *Sendero Luminoso*.

Ships and Shipping

See *Fleet Systems, Colonial; Manila Galleon*.

Sierra Madre

The Sierra Madre is a large system of mountains stretching the length of MEXICO. The range is an interconnected set of five mountain groups that divide Mexico into its various regions and influence its climate. The Sierra Madre reaches as far north as the southwestern United States and as far south as Guatemala.

MINING of metals such as silver, gold, iron, and zinc first brought the Spanish to the Sierra Madre. Mining remains important, but forestry and dam construction also developed during the 1900s.

Four of the mountain groups form the edges of Mexico's vast central plateau. The Sierra Madre Occidental and the Sierra Madre Oriental mark the plateau's western and eastern edges. The Occidental range is volcanic and runs along Mexico's western coast. Some of the country's most valuable evergreen forests grow on its higher slopes. Water rushing down the canyons on its western side powers hydroelectric* plants. East of the plateau, the Sierra Madre Oriental runs parallel to the Gulf of Mexico. At its southern end is Mount Orizaba, the highest peak in Mexico.

The Sierra Madre del Sur is a region of ridges and steep valleys between Mount Orizaba and the Pacific coast. Its eastern portion is called the Sierra Madre de Oaxaca. This area was home to several important pre-Columbian* Indian groups, including the MIXTECS and the ZAPOTECS.

The fifth and smallest mountain group is the Sierra Madre de Chiapas. Located in the southernmost corner of Mexico, it reaches into neighboring Guatemala. Forestry and coffee growing are the main economic activities of this sparsely populated region. (*See also* **Geography**.)

* **hydroelectric** referring to electricity harnessed from waterpower

* **pre-Columbian** before the arrival of Christopher Columbus and other Europeans in the Americas in the 1490s

Silva Xavier, Joaquim José da

1746–1792
Brazilian independence fighter

Joaquim José da Silva Xavier, also known as Tiradentes, became a Brazilian national hero for his role in a plot to overthrow Portuguese colonial rule and make BRAZIL independent. Silva Xavier was born in MINAS GERAIS, Brazil's mining province. Orphaned at an early age, he was raised by his older brother, who was a priest. Silva Xavier's godfather was a dentist, and the young man probably learned the basic techniques of the profession from him. From time to time, Silva Xavier practiced dentistry and his nickname, Tiradentes, means "Toothpuller."

Silva Xavier enlisted in the royal army and soon rose in the ranks to troop commander. In 1788, he joined a group of elite citizens of Minas Gerais who were plotting independence. Among the members of this group were a royal judge, a town councillor, a military commander, a priest, and the son of the local tax collector. The group hoped to win support in other provinces and make Brazil a republic*, but the governor learned of the plot, which became known as the Inconfidência Mineira, and had the plotters arrested before they could implement their plan.

Of all those involved in the plot, only Silva Xavier took full responsibility for it and was executed. The others, all of whom had higher social status than Silva Xavier, did not even stand trial. Although the

* **republic** government in which citizens elect officials to represent them and govern according to law

Inconfidência Mineira failed, it was a sign of growing unrest under Portuguese rule. In the years since Brazil won its independence, Silva Xavier has become one of the major heroic figures of the nation's past, a symbol of the ordinary Brazilian's desire for liberty and independence.

See color plate 3, vol. 4.

Slave Revolts

For almost 400 years, from the early 1500s until the late 1800s, Latin Americans held slaves, mostly Africans and their descendants. Slaveholders treated these enslaved people like property, often punished them cruelly, and forced them to labor in miserable and dangerous conditions. It is no surprise that slaves often resisted this treatment by running away or rebelling against their owners.

Some MAROONS, as runaway slaves were called, formed communities in remote areas where they were unlikely to be pursued. Others, however, led insurrections* or joined them. From the earliest days of slavery in the Spanish-ruled Caribbean islands until the freeing of the last slaves in Brazil, slave revolts broke out throughout Latin America.

* **insurrection** violent uprising against authority; rebellion

Slave Uprisings in Spanish America.
The first serious revolt by African slaves in the Americas occurred in 1522, just a few decades after European colonization began, on the island of Hispaniola. Forty slaves took part in the uprising, which occurred on a sugar estate owned by the son of Christopher Columbus. In the years that followed, many similar revolts took place throughout Spain's American empire, especially where large numbers of slaves were concentrated on plantations and in mines.

Revolts usually began as conspiracies, and sometimes authorities uncovered these plots before open rebellion erupted. Many plots and uprisings involved African slaves working with Indians, free people of color, and a few Creoles* who supported the abolition of slavery or who had reasons of their own for wanting to overthrow the local government. Slaves in privileged positions—drivers and domestic workers rather than field-workers—led many of the conspiracies and uprisings.

* **Creole** person of European ancestry born in the Americas

As early as the 1550s, a runaway slave tried to unite Africans and Indians in an anti-Spanish rebellion. The 1700s brought a series of bloody slave revolts to the sugar-growing area around Veracruz, Mexico. The largest of these, in 1735, may have involved as many as 2,000 slaves. Spanish Louisiana experienced a revolt and a revolutionary conspiracy in the 1790s, and Cuba had some of the most intense slave resistance in Spanish American history during the sugar boom of the 1800s. Several conspiracies involved large networks of both slaves and free people. Coastal Venezuela's uprisings and conspiracies, however, were the most serious in Spanish America. Colombia and Peru also experienced large-scale slave revolts, both before and after their independence from Spain. Two uprisings on sugar plantations in Peru in 1851 were among the last in Spanish America.

The collective resistance of slaves in Latin America contributed to the abolition of slavery. Many of the slave revolts in the region were large, violent, and well organized. This engraving, taken from a German report of a 1791 slave revolt, depicts the uprising against plantation owners and their families in Santo Domingo, Hispaniola.

Slave Uprisings in Brazil.
Slaves in all parts of the Portuguese colony of Brazil escaped bondage by forming and defending runaway

89

Slave Trade

° **autonomous** self-governing
° **militia** army of citizens who may be called into action in a time of emergency

Rebellion in Venezuela

In the early 1730s, Andrés López del Rosario, known as Andresote, led one of the largest slave revolts in Spanish South American history. Andresote was a smuggler of mixed black and Indian ancestry who, with help from the Dutch, clashed with authorities in the Yaracuy River valley of Venezuela.

He led black and Indian followers in a great insurrection against the Caracas Company, which exported cacao and imported slaves. The rebellion lasted several years before a force of 1,500 soldiers crushed it. Andresote fled to the Dutch Caribbean island of Curaçao, where he died a few years later.

slave communities called *quilombos*. More than 100 *quilombos* are believed to have existed in the single province of Minas Gerais in the 1600s and 1700s. The largest *quilombo* in Brazil's history was PALMARES, which flourished for almost half a century and functioned like an autonomous* state.

Many slave revolts in Brazil occurred in the sugar plantation areas of the northeast during the first half of the 1800s. The Bahia region experienced a great number of revolts, including the most serious ones. Later in the 1800s, many smaller rebellions occurred in the coffee-growing region to the south.

Rebellions and *quilombos* were closely linked. Many uprisings led to the formation of new runaway slave communities, and people from such communities often encouraged or led new revolts. For example, in 1826 a *quilombo* called Urubu (Vulture), strengthened by newly escaped slaves, tried to take over the city of Salvador on Christmas Eve. A woman named Zeferina led the warrior-slaves, but militia* and regular troops overcame them. A few years later, African Muslims led a revolt that pitted 500 rebels against police in house-to-house fighting in Salvador.

Many slave uprisings during the second half of the 1800s were tied to revolutionary or abolitionist movements. The 1870s and 1880s, especially the years before Brazil ended slavery in 1888, saw many small revolts, escapes, and conspiracies, as well as the formation of new *quilombos*. These actions probably helped bring about the end of slavery in Brazil, the last country in the Americas to free its enslaved people. (*See also* **Slave Trade; Slavery; Slavery, Abolition of.**)

Slave Trade

Of the 10 million or more enslaved Africans who were transported across the Atlantic Ocean between the 1490s and the 1860s, more than 85 percent ended up in Latin America. About 10 percent of all African slaves in the Americas went to the Spanish mainland colonies. Another 35 percent went to the Portuguese colony of Brazil. Most of the remaining slaves—the largest percentage—went to the Caribbean islands, which included French, Dutch, and British colonies as well as Spanish ones.

The trafficking of slaves was a critical element in the economies of colonial Latin America. Although slavery contributed to the formation of the richly diverse multicultural population that is one of the region's unique characteristics today, the slave trade was a tragic chapter in the history of European activities in the Americas.

° **Creole** person of European ancestry born in the Americas

The Traders. The Portuguese were the leading slave traders of the 1400s and 1500s. The Dutch joined them in the 1600s, and by the 1700s, the British and French were carrying the majority of captive Africans across the Atlantic. Merchants and shippers based in Europe rather than colonists or Creoles* organized most of the slave trade. Brazilians in the ports of Salvador and Rio de Janeiro, however, were responsible for a considerable portion of the slave trade to those ports during the 1700s.

As the British began to withdraw from the slave trade in the early 1800s, the Brazilians and Portuguese became the major suppliers of slaves. The Spaniards, a few from the United States, and some French also remained involved in the slave trade until it officially ended in the mid-1860s.

During the 1500s and 1600s, the Spanish and Portuguese tried to regulate and tax slave trading. By the late 1600s, however, companies of private merchants in several nations had taken over the slave trade, some engaging in illegal commerce as well. During stops in Spanish colonial ports to unload legal shipments of slaves, they often smuggled manufactured goods into the colonies and took silver out of them.

The Queirós Law

Passed in 1850 by the Brazilian legislature and named for Minister of Justice Eusébio de Queirós, the Queirós Law ended the slave trade between Africa and Brazil. Although a similar law had existed for nearly 20 years, Brazilians had effectively ignored it until 1845. That was when the British claimed the authority to search and seize slave ships in Brazilian ports. Within a few years after the passage of the Queirós Law, the Brazilian slave trade virtually disappeared.

Development of the Slave Trade. The European slave trade began in the 1400s as an outgrowth of the Portuguese trade with West Africa. At first, the Portuguese were more interested in gold than in slaves. As droughts and wars created turmoil in that region of Africa, local warlords began to kidnap refugees and prisoners of war and sell them to other Africans and to Europeans. A new area of the African economy emerged, one that exchanged slaves for European manufactured goods, such as cloth, metal items, liquor, and firearms. Gradually, the dominant states in the region grew dependent on selling slaves.

In the Americas, the demand for slaves arose from the combination of Europeans' desire to exploit the mineral and agricultural resources of their colonies and the shortage of labor needed to do so. Since European diseases and cruel treatment had already reduced the Indian population in Latin America, Europeans turned to the forced labor of Africans.

The Traffic in Human Beings. Slave traders brought about twice as many men as women to the Americas. Over time, the average age of slaves carried across the Atlantic dropped, so that by the 1800s, the typical slave was a teenage boy. European and African slavers established outposts—factories and forts at which captives were held for shipping—along the African coast. Slavers at these outposts loaded their human cargo onto ships for the arduous "Middle Passage" across the Atlantic from West Africa to the Caribbean, a voyage that took from 80 to 120 days, or from Angola to Brazil.

In the early years, the slave traders used ships that had been designed to carry goods, not human beings. Shortages of water and food killed many of the Africans, who were crammed into the cargo holds. During the early years of the slave trade, perhaps as many as one-fourth of all the captives died during the passage. By the early 1700s, professional slavers had developed vessels that could carry 300 to 400 prisoners, chained closely together below decks. Over time, slavers learned that by providing enough food and water, and sometimes even allowing exercise on deck, they were able to keep a greater proportion of their valuable human cargo alive. The death rate among slaves dropped to about 10 percent.

Pirates, war, and storms at sea brought disaster to many slave ships, but disease was the slaves' worst enemy. The crowded, filthy cargo holds in which they traveled were breeding grounds for disease, and the Africans could do nothing to improve their condition. Most prisoners

Slavery

spent the months before boarding the ships marching in captivity or enduring imprisonment in a coastal trading post or fortress. Those who were originally from the highlands of interior Africa easily succumbed to the illnesses and infections they encountered in these coastal prisons. By the time they were loaded onto the ships, many were already weak, malnourished, and ill.

In the early 1800s, Britain spearheaded a movement to abolish the slave trade, and after 1811, the British navy began to drive slavers from the seas. Still, the Europeans and Africans involved in the trade sought out remote, hidden ports in Africa and the Americas where they could continue their commercial activities. Ironically, in the last years of the slave trade, when slaving had become illegal, traders used faster ships and took greater precautions than ever to make their voyages profitable, and the death rate among the slaves they carried dropped to 5 percent. (*See also* **Africans in Latin America; Slavery; Slavery, Abolition of.**)

Slavery

* **pre-Columbian** before the arrival of Christopher Columbus and other Europeans in the Americas in the 1490s
* **immigrant** one who settles in a new country

Slavery existed in Latin America for well over 1,000 years—from the time of the pre-Columbian* kingdoms through the colonial period and until long after the wars of independence had freed the region from European control. Pre-Columbian societies sold people into slavery or conquered them. During the colonial period, many economies depended on the labor of enslaved Africans and INDIANS who worked on plantations, in mines, as servants, and in many other jobs. Over the centuries, Europeans brought between 5 and 6 million Africans to Spanish America and Brazil as slaves. These unwilling immigrants* not only powered the Latin American economy but also shaped the racial, ethnic, and cultural landscape of modern Latin America.

Slavery in Spanish America.

* **exploitation** relationship in which one side benefits at the other's expense
* **indigenous** referring to the original inhabitants of a region

Slavery was a feature of Spanish society before the colonization of the Americas began. The Spanish had enslaved Africans, Jews, Muslims, and other Spaniards. When Spain began colonizing the Americas, it turned to slave labor, already a familiar form of exploitation*. The Spanish first enslaved Indians in the Caribbean, but disease and ill treatment soon killed many of these indigenous* peoples. In 1501, the Spanish crown granted permission to the governor of HISPANIOLA, Spain's first American colony, to import Africans as slaves to that island.

Once slavery was established in Hispaniola, it soon spread to Cuba, Puerto Rico, Jamaica, and Mexico. Eventually, Africans worked as slaves in every colony in Spanish America. Cuba, which flourished as a sugar-producing colony in the 1800s, imported the largest number of Africans in Spanish America, about 700,000. Another 200,000 went to Mexico, 121,000 to Venezuela, 95,000 to Peru, and 80,000 to Puerto Rico.

Spanish American slaveholders regarded their slaves as human property and used them in many ways. Enslaved Africans made up a large part of the labor force in the silver mines of Mexico and Peru and on the sugarcane plantations of Cuba, Puerto Rico, Mexico, and Peru. They also worked on cattle ranches and cultivated ginger, cacao*, coffee, and

* **cacao** bean from which chocolate is made

92

tobacco for their owners. In the cities, especially in Mexico and Peru, they worked in textile factories under extremely difficult conditions. Many other Africans worked as domestic servants or in such trades as carpentry and shoemaking.

The lives of most slaves were short. Overwork, poor diet, and disease killed many. Slaves had certain rights under Spanish law, which was supposed to protect them from mistreatment. They had the right to marry, to have families, and to be freed if their owners chose to free them. These rights, however, were not always observed. The colonists enacted their own laws that limited slaves' rights, regulated their behavior, and allowed for harsh punishments.

Despite the hardships and indignities of slavery, Africans in the Americas struggled to support their families, maintain their African heritage, and practice their religions. Many adopted beliefs and traditions that combined African and Roman Catholic elements. Although slaves often married within their own group, intermarriage between different groups and races gradually produced a population of mixed Spanish, African, and Indian ancestry.

One important feature of Spanish American slavery was the act of manumission, the freeing of slaves by their owners. Most slaves who were manumitted were elderly people, children, and those who were able to buy their freedom. By the late 1700s, a substantial free black population had emerged. Peru had 41,000 free blacks and 40,000 slaves, while Panama had 33,000 free blacks and 3,500 slaves. Millions of Africans never obtained their freedom, however, and many tried to escape the nightmare of enslavement by running away or rebelling against their owners.

African Slavery in Brazil.

The main centers of African slavery in colonial Brazil were in the northeastern provinces and in Minas Gerais and other interior provinces. However, African slavery also existed in the Amazon region of northern Brazil and in the far south. Their labor on agricultural plantations and in gold mines was the foundation of Brazil's export economy. Some historians estimate that Brazil imported between 3.5 and 4 million Africans as slaves.

The first Africans in Brazil were brought from Portugal, where they had been serving as slaves since the 1450s. After the European conquest, black troops played a vital role in defending coastal Brazil from foreign attackers. Most of the Africans in Brazil, however, worked on the sugar plantations that the Portuguese established in the mid-1500s. As sugar became the leading export, Africans replaced the Indian slaves. Half a million Africans were imported to work on the plantations before 1640. Plantation work was demanding and dangerous, and the death rate among slaves was high. As a result, more Africans were brought to Brazil to replace those who had died.

Africans' traditional skills also made them useful in other segments of the colonial economy. Their experience tending livestock made them good at herding cattle, leading mule trains, and driving oxcarts. The African tradition of carrying heavy loads balanced on one's head became an important part of colonial Brazil's transportation industry.

African Homelands

It is estimated that from the mid-1500s to the late 1800s, more than 3 million slaves were brought to Brazil. They came mainly from West Africa and west-central Africa. The greatest number of slaves arrived from Costa da Mina (present-day Ghana) and Guinea and were known as Mina or Minas. The second major region of slave export was present-day Angola, and Africans from this area were known in Brazil as Angolans or Congos (named after the old kingdom of Kongo in northern Angola). A relatively small number of slaves came from countries in East Africa, principally Mozambique.

See color plate 6, vol. 2.

Slavery

In the late 1800s, a majority of African slaves in Brazil worked on coffee plantations. However, plantation labor, shown in this painting by Johann Moritz Rugendas (1835), was not the only area in which slaves served. Many worked as domestic servants, fishermen, and miners. Slavery of Afro-Brazilians was abolished in 1888.

Taking the place of "beasts of burden," Africans were made to carry water, haul and load cargoes, and even carry their owners in chairs or hammocks on their shoulders.

African slavery was also essential to Brazil's mining industry. Miners who hoped to become rich bought young Africans in coastal ports and led them to the gold-rush camps to pan for gold and diamonds. A few African women worked the mines, but most served as cooks or domestic servants in the growing towns.

Slave labor existed at all levels in Brazilian society. Some large and wealthy urban households had many slaves, including nurses, coachmen, footmen, and seamstresses. Additional slaves were sent into the streets as workers for hire to earn money for their owners. But the vast majority of African slaves, including women, were forced to work in the fields or at hard labor as porters carrying loads. Although those who resisted the demands of slavery faced severe punishments, many Africans struggled to buy their freedom, to escape, or to strike back against their owners.

Indian Slavery in Brazil. Indian slavery, like African slavery, was an important element of the colonial Brazilian economy, especially in areas that contributed to the export economy. Although African slaves gradually replaced Indian laborers in the sugar-growing regions, Indian slavery reached massive levels in the southern coastal province of São Paulo and in the northern state of Maranhão, whose economies relied on Indian agricultural workers and porters. During the 1600s, colonists in São Paulo made several large raids into the territory of the GUARANI Indians, bringing thousands of slaves back to the Portuguese

settlements. Because Indian slavery was against Portuguese law after 1570, the colonists referred to their Indian captives as "freedmen" even though they treated them as slaves. (*See also* **Africans in Latin America; Maroons; Race and Ethnicity; Slave Revolts; Slave Trade; Slavery, Abolition of.**)

Slavery, Abolition of

* **diplomatic** demonstrating tact and skill at conducting negotiations among nations

* **Creole** person of European ancestry born in the Americas

The abolition of slavery in Latin America during the 1800s was part of a worldwide movement, led by the British, to end the practice of owning human beings as property. In Latin America, abolition consisted of two distinct steps: ending the trade that brought new slaves into the region and enacting governmental emancipation, or freeing the people who were enslaved. In the many countries and colonies of the region, these steps were taken at different times.

Spanish America. The great majority of the enslaved Africans brought to the Americas between 1650 and 1800 went to the Portuguese, English, and French colonies. The Spanish colonies had depended on African slaves for their silver-mining operations but also used Indian labor. After 1770, however, changes in world markets led to the rise of sugar plantations in Spanish America, especially in Cuba and PUERTO RICO, and the demand for African slaves increased sharply.

The early 1800s marked the beginning of the British abolition movement. Great Britain used diplomatic* pressure—and its powerful navy—to attack the international slave trade. At the same time, independence movements gained strength in most of Spain's American colonies. Many of the Creoles* who had fought for independence were opposed to slavery, and the notion of emancipation became linked to the new visions of liberty and citizenship that shaped the newly independent republics of the 1820s.

Chile, Central America, and Mexico outlawed slavery in the 1820s. Fears of angering the elite property owners delayed the full abolition of slavery in most of South America. Between 1846 and 1870, however, Uruguay, Colombia, Argentina, Venezuela, Peru, and Paraguay outlawed slavery, although as nonwhites, the freed people continued to suffer from economic and social inequality.

Cuba and Puerto Rico remained in Spanish hands until the end of the 1800s. Under pressure from Great Britain and the United States, Spain strengthened its laws against slave trading in the 1860s. Although an illegal trade continued to flourish for a few years, Spain finally ended slavery in Puerto Rico in 1873 and in Cuba in 1886.

Brazil. The economy of Brazil, Portugal's colony in South America, remained dependent on slave labor, mostly on the plantations that produced products for export. In the early 1800s, however, Britain began a vigorous campaign against the shipping of enslaved people to Brazil, forcing the Portuguese government to pass laws limiting the slave trade. In practice, however, Portuguese and Brazilian officials did little to curb the traffic, sometimes actually aiding the slave traders.

Brazil's Golden Law

Brazil was the last country in the Americas to abolish slavery. On May 13, 1888, Princess Isabel of Brazil gave formal approval to legislation that became known as the Golden Law and that freed the remaining 600,000 slaves in the country. Even before the Senate passed the Golden Law, slavery in Brazil was on the wane. Thousands of slaves had already run away from their owners, and many planters had freed their slaves, hoping to keep them as wage laborers. Although slaveholders bitterly opposed the Golden Law, they recognized that slavery's time had passed.

In 1830, seven years after Brazil became independent, the Brazilian government reluctantly outlawed all slave trading. Yet the trade continued for more than 20 years. The Brazilian government stamped it out only after the threat of attack by Britain's powerful navy. Even so, because of the lingering power of the Brazilian slaveholding elite, it took almost 40 more years before the enslaved people already in the country were freed. (*See also* **Slave Revolts; Slave Trade; Slavery.**)

Smuggling

Smuggling is the illegal transport of goods into or out of a country or region. For 300 years, smuggling and other forms of illegal trade formed an important part of the economy of colonial Spanish America as it did in the 13 British colonies. Despite Spain's efforts to halt smuggling, goods flowed in and out of the colonies outside the control of Spanish taxation and regulation.

Because the law prohibited trade between foreigners and Spanish colonists, such transactions were referred to as illicit commerce. The term *contraband* referred to Spanish or Spanish colonial products that were illegally traded. Often, however, the term was used to describe other types of illegal trade as well.

Most contraband involved external trade between a Spanish American colony and a foreign merchant or smuggler. Smuggling occurred along the coasts. It was extremely difficult for the authorities to stop, partly because the smugglers developed clever ways of hiding their activities and partly because the coastlines of the colonies were too long to be effectively guarded. Coastal smuggling was especially common between present-day Panama and Venezuela. The delta of the Río de la Plata on the southeastern coast of South America was another busy smuggling region.

Smuggling was well established by the late 1500s. Wars in Europe during the 1700s interfered with normal trade and led to an increase in illegal trade through Spanish American ports. The British smuggled throughout the region; the Dutch conducted their illegal trade in the Caribbean Sea; Portuguese smugglers were active in the Río de la Plata delta; and the French traded on the Pacific coast.

Spanish authorities blamed the exchange of contraband on the exaggerated demands of colonial consumers and on the colonists' general disrespect for the law. The colonists, on the other hand, accused Spain of failing to meet their needs at a fair price. Spanish authorities considered smuggling a drain on profits that rightfully belonged to the crown. They also believed that illegal trade undermined royal authority in the colonies. The Spanish crown's efforts to halt smuggling generally failed because the rewards of illegal trade far outweighed the government's ability to punish smugglers.

Contraband played a key role in colonial trade. When legal trade fell short or was absent, contraband trade was all that kept colonial ports and merchants active. In addition, contraband cut across social lines. Government officials, priests, soldiers, merchants, Indians, and even slaves took part in illegal trade. Because contraband trade was almost entirely unrecorded, historians are unable to determine precise amounts or

Illegal Goods

Some goods were so valued by Spanish American colonists that they were willing to engage in illegal trade to obtain them. Contraband goods included slaves; new and used clothing; wheat, flour, spices, and other foods; and ordinary items such as scissors, toys, and candles. Smugglers provided these goods at prices that were far lower than those of legal importers and merchants. To pay for these imports, colonists sold or traded such Spanish-outlawed colonial products as silver, gold, gems, tobacco, livestock, hides, and wood.

values. In 1800, however, one well-informed Spanish American official estimated that the value of the smuggling trade between Jamaica and Cartagena, Colombia, alone was a million pesos a year. (*See also* **Trade and Commerce**.)

Soccer

See *Sports and Recreation*.

Social Structure

See *Class Structure, Colonial and Modern; Race and Ethnicity*.

Soldaderas

* **Mesoamerican** referring to Mesoamerica, a culture region that includes central and southern Mexico, Guatemala, Belize, El Salvador, and parts of Honduras, Nicaragua, and Costa Rica; an inhabitant of Mesoamerica

Derived from the Spanish word *soldada,* meaning "pay of the soldier," a *soldadera* is a female servant who takes the *soldada* of a soldier and buys him food and other essentials. The term also refers to women who served in armies as camp followers and soldiers during wars. The custom of women fighting in wars dates to Mesoamerican* times, when women defended tribes, accompanied warriors to battles, or functioned as cooks, nurses, laundresses, baggage carriers, and prostitutes. Sometimes called *viejas* (old ladies) or *galletas* (cookies), *soldaderas* also worked as gunrunners, spies, and guards. Because of the variety of their roles and their semiofficial acceptance in the military until 1925, *soldaderas* occupy an ambivalent position in Mexican society and popular culture. They are considered variously as silent bystanders, selfless patriots, loose women, or valiant fighters for justice. (*See also* **Armed Forces; Militias**.)

Somoza Family

* **dynasty** succession of rulers from the same family or group

* **guerrilla** referring to a group that uses surprise raids to obstruct or harass an enemy or overthrow a government

* **regime** prevailing political system or rule

The Somoza family controlled NICARAGUA for more than 40 years. The Somozas ruled as dictators, often using repression to silence their opponents. The dynasty* ended in 1979, when the success of the SANDINISTAS and accusations of HUMAN RIGHTS violations led to the resignation of the last Somoza leader.

Born to a wealthy family, Anastasio Somoza García was educated in the United States. In 1927, he was appointed commander of the Nicaraguan National Guard, a position he used to his advantage. In 1936, with the help of the National Guard, Anastasio ousted ruling president Juan Bautista Sacasa and took over the presidency. Anastasio used cunning, deceit, and ruthlessness to build a political dynasty. In fact, he is usually blamed for the murder of guerrilla* leader Augusto César SANDINO. Anastasio's power was bolstered by the National Guard and support from the United States, which considered him a strong ally. He also controlled the Nicaraguan economy and amassed a huge personal fortune. In 1956, amid increasing discontent with his repressive and dictatorial regime*, Somoza was assassinated. He was succeeded by his oldest son, Luis Somoza Debayle.

Soto, Hernando de

Anastasio Somoza García, (left) is shown here with President Franklin Delano Roosevelt of the United States. Somoza was the patriarch of the family that controlled Nicaragua for more than 40 years. Although the United States considered Somoza an ally, it disapproved of his repressive tactics and the corruption in his government.

* **liberal** supporting greater participation in government for individuals; not bound by political and social traditions

Luis Somoza began his career in politics as a member of the Nicaraguan Congress. As president, Luis was more liberal* than his father. He relaxed political repression, initiated social reforms, and encouraged freedom of the press. Yet the country remained under strict military control, and Luis continued to expand his family's business interests and fortune.

After his death in 1967, his younger brother, Anastasio Somoza Debayle (Tachito), became president. Tachito, who resembled his father in greed, cruelty, and ruthlessness, also rose to power through the military. His dictatorship was marked by corruption and violent repression. In the early 1970s, the Sandinista National Liberation Front (FSLN), a revolutionary group, began to pose a serious political threat to the Somoza regime. Increasing numbers of discontented Nicaraguans joined the FSLN in its struggle against the Somoza dictatorship. In the late 1970s, the United States and other nations accused Somoza of human rights violations and threatened to withdraw their support. In 1979, following these incidents and the increasing political successes of the FSLN, Tachito resigned and was forced into exile in Paraguay. He was assassinated by a car bomb the following year, ending the Somoza dynasty.

Soto, Hernando de

ca. 1496–1542
Spanish explorer

Hernando de Soto, a successful conquistador*, came to America in 1514 as a member of Pedro Arias de Ávila's expedition to Darién in present-day Panama. He soon became rich from the slave trade in Central America, and in 1532, he joined Francisco PIZARRO to conquer the Inca of Peru. Soto was present when Pizarro captured the Inca ruler ATAHUALPA, and he helped seize the Inca capital of Cuzco. Although by this time, Soto was extremely rich, he sought the governorship of Florida, in the hope of finding even greater riches. He landed in

° **conquistador** Spanish explorer and conqueror

Florida in 1539 and traveled through present-day Georgia, Tennessee, Arkansas, and Texas, terrorizing the Indians he encountered. Soto and his men were the first Europeans to sail down the Mississippi River and to cross the Gulf of Mexico. When Soto died in present-day Louisiana, his soldiers, afraid that the Indians would attack if they learned of his death, threw his corpse into the Mississippi River. (*See also* **Explorers and Exploration**.)

Soulouque, Faustin Élie

1785–1867
President and emperor of Haiti

° **illiterate** person who is unable to read and write

° **mulatto** person of mixed black and white ancestry

° **oust** to remove from office

An illiterate*, former black slave, Faustin Élie Soulouque ruled as president and emperor of HAITI from 1847 to 1859. His reign was one of corruption, bloodshed, and terror, and it resulted in the destruction of the Haitian economy.

In 1803, Soulouque participated in the revolt that freed Haiti from French rule. After independence, he served in the army and steadily rose in rank. In 1847, mulatto* leaders from the Haitian assembly elected him to succeed President Jean-Baptiste Riché because they mistakenly thought that they would be able to manipulate him.

Once in power, Soulouque began a 12-year reign of terror conducted by his secret police. After a failed plot to eliminate him during his first year in power, Soulouque named himself Emperor Faustin I and created an aristocracy consisting of loyal black generals from the army. He was also the first Haitian leader to practice VOODOO openly. In 1849, he created a new constitution to provide a legal basis for his reign. Soulouque lived as an aristocrat and squandered the Haitian treasury. His greed for power and conquest drew him into several costly wars against the Dominican Republic.

Soulouque's unpopularity grew steadily during his reign, and political opposition increased. In 1859, he was ousted* from power by a group of mulattos. Soulouque fled Haiti and died in exile.

Sousa, Tomé de

ca. 1502–1579
First governor-general of Brazil

° **evangelize** to preach Christian beliefs; to convert to Christianity

° **captaincy** administrative unit in colonial Brazil

° **Jesuit** popular name for the Roman Catholic religious order officially known as the Society of Jesus; also, a member of that order

Tomé de Sousa was a descendant of Portugal's king Afonso III. He spent his youth at the Portuguese court and later fought in Morocco and worked in the spice trade with India. In 1549, he was appointed the first governor-general of Brazil. Sousa set sail with six ships and 1,000 settlers to establish royal control over Brazil, to defend it from French pirates, and to conquer and evangelize* the Indians there.

Arriving in Brazil, Sousa bought land from a Portuguese nobleman and founded the city of SALVADOR, the new capital of the colony. He helped in the construction of the capital, toured all the captaincies* except Pernambuco, and evicted some hostile Indians, giving their land to the new settlers. He formed a close relationship with the Jesuits*, whom he later sent to inspect the captaincies. Under Sousa's leadership, the colonists built new missions, forts, towns, and courts; established sugar mills; and introduced livestock—thus creating the backbone of Brazil's colonial economy.

South America, Pre-Columbian History

° **pre-Columbian** before the arrival of Christopher Columbus and other Europeans in the Americas in the 1490s

° **archaeology** science of studying past human cultures, usually by excavating ruins

° **anthropologist** scientist who studies human beings, especially in relation to origins and cultural characteristics

° **artifact** in archaeology, a human-made object such as a tool, household utensil, or work of art

° **indigenous** referring to the original inhabitants of a region

The South American continent was inhabited for several thousand years before the first Europeans arrived in 1492. A number of pre-Columbian* societies occupied the continent, which is characterized by environments ranging from tropical rain forests in the AMAZON REGION to high mountain plateaus and valleys in the ANDES.

The Amazon Region

The Amazon region, or Amazonia, is a humid tropical forest that covers an area of more than 2 million square miles. It includes the basins of thousands of large and small rivers, most notably the Amazon River. Compared with other geographic regions of Latin America, little attention has been paid to the archaeology* of Amazonia because of the region's size and remoteness and the density of its forests. Thus, the prehistory of Amazonia has been the subject of much debate.

Early Ideas About the Region.

For many years, archaeologists and naturalists characterized Amazonia as a region almost completely untouched and unsettled by humans until the arrival of Europeans. They believed that the region consisted of rich land, teeming with fish and game and with unlimited potential for agriculture.

By the 1900s, anthropologists* began to challenge this view. They argued that the region had remained uninhabited or sparsely inhabited because of poor soil conditions and environmental factors that had limited agriculture. They also suggested that the animal and plant resources of Amazonia were insufficient to support large societies.

Current Knowledge About Amazonia.

Recent discoveries, have led to a new view of Amazonian prehistory, however, Archaeologists have found artifacts* dating from as early as 9000 B.C., including stone tools (axes, scrapers, arrowheads, and spear tips), suggesting the existence of pre-agricultural hunting and gathering societies. They have also discovered ancient pottery in Amazonia, some of which is about 7,000 years old—among the oldest in the Americas. In fact, when archaeologists found hunting and gathering implements and pottery at the same sites, they began to challenge long-held beliefs that pottery and agriculture developed in tandem. Because the earliest evidence of agriculture in Amazonia dates only to about 4000 B.C., they proposed that pottery may have developed before agriculture, at least in the Amazon region if not in the rest of the Americas.

Similarities in pottery styles from various areas in the region indicate that the Amazon region had a vast network of interacting societies by the 1000s B.C. This network, based on canoe travel along rivers, connected small farming and fishing communities located on the fertile flood plains of major waterways. By the A.D. 1000s, many of these communities had developed into complex societies called chiefdoms. The chiefdoms made colorful pottery, had elaborate burial practices, and constructed large earthworks. Around the same time, in the areas where the rain forests merged with grasslands, indigenous* peoples built extensive networks of raised agricultural fields, irrigation canals, and earthen mounds for houses.

South America, Pre-Columbian History

When Europeans began exploring Amazonia in the mid-1500s, they found highly organized societies stretching along its major waterways. These societies had large settlements and political systems that enabled them to mobilize sizable forces to defend their territories.

The Andean Region

The pre-Columbian history of the Andean region is complex and poorly understood. In the absence of indigenous writing systems, most

During the pre-Columbian period, the Andes region of South America was the most populated on that continent. This map shows where some of the major Indian groups were living before the arrival of Europeans.

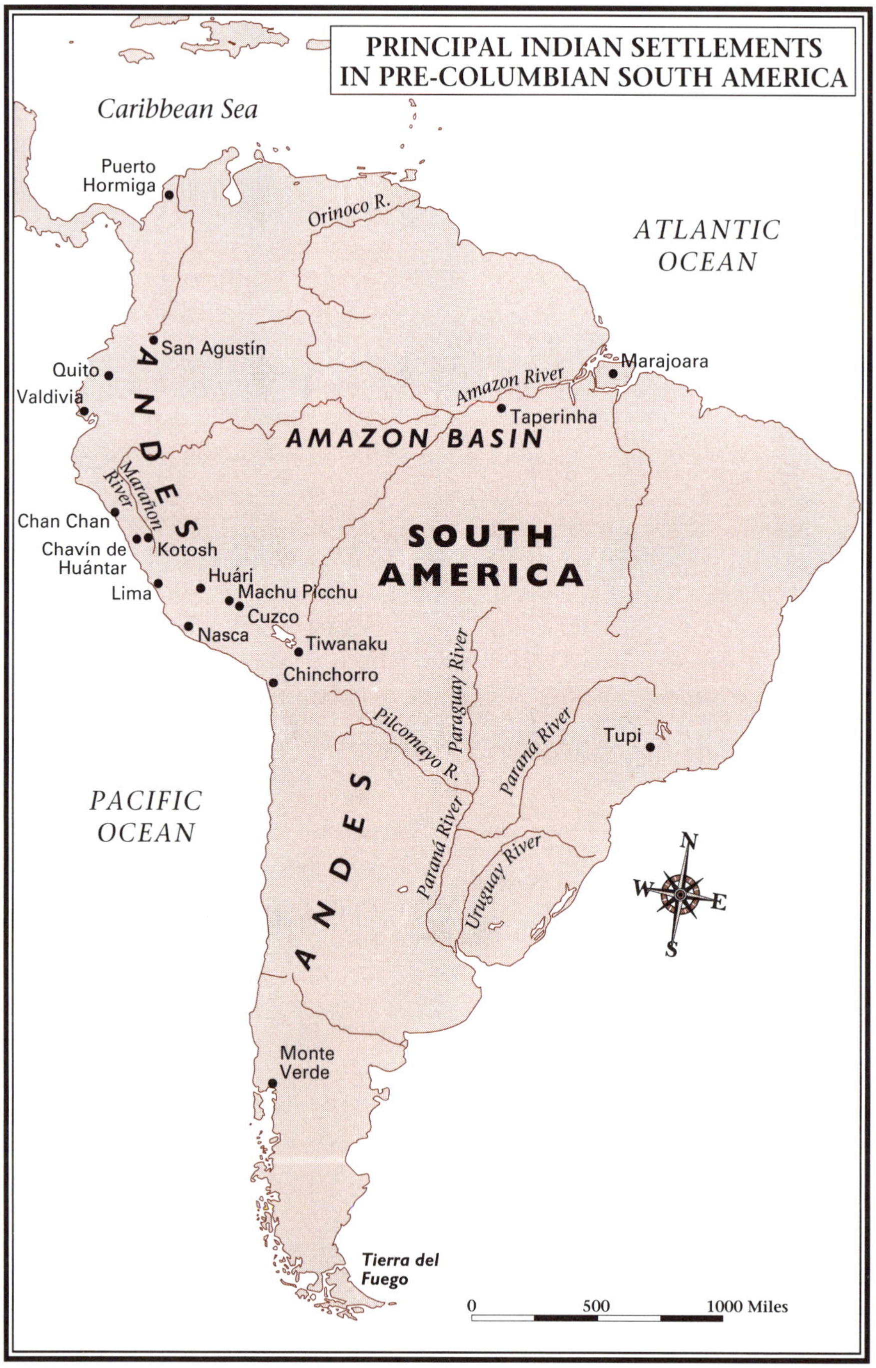

PRINCIPAL INDIAN SETTLEMENTS IN PRE-COLUMBIAN SOUTH AMERICA

101

South America, Pre-Columbian History

information about the region's prehistory comes from archaeology. Yet in many areas, little archaeological research has been carried out.

The Andean region, stretching from Venezuela in the north to Tierra del Fuego in the south, consisted of four main cultural regions: the northern Andean area (Venezuela, Colombia, and Ecuador), the Peruvian or central Andean area (Peru and northern Bolivia), the south Andean area (Bolivia, northern Chile, and northwest Argentina), and the Fuegian area (southern Chile). Contact among these cultural areas was limited until the 1400s, when the INCA created a vast empire that incorporated portions of them. Although the Inca created a semblance of similarity in the region, they were unable to wipe out the fundamental cultural diversity of the pre-Columbian Andes.

Settlement of the Andean Region.

Archaeological evidence suggests that several indigenous groups inhabited the Andean region more than 12,000 years ago. These early people are known mainly from the stone tools and other artifacts that remain. Evidence of ancient dwellings is rare, but at Monte Verde in Chile, archaeologists have unearthed a settlement of small rectangular huts built of wood and animal skin dating to about 11,000 B.C.

Archaeological evidence also suggests that early Andean peoples sometimes hunted large animals but that their diet consisted mainly of small animals and wild plants. Their hunting and gathering lifestyle gave way to a sedentary lifestyle, one in which people remained in one place. By about 3500 B.C., Peruvian peoples had begun herding llamas and had begun to experiment with plants yielding potatoes, quinoa*, peanuts, cotton, and coca.

Beginnings of Andean Civilization.

The emergence of permanent communities led to an increase in population, which in turn reinforced the dependence on subsistence farming*, breeding livestock, and engaging in year-round fishing. Settled farming villages appeared in the northern Andes sometime before 3000 B.C. Evidence of such communities has been found at Valdivia in Ecuador and Puerto Hormiga in Colombia. Around the same time, large settlements focused on fishing were established along the coast of the central Andes. The coastal settlements also cultivated cotton to make fishing lines and gourds to make floats. The inhabitants grew domesticated* plants and maintained strong ties with farming settlements located farther inland. The coastal cultures constructed some of the oldest large structures in the Americas, including several step-shaped pyramids for public ceremonies and religious rituals.

Between 3000 B.C. and 2000 B.C., the farming communities in the highland regions of the central Andes also constructed small ceremonial structures for burials and religious offerings. Rebuilt often, these structures gradually grew into large pyramid-platforms, such as those found at KOTOSH in Peru. Agricultural settlement expanded throughout much of the central Andes between 2000 B.C. and 1000 B.C., and coastal communities expanded their farming lands with the help of irrigation canals that brought water from inland regions. They also built many

---

* **quinoa** type of plant whose seeds have been a basic food source in the Andes region since precolonial times

* **subsistence farming** system of farming that provides all or almost all the food needed by the farm family without a surplus for sale

* **domesticated** referring to animals or plants adapted for use by humans

Mummies of the Americas

The oldest mummies in the Americas are from the Chinchorro culture of northern Chile and southern Peru. Between 5500 B.C. and 2000 B.C., these coastal peoples introduced mummification of their dead. They preserved the corpse by removing its internal organs, drying the body, and rebuilding it with fillers, clay modeling, and a wig. Some Andean cultures also used natural processes to mummify the dead, leaving bodies high in the mountains, where they were preserved by cold and dryness.

large public structures, suggesting an extended period of cultural and political stability in the region.

By about 2000 years ago, most of the coastal communities in the central Andean region had been abandoned, but the highland settlements continued to flourish. One of these centers, CHAVÍN DE HUÁNTAR, gained special prominence around 500 B.C. because of its role as a ceremonial and trading center. During that period, the CHAVIN culture emerged and spread throughout Peru, becoming one of the earliest civilizations in South America. The collapse of the Chavin culture in about 200 B.C. left the central Andes with several small, warring states. Over the next several centuries, these states struggled to expand into neighboring territories and to establish larger states. One of the first large states formed in the region was that of the Gallinazo culture, which dominated northern Peru from A.D. 100 to A.D. 300. Between 300 and 500, power shifted to the MOCHE culture, which occupied more than 250 miles along Peru's northern coast.

Andean Empires and Their Collapse. The earliest large state in the Andean highlands was centered at TIWANAKU in Bolivia. The Tiwanaku culture, which reached its height in about 600, established a network of long-distance trade links that extended from the desert coastal regions of northern Chile to the tropical forests of eastern Bolivia. In the 500s, the HUARI peoples of southern Peru created the first true empire in the Andean region. The Huari conquered other cultures and expanded their territory, which reached into the northern and southern highlands of the central Andes. They unified diverse cultures and established a centralized government. The Huari empire collapsed around 800 and the Tiwanaku state around 1000, causing political fragmentation and increased cultural diversity in the region. New cultural centers emerged, such as CHAN CHAN, which spanned all of Peru's northern coast and part of its central coast.

In the 1400s, a small highland group emerged from this diversity of cultures to become the greatest pre-Columbian civilization of South America, that of the Inca. Through a remarkable series of conquests and alliances, the Inca united the Andes region and created a large and formidable empire. However, their empire lasted less than a century before it was destroyed by the Spanish in the 1530s. (*See also* **Amazon River; Art, Pre-Columbian; Chimu; Cultures, Pre-Columbian; Mesoamerica: Pre-Columbian History; Nasca and Nasca Lines.**)

Southern Cone

The Southern Cone comprises the three southernmost countries of Latin America—Argentina, Chile, and Uruguay—which share similar climates, geographic features, and a rich supply of natural resources. These countries are unique among Latin American nations in that their populations are substantially European in origin because of significant immigration in the late 1800s. During the first half of the 1900s, these nations adopted democratic governments and led the rest of Latin America in economic growth. The United States and

Soviet–Latin American Relations

Europe viewed them as important economic and political allies, and other Latin American nations envied their level of modernization. However, conditions changed after World War II, when the Southern Cone nations began to experience serious economic problems. Political upheavals in the 1970s brought repressive regimes* to power, worsening conditions and isolating the Southern Cone from Europe and the United States. Despite political reforms since then, the Southern Cone nations continue to struggle to regain their leadership status in Latin America.

* **regime** prevailing political system or rule

Soviet–Latin American Relations

* **diplomatic** demonstrating tact and skill at conducting negotiations among nations
* **Communist** referring to a social system in which land, goods, and the means of production are owned by the state or community rather than by individuals

Communist Parties Today

After the breakup of the Soviet Union in 1991, Russia sought to mend relations with the United States. The desire for better relations with the United States prompted Russia to abandon financial support for all Communist parties in Latin America. Since then, these parties have split into separate factions and have lost much of their popular support. Many Latin Americans maintain that the parties are more concerned with disseminating Communist ideas than with solving the real problems of the people and their nations.

* **radical** favoring extreme changes or reforms
* **socialist** promoting socialism, a system in which the means of production and distribution of goods in a society are owned and controlled by the state

Between the 1950s and the 1980s, the United States and the Soviet Union participated in a struggle known as the Cold War, in which they competed to influence the world. During this time, the Soviet Union expanded its diplomatic* and political presence in Latin America despite the huge distance that separated the two regions and their limited common interests.

Before the 1940s, only Mexico and Uruguay had established diplomatic relations with the Soviet Union, which focused on two issues to gain support in the region. Soviet-sponsored Communist* parties tried to organize industrial and agricultural workers against exploitation by the ruling classes and rallied against foreign domination of the region. By the late 1930s, Communist parties had been formed in most Latin American countries. They controlled trade unions in Chile, Cuba, and elsewhere but had limited electoral support. The foreign policies of these parties were identical to those in the Soviet Union. By the end of World War II, most governments in the region formally recognized the Soviet Union and established and maintained close ties with the Soviet government.

The CUBAN REVOLUTION of 1959 was a turning point in Soviet–Latin American relations. The Soviets began to support Fidel CASTRO after he overthrew Cuban dictator Fulgencio Batista y Zaldívar. Castro initially disagreed with the Soviets over domestic policy and revolutionary tactics, but by 1970, he had adopted Soviet political ideas and was supporting Soviet foreign policy in China and Africa. In return, the Soviet Union provided financial and technical assistance to Cuba, including military equipment and arms. In 1962, the Soviets attempted to establish nuclear missiles in Cuba, creating the threat of a global nuclear war. Besides Cuba, the Soviets backed other revolutionary movements as well. In Nicaragua, they provided the SANDINISTAS, a radical* rebel group, with economic and military aid in their war against the CONTRAS, a group supported by the United States. In El Salvador, the Soviets backed the radical Farabundo Martí Front for National Liberation (FMLN) in a civil war that lasted until the early 1990s.

Still, Communist parties had little success in Latin American elections. Their greatest victory was in Chile in 1970, when the Chilean Communist party helped elect the socialist* candidate, Salvador ALLENDE, to the presidency. However, his victory was short-lived. Allende

was overthrown in a coup* in 1973, and the military established a dictatorship that was hostile to communism. Soviet efforts to expand trade relations with Latin America had only modest success, and Soviet political efforts had limited results, triumphing only in Cuba. The creation of a network of Communist parties throughout Latin America was a significant achievement, but no Soviet-backed Communist party ever gained control of a Latin American government. The parties that gained control were nationalist* rather than Communist, and except in Cuba, these have all lost power and influence.

After 1985, domestic problems forced the Soviet Union to withdraw its support to Latin American nations. The fall of the Soviet Union in 1991 ended the Cold War and Soviet involvement in Latin America. (*See also* **Communism; Cuban Missile Crisis; United States–Latin American Relations.**)

* **coup** sudden, often violent overthrow of a ruler or government

* **nationalist** promoting the culture and interests of the nation

Spain and the Spanish Empire

Once Christopher COLUMBUS sailed westward in 1492 and encountered a "New World," Spain began to focus its attention on the exploration and settlement of the Americas. In the years that followed, Spain claimed a vast overseas empire and emerged as a major power in Europe. By the 1600s, however, Spain's power began to decline, and by the mid-1800s, the empire had lost most of its overseas colonies and had fallen to the rank of a minor power.

Unification of Spain. Spain did not exist as a single, unified nation in the mid-1400s. Instead, the term *Spain* referred to the Iberian Peninsula, which contained several independent kingdoms that had been retaken from the Moors*, who had conquered much of Iberia in the 700s. Christian forces gradually reconquered the region and established independent kingdoms, including those in Castile, Aragon, and León. The reconquest was accompanied by a long process of political unification that occurred through marriage, inheritance, and warfare. The marriage of Isabella I of Castile and León and Ferdinand II of Aragon in 1469 marked the beginning of a unified Spain. In 1492, when Isabella and Ferdinand took Granada from the Moors, the reconquest was complete, and they became the rulers of all Spain. The same year, Columbus sailed westward to the "New World," and Spain embarked on an era of overseas exploration and colonization.

* **Moors** North African Muslims who conquered Spain in the A.D. 700s

Expansion of the Empire. Spain quickly expanded its territorial claims in the Americas. By the early 1500s, the monarchy had colonized HISPANIOLA, PUERTO RICO, and CUBA. From there, they ventured into FLORIDA, the MISSISSIPPI VALLEY, MEXICO, CENTRAL AMERICA, and South America. The conquests of Mexico and PERU gave the Spaniards access to enormous wealth in GOLD AND SILVER. These regions became the focus of Spanish colonial efforts, and Spain became the wealthiest and most powerful nation in Europe.

Spain and the Spanish Empire

Throughout the 1500s, Spain continued to expand its overseas empire, especially when King Charles I and his son, PHILIP II, were in power. They established colonies and outposts from the Pacific Northwest and CALIFORNIA to Florida, as far south as TIERRA DEL FUEGO, and as far west as the islands of Micronesia and the PHILIPPINES. The expansion of the empire was also accompanied by cultural, artistic, and intellectual achievements in Spain.

Although Spain's American empire expanded, Charles and Philip faced many challenges in Europe. Spain controlled a large European empire that included the present-day Netherlands, Austria, and parts of France and Italy. Spanish control of these regions led to local rebellions and conflict with other European nations. Moreover, Spain—a devoutly Catholic nation—also became embroiled in religious conflicts between Catholics and Protestants.

The Empire in Decline. Spain began to decline in the 1600s, when England, France, and the Netherlands established colonies in North America and in the Caribbean, challenging Spanish power there. The

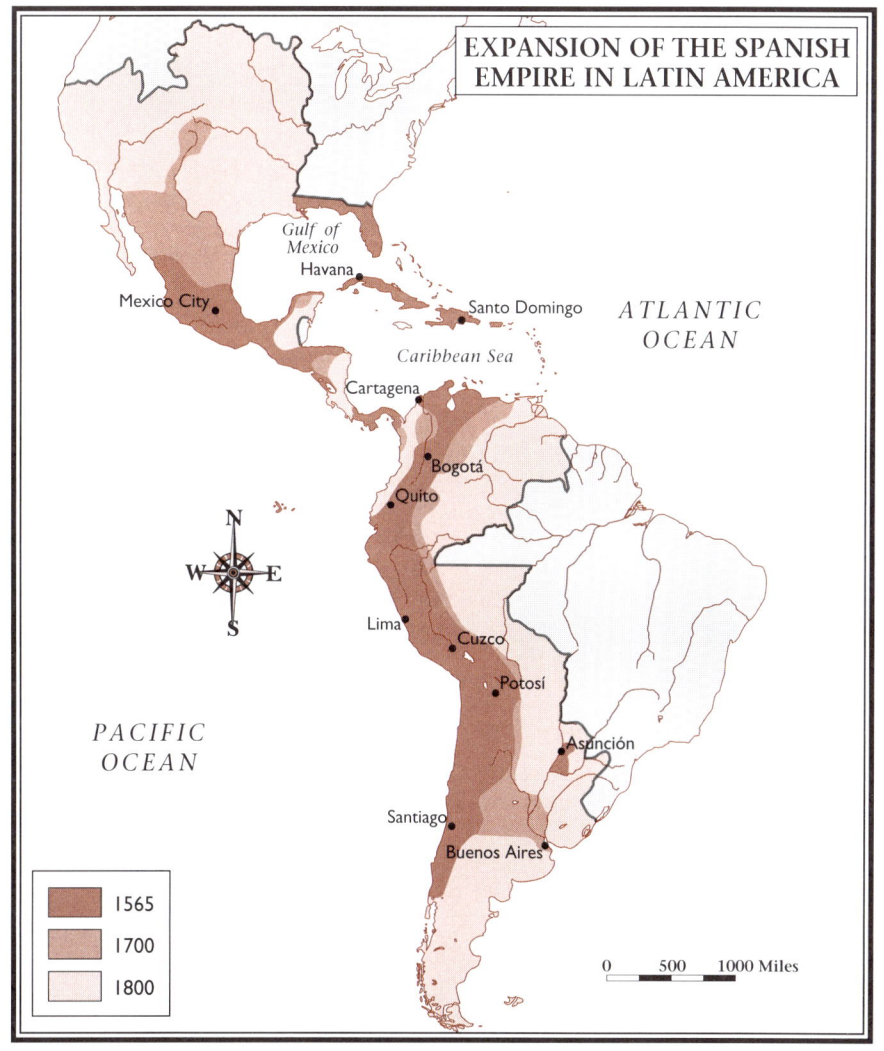

Spain quickly expanded its territorial claims in the Americas following Christopher Columbus's first voyage to the "New World" in 1492. Starting with colonies on the Caribbean islands, Spain extended its rule to large parts of North, Central, and South America. Spain's power began to decline in the early 1800s, and by 1898, Spain had lost control of its last colonial possessions in the Americas.

monarchy also faced territorial challenges in South America as Portugal expanded its colonies in Brazil. Spain's involvement in European conflicts contributed to the nation's decline as well. The expense of funding European wars, as well as maintaining a vast empire, led to serious economic decline, which was reflected in Spain's reduced control and sale of offices in the colonies.

In the early 1700s, following the War of the Spanish Succession, the Bourbon prince Philip of Anjou gained the Spanish throne as Philip V. He strengthened royal administration, and the Spanish economy improved. In the Americas, the monarchy enacted the BOURBON REFORMS, which reorganized the region's economy, administration, and military. The reforms strengthened Spanish rule in the Americas and brought some prosperity to Spain, but the empire was never able to regain its former glory.

The End of Empire. Spain's involvement in the French Revolution and in wars with England in the late 1700s and early 1800s further weakened the empire. In 1808, France's Napoleon I invaded Spain and placed his brother Joseph on the Spanish throne. During the period that France controlled Spain, Spaniards on the mainland and colonists in the Americas rebelled against imperial rule, and several colonies declared their independence. In 1814, the Spanish monarchy returned to power, but its efforts to reassert control over its overseas empire faced strong resistance throughout Spanish America. By 1824, Spain had lost most of its American colonies. After its defeat in the SPANISH-AMERICAN WAR in 1898, Spain lost Cuba and ceded Puerto Rico, the Philippines, and several islands in Micronesia to the United States in exchange for 20 million dollars.

In the early 1900s, the once-mighty Spanish empire consisted of only a few possessions in Africa. Today Spain's overseas possessions include Ceuta and Melilla, two small seaports on the coast of North Africa. (*See also* **Explorers and Exploration; Imperialism; Inquisition, Holy Office of the; Spanish Monarchs; Wars of Independence.**)

"Golden Ages" of Spain

Between the 900s and 1200s, a period known as the golden age, the Moors in Spain produced great works of architecture, literature, and art. Their achievements greatly influenced the rest of Europe, generating new ideas in science, mathematics, and medicine, and reintroducing the works of ancient Greek and Roman scholars. During the 1500s and 1600s—Spain's second "golden age"—such painters as Diego Velázquez, Bartolomé Murillo, and El Greco created magnificent works of art, while such writers as Lope de Vega, Tirso de Molina, and Miguel de Cervantes produced brilliant literary masterpieces.

Spanish Borderlands

° **viceroyalty** region governed by a viceroy, a royally appointed official

The Spanish Borderlands were areas of Spanish America that extended into the present-day United States. During the colonial era, this frontier region served as a buffer between the Viceroyalty* of NEW SPAIN and the British and French colonies in North America. The Borderlands included the present-day states of New Mexico, Arizona, Texas, California, Louisiana, Mississippi, Alabama, Georgia, Florida, and the Carolinas.

The Spaniards explored the region in the 1500s and established the first settlement at ST. AUGUSTINE, Florida. New Mexico, the most successful and populous colony, was first settled in the late 1500s; Arizona was settled as a colony in the mid-1600s; and California, the last area to be colonized, was settled in the late 1700s. The Borderlands attracted few settlers because of the great distances between the region's settlements,

Spanish Borderlands

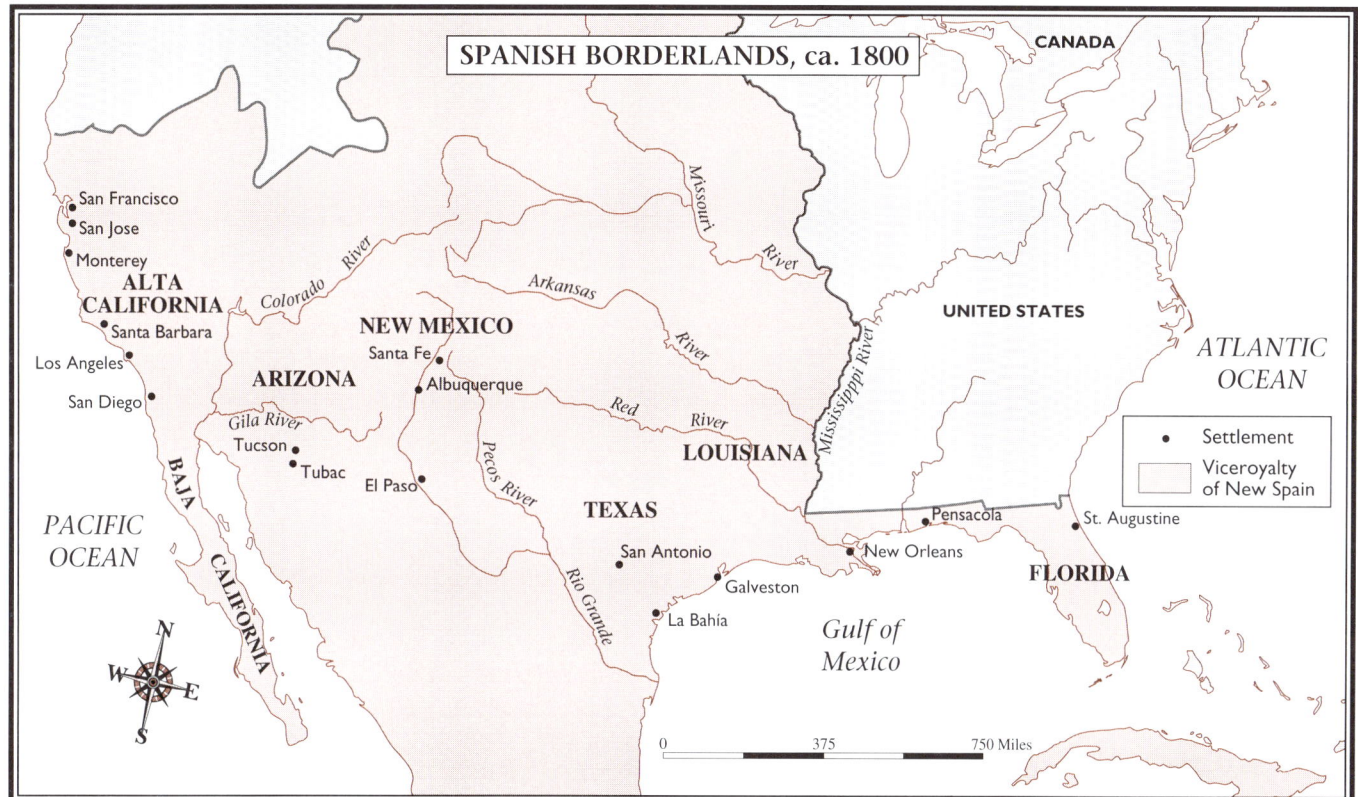

During the colonial period, the Spanish Borderlands marked the northern frontier of Spain's empire in the Americas. Most of the early settlements in the Borderlands were founded as missions to convert Indians to Christianity. Some of these original settlements continue to thrive and have grown into major cities.

° *encomienda* right granted to a conqueror that enabled him to control the labor of and collect payment from an Indian community

° **presidio** Spanish fort built to protect mission settlements

° **missionary** person who works to convert nonbelievers to his or her faith

° **assimilate** to adopt the beliefs or customs of a society

the often harsh climate, and the hostile Indians. To encourage settlement and promote economic development in the Borderlands, the Spanish monarchy awarded *encomiendas** to the colonists. Gradually, the Borderlands developed diverse economies based on AGRICULTURE, LIVESTOCK, and CRAFTS.

Despite their isolation from the rest of Spanish America, the Borderlands shared certain characteristics. As in other settlements, the monarchy established mission communities, presidios*, and towns to help colonize and settle the region. Once the settlements were established, missionaries* began the work of converting Indians to Christianity and assimilating* them into Spanish culture. After a mission community was established, the monarchy built a presidio to defend and enforce its territorial claims and to protect the settlers and Indians from hostile attacks. Then the monarchy proceeded to establish civilian villages and towns.

Although the monarchy had established a centralized system of colonial government for its empire, the isolation of the Spanish Borderlands allowed the region to develop considerable political independence. The task of enforcing colonial policies fell to the local governors and officials, who often took matters into their own hands. In the late 1700s, however, the monarchy reorganized the Borderlands into a new administrative unit called the PROVINCIAS INTERNAS, or Internal Provinces of the North.

The Borderlands were linked to the trading network of the Spanish empire. However, strict regulations on imports and exports limited the

potential for the expansion of trade. As a result, settlers in the Borderlands engaged in SMUGGLING and other forms of illegal trade with the French and British colonists. Life in the Borderlands was difficult as colonists faced threats from Indians, disease, and crop failures. With little access to manufactured goods, the Spaniards depended on trade with the foreign colonies. Most lived on farms or ranches near tiny rural communities since large towns were few and scattered throughout the region.

The Spanish Borderlands remained under Spanish rule until the early 1800s. In 1819, Spain sold Florida to the United States, and the remaining regions were incorporated into Mexico in 1821. In the mid-1800s, after its defeat in the MEXICAN-AMERICAN WAR, Mexico ceded* most of the Borderlands to the United States. The final consolidation occurred in 1854, when southern Arizona was transferred to the United States in the GADSDEN PURCHASE.

* **cede** to yield or surrender, usually by treaty

Spanish Monarchs

* **Iberian** from or related to Spain and Portugal, the countries that occupy Europe's Iberian Peninsula
* **Moors** North African Muslims who conquered Spain in the A.D. 700s

See color plate 3, vol. 4.

Between the 1200s and the mid-1400s, several small Christian kingdoms, each ruled by its own monarch, struggled to reconquer the Iberian* Peninsula from the Moors*. In 1474, when Ferdinand of Aragon married Isabella of Castile and León, all the Christian kingdoms of Spain were united. However, the kingdom of Granada remained under the control of the Moors. As Catholic rulers, Ferdinand and Isabella increased the power of the monarchy and strengthened religious and political unity in the kingdom. They established the Holy Office of the INQUISITION in 1478, conquered Granada by 1492, and funded Christopher Columbus's voyages to the "New World."

In 1516, Charles I, the grandson of Ferdinand and Isabella, inherited a vast empire that included the Netherlands, Austria, and parts of France and Italy. For most of his reign, Charles was preoccupied with political problems in Europe and religious conflicts between Catholics and Protestants. Nevertheless, the Spanish empire in the Americas expanded tremendously under his rule, and gold and other riches from the colonies helped make Spain the greatest power in Europe.

In 1556, Charles was succeeded by his son, PHILIP II, who also faced many challenges in Europe, including several revolts in the Netherlands. In 1580, he successfully conquered the throne of Portugal. During his reign, the monarchy completed the conquest of the Americas and turned its attention to administering its territories there. Philip established colonies and military outposts in the SPANISH BORDERLANDS, and in the Pacific, the Spanish fleet conquered the PHILIPPINES, which was so named in his honor.

Between 1598 and 1700, during the reigns of Philip III, Philip IV, and Charles II, Spain entered a period of political and economic decline. Burdened with problems in Europe, these monarchs paid little attention to Spanish America. When Charles II died childless in 1700, Spain found itself in the midst of a war between England, allied with the Hapsburgs of Austria, and Louis XIV of France over the succession to the throne. Spain's power was greatly reduced, and the monarchy lost many

The Succession

1474–1504	Isabella I
1474–1516	Ferdinand I
1516–1556	Charles I
1556–1598	Philip II
1598–1621	Philip III
1621–1665	Philip IV
1665–1700	Charles II
1700–1746	Philip V
1746–1759	Ferdinand VI
1759–1788	Charles III
1788–1808	Charles IV
1808–1833	Ferdinand VII

* **abdicate** to give up power formally

territories in Europe. Still, under Philip V (Charles's named successor and grandson of Louis XIV), the monarchy slowly recovered from the economic decline of the 1600s.

During the 1700s, a succession of Bourbon monarchs—Philip V, Ferdinand VI, and CHARLES III—ruled the Spanish empire. Their most notable achievement was the institution of the BOURBON REFORMS, which reorganized the economic, administrative, and military structures of the empire. Charles III, considered the most successful Bourbon ruler, was succeeded by his son Charles IV, who handed over the governance of Spain's American colonies to Manuel de Godoy, his chief minister. During the reign of Charles IV, Spain became involved in the French Revolution and in costly wars with England. In 1808, Charles was forced to abdicate* the throne in favor of his son Ferdinand VII. Shortly thereafter, Napoleon Bonaparte invaded Spain and persuaded Charles and Ferdinand to abdicate the throne in favor of his brother, Joseph Bonaparte, who ruled Spain until 1814. During the time that Spain was in revolt, its American colonies were left to govern themselves. When Ferdinand was restored to the throne, he attempted to reassert control over the colonies, but movements for independence were already under way throughout Spanish America. By the end of his reign in 1833, most of the American colonies had gained their independence, and Spain had lost most of its colonial empire.

Spanish-American War

See color plate 7, vol. 4.

The Spanish-American War was a short and decisive conflict fought in 1898 between Spain and the United States. The war marked the end of Spanish colonialism in the Americas and the emergence of the United States as the dominant power in the Caribbean.

When CUBA revived its struggle for independence from Spain in 1895, several groups, including people in the United States who were sympathetic to its cause, encouraged the United States to intervene in the conflict. Newspapers in the United States inflamed the "war fever" by printing sensationalized stories about atrocities committed by the Spanish. Wealthy Cuban landowners supported United States intervention in the hope of restoring order to their country, but prominent leaders, such as José Marti, advised against it. The United States found a pretext for war on February 15, 1898, when the battleship USS MAINE exploded and sank in Havana's harbor, killing all 260 sailors aboard. Although an official investigation into the explosion was inconclusive, the United States demanded Spain's withdrawal from Cuba. On April 24, Spain declared war on the United States, and the following day, the United States declared war as well. The United States declaration included the Teller Amendment, which stated that the United States would not attempt to control Cuba.

The war lasted less than four months. The first battle was fought in the PHILIPPINES, a Spanish colony in Asia. On May 1, the U.S. Navy entered Manila Bay and destroyed the Spanish fleet there, prompting the Spanish to quickly surrender the islands to the United States. Back in the Caribbean, the U.S. Navy destroyed another Spanish fleet, and the

Spain was expelled from Latin America following the Spanish-American War, a short but decisive conflict. During the war, United States troops stormed Spanish outposts at San Juan Hill, Cuba, shown in this drawing by Frederic Remington. Although many artists and writers tended to romanticize the ensuing battle of San Juan Hill, losses and casualties on both sides were heavy.

* **cede** to yield or surrender, usually by treaty

combined United States and Cuban ground troops won several victories against Spanish forces on land. Finally, on August 12, the remaining Spanish forces surrendered and signed a formal truce agreement. On December 10, the two nations also signed the Treaty of Paris. Spain agreed to withdraw from Cuba and ceded* Guam, Puerto Rico, and the Philippines to the United States, marking the end of Spain's colonial empire in Asia and the Americas.

Although the Cuban struggle for independence had initiated the war, Cuba was excluded from the peace negotiations that resulted in the Treaty of Paris. Moreover, the United States, which had earlier promised not to take control of Cuba, went back on its word and established a military occupation of the island until 1902. The United States claimed the right to intervene in Cuba's affairs to maintain order there until 1934. (*See also* **Imperialism; Spain and the Spanish Empire; United States–Latin American Relations.**)

Spices and Herbs

* **colonial** referring to the period between the European conquest and independence, generally from the early 1500s to the early 1800s
* **indigenous** referring to the original inhabitants of a region

Long before the colonial* period, Europeans, Africans, and the indigenous* peoples of the Americas had been using spices and herbs to flavor their foods. During the colonial era, local spices were used in European cooking, and they also became important trade goods.

The Europeans' desire for Asian spices, such as black pepper, cinnamon, and cloves, greatly motivated their expeditions to Asia, the Americas, and elsewhere. Although overland trading routes linking Europe and Asia had existed for centuries, they were long and dangerous. In the 1400s, Europeans began searching for new ocean trade routes to Asia, and it was during this quest that Christopher Columbus stumbled on the Americas.

Throughout the colonial period, Asia remained the focus of the spice trade, which the European powers struggled to control. They introduced Asian spices to the Americas and tried to grow some of these spices there. Because of the similar tropical climates, some herbs grew well and became popular flavorings in Latin American cooking. Among these were cilantro, cumin, gingerroot, anise, and cardamom. In addition to Asian spices, the Europeans also brought onion, garlic, parsley, and oregano to the Americas. These herbs have all become essential flavorings in Latin American cooking.

The indigenous peoples also used several native herbs and spices to flavor their dishes. One of the best-known native plants is vanilla. In pre-Columbian* times, the Aztec nobility used vanilla to flavor their chocolate drinks; others used it as a perfume or for medicinal purposes. During the colonial period, vanilla became popular among European colonists as a sweetener, but their attempts to grow the plant in Africa and Asia failed until the 1800s, when a former French slave developed a special technique for its cultivation.

* **pre-Columbian** before the arrival of Christopher Columbus and other Europeans in the Americas in the 1490s

Perhaps the most important Native American plants were chili peppers, or CHILES. Since pre-Columbian times, several varieties of chiles have been cultivated throughout Latin America and used variously as spices, medicines, insect repellent, and the hottest ones as a weapon against the Spanish. During the colonial period, chili peppers were exported from the Americas and grown successfully in various places around the world. Today all Latin American countries use chili peppers in their cooking, either in sauces or as flavoring for other dishes.

Two other important Native American plants are *achiote* and allspice. *Achiote* is a seed that serves as both a red coloring agent and a spice. Indians painted their bodies with *achiote* for ceremonial occasions and during times of war. Nicaraguans added it to chocolate drinks to give them a bloodlike color, and the Spaniards used it as a substitute for saffron. Today, *achiote* is used throughout Latin America to flavor and color dishes, such as *arroz con pollo* (chicken and rice). Allspice, a seed native to the Caribbean, was exported to Europe in the early 1600s. It became a popular flavoring for sausages and other dishes. (*See also* **Food and Drink**.)

Southwestern Chili Powder

Chili powder is a combination of spices, based on chili peppers, that is used to flavor dishes from both Mexico and the southwestern United States. To make a mild chili powder, combine the following ingredients: **5 tablespoons of dried, ground chili peppers** (such as *pasillas* or *anchos*); **2 tablespoons dried oregano; 1½ tablespoons ground cumin; and ½ teaspoon ground red pepper.** Place the spices in a skillet and toast over low heat until you can smell the spices, about 2 minutes.

Spiritism

Spiritism encompasses a wide range of beliefs involving spirits and the ability of mediums to communicate with those spirits. In the 1850s, a French educator named Allan Kardec founded a spiritist movement that gained many followers in Latin America.

Spiritist beliefs and practices blended easily with Latin American religions through the process of syncretism*. This occurred largely because of the similarities between spiritist ideas and those of African, Native American, and Iberian* religions. Today spiritism remains a strong belief in many Latin American countries, especially in Brazil, where it has millions of followers. Spiritists meet at special centers to study the works of other spiritists, develop their skills as mediums, and provide charitable

* **syncretism** assimilation of different beliefs or practices
* **Iberian** from or related to Spain and Portugal, the countries that occupy Europe's Iberian Peninsula

services. In Brazil, spiritists run hospitals, orphanages, pharmacies, and free services for the poor.

An important element of spiritism is its connection to alternative forms of healing. Spiritists believe that earthbound spirits cause illnesses by attaching themselves to people and causing mental or physical distress. Spiritist centers thus offer various types of spiritual healing, such as a type of exorcism* known as disobsession. Some mediums practice psychic, or spirit, surgery and may operate on a person's spirit without actually touching his or her body.

* **exorcism** ritual to cast out evil spirits that inhabit a person's body

Historically, spiritists have suffered persecution by the Catholic Church and the state. However, they continue to practice spiritism and to defend the freedom of religion and the rights of spiritual healers. (*See also* **Candomblé; Medicine; Religions, African–Latin American; Religions, Indian; Voodoo.**)

Sports and Recreation

Sports and recreation are an integral part of Latin American society. The history of sports in the region has been marked by great variety, both socially and geographically. It reflects the historical processes that contributed to the development of modern Latin American culture.

Native American Sports and the European Conquest.
During the pre-Columbian* period, the indigenous* peoples of Mesoamerica* played complex ball games that were linked to religious rituals or had political and military significance. The people of South America also played several ball games, such as *chueca,* a game similar to field hockey.

* **pre-Columbian** before the arrival of Christopher Columbus and other Europeans in the Americas in the 1490s
* **indigenous** referring to the original inhabitants of a region
* **Mesoamerica** culture region that includes central and southern Mexico, Guatemala, Belize, El Salvador, and parts of Honduras, Nicaragua, and Costa Rica
* **Iberian** from or related to Spain and Portugal, the countries that occupy Europe's Iberian Peninsula

During the conquest of Latin America, the Spanish and Portuguese colonists attempted to abolish indigenous sports in their effort to establish cultural domination in the region. Yet some of these games survived in isolated communities. The colonists introduced several competitive and recreational activities based on Iberian* traditions. These activities typically involved animals (horse racing, cockfighting, and bullfighting) or chance (card and board games). Work-related competitions and festivals were also important.

Beginnings of Modern European Sports.
By the mid-1800s, sports in Latin America had become increasingly tied to European culture and the recreational practices there. New sporting activities were brought to Latin America by businesspeople, missionaries, teachers, and immigrants from Britain, France, and elsewhere in Europe, as well as by Latin American students who had attended school in Europe. These activities were first introduced in schools and social and athletic clubs run by foreigners and progressive* locals. The new sports and games spread in the cities and eventually reached rural areas. They changed the nature of recreation in Latin America, causing many traditional sports and games, such as *patolli* (a Mexican board game), *pato* (gaucho basketball

* **progressive** inclined to support social improvement and political change by governmental action

Sports and Recreation

Baseball is one of the most popular sports in Latin America, particularly in the Caribbean region. In this photograph, taken during the 1987 Pan American Games in Indianapolis, Cuba's Alejo O'Reilly scores the winning run against the United States. Many Cuban players have signed with major league baseball teams in the United States.

Mexico's Rodeo

The *charreada* is a roping and riding contest in Mexico and is the precursor of the North American rodeo. Events in the contest include *coleadero* (downing a bull by twisting its tail), *jineteo* (riding wild mares and young bulls), and *paso de la muerte* (death pass: jumping from a tame horse onto the back of a wild horse). *Charreadas* were very popular in the 1800s during hacienda fiestas but declined after the Mexican Revolution and the breakup of the haciendas. In 1921, to preserve the tradition, a group of *charros* founded amateur *charreada* clubs. Today the *charreada* is held in a special area called *lienzo*, and includes the traditional events as well as some new ones. As in the 1800s, *charreadas* end with the *jarabe tapatío* (Mexican hat dance).

on horseback), and cockfighting, to disappear or survive regionally in modified forms.

Latin American Sports Today. The popular competitive sports in Latin America today are soccer, baseball, basketball, tennis, volleyball, cycling, boxing, swimming, and car racing. Commonly practiced recreational activities include hiking, camping, boating, and sport fishing. Bullfighting and some other traditional sports are also popular, especially in regions where the colonial presence was strong and traditional lifestyles remain unchanged. Mexico, Columbia, Peru, and Venezuela have strong bullfighting establishments, and court-related ball games such as jai alai—derived from sports in the Basque region of Spain—are popular in Cuba, Mexico, and the Andean region.

In most Latin American countries, many sports are played exclusively at professional levels, while others are played by professionals as well as amateurs. Soccer and Formula One auto racing are solely professional; baseball, basketball, tennis, and cycling are both amateur and professional; and volleyball, swimming, and track and field events are almost entirely amateur. Professional sports, in which the players are highly paid and idolized by fans, attract the most spectators.

The most popular sport in Latin America is soccer (*fútbol* in Spanish; *futebol* in Portuguese). Professional teams participate regularly in regional and international competitions. In fact, Latin American teams have won the World Cup eight times—four times by Brazil and twice each by Uruguay and Argentina. In the Caribbean, baseball (*béisbol*) has been the "king of sports" since the early 1900s, primarily because of the influence of the United States. Some Caribbean players, especially Dominicans, Venezuelans, Cubans, and Puerto Ricans, play for professional teams in North America. Since the 1950s, Latin American tennis players have risen in the world rankings, and their success has promoted

tennis as a recreational activity. Prominent tennis players include Gabriela Sabatini of Argentina, Guillermo Vilas of Ecuador, and Pancho González of Mexico.

Latin America has also produced world champions in professional boxing, especially in the lighter weight divisions. The region also has a strong tradition in amateur boxing, and boxers have fared well at amateur competitions, such as the Olympics and the Pan-American Games. In recent years, basketball has gained popularity in many countries and is an important part of school physical education and recreation programs.

Private and public agencies in Latin America use sports and recreation to improve physical health, teach moral values, reduce crime, develop a sense of community and cooperation, and promote patriotism. All Latin American countries have national associations for most sports, physical education institutes, and agencies with links to international sporting associations. (*See also* **Ball Game, Pre-Columbian; Education; Pelé**.)

See color plate 15, vol. 2.

State Corporations

See *Public Sector*.

Storni, Alfonsina

1892–1938
Argentine poet and journalist

Alfonsina Storni, a leading Latin American poet, was born in Switzerland and moved to Argentina with her family in 1896. She went to work when she was ten, washing dishes and waiting tables. In 1912, Storni had a child out of wedlock and moved to Buenos Aires, where she became a teacher. She had begun writing poetry in 1910, and her first book, *La inquietud del rosal* (The Disquiet of the Rosebush), was published in 1916. By 1925, after the publication of *El dulce daño* (Sweet Harm) and *Ocre* (Ochre), Storni attained great critical acclaim. Her poems expressed erotic themes and her resentment against women's submissive role in society. Storni became a symbol of the rebel, the feminist, and the fighter against a male-dominated society. However, her personal life was filled with disillusionment. She was unable to find fulfillment in love and underwent surgery for cancer. In 1938, Storni committed suicide. Her last book, *Mascarilla y trébol* (Death Mask and Clover), was published that same year. (*See also* **Literature**.)

Street Vendors

Throughout Latin America, thousands of men, women, and children have congregated on city streets each day since ancient times to sell merchandise: flowers, foods, drinks, candy, clothing, electronic equipment, books, and handicrafts. Some vendors are performers, amusing passersby with music, magic tricks, skits, and other types of entertainment.

Street Vendors

Some cities control street vending by restricting sellers to certain areas and making them pay a vending fee. Despite such measures, street vending comprises a large portion of the region's total economic activity and is a means of survival for the poor.

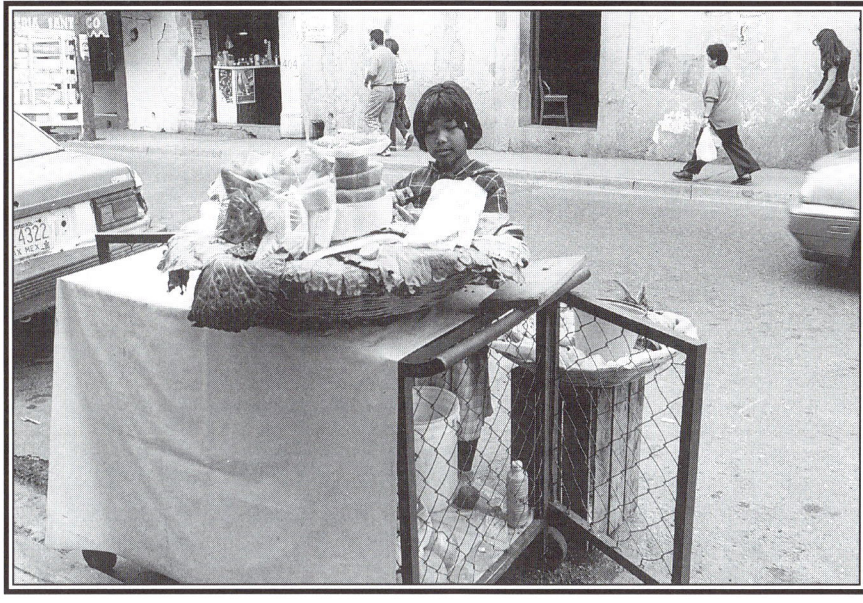

* **pre-Columbian** before the arrival of Christopher Columbus and other Europeans in the Americas in the 1490s

The tradition of street vending in Latin America can be traced to the street markets of pre-Columbian* cultures. The practice continued through the colonial period and the 1800s, largely as a refuge for women who needed to support their families. Today street vendors form part of Latin America's "informal economy"—economic activities occurring outside the law and beyond regulation. Most vendors within the informal economy do not pay taxes, and their income is never included in national income measurements. Still, this sector of the economy makes up a significant portion of the total economic activity of Latin America.

Unemployment is high in Latin America, and street vending is a means of survival for the urban poor. However, the activity has long been a source of controversy. Government officials believe that street vending is a hotbed of corruption and is directly related to the increasing crime rate in the cities because many vendors sell stolen or smuggled goods. In recent years, some governments have tried to crack down on illegal street vending and to regulate the activity. As a result, many vendors belong to associations that control their activities, collect dues, assign spots, and provide protection from other vendors, the police, and city inspectors. In some countries, such as Mexico, vendors pay dues to a leader who negotiates with government officials on their behalf.

However, these efforts have had little success, and many thousands of vendors remain unregulated. In the 1980s, Peruvian economist Hernando de Soto studied vendors' reluctance to formalize their activity. He discovered that it takes 289 days and the equivalent of $1,000 to register a new business, 83 months and more than $500,000 to own a piece of land legally, and 43 days and almost $600 to open a store. He concluded that the Lima elite had purposely created such obstacles to prevent the poor from legalizing their efforts, thus keeping them from fully participating in Peruvian society. (*See also* **Cities and Urbanization; Labor and Labor Movements.**)

Stroessner, Alfredo

born 1912
President of Paraguay

° **coup** sudden, often violent overthrow of a ruler or government

See color plate 11, vol. 3.

° **inflation** sharp increase in prices due to an increase in the amount of money or credit relative to available goods and services

° **oust** to remove from office

Alfredo Stroessner, one of Latin America's longest-ruling dictators, was the president of PARAGUAY for 35 years—from 1954 to 1989. Stroessner governed Paraguay through a combination of political skill, hard work, attention to detail, and a genius for organization. He created a system in which he tied almost every social group in Paraguay to his political machine.

Born to a German father and a Paraguayan mother in the southern Paraguayan town of Encarnación, Stroessner entered the Military Academy in Asunción at the age of 16. Three years later, he fought in the CHACO WAR and was decorated for his bravery. He rapidly advanced in rank in the military and rose to prominence during Paraguay's civil war in 1947. After the war, the Colorado Party (one of Paraguay's two traditional political parties) gained control of the country. Between 1947 and 1954, the leaders of the Colorado Party competed among themselves to control the nation; Paraguay had five different presidents during that period. Stroessner was deeply involved in the political plotting that occurred at the time. In 1948, he backed the wrong side in a coup* and was forced to flee the country hidden in the trunk of a car. Three months later, however, Stroessner slipped back into Paraguay and supported the winning side in a new coup. Finally, in 1954, he seized the presidency for himself.

By 1959, Stroessner had eliminated or suppressed any opposing officials and dominated the army and the Colorado Party. Soon his military dictatorship gained popular support because businesspeople, professionals, young people, women, veterans, and peasants in every corner of the nation were connected to the regime through the Colorado Party. Although his economic policies favored large landowners and foreign investors, Stroessner implemented several public works projects that brought jobs, contracts, and prosperity to his followers. He governed ruthlessly, persecuting his critics and others who refused to conform to his methods, including members of the Liberal Party and the Catholic Church.

During the 1980s, Stroessner's regime began to crumble as economic problems, including inflation*, developed and the new middle class began challenging his authority. Stroessner, by now an elderly man, was ousted* in 1989 by General Andrés Rodríguez and forced into exile in Brazil. (*See also* **Dictatorships, Military; Political Parties**.)

Suárez, Inés de

ca. 1512–ca. 1580
Collaborator in the conquest of Chile

° **conquistador** Spanish explorer and conqueror

Inés de Suárez played a forceful part in the Spanish conquest of CHILE. In her 20s, she left Spain for America, where she became the mistress of conquistador* Pedro de VALDIVIA. In 1541, when SANTIAGO came under attack from the Indians, Suárez, acting on Valdivia's behalf, hatched a plan to retaliate. She ordered the Spaniards to kill the seven caciques* whom they were holding captive and to throw their corpses into the crowd of attacking Indians. She then put on armor and led the Spaniards during the rest of the battle. As the only spanish woman in the colony, Suárez devoted herself to caring for the wounded and supervising supplies. Later she was awarded an

Sucre Alcalá, Antonio José de

- **cacique** Indian leader at the town or village level
- **encomienda** right granted to a conqueror that enabled him to control the labor of and collect payment from an Indian community

encomienda* for her contributions to the conquest. She married one of Valdivia's lieutenants, Rodrigo de Quiroga, who later became the governor of Chile. As an act of repentance for her murderous acts, Suárez supported a small church in Santiago, which she presented to the Dominicans in 1553.

Sucre Alcalá, Antonio José de

1795–1830
Venezuelan military leader

- **royalist** supporter of the king or queen, especially in times of civil war or rebellion

Antonio José de Sucre Alcalá was one of the most distinguished generals of Latin America. He served as Simón BOLÍVAR's chief lieutenant and helped liberate ECUADOR and BOLIVIA. Sucre was also the first constitutionally elected president of Bolivia.

Sucre was born in Cumaná, Venezuela, and joined the WARS OF INDEPENDENCE as a youth. He displayed great military skills and soon became Bolívar's chief of staff. In 1820, Sucre led the expedition to liberate Ecuador, which he accomplished in 1822. He then joined Bolívar, who was on an expedition to liberate Peru. There Sucre's brilliant strategies won crucial battles at Junín and Ayacucho, guaranteeing Peru's independence.

In 1825, by defeating the royalists* in Upper Peru (present-day Bolivia), Sucre had overcome the last obstacle to the independence of Spanish South America. Appointed president of Bolivia, he implemented far-reaching economic and social reforms. However, his ideas were opposed by Bolivia's elite, and he resigned in 1828, retiring to Ecuador.

In 1829, when war broke out between Peru and GRAN COLOMBIA, Sucre returned to successfully lead an army against Peruvian forces in southern Ecuador. The following year, Sucre presided over a congress that met in BOGOTÁ to discuss how to preserve the unity of Gran Colombia. Despite Sucre's prestige, the congress failed, and Gran Colombia broke up into three independent republics: Colombia, Ecuador, and Venezuela. On his way home, Sucre was assassinated. The identity of his killers remains a mystery.

Suffrage Movement

- **literacy** ability to read and write; illiteracy is the inability to read and write

Following the WARS OF INDEPENDENCE in the early 1800s, many Latin American countries adopted a representative form of government based on a constitution. Since the newly independent countries did not immediately become full-fledged democracies, suffrage, or the right to vote, was limited to free men who owned a certain amount of property or who engaged in specific occupations. In some countries, literacy* was an additional criterion for voting. As a result, only 5 to 10 percent of the population was eligible to vote and participate in the government.

Universal male suffrage, or voting rights for all men, was incorporated into the constitutions of several countries in Latin America in the mid-1800s. Colombia enacted such a constitution in 1853, although

many doubted whether the average man would know how to use the right to vote effectively. Other countries that adopted the universal male suffrage policy during this period include Mexico and Venezuela. Although these countries had adopted universal male suffrage legally, the governments continued to impose restrictions on voter eligibility. For example, although 50 percent of Brazil's male population was legally eligible and registered to vote in the mid-1800s, the government passed new laws raising the income requirements. In Chile, property qualifications for voting were abolished in 1874, but the literacy requirement remained.

According to the Sáenz Peña Law of 1912, Argentina made universal male suffrage compulsory for all males over the age of 18, making possible the 1916 election of Hipólito YRIGOYEN, the first popularly chosen president in South America. The following year, Mexico enacted a constitution that was hailed as the most advanced social and political document of its day. The Mexican Constitution of 1917 granted political rights, including the right to vote, to all Mexican citizens with the exception of women.

Women's suffrage was the topic of much debate at national and international conferences throughout Latin America until the mid-1900s. In 1929, Ecuador became the first nation to grant women the right to vote. By 1933, Uruguay, Brazil, and Cuba had followed. Argentina and Mexico, two nations where women had organized early, did not grant voting rights to women until 1947 and 1953, respectively. (*See also* **Political Parties; Women.**)

Remember: Consult the index at the end of this volume to find more information on many topics.

Sugar Industry

Latin America is one of the world's major sugar-producing regions. Brazil, Cuba, and Mexico are among the leading sugar-producing countries in the world, and the sugar industry is an important part of the economies of the Dominican Republic, Guyana, and Barbados.

Introduction in the "New World." Sugarcane was first brought to the Americas by Christopher Columbus in 1493, during his second voyage to the region. It came from the Canary Islands off the northwestern coast of Africa and was first grown in Santo Domingo on the island of Hispaniola. By 1526, the Portuguese had begun to grow sugarcane in Brazil and to export the processed sugar to Europe. At first, sugarcane thrived in fertile valleys in Mexico and Paraguay and along the Pacific coast of South America. Eventually, the growing and processing of sugar spread to other islands in the Caribbean. In addition, the Spanish and Portuguese colonists also imported slaves from Africa to work on sugarcane plantations and in processing mills.

Colonial Sugar Plantations. During the colonial period, a typical sugar plantation had 15 or 20 Portuguese or Spanish workers and more than 100 African and Indian slaves. Each plantation typically consisted

Sugar Industry

of a chapel, workshops, a processing plant, a big house for the owner and his family, and a senzala, or slave quarter.

When the sugarcane was ready for harvesting, slaves cut it by hand with a large knife, or machete. It was then taken to a mill, where a waterpowered or oxen-powered grinder extracted the juices from the cane by pressing it through large rollers. The raw sugar juice was then heated and cooled until it formed crystals. At the time, large mills could produce between 200,000 and 320,000 pounds (100 to 160 tons) of sugar annually, much of which was exported to Europe. Molasses, a thick brown syrup that was extracted from the sugar juice, was also exported and distilled* into a liquor called rum.

* **distill** to manufacture alcoholic beverages by heating the liquid until it begins to evaporate and then cooling it

Triangular Trade.

The slave-based sugarcane plantations in the Americas reached their peak of operation during the 1700s. Great Britain and France had established a presence in the Caribbean and became great sugar makers and exporters of the "New World." During that time, a trading network known as the triangular trade emerged between Africa and the Americas. First, the Europeans sold goods in Africa and used the proceeds to buy African slaves, whom they transported to the Americas for sale. Then they used the profits from the sale of slaves in the Americas to purchase regional goods, especially sugar, which they exported to Europe.

In the late 1700s and early 1800s, the sugar colonies in the Americas experienced dramatic changes caused by the revolutions for independence

The Latin American sugar industry was started on the Caribbean islands. However, sugar cultivation spread quickly throughout Latin America. Today South America accounts for 75 percent of the sugarcane grown in the region, with Brazil producing more sugar then all other Latin American nations combined.

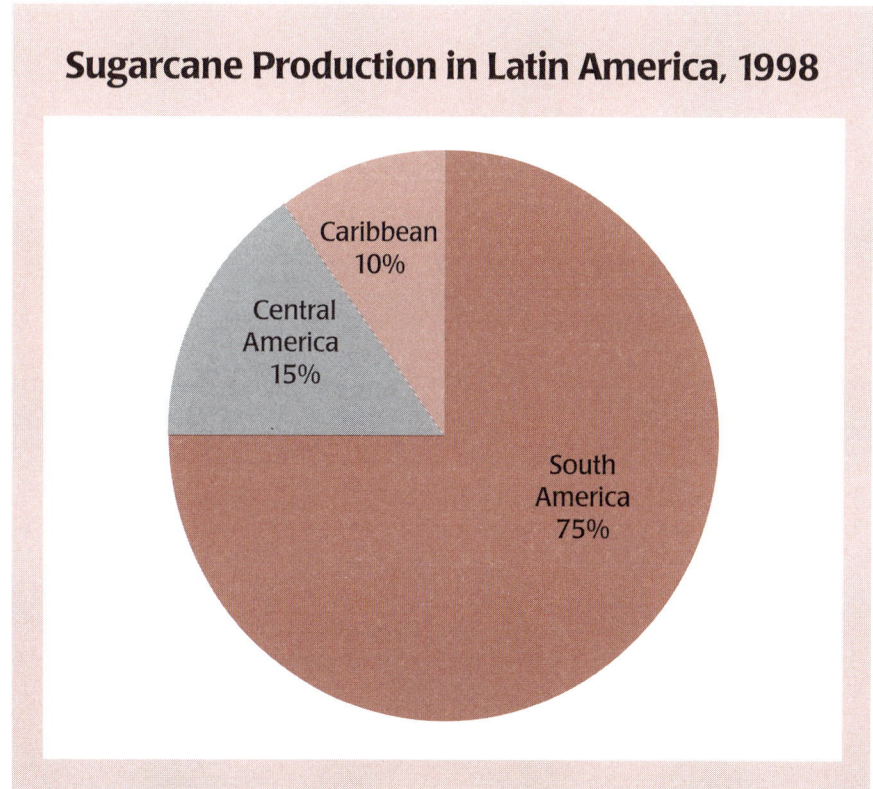

Source: Food and Agricultural Organization of the United Nations.

and by the abolition of the slave trade. Moreover, the demand for American sugar decreased as Europeans began producing sugar from beets, which grew abundantly in Europe.

Cuba's Sugar Industry. Cuba was the last island in the Caribbean to develop its sugar industry, but by the early 1800s, sugar had become Cuba's main export. Before the TEN YEARS' WAR in the mid-1800s, Cuban plantation owners grew sugarcane and processed it in their own mills. However, after the war, the destruction of property throughout the island and the abolition of slavery resulted in economic hardships. Many sugar mills in Cuba were purchased by foreign investors, largely from the United States. However, the sugar industry continued to dominate the Cuban economy until the mid-1900s. In 1959, following the CUBAN REVOLUTION, Fidel CASTRO began to enact agricultural reforms to end the island's dependence on the sugar industry. Despite the efforts of many Cubans to diversify agriculture and industrialize, they continued to depend on sugarcane for their livelihood.

Modern Trends in the Industry. Today the process of refining sugar is highly mechanized. Still, several companies continue to employ poorly paid workers to produce sugar manually, especially on large estates. Since the 1980s, sugar production has been steadily declining in some Latin American nations, such as Guatemala, because of falling world prices; competition from sugar substitutes, such as corn syrup, a thick, sweet liquid made from cornstarch; and increased diet consciousness. Food manufacturers worldwide have begun to use certain sugar substitutes because they are nonfattening or because they are sweeter and cheaper than sugar made from sugarcane. (*See also* **Agriculture; Slave Revolts; Slave Trade; Slavery; Slavery, Abolition of; Technology; Trade and Commerce; United States–Latin American Relations.**)

Dance of the Millions

During World War I, Europe's beet sugar production was severely reduced. As a result, there was a great demand for Cuban sugar. During this period, known as the Dance of the Millions, the Cuban sugar industry expanded rapidly and the price of sugar soared. Although the United States had set price controls on sugar, the price reached almost 23 cents per pound in May 1920. When Europe's beet sugar production resumed at the end of that year, Cuban sugar prices fell to just 4 cents per pound. Many of those who had made quick fortunes in Cuba lost them just as quickly.

Suriname

Suriname is the smallest country—in size and population—in South America. It lies just north of the equator and has a hot, humid climate. Most of its population lives along the Atlantic coastal plain, which stretches some 200 miles. Mountainous RAIN FORESTS cover about 80 percent of Suriname.

In pre-Columbian* times, Suriname was inhabited by the Surinen, and later, by the Carib, Arawak, and Awarao Indians. Today East Indians form the largest ethnic group, followed by Creoles (people of African and European descent), Indonesians, American Indians, Africans, Europeans, and Chinese. Dutch is the official language, but Sranan Tongo—a Creole language based on English, Dutch, and African dialects*—is also widely spoken.

The Spaniards first sighted Suriname in 1498, and two years later, explorer Vicente Yáñez Pinzón visited the region. From then until the mid-1600s, the Spaniards, the Dutch, the English, and the French attempted

* **pre-Columbian** before the arrival of Christopher Columbus and other Europeans in the Americas in the 1490s

* **dialect** regional form of speech that differs from the standard language in pronunciation, vocabulary, and grammar

Syncretism

- **indigenous** referring to the original inhabitants of a region

- **bauxite** mineral ore that is the principle source of aluminum

- **left-wing** very liberal

- **coup** sudden, often violent overthrow of a ruler or government

- **guerrilla** referring to a group that uses surprise raids to obstruct or harass an enemy

to settle Suriname but failed because of the violent resistance of the indigenous* peoples. Finally, in 1651, the English established a plantation-based settlement there. In 1667, the Dutch seized Suriname from the English and retained control of it until the Surinamese declared their independence in 1975.

In the early colonial period, Suriname was a plantation colony based on sugar. By the mid-1800s, however, the SUGAR INDUSTRY had become less profitable because of the abolition of slavery. Although the colonists encouraged the immigration of laborers from China, Madeira, India, and Indonesia, sugar production eventually failed. In 1916, the Dutch began to mine newly discovered reserves of bauxite*, and the economy revived.

In 1954, Suriname became a self-governing territory of the Netherlands, and a multiparty system based on the nation's ethnic groups emerged. The parties included the Suriname National Party (NPS), composed mainly of Creoles; the Progressive Reform Party (VHP), which consisted of East Indians; and the Indonesian Peasants' Party (KTPI). During the next 20 years, several coalition governments came to power, and many new political parties emerged. In 1975, the Suriname National Party and the left-wing* Nationalist Republican Party (PNR) led the country to independence.

In 1980, the National Military Council (NMR), led by Lieutenant Desi Bouterse, staged a coup* and seized power. After the coup, the economy deteriorated rapidly, forcing Bouterse to ask the leaders of Suriname's traditional parties for help in forming a new civilian government. Over the next few years, power continued to change hands frequently, civil strife prevailed, and the economy suffered. The government faced another crisis when a guerrilla* war broke out after raids by the Surinamese Liberation Army (SLA), which disrupted bauxite mining and caused the death of many civilians. In 1985, the military opened talks with the leaders of the main political parties and formed a new national assembly.

In 1988, the Front for Democracy and Development (FDO) formed a new coalition government and began negotiations with the SLA. Two years later, the military forced the FDO out of office and resumed control of Suriname. The FDO returned to power in the 1991 elections, gained control over the military, and negotiated cease-fires with the SLA. In 1996, Bouterse's National Democratic Party (NDP) came to power, assuring the military's influence in Suriname for years to come. (*See also* **Dutch in Latin America**.)

Syncretism is the merging of beliefs and rituals of different religions. Christianity, for example, incorporated features of Judaism, and the first part of the Roman Catholic Mass is based on the Jewish religious service of the first century. Syncretism was common among the indigenous* peoples in pre-Columbian* times. The AZTECS adopted the gods of the peoples they conquered. The MAYA began

- **indigenous** referring to the original inhabitants of a region
- **pre-Columbian** before the arrival of Christopher Columbus and other Europeans in the Americas in the 1490s

to worship the Toltec god Quetzalcoatl and as a result, the practice of human sacrifice gained greater importance in Mayan culture. Following the European conquest, Catholicism became so intertwined with indigenous religions that it was often difficult to separate pre-Christian elements from original Catholicism. In many instances, however, people retained their old practices, especially people living in isolated regions of Latin America. (*See also* **Catholic Church; Jews in Latin America; Protestantism; Religions, African–Latin American; Religions, Indian.**)

Taxes and Taxation

Even before the arrival of the Europeans, many people living in Latin America paid taxes. Dominant powers, such as the Aztec and the Inca empires required those they ruled to provide food, labor, and goods in support of the imperial government. The Inca empire, for example, used a system of taxation-by-service. Subjects of the empire were required to work a certain number of days to help build roads and bridges or as messengers for government officials. As a form of taxation, a percentage of each harvest or a share of woven textiles was also taken. The food enabled Inca rulers to feed government workers and distribute food during crop failures.

During the colonial rule of Latin America, taxes were used by royal governments to ensure that they received a percentage of the wealth that was being discovered in the "New World" to pay for the costs of maintaining their empires. One important source of money for the rulers of Latin America was known as the quinto, or "king's fifth." This tax required mine owners to share a fifth of all precious metals with the king. Another source of money at this time was a tax on imports and exports known as the *avería*. The money generated from this tax was used to pay the cost of protection provided by the king's naval forces to merchant ships.

Not all taxes were used to support royal governments, however. The *diezmo* was used to support the Catholic Church. Also known as a tithe*, the *diezmo* required all Catholics to give 10 percent of their agricultural production to the church. For example, if a farmer harvested ten bushels of wheat, one bushel would go to the church. The goods collected through this tax were used to support religious leaders, hospitals, and the local cathedral.

After winning independence from colonial rule, the newly formed governments of Latin America needed to raise money to rebuild their countries. Taxes on exports and imports became a chief source of money for the young nations. Because the demand for exports fluctuates, this proved to be an unreliable source of revenue. Many governments were slow to introduce progressive income or property taxes, which require wealthy people to pay a greater percentage of taxes than poorer people. Instead, governments used sales taxes. Foreign companies working in Latin America paid little in taxes, and their profits were often taken out of the region.

- **tithe** payment or gift of a tenth of one's salary for the support of the church

Tayasal

Latin American nations are now attempting to address these and other problems, such as a more equitable distribution of government resources and the efficient collection of income and property taxes.

Tayasal

* **conquistador** Spanish explorer and conqueror

* **musket** heavy shoulder gun used from the late 1500s through the 1700s

Tayasal was the last MAYA site to be conquered by the Spaniards. Ancient Maya chronicles report that the last of the Maya fled to the south after the Spanish conquered CHICHÉN ITZÁ and settled at Tayasal, on the southern shore of Lake Petén in present-day Guatemala. When conquistador* Hernán CORTÉS arrived in Tayasal in 1525, the Maya chief there promised Cortés that the Indians would convert to Christianity. However, over the next 100 years, the Maya resisted conversion. Moreover, when the Spaniards attempted to conquer the region, the Indians stood firm. In 1696, some 235 Spanish soldiers arrived at the lake and tried to convince the Maya to surrender, but they failed to do so. The Spanish force then crossed the lake and with heavy musket* fire, defeated the Maya. By early 1697, the Spanish troops had seized Tayasal, destroyed Maya idols, and completed the conquest of the Maya. (*See also* **Conquistadors; Indian Policy; Indians; Tikal.**)

Technology

* **pre-Columbian** before the arrival of Christopher Columbus and other Europeans in the Americas in the 1490s

* **indigenous** referring to the original inhabitants of a region

* **archaeological** relating to the study of human cultures, usually by excavating ruins

* **terrace farming** creating a series of horizontal ridges on a hillside to increase land that can be cultivated, conserve moisture, and minimize erosion

In pre-Columbian* times, Latin America's indigenous* peoples developed complex technologies for use in agriculture, mining, and industry. During the colonial period, technological development reflected the development in Europe and was used to achieve colonial dominance and to accumulate wealth for the crown. Since independence and especially in recent years, technology has advanced by leaps and bounds. Today's sophisticated information technology is bringing Latin American nations closer to each other and to the world.

Technology of Native Americans.
The pre-Columbian peoples were skilled architects. Their talent is evident from an examination of the archaeological* sites at MACHU PICCHU, TEOTIHUACÁN, and TIKAL. Around 1400 B.C., the peoples of northern Peru constructed irrigation systems to bring water to the farms. The MAYA were experts in the field of astronomy. The INCA used terrace farming* to cultivate beans, corn, and potatoes on the slopes of the Andes. They also developed a method for predicting the weather by observing the stars, the sky, and the ocean, as well as the behavior of plant and animal life.

Improved Production Techniques.
Technological advances in Latin America were propelled by the desire to increase productivity. In pre-Columbian times, Indians mined silver, gold, copper, and lead from shallow pits. During the colonial period, Spaniards introduced

Technology

Refrigeration Brings Risk

In the early 1800s, Argentine beef produced for export was shipped either dried or salted. With the development of refrigeration technology in the 1870s, *frigoríficos* (refrigerated ships) came into use. Although the refrigeration technology worked well, problems existed in the managerial and marketing phases of the industry. The need for precise timing in loading, unloading, and selling the beef left little room for error and posed high risks for beef exporters, thus paving the way for foreign ownership.

the deep-shaft technique of MINING, which significantly increased the amount of ore that could be reached. Another major breakthrough in the mining industry was the development of a new silver-refining procedure. In the mid-1550s, Bartolomé de Medina developed a new amalgamation process that used large amounts of mercury to produce enormous amounts of silver.

In the sugar industry, cane growers in the 1800s experimented with different varieties of sugarcane to cultivate a robust plant that contained more sugar and was resistant to drought. They also made advances in sugar-processing technology by replacing vertical rollers with horizontal rollers, making the grinding and extraction processes more efficient, and developing techniques for faster evaporation in sugar processing.

The invention of the steam engine revolutionized many industries. Steam engines were used in mining from the early 1800s and eventually replaced animal power in the sugar mills. The invention of a steam-powered machine to strip fibers from the henequen plant enabled Mexico's rope-making industry to engage in mass production. Still, in some areas, cheap land and labor reduced the incentive to seek improved methods of production, and new technologies were adopted slowly.

Later Technological Advances.

A major thrust in technological research and development has been in the field of energy production. In 1974, Argentina became the first Latin American nation to build a nuclear power plant, followed by Brazil, Mexico, Colombia, Chile, Peru, and Venezuela. In the 1970s, Brazil launched a research and development program to produce ethanol* from sugarcane as a substitute for

* **ethanol** colorless, flammable liquid; alcohol

This photograph shows the interior of an airplane factory in Brazil, one of the most technologically advanced nations in Latin America. Brazil not only exports traditional items, such as textiles and clothing, but automobiles and household appliances as well. Because of the new jobs created by these manufacturing industries, more people move to the cities, increasing the urban population by 5 to 7 percent annually.

gasoline. By 1990, ethanol production met about 15 percent of Brazil's liquid fuel requirements.

Manufacturing productivity has also increased as a result of the constant stream of innovations. Mexican researchers have developed and exported glass-manufacturing equipment, technologies for deep drilling of petroleum, and a method of producing paper from bagasse, a by-product of sugar production. Chile and Peru lead experimental research in copper mining extraction. In Mexico, iron ores are transported by the most advanced computer-driven pipeline system in the world.

However, Latin American efforts to develop technology have encountered several problems, including a lack of funds. In general, only modest research and development is undertaken outside the largest cities. In recent years, there has been increased cooperation among countries to consolidate technological growth in Latin America. Argentina, Brazil, and Mexico are achieving success in growing fields such as biotechnology*.

* **biotechnology** technology applied to the biological sciences

Latin American nations are progressing significantly by pursuing the latest in communications and information technologies. Microcomputers, which first appeared in the 1980s, have made computing affordable for small businesses and educational institutions in Latin America and have created markets for locally produced software. By the 1990s, most Latin American countries, including Brazil, Argentina, Peru, Mexico, Costa Rica, and Chile, were linked to the Internet and were developing networks within their borders. (*See also* **Agriculture; Energy and Energy Resources; Science; Sugar Industry.**)

Tegucigalpa

* **provincial** having to do with the provinces, outlying districts, administrative divisions, or conquered territories of a country or empire
* **New Spain** Spanish colony in Mexico

See map in Central America (vol. 1).

Tegucigalpa, which according to folk legend means "hill of silver," is the capital and largest city of HONDURAS. Surrounded by mountains, the city lies in a fertile plain along the Choluteca River in south central Honduras, about 75 miles from the Pacific Ocean.

The city was founded in the 1570s, after Spanish explorers discovered silver mines in the region. When reports of the silver deposits reached the king, he named Tegucigalpa an *alcaldía mayor,* a provincial* unit of the Viceroyalty New Spain*. In 1578, Tegucigalpa became independent of the provincial capital at Comayagua, thus beginning a rivalry between the two cities. When silver production declined, the city decreased in size but remained a center for cattle ranching and commerce and served as the political and religious center of Honduras. Along with some minor mining efforts, these activities sustained Tegucigalpa as the largest and most prosperous city in Honduras.

In 1824, after CENTRAL AMERICA gained its independence from Spain, the political leaders agreed that the capital of the Province of Honduras would alternate between Tegucigalpa and Comayagua. This arrangement continued until 1880, when the capital was moved permanently to Tegucigalpa. However, it is one of few capitals in the world without a railroad. Tegucigalpa depends largely on the international airport at Toncontín and on the Pan-American Highway, which passes some 50

miles south of the city. Today Tegucigalpa is a rapidly growing city, with a population exceeding 750,000, due largely to the migration of *campesinos,* or rural workers, from the countryside.

Templo Mayor

- **Franciscan** member of the Order of Friars Minor, a religious brotherhood
- **archaeologist** scientist who studies past human cultures, usually by excavating ruins
- **artifact** in archaeology, a human-made object such as a tool, household utensil, or work of art

Templo Mayor is the ceremonial center at TENOCHTITLÁN, the capital of the AZTEC empire in Mexico, and more specifically its main pyramid temple. According to Franciscan* priest Bernardino de Sahagún, the main ceremonial center contained 78 structures, including temples and shrines to deities, a residence and school for priests, a ball court, and a skull rack. The main temple was constructed in the 1300s and consisted of a base of four progressively smaller stacked platforms. At the top were shrines to Huitzilopochtli, the sun god of warfare, and Tlaloc, the god of rain. Templo Mayor was unearthed in 1978, when workers were digging up power lines in Mexico City. After extensive excavations that lasted for more than 20 years, archaeologists* found many ceremonial structures and unearthed sculptures, ritual items, and artifacts*. Mexicans willingly sacrificed valuable real estate in downtown Mexico City to preserve this monument. (*See also* **Archaeology; Ball Game, Pre-Columbian; Divinities.**)

Ten Years' War

- **emancipation** liberation

- **conservative** inclined to maintain existing political and social views, conditions, and institutions
- **annexation** addition of a territory to an existing state
- **republican** referring to a government in which citizens elect officials to represent them and govern according to law
- **suffrage** the right to vote

The Ten Years' War, fought from 1868 to 1878, was the first major Cuban struggle for independence. The war stemmed from serious social, political, and economic problems in CUBA and from the failure of the Spanish to grant various reforms. Although the rebellion failed to liberate Cuba from Spanish rule, it began the process of slave emancipation*.

In the 1820s, after most of Spanish America had gained independence, Spanish rule in Cuba became more oppressive. Although earlier governments had raised expectations of reforms, subsequent conservative* rulers enacted repressive policies that alienated many Cubans. By the mid-1800s, the failure to win reforms had provoked widespread unrest, and Cubans began to call for independence or annexation* to the United States. In 1868, a Cuban planter, Carlos Manuel de Céspedes, proclaimed Cuban independence and began a war against the Spaniards. He organized a republican* government that called for universal male suffrage* and a gradual end to slavery and supported Cuba's annexation to the United States. The issue of slavery, however, divided the rebel movement and cost the support of some plantation owners. Nevertheless most of the rebels were Afro-Cubans and favored abolition as did the movement's military leaders, Antonio MACEO and Máximo Gómez.

By 1878, the fighting had cost more than 250,000 lives and had severely damaged Cuba's SUGAR INDUSTRY. The same year, the monarchy proposed the Pact of Zanjón, by which it agreed to some political reform

and immediate freedom for the slaves who had fought in the war. The remaining slaves were to be given freedom gradually, and their owners were to be compensated for the loss. However, the agreement did not satisfy the rebels who desired autonomy*. Shortly after the pact was signed, Maceo issued the "Protest of Baraguá" and continued to fight until his defeat later that year.

The war led to a major reorganization of the sugar industry in Cuba, with major capital* investment from the United States. The Spaniards' failure to enact reforms, along with the continued social and economic problems in Cuba, contributed to the resumption of the struggle for independence in 1895. Although the Ten Years' War failed to win independence for Cuba, it produced several leaders, including José MARTÍ, who later led the nation to freedom. (*See also* **Slavery, Abolition of; United States–Latin American Relations; Wars of Independence.**)

* **autonomy** independent self-government

* **capital** money invested to start a business or industry

Tenentismo

Tenentismo was a powerful politico-military movement in Brazil during the 1920s and 1930s. Its members, called *tenentes*, were military officials and intellectuals involved in revolts to protest corruption and to force government reforms. They first revolted in 1922 and again in 1924, when they captured the city of São Paulo for a month. Following a guerrilla* war against the government, the *tenentes* escaped to the interior, from where they set out on a great march known as the Prestes Column (named after their leader Luís Carlos Prestes). They covered more than 15,000 miles in 11 states, crossing into Bolivia in 1927. In 1930, presidential candidate Getúlio VARGAS recruited them to initiate a revolt. After Vargas won the election, the *tenentes* pressured him to give them more influence in government. Vargas, whose hold on power was shaky, came to depend on the *tenentes,* and they became very powerful during his regime*. The *tenentes* succeeded in instituting several reforms, but after they provoked a civil war in São Paulo in 1932, Vargas removed them from power. A few *tenentes* continued to hold political positions, but the movement itself was disbanded the same year. *Tenentismo* was uniquely Brazilian and has never appeared anywhere else in Latin America. (*See also* **Federalism.**)

* **guerrilla** referring to a group that uses surprise raids to obstruct or harass an enemy or overthrow a government

* **regime** prevailing political system or rule

Tenochtitlán

Tenochtitlán, the capital of the AZTEC empire, was located at the center of present-day Mexico City. According to accounts written by indigenous* historians, in 1325, the Aztec patron and god of warfare, Huitzilopochtli, led the Mexica* to a spot where an eagle was perched on a prickly pear cactus, or *tenochtli*. It was at that spot—a marshy island in Lake Texcoco—that they founded Tenochtitlán, which means "by the prickly pear fruits." The Mexica developed the island by trading food from the lake for wood and stone from the mainland. They gained political control over the region and eventually dominated the Aztec

* **indigenous** referring to the original inhabitants of a region
* **Mexica** proper name of the people who came to be known as Aztecs

Conflict and Revolution

Plate 1
This painting shows Hernán Cortés preparing to seize the Aztec island capital of Tenochtitlán. Cortés (seen on horseback at bottom right) ordered the building of 13 brigantines (two-masted sailing ships) to blockade the island. The Spaniards and their Indian allies attacked the Aztec capital from the surrounding waters and on horseback via the causeways that linked the city to the mainland. Tenochtitlán fell in August 1521.

Plate 2

When Atahualpa, the last Inca emperor, refused to convert to Christianity, conquistador Francisco Pizarro ordered his troops to massacre Atahualpa's men and capture the Inca king. Atahualpa offered a room filled with gold as ransom for his release. Pizarro accepted the ransom, but after the payment was made, he reneged. Although Atahualpa accepted Christianity at the end, Pizarro had him killed anyway. His death in 1533 marked the end of the Inca empire.

Plate 3

During the late 1700s, Joaquim José da Silva Xavier, known as Tiradentes (Toothpuller), joined a group of upper-class citizens who were plotting to overthrow the Portuguese colonial government in Brazil. However, the plot was discovered before the conspirators could act and they were arrested. Silva Xavier was the only plotter to be executed because the others were protected by their high social rank. This painting by Francisco Aurélio de Figueiredo e Melo (1854–1916) shows Silva Xavier (in white) preparing to die on the gallows. Today, he is honored as a symbol of courage, liberty, and independence in Brazil.

Plate 4

Many slave revolts occurred during the more than three centuries of colonial rule in Latin America. The first serious rebellion may have erupted in 1522 in Hispaniola. In 1786, the region experienced one of its most violent revolts on a large sugar plantation called Boca Nigua, near the city of Santo Domingo. This was followed by several smaller insurrections, such as the one depicted in this engraving.

Plate 5

Patriot leader José Francisco de San Martín and Chilean general Bernardo O'Higgins are shown here leading troops across the hazardous mountain passes of the Andes. After defeating the Spanish royalists at the battle of Chacabuco, San Martín entered Santiago and proclaimed Chile's independence. By 1820, the royalists had retreated from the region, and San Martín declared Peru independent. However it was not until 1824 that Peru achieved true independence.

Plate 6

Built in the 1780s, Chapultepec Castle housed the National Military Academy during the Mexican-American War. When United States soldiers began bombing the castle, the young cadets refused to withdraw. On September 12, 1847, U.S. General Winfield Scott stormed the castle (shown here) killing more than 200 defenders. Some of the cadets who jumped from the castle rather than surrender became known as Los Niños Héroes (The Boy Heroes).

Plate 7

The Rough Riders, a regiment of the U.S. Cavalry Volunteers in the Spanish-American War, fought in Cuba in 1898. Led by Theodore Roosevelt, the regiment consisted of cowboys, miners, law-enforcement officials, and students from universities in the eastern United States. The Rough Riders gained extensive publicity because of their colorful exploits and unconventional methods, especially when they undertook the uphill charge, shown here, during the capture of San Juan Hill. Two weeks later, the Spaniards surrendered Cuba, ending the war.

Plate 8
In 1913, General Victoriano Huerta ousted President Francisco Madero from office. However, when Huerta tried to form a new government, he was opposed by Emiliano Zapata, Venustiano Carranza, "Pancho" Villa, and U.S. President Woodrow Wilson. This cartoon shows a stern-faced Uncle Sam threatening to use force if necessary to remove Huerta from his position. Huerta eventually fled the country and died in a Texas prison.

Plate 9
The Falklands/Malvinas War broke out in 1982 when Argentina decided it was time to recapture the group of islands from the British, who had occupied them since 1833. A British invasion force recaptured the islands after two months of air and sea battles.

Plate 10

The Duvaliers ruled Haiti as dictators for nearly 30 years. Their regime was known for its cruelty and corruption, and there was much celebration when it ended. When Jean-Claude Duvalier fled the country in 1986, Haitians rejoiced in Port-au-Prince, shown here, and elsewhere in the country.

Plate 11

Pôrto Alegre, Brazil, was the site of protest demonstrations in 1988. The protest involved the rights of squatters to occupy unused land in the region. The settlers and members of the clergy, shown here calling for land reform, occupied City Hall for months in support of their cause.

Plate 12

Conflicts between Sandinistas and contras (backed by the United States) erupted in Nicaragua throughout the 1980s. This photo shows the Sandinistas celebrating one of their victories over the contras. In 1989, several Central American presidents joined together to bring an end to the fighting.

Plate 13

In March 1992, a car bomb exploded near the Israeli embassy in Buenos Aires, Argentina, destroying the building, killing 29 people, and injuring more than 200 others. The Islamic Jihad claimed responsibility for the bombing, maintaining that it was in retaliation for an earlier attack against one of their leaders. However, Argentine officials believed that the bombing was an effort to hamper the Middle East peace process and to create hostility between Argentina's Jews and their neighbors. The attack was directed at the largest Jewish community in Latin America, which is estimated to be between 250,000 and 400,000 people.

Plate 14

This photo shows young Indian boys in Chiapas, Mexico, training for the Zapatista Army of National Liberation (EZLN), which became a significant political force in the region in the 1990s. The Zapatistas gained the public's attention when they demanded social justice and economic benefits for the poor and protested the North American Free Trade Agreement (NAFTA). EZLN forces consist largely of indigenous peasants from the highland regions of Chiapas, a rural state in southern Mexico that borders Guatemala.

Plate 15

Chilean demonstrators carry photos of their "disappeared" relatives with the caption "Where are they?" in a December 1998 show of support for the continued detention of former dictator Augusto Pinochet Ugarte. Pinochet was arrested in London after a Spanish judge ordered that he stand trial for his role in the deaths or "disappearances" of more than 3,000 Chileans during the 1970s and 1980s.

Teotihuacán

This drawing shows how archaeologists imagine the central square of the Aztec capital of Tenochtitlán might have looked before the arrival of the Spaniards. These pyramids were similar in size to those of the ancient Egyptians. Unlike the Egyptian pyramids, which were burial monuments, the Aztec pyramids were temples.

empire. By the time the Spaniards arrived in the early 1500s, Tenochtitlán had a population of more than 125,000.

The city was divided into four sectors, each separated by a major canal, which was used for canoe transportation. Each sector contained a temple, schools, and several *calpulli,* or big houses, that served as administrative centers. The political and ceremonial district, located at the center of the city, contained the royal palaces and temples for the Aztec gods. Two major causeways connected the city to the mainland. The Aztecs cultivated fresh vegetables on raised fields (called *chinampas*) outside the city and used an aqueduct to bring in freshwater because the lake water was too salty. The main market was located on the island of Tlatelolco, a settlement conquered by Tenochtitlán in 1473. In 1521, the Spaniards, led by conquistador Hernán CORTÉS, defeated the Aztecs, destroyed Tenochtitlán, and founded Mexico City—the colonial capital of New Spain*—on the ruins.

° **New Spain** Spanish colony in Mexico

Teotihuacán

° **pre-Columbian** before the arrival of Christopher Columbus and other Europeans in the Americas in the 1490s

Between 100 B.C. and A.D. 750, Teotihuacán served as the center of religious, economic, and political power of central MEXICO. Located about 30 miles northeast of Mexico City, Teotihuacán was the first true city in the Americas, and it influenced all later pre-Columbian* civilizations in the region, including the Aztecs. Today parts of the city lie in ruins, but much of it is buried under a military base, commercial centers, and farms.

Teotihuacán was built as the ceremonial center for a religion that featured extravagant rituals, including human sacrifice. The main feature of the city was the Avenue of the Dead, a wide north-south thoroughfare that ran through the center. The avenue was dominated by three immense pyramid complexes: the Pyramid of the Moon at the north end, the Pyramid of the Sun along the east, and the *Ciudadela* on the southeast, which served as the administrative center of the city. The

Texas

Many aspects of the culture of Teotihuacan, shown here, are still a mystery to archaeologists and historians. Scientists know very little about the origin, language, and social organization of the Teotihuacános. However, recent archaeological surveys suggest the existence of a writing system.

city, which also contained scores of smaller temples, was ruled by priests who governed in the name of the gods.

During the city's construction, its population grew rapidly. Many foreign residents, probably merchants and representatives from other regions in Mexico, moved there. More than 2,000 stone-walled apartment compounds, each housing 60 to 100 people, were built to accommodate the rapidly growing population. These single-story, windowless structures were divided into separate units arranged around open patios.

About two-thirds of the residents were farmers who worked on fields surrounding the city, using the area's natural springs for irrigation. The basic foods consisted of corn and beans, a variety of wild plants, game, turkeys, and even dogs. Another segment of the population consisted of full-time crafts workers, who produced ceramics and worked with obsidian (a black stone used in jewelry), bone, and feathers. Others worked as plasterers, painters, warriors, merchants, and bureaucrats. The state exercised strong control over the economy, managing resources, production, and the exchange of goods in locations as far away as Guatemala. At its height, around A.D. 500 to A.D. 600, Teotihuacán had a population of between 125,000 and 200,000.

Teotihuacán existed around the same time as the Roman Empire and lasted longer. In the A.D. 700s, the ceremonial center of the city was burned. After that, the city's population dropped sharply, its culture disintegrated, and Teotihuacán never regained its former glory.

Texas

Texas, the second-largest state of the United States, is a region with strong cultural and historic ties to Mexico. Texas was explored and settled by the Spaniards relatively late and served as an important point of contact between Latin America and the United States.

Preconquest History and Spanish Exploration. Historians generally agree that the region that is now Texas was probably first settled

by humans around 10,000 B.C. These early people had no advanced technologies, and when the Europeans arrived in the 1500s, little existed in the way of crafts or agriculture. At the time, the Caddo was the most technologically advanced culture in the region, having developed a village-based, agricultural society in northeastern Texas. In fact, the word *Texas* (*Tejas* in Spanish) comes from *tayshas,* a Caddo term meaning "friends or allies."

The Texas coast was first explored by Spaniard Alonso Álvarez de Pineda, who sailed into the mouth of the RIO GRANDE in 1519. In 1528, four survivors of the ill-fated expedition of Pánfilo de NÁRVAEZ washed up on the Texas coast. The group, led by Álvar Núñez CABEZA DE VACA, wandered through Texas for eight years before reaching the west coast of Mexico. After that, the Spanish colonists largely ignored Texas for the next 150 years. They considered the region too far from their outposts in Florida and the Mexican highlands for successful settlement. In fact, the first Spanish missions* and towns in Texas were not founded until the late 1600s.

See map in Spanish Borderlands (vol. 4).

* **mission** settlement started by Catholic priests whose purpose was to convert local people to Christianity

Spanish Colonization.
In 1685, following the establishment of a French fort on the coast of the Gulf of Mexico, Spain developed an interest in Texas. Four years later, the Spaniards drove the French from the region and established many mission-forts across Texas and placed them under the control of a general. Spain's fear of the French eased until the early 1700s, when France sent reinforcements to its colony in Louisiana. In 1718, the Spaniards built a mission and a fort in the present-day city of San Antonio, and four years later, they founded another fort and mission on Matagorda Bay.

By the early 1800s, Mexicans had begun to revolt against Spanish rule, beginning the MEXICAN WAR OF INDEPENDENCE. In 1813, Texas declared its independence from Spain and became a Mexican state with its capital at San Antonio. Shortly thereafter, several Anglo-Americans arrived in Texas to aid in the struggle for independence on behalf of Mexico. When the Spaniards finally admitted defeat in 1821, Texas was a Mexican province with an Anglo-American population of about 7,000. The same year, Stephen F. Austin, pioneer and founding settler, promised huge plots of land to attract settlers to the region. This brought 300 Anglo-American families to central Texas, increasing the region's Anglo-American population.

The Texas Revolution.
By 1835, the population of Texas had grown to about 21,000, most of whom were Anglo-Americans who cared little for Mexican culture and lived in the hope that the region would come under United States control. To this end, in 1826, Haden Edwards tried to drive the Mexicans from East Texas but was forced to flee the region himself. The same year, his brother Benjamin led 30 men into Nacogdoches and proclaimed the Republic of Fredonia (a brief revolt by Anglo-American adventurers in East Texas). Shortly thereafter, the Mexican government abolished slavery and enacted the Law of 1830, which forbade new immigration and levied taxes on all imports. The Anglo-Americans responded to the law with anger, and in

---

Tex-Mex: A Cultural Blend

In Texas towns along the Rio Grande—the river that marks the border between Texas and Mexico—two powerful cultures come together. The river nurtures a string of twin cities, such as El Paso and Ciudad Juárez, Laredo and Nuevo Laredo, McAllen and Reynosa, and Brownsville and Matamoros, where the blending of cultures is an everyday occurrence. In Laredo, Texas, about 94 percent of the residents are of Mexican ancestry, and at least 75 percent are bilingual. In another Texan town, more than 98 percent of the high school's 2,200 students are of Mexican ancestry. As a result, Mexican culture, food, and music, as well as the Spanish language, are as natural in these Texas towns as they are in towns south of the border.

Texas

° **tariff** tax on imported or exported goods

1833, when General Antonio López de SANTA ANNA overthrew the Mexican president, they sent Austin to Mexico City to ask Santa Anna to repeal the Law of 1830. On his return to Texas, Austin was arrested, and Santa Anna continued to collect tariffs*. When the Anglo-Texans objected, he placed the region under military command. In 1835, the Texan and Mexican forces engaged in a minor skirmish, beginning the Texas Revolution.

The Anglo-Texans formed a provisional government and requested the assistance of the United States in their struggle against Mexico. The United States appointed Sam Houston commander in chief of the Texas army. In 1836, in the hope of marching deeper into Texas to crush the rebellion there, Santa Anna led an army across the Rio Grande and attacked the ALAMO—a mission-fort outside San Antonio. In the ensuing battle, all the Anglo-Texans and at least 7 Mexican Texans defending the Alamo were killed; about 342 other Texans who surrendered to Santa Anna were also massacred. These tragedies convinced most Anglo-Texans and some Mexicans that they could not remain under Mexican rule and that they had to defeat Santa Anna to gain independence. In mid-1836, the Texas army, led by Sam Houston, surprised and defeated Santa Anna at the battle of SAN JACINTO. More than 1,500 Mexicans were killed, wounded, or captured, compared to only 39 casualties for the Texans. This decisive victory freed Texas, which then declared itself an independent republic*.

° **republic** government in which citizens elect officials to represent them and govern according to law

The Mexican-American War. The new "Lone Star" republic was recognized by the United States, as well as several European nations. However, Texas was heavily in debt and unable to survive on its own. The republic was also unable to reach an agreement with Mexico regarding its border. In 1845, Texas joined the United States, which tried to negotiate a treaty with Mexico to purchase the disputed territory between the Rio Grande and the Nueces River, as well as the present-day states of California and New Mexico. However, Mexico saw things differently and perceived the annexation of Texas as an attack on its sovereignty, provoking the MEXICAN-AMERICAN WAR (1846). Within a year, the United States defeated Mexico, which signed the Treaty of Guadalupe Hidalgo, ceding to the United States the disputed territory, the present-day states of Arizona, California, New Mexico, and parts of Utah, Colorado, and Nevada and renouncing its claim to Texas. This amounted to more than half of Mexico's land.

See color plate 6, vol. 4.

Texas Today. Although Texas has been a part of the United States for more than 150 years, some areas maintain a strong Mexican character. In the late 1990s, the state had more than 5 million inhabitants of Mexican origin, and that number is expected to double by 2005. Mexico is Texas's largest trading partner, and because of the North American Free Trade Agreement (NAFTA), business and cultural ties between the two regions have increased. (*See also* **Guadalupe Hidalgo, Treaty of; North American Free Trade Agreement; United States–Latin American Relations; United States–Mexico Border.**)

Textiles and Textile Industry

Weaving is one of the oldest craft traditions in Latin America, and it remains a cultural expression for many of the region's indigenous* groups. In pre-Columbian* times, woven cloth was traded and used as a form of tribute*. During the colonial era, fabrics were produced for profit, and a true textile industry was established.

* **indigenous** referring to the original inhabitants of a region
* **pre-Columbian** before the arrival of Christopher Columbus and other Europeans in the Americas in the 1490s
* **tribute** payment made to a dominant power
* **encomienda** right granted to a conqueror that enabled him to control the labor of and collect payment from an Indian community

The Colonial Textile Industry

The Spaniards hoped to continue the practice of using textiles as tribute through the *encomienda** system, but the system failed when the Indian population declined as a result of conquest, disease, and warfare. Spanish attempts to increase cloth production by forced Indian labor also failed, and much of the production of cloth shifted to individual households. Soon the colonists began to import textiles from Europe and Asia, but a great majority of the people could not afford these fabrics. Within 20 years of the conquest of Mexico, a colonial textile industry emerged to meet the demand for inexpensive cloth.

Woolens. In the mid-1530s, large workshops called *obrajes* emerged in central Mexico. They supplied fine woolen cloth to markets in Mexico and Peru. By the late 1500s, similar workshops were operating in Quito and providing cloth to markets from Colombia to Argentina. By the 1630s, however, the Mexican wool industry had begun to decline because of the restrictions on the use of Indian labor and Spain's prohibition of trade between New Spain* and Peru. Quito's *obrajes* continued to make fine wool until the early 1700s, but throughout Latin America, production shifted to ordinary, cheaper cloth, and small shops replaced the *obrajes* as the centers of wool production.

* **New Spain** Spanish colony in Mexico

See color plate 9, vol. 1.

Cottons. In the late 1600s, when the Indian population began to increase, cotton manufacturing in Indian villages revived. Moreover, non-Indians in Mexico began to specialize in cotton weaving and spinning. Using the spinning wheel and loom technology imported from Europe, the Mexican cotton industry produced cloth for local and foreign markets. Several factors aided the rapid growth of Mexico's cotton industry: the urban location of Mexico's cotton weaving, which reduced the transportation costs; the large domestic market for cloth; greater involvement by merchants in the industry; and the willingness of state officials to protect the young industry from foreign competition. Cotton weaving also flourished in the Andean region, but it was largely a rural and Indian occupation, and the industry did not expand here as it had in Mexico.

Modern Textiles

The first modern textile factories appeared in Mexico in the 1830s, and until World War II, textiles comprised a large segment of Latin America's

Textiles and Textile Industry

° **capital** money invested to start a business or industry

industrial output. Mexico and Brazil were the centers of the textile industry, producing mostly lower-quality goods for the local market.

Early Factories. Mexican merchants built the earliest factories for spinning cotton yarn with capital* from their business activities and government-sponsored loans from banks eager to support industrial development. By the 1850s, the factory system had spread to other Latin American countries, and by the 1870s, nearly every country in the region was producing at least some cotton goods by machine. However, Mexico and Brazil were clearly the two most important producers.

Expansion. By the 1890s, the textile industry had grown rapidly. The boom in exports from Latin America increased income, especially among the merchants who provided the capital for the industry. Newly constructed RAILROADS opened new markets and reduced the cost of transporting goods. By 1920, the textile industry employed more than 35,000 workers in Mexico and nearly 80,000 in Brazil. Large firms dominated the industry—almost 30 percent of Mexico's cotton cloth was produced by just four firms, and only two companies produced more than one-third of its machine-made wool cloth.

Brazil had surpassed Mexico as the region's largest textile producer primarily because of the growth of the stock exchange in Rio de Janeiro. This stock exchange enabled the owners of cotton factories to finance their businesses through the sale of company stock to the public. As in the United States and Europe, only merchants had the capital that was needed for such investments. The merchants who owned shares of stock in the factories would sell the cloth to their own stores at a discount, enabling them to offer it to their customers at a lower price.

Pre-Columbian Textiles

Pre-Columbian cultures used a variety of fibers in addition to cotton and wool. Some of these fibers included hair from llamas, alpacas, vicuñas, and rabbits, as well as spider webs and feathers. The indigenous peoples colored these materials with natural dyes such as walnut leaves, indigo, and even soot. Many beautifully preserved pieces from colorful garments from this period have been found in the dry regions of the Andes. However, almost no pre-Columbian fabrics have been found in Mexico or Central America because of the humid conditions and very acidic soil there, both of which can damage fabrics over time.

Decline of the Industry. Despite its local success, Latin America's textile industry was never internationally competitive. The cost of building a factory was very high because manufacturing equipment was imported and foreign expertise was needed to set up the plants. Labor productivity was also low because workers resisted attempts to make work more mechanized. A typical factory in Latin America employed two to three times as many people as one in a more industrially advanced country. These extra costs made regional textiles too expensive to sell overseas. Therefore, almost all goods produced were sold to the local market. As a result, many governments levied high tariffs* on imported textiles to protect their domestic industries.

° **tariff** tax on imported or exported goods

° **depression** period of little economic activity during which many people become unemployed

With the onset of World War I and a worldwide depression*, Latin America's textile industry suffered. The region's economies failed to revive until after World War II, and by that time, the industry was far behind the rest of the world. Still, textile plants in Colombia and elsewhere produced low-cost clothing for those who could not afford the imports. After 1945, heavy industries, such as paper, steel, and cement, replaced textiles as the focus of industrial development. (*See also* **Industrialization**.)

Theater

- **pre-Columbian** before the arrival of Christopher Columbus and other Europeans in the Americas in the 1490s

Latin Americans had developed drama and other forms of performance for their rituals and entertainment long before the colonial period. The INCA produced comedies and tragedies, and the AZTECS developed forms of dance and theatrical spectacle. However, none of these have survived. The only surviving theatrical piece from pre-Columbian* times is the *Rabinal Achí*, a K'iche' MAYA drama about the capture, interrogation, and death of a warrior. Other plays are the work of colonial and modern Latin American writers and playwrights.

- **clergy** priests and other church officials qualified to perform church ceremonies

- **indigenous** referring to the original inhabitants of a region
- **secular** nonreligious; connected with everyday life

Colonial Theater.

The earliest examples of colonial theater are short religious pieces developed by the clergy* to aid them in converting the Indians to Catholicism. These works, called *autos, loas,* or *mojigangas,* used local settings and artistic forms, and concepts familiar to the indigenous* peoples. These short plays were important in the colonization of Latin America. By the mid-1500s, a secular* theater had emerged in response to the interests of settlers in major cities such as Lima and Mexico City.

The 1600s were a golden age of theater in Spain. During this period, Latin American theater borrowed heavily from European ideas and forms. Most works, such as *Las paredes oyen* and *La verdad sospechosa* by Mexican-born Juan Ruíz de Alarcón, reflected the tastes and interests of the upper classes, who looked to Europe for cultural fashions. The greatest regional writer of the time was the Mexican poet Sor JUANA INÉS DE LA CRUZ. By the late 1700s, the literature of Spain had declined, and the lack of originality had become apparent in Latin American theaters.

Independence and Theater.

Between 1810 and 1825, the Latin American wars of independence broke the region's political ties with Spain, but the cultural ties remained. Writers continued to adapt or translate European works, placing emphasis on reason over passion. These works served not only as entertainment but were intended to teach lessons about proper conduct to a people who had a reputation for violence and emotionalism. However, between the 1830s and the 1870s, a split began to emerge between those writers. Some Mexican playwrights, such as Fernando Calderón, preferred European themes, whereas others, such as Ignacio Rodríguez Galván in *Muñoz, Visitador de México,* explored the identity, customs, and values of the Americas.

- **conservative** inclined to maintain existing political and social views, conditions, and institutions

The literary and political freedom of the time also enabled some writers to use the stage for propaganda. The conservative* dictatorship of Juan Manuel ROSAS prevented the theater from developing freely in Argentina, and much of its work praised the government. However, in 1851, exiled writer Pedro Echagüe staged his play *Rosas* in Bolivia, severely criticizing the Argentine dictator. In Brazil, playwrights had more freedom to experiment with new techniques and to make political statements. By the end of the 1900s, Spanish theater in Latin America was producing works that attempted to capture a realistic view of life, and some playwrights began to explore important social issues. More successful, however, was the *revista* (review), a form popularized by Artur

135

Theater

This is an illustration of the Iturbide Theater in Mexico. Latin American theater was greatly influenced by the cultural developments in Europe during the colonial period. In the 1830s, however, a split began to emerge. Some theaters continued to stage plays with European themes and written by European playwrights, while others began to focus exclusively on the traditions and themes of Latin America.

° **Creole** person of European ancestry born in the Americas

> ### Shakespeare of the Convent
>
> One of the greatest Latin American playwrights and poets of the colonial era was the Mexican nun Sor Juana Inés de la Cruz. Her theatrical works consist of several *loas*, short, dramatic mythical prologues with Aztec female characters. She also wrote many *autos* (short religious pieces) and two full-length plays. Her *loas* and *autos* reflect religious themes and defend Christian practices. Of the *autos*, *El cetro de José* (Joseph's Scepter) is based on a story from the Bible; *El mártir del Sacramento, San Hermenegildo* (The Martyr of the Sacrament ...) is about the life of a saint; and *El Divino Narciso* (Divine Narcissus) portrays Narcissus as the redeeming Christ. Her plays, *Amor es más laberinto* and *Los empeños de una casa*, however, are secular. They have strong female characters and reflect Sor Juana's concerns as a woman and a Creole.

Azevedo, which took a light, comical view of Brazilian customs and politics. In the Río de la Plata region, Spanish traditions were combined with local elements in the *sainete criollo* (Creole* farce). This theatrical form focused on the moral values, social problems, and ethnic complications of a land settled by European immigrants and drew on both indigenous and GAUCHO traditions.

Theater After 1900. Many of the theater traditions of the 1800s continued into the 1900s, and a truly modern theater did not develop until the late 1920s. In 1928, the Teatro de Ulises opened in Mexico, bringing in the latest techniques in staging, lighting, and direction. The new format required small theaters, electric lighting, less dominance by the lead actor or actress, and increased involvement of the director in all elements of the performance. During the 1930s and 1940s, theater groups in Puerto Rico, Argentina, and elsewhere adopted similar techniques and began to produce more plays with social messages. Argentina's Roberto Arlt wrote *Saverio el cruel,* which deals with class struggle and conflicts, and Brazil's Joracy Camargo wrote several plays exploring the theories behind such struggles. In Chile, theater reform occurred in the universities, where semiprofessional theater companies brought new ideas to the stage.

The experimentation of the 1930s and 1940s led to a theater boom in the 1950s and 1960s. Plays such as Argentine Carlos Gorostiza's *El puente* moved theater to the commercial stage and into a new era. During this period, theater expanded, writers created exciting new plays, and directors developed imaginative methods of staging these plays. Playwrights sought to capture the human spirit through believable characters who reflected the political, social, religious, and personal conflicts of individuals in modern society. By the 1960s, writers had begun to look within Latin America for inspiration rather than to Europe or the

United States. The year 1968 marked a turning point, when theater festivals were organized in several cities, including Lima, Peru; San José, Costa Rica; Manizales, Colombia; and Mexico City. The festivals provided an opportunity for Latin American playwrights to share their ideas, see each other's works, and develop a sense of solidarity in the regional theater community.

At this time, theater began to favor a system based more on equality. Directors assumed less authority and allowed actors to create their own works. In Brazil, the *teatro de coringa* placed its actors in direct contact with the writers and the viewing public. In Cuba, Fidel Castro used the theater as an instrument for social change and to reinforce his Communist* ideas. In the 1960s and 1970s, with the emergence of right-wing* dictatorships, theaters staged plays with political and social messages. By the late 1980s, democratic governments had returned to most countries, but the issues, such as inflation*, poverty, overpopulation, and drugs, and the need for social reform remained. Regional theater companies continue to respond to these issues and to anticipate the needs of the different segments of Latin American society. (*See also* **Literature**.)

* **Communist** referring to a social system in which land, goods, and the means of production are owned by the state or community rather than by individuals
* **right-wing** very conservative
* **inflation** sharp increase in prices due to an increase in the amount of money or credit relative to available goods and services

Thousand Days, War of the

See *War of the Thousand Days*.

Tierra del Fuego

* **islet** small island
* **fjord** long, narrow arm of the sea bordered by mountains

Tierra del Fuego is a group of islands at the southernmost tip of South America and is separated from the mainland by the Strait of Magellan. It consists of the island of Tierra del Fuego, several other large islands, and many islets*. ARGENTINA controls the eastern half of the main island, which consists of flat plains carved out by glaciers. The western half, which belongs to CHILE, consists of the ice- and snow-covered mountains of the southern Andes and several fjords* and channels. Most of the inhabitants live in the Argentine-controlled sections of Tierra del Fuego, which also are home to many sheep ranches and the duty-free port of Ushuaia, the southernmost city in the world. The Beagle Channel marks the southern boundary of the main island. The major Chilean centers of Tierra del Fuego are the naval base at Puerto Williams and the town of Cerro Sombrero, Chile's main oil-producing center. The Chilean-owned regions of Tierra del Fuego are also rich in petroleum.

Tikal

Tikal, located in the dense jungles of the department of Petén in GUATEMALA, was an important MAYA center. It is the largest and most thoroughly studied Maya site. Dating from about A.D. 292 to A.D. 869, the site consists of several major temple-pyramid complexes constructed on high, rocky ground. These complexes were linked to one another by causeways and were surrounded by more than 20 square miles of residential areas and defensive fortifications. At its peak, around A.D. 700, Tikal had a population of about 10,000.

Tin Industry

See color plate 10, vol. 1.

Carved stelae (upright stone slabs), ceramics, and burial offerings found at the site show that Tikal maintained close ties with TEOTIHUACÁN in Mexico as early as the late A.D. 300s. One stela dating from about A.D. 435 shows attendants dressed in Teotihuacán military attire carrying Teotihuacano weapons. However, these ties vanished after A.D. 534, when Teotihuacán declined. Around the same time, Tikal experienced a period of reduced construction and activity until about A.D. 700, when the Great Plaza, containing two east-west facing temple-pyramids, was constructed. Temple I on the plaza was the burial pyramid of the ruler Ah Cacau. Next to the Great Plaza is the north acropolis, consisting of large temple-pyramids built above the tombs of other Tikal rulers. To the south was a large residence for Tikal's most important families. West of the Great Plaza is Tikal's largest pyramid, which is probably the tomb of Ah Cacau's son. Although artifacts* dating from the late 800s were found at Tikal, archaeologists* believe that the site was abandoned in the 900s.

* **artifact** in archaeology, a human-made object such as a tool, household utensil, or work of art
* **archaeologist** scientist who studies past human cultures, usually by excavating ruins

Tin Industry

* **commodity** article of trade

Bolivia is the world's second largest producer of tin. In 1996, tin accounted for 16 percent of the country's total mineral export earnings. Because of the falling prices of tin, Bolivia's mining output of the metal has declined since 1993, as shown by this bar graph.

The Latin American tin industry is largely concentrated in BOLIVIA, the world's largest producer of tin after Malaysia. Between 1900 and 1980, tin was Bolivia's largest export commodity*, and during that period, the owners of the nation's tin mines were among the wealthiest people in the world.

Tin mining became important in Bolivia around 1900, when silver mining, the country's most important economic activity during the 1800s, became unprofitable. Nevertheless, systems established for the silver industry contributed to making the Bolivian tin industry a profitable venture. For example, railroads that were built to connect the highland silver-mining areas to ports on the Pacific Coast made it possible to transport tin ore inexpensively. Even so, only one important

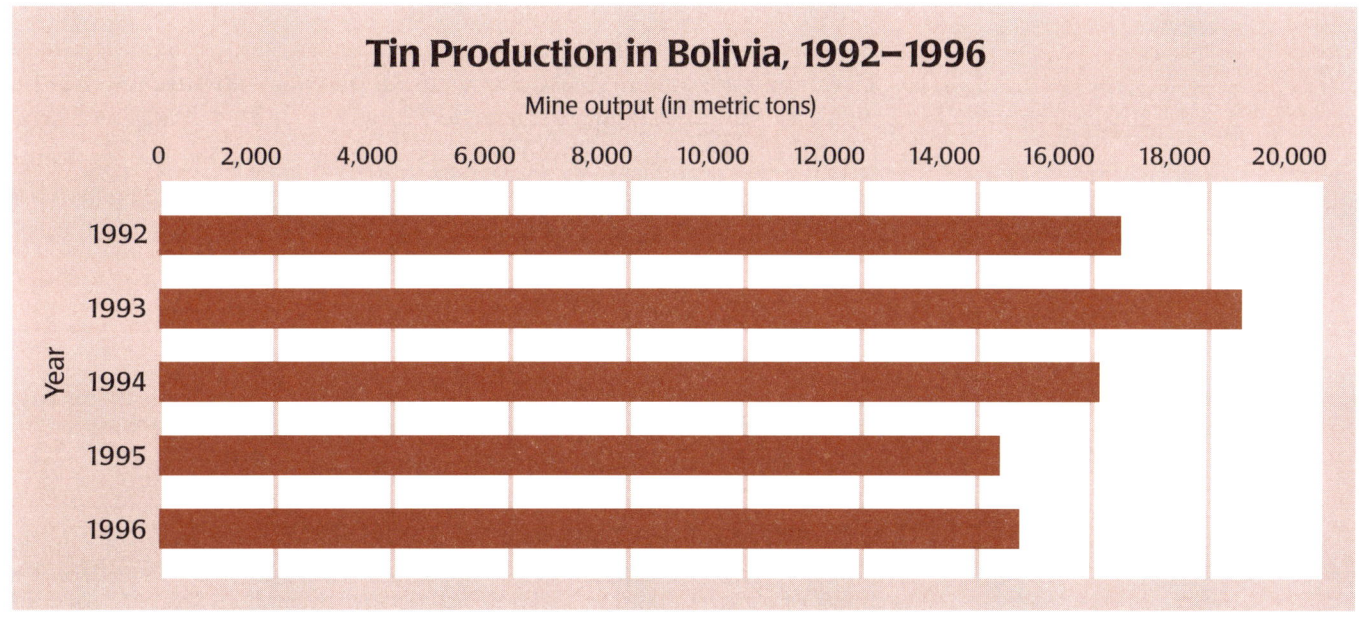

Source: United States Geological Survey.

silver-mining family—the Aramayos—successfully made the transition from silver to tin. Eventually, three major companies from northern Bolivia, controlled the tin industry. Despite heavy FOREIGN INVESTMENT, the industry was controlled by Bolivians throughout the 1900s.

The tin industry greatly influenced Bolivian politics. Political power shifted from its former base in the south to cities in the north, including La Paz and Oruro, and the mine owners became powerful political figures in the nation. The owners also maintained tight control over their workers, which led to strikes that were violently suppressed by the Bolivian military. However, in 1942, following a bloody massacre, left-wing* political parties, such as the National Revolutionary Movement (MNR), which opposed the interests of the mine owners, allied themselves with the mine workers.

In 1952, the MNR, supported by the laborers, overthrew the Bolivian government, seized the mines, and nationalized* the tin industry. Although the mine owners and foreign investors were compensated for their losses, they were stripped of their political power. In 1964, the tables turned again when the military defeated the MNR, occupied the mines, and dismantled the labor unions. This type of repression occurred again in 1971 and 1981, when right-wing* military dictators controlled the government. In the 1980s, declining world prices for tin led to the closing of most mines, and many mine workers relocated to the Bolivian jungles or to cities such as Sucre, Cochabamba, and Santa Cruz. (*See also* **Labor and Labor Movements**.)

* **left-wing** very liberal

* **nationalize** bring land, industries, or public works under state control or ownership

* **right-wing** very conservative

Titicaca, Lake

* **navigable** deep and wide enough to provide passage for ships
* **archaeologist** scientist who studies past human cultures, usually by excavating ruins

See color plate 9, vol. 2.

Lake Titicaca, located on the border between Bolivia and PERU, is the highest navigable* lake in the world. The lake is actually an inland sea that stands at an elevation of 12,467 feet above sea level and covers an area of more than 3,200 square miles.

The waters and shoreline of the lake have supported fishing and agriculture for thousands of years. Archaeologists* have discovered the remains of complex societies that lived in the region and benefited from Titicaca's resources and climate. The lake has also been an important link between southern Peru and northern Bolivia, especially since the beginning of steam-powered water transportation in the late 1800s. The ability to refrigerate and quickly transport fish products has also increased the economic significance of Lake Titicaca. The lake contains several habitable islands. (*See also* **Geography**.)

Tiwanaku

Tiwanaku, or Tiahuanaco, was a pre-Columbian* empire in the Andes that dominated the region around LAKE TITICACA. Although historians disagree on the exact dates of the Tiwanaku culture, they generally believe that the Tiwanaku dominated the region from about A.D. 100 to A.D. 1200. Their most important political and religious center was a city of the same name, located on the ALTIPLANO, in present-day Bolivia.

Tlaloc

- **pre-Columbian** before the arrival of Christopher Columbus and other Europeans in the Americas in the 1490s
- **archaeologist** scientist who studies past human cultures, usually by excavating ruins

The ancient city of Tiwanaku was located at an altitude of 12,600 feet. It consisted of a political and ceremonial center that featured monumental stone architecture and was surrounded by residential areas. Most of the main temples, courtyards, and stelae (carved stone slabs) were constructed between A.D. 100 and A.D. 725. Archaeologists* believe that the city covered an area of about 1,000 acres and had a population of between 20,000 and 40,000. Tiwanaku society was highly stratified. Its people engaged in extensive agricultural and herding activities and imported products from other zones when they were unable to produce them in the highlands.

After about A.D. 375, the Tiwanaku culture spread throughout the Andean region, including valleys in Bolivia and coastal Chile and Peru. In the 600s, another major center of Tiwanaku culture emerged at HUARI in the central highlands of Peru. However, the origins of the settlement at Huari and its connections to the Bolivian Tiwanaku are unclear; the site may have been established by conquest. The Huari culture declined in the 800s, while the Tiwanaku survived until about 1200.

Tlaloc

See *Divinities*.

Tobacco Industry

- **pre-Columbian** before the arrival of Christopher Columbus and other Europeans in the Americas in the 1490s
- **commodity** article of trade
- **cash crop** crop grown primarily for profit rather than for local consumption

The tobacco plant is native to the Americas and has been cultivated in the region since about 3500 B.C. Many pre-Columbian* societies smoked tobacco as part of their religious ceremonies or as a form of ritual healing. In fact, some of these rituals continue to be practiced in certain African–Latin American religions, such as CANDOMBLÉ and UMBANDA. In the early years of exploration and conquest, explorers brought tobacco samples back to Europe. It took until the late 1500s for tobacco use to gain popularity there, after which it became an important export commodity*.

Tobacco was cultivated as a cash crop* by small farmers because it did not require great amounts of land or significant cash outlays. However, it required a great deal of labor, and in many Latin American countries, the crop was mostly harvested by slaves or other forced laborers. In addition to being exported, tobacco was an important commodity in domestic trade.

Brazil was the first to export tobacco in the form of twists, tightly woven ropelike cords of tobacco that were coated with molasses and herbs. The higher-quality twists were sent to Portugal, and lower-quality tobacco was shipped to West Africa, where it was used to barter for slaves. Tobacco became crucial to the development of slave-based agriculture and mining. By the 1700s, more than two-thirds of the Brazilian crop was exported.

Almost all the countries of Latin America grow tobacco. Brazil was one of the first colonies in the "New World" to grow tobacco for export. This table shows the leading producers of tobacco grown for export and indicates that Brazil produces more than four times as much tobacco as the next leading producer, Argentina.

Tobacco Leaf Production in Latin America, 1998

Country	Production in Metric Tons
Brazil	506,222
Argentina	116,500
Dominican Republic	42,683
Cuba	31,485
Mexico	19,100
Latin America (total)	**820,867**

* **monopoly** exclusive control or domination of a particular type of business

* **snuff** powdered tobacco that is inhaled, chewed, or placed against the gums

Because of its profitability, the tobacco industry was regulated by the colonial government. The Portuguese crown established a monopoly* that controlled the production, storage, price, and quality of Brazilian tobacco. In 1822, however, when Brazil gained its independence from Portugal, the Brazilian tobacco industry declined, partly because European customers preferred cigars—which were usually made from a type of leaf tobacco grown in Cuba—to snuff* and pipe tobacco. (In fact, English customers sought hand-rolled "Havanas" as early as the 1820s.) The industry revived in Brazil after 1840, when growers there began producing tobacco more suitable for cigars.

By the mid-1800s, Latin America had a well-developed tobacco industry, and cigarette and cigar factories employed thousands of workers in Mexico, Cuba, and Brazil. During the 1900s, many governments reestablished monopolies or formed state-owned companies. Today tobacco is a widely cultivated cash crop, but the industry is dominated by foreign firms.

Tobago

See *Trinidad and Tobago*.

Toledo y Figueroa, Francisco de

1515–1582
Viceroy of Peru

Francisco de Toledo y Figueroa, a Spanish nobleman, served as the viceroy* of Peru from 1568 to 1581. As viceroy, Toledo attacked and reduced the authority of the *audiencias** of Lima and La Plata, the clergy, the *cabildos*, (town councils) and the independent INCA state of Vilcabamba.

Born in Oropesa, Spain, Toledo served in the monarchy's military and diplomatic service until he was appointed viceroy of Peru in 1568. Two years later, he began a five-year *Visita General* (General Inspection) of his viceroyalty that took him through Peru's political and economic

Toltecs

- **viceroy** one who governs a country or province as a monarch's representative; royally appointed official
- ***audiencia*** highest regional court in a Spanish colony; also, the district under its jurisdiction
- **indigenous** referring to the original inhabitants of a region

centers. During his *visita,* he executed the last Inca ruler, Tupac Amaru, eliminating all Inca resistance. Toledo resettled many indigenous* groups in new towns for more efficient government administration, religious conversion, and the use of their labor. He also formulated the colonial version of the *mita* system, which ensured a steady supply of forced labor for the Spanish mines, and adopted a silver-refining process using mercury, both of which enhanced silver production. Moreover, he issued regulations on many other political, economic, and social matters.

Although Toledo built a strong foundation for colonial government in South America, he was severely criticized for his actions toward the indigenous peoples. Nevertheless, he is considered the organizer of Spanish Peru, and his legislation established a model for governors throughout the Spanish colonial empire.

Toltecs

- **archaeologist** scientist who studies past human cultures, usually by excavating ruins

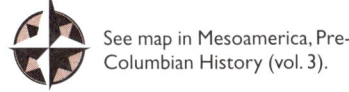
See map in Mesoamerica, Pre-Columbian History (vol. 3).

The Toltecs were a people who controlled much of central Mexico and influenced much of modern Mexico and Central America from about 950 to 1200. Their capital was at Tula (Tollan in their Nahuatl language), a city in the state of Hidalgo, about 40 miles northwest of Mexico City. Although archaeological evidence suggests the existence of a Toltec empire, its size and duration are unknown. Some archaeologists* believe the empire stretched from the Pacific coast of Guatemala and the Mexican state of Chiapas to the Yucatán peninsula and included the Toltec-Maya center of Chichén Itzá and much of north and west Mexico. However, other scholars challenge such claims for a Toltec empire.

The origins of Toltec culture are also difficult to reconstruct because of unreliable historical records. In the chronicles about their ancestors, the Aztecs praised the Toltecs as warriors, master craftsmen, builders, and wise men. However, historians believe that the Aztecs created these exaggerated, although justifiable, accounts to validate their own status as rulers of Mexico. Spanish accounts of the Toltecs and their legendary ruler Quetzalcoatl are filled with contradictions and are also unreliable. Moreover, the information derived from archaeological studies has also been inconsistent with these historical accounts.

Historical records suggest that Toltec society consisted of members from several groups that migrated to Hidalgo after the fall of the city of Teotihuacán as well as farmers fleeing from the frontiers of northern Mexico, which was becoming increasingly turbulent. The Toltecs generally spoke Nahuatl, used later by the Aztecs, although speakers of other languages were also present in their communities in significant numbers.

Toltec society was based on agriculture, and maize was the staple crop. Their diet also included beans, squash, cactus fruits, and the meat of dogs, deer, and rabbits. In addition to agriculture, their economy depended on the production and trade of handicrafts, such as pottery, stone tools, textiles, and personal ornaments. Merchants imported luxury goods, such as

fancy pottery, rare animal skins and feathers, exotic foods, and cacao* and exported Toltec products to regions far from their homeland.

Although the Toltecs built irrigation systems where possible, they were frequently plagued by water shortages. In fact, some recorded legends suggest that famine, possibly triggered by insufficient rainfall, led to the civil war that caused the Toltecs to abandon Tula around 1200. Other legends suggest that the Toltec culture began declining around the mid-1100s, when the Aztecs invaded the region and destroyed Tula.

* **cacao** bean from which chocolate is made

Tonton Macoutes

The Tonton Macoutes were members of the secret police force created by Haitian dictator François DUVALIER in the late 1950s to suppress his opposition. The name was derived from a folk character, Uncle Knapsack, who snatched children into a knapsack or basket *(makout)* and often ate them.

At first, Duvalier denied the existence of the secret police, but in 1962, he introduced the Volontaires de la Sécurité National (VSN) as the official Tonton Macoutes. In reality, the Tonton Macoutes were members of the middle class and did not belong to the VSN, which was a peasant militia*. The Duvalier regime did its best to merge the identity of the two groups, and throughout the 1960s, the VSN served to distract attention from the activities of the dreaded Tonton Macoutes. The VSN played a symbolic role, marching in government parades wearing colorful uniforms, which evoked the costume of the peasant god Zaka, the colors of the Haitian flag before Duvalier's reign, and the colors of the peasant armies of the 1800s.

The Tonton Macoutes became a powerful force and a counterpart of the Haitian army. Duvalier's son Jean-Claude forged stronger links between the active branches of the political police, the army, the militia, and the bodyguards of the Duvalier family. By the mid-1980s, the 9,000-strong VSN consisted of members of all these groups, and the term *Tonton Macoutes* referred to militiamen, informers, and torturers alike. Consequently, when Jean-Claude was overthrown in 1987, many members of the Tonton Macoutes escaped arrest because it was hard to tell who had been involved in the worst excesses.

* **militia** army of citizens who may be called into action in a time of emergency

Tordesillas, Treaty of

The Treaty of Tordesillas was an agreement between Spain and Portugal that divided the administration of all overseas possessions between the two countries. In 1493, Pope Alexander VI awarded Spain control over all newly discovered lands that lay 100 leagues* to the west and south of the Azores and Cape Verde islands and were not already controlled by a Christian prince. Although Portugal then had claim to all lands east of the line of demarcation, the Portuguese protested its location and demanded a meeting to discuss the issue. In 1494, the negotiators met in the small town of Tordesillas, Spain,

* **league** unit of distance; one league is between 2.4 and 4.6 miles

Torrijos Herrera, Omar

and signed a treaty by which they agreed to push the line of demarcation some 270 leagues farther west. According to this treaty, Portugal legally owned a large strip of the Brazilian coast that was subsequently discovered by Pedro Alvares CABRAL in 1500.

Torrijos Herrera, Omar

1929–1981
Leader of the Panamanian Revolution

° **Canal Zone** ten-mile-wide strip of land along the length of the Panama Canal that belongs to the United States until 2003

° **mulatto** person of mixed black and white ancestry

Omar Torrijos Herrera was born in Santiago de Veraguas, PANAMA, and educated in a military school in El Salvador. In 1952, he joined Panama's National Guard as a second lieutenant. In 1968, Torrijos joined several colonels of the guard to overthrow president Arnulfo Árias Madrid. Shortly thereafter, he emerged as the leader of the guard and virtual dictator of Panama.

Torrijos is best remembered for the 1977 Torrijos-Carter Treaty that guaranteed the transfer of control of the PANAMA CANAL from the United States to Panama on January 1, 2000. The treaty guaranteed the fulfillment of a long-standing national goal and the end of United States control over a valuable economic resource. Moreover, the Canal Zone* would be eliminated in 2003, United States citizens in Panama would no longer enjoy special privileges, and Panama would greatly benefit from canal revenues.

Torrijos's revolution greatly influenced Panamanian politics by ending the dominance of the elite classes and opening the political system to laborers and the middle class, which consisted largely of mulattos* and blacks. Torrijos established a minimum wage and placed the economy in the hands of the state, further weakening the power of the upper classes. He also launched a housing and public works construction program in the cities and instituted programs to give land to peasants and to increase grain production.

Torrijos overhauled the economy by removing many restrictions on the nation's banking industry. As a result, Panama became a haven for foreigners seeking to hide money in secret bank accounts. He also commissioned the building of roads, an oil pipeline, an international airport, and container ports to make Panama a transportation hub to enhance the revenue-generating potential of the canal.

° **blockade** closing off of a port to prevent ships from entering or leaving, thus crippling trade

Torrijos restored pride to Panama by resisting United States pressures. For example, he confronted the UNITED FRUIT COMPANY regarding taxes, opposed the United States blockade* of Fidel Castro's Cuba, and allowed Cubans to supply arms to Nicaragua's SANDINISTA rebels through Panama. However, he cooperated with the United States in security matters and accepted compromises on the canal, such as sharing responsibility for its defense. In 1981, Torrijos's death in an unexplained airplane crash cut short his revolution. (*See also* **United States–Latin American Relations**.)

Totonacs

See *Indians*.

Tourism

° **archaeological** relating to archaeology, or the science of studying past human cultures, usually by excavating ruins

° **Great Depression** period in the 1930s marked by low economic activity and high unemployment

° **indigenous** referring to the original inhabitants of a region

The Fall and Rise of Cuban Tourism

Before the Cuban Revolution in 1959, Cuba was possibly the most popular vacation spot in Latin America for international tourists. During the 1920s, Havana boasted fabulous hotels, country clubs, casinos, and beaches that attracted the wealthy from the United States and Europe. In 1928, United States–based Pan American Airways established the first commercial air route to Latin America with flights from Miami to Havana. After World War II, Cuba again dominated regional tourism until the revolution, when tourism fell into a steep decline. In recent years, Cuba has again begun to promote tourism, competing for visitors from Europe, Latin America, and Canada. In fact, the tourism industry has become its primary source of revenue.

Each year, millions of tourists visit Latin America to enjoy its mountains, beaches, rain forests, towns, cities, and archaeological* sites and to experience the region's cultural traditions. About 85 percent of the tourists come from the United States, Canada, and Europe, and most of them travel to MEXICO or the islands of the CARIBBEAN. Latin America accounts for about 10 percent of all money spent on international tourism. The industry brings valuable foreign currency, provides employment, and creates a market for the region's folk arts and CRAFTS.

Before 1900, most travelers to Latin America were adventurers, explorers, scientists, and others motivated by personal gain or interested in the region's unique features. Commercial tourism to the region began only after the advent of the steamship and the building of railroads, both of which made travel more pleasurable. JAMAICA and CUBA were the first to become tourist spots, attracting sightseers and travelers seeking warm climates. In the 1920s, Mexico and Cuba were popular tourist destinations because of their proximity to the United States. Cuba, however, declined as a vacation spot in the mid-1930s as a result of political unrest and the effects of the Great Depression*, but revived soon after. During World War II, tourism declined throughout Latin America, especially when the military took over most of the cruise ships to transport troops.

After the war, overall prosperity and major improvements in air travel facilitated the creation of the modern tourist industry. More people could afford international travel, and with Europe mostly in ruin from the war, many people in the United States chose to vacation in Latin America. Even before the end of the war, President Franklin Roosevelt of the United States encouraged Latin American nations to promote tourism because the foreign currency would enable Latin Americans to buy goods from the United States. Mexico was one of the first countries to adopt this policy. The government turned ACAPULCO into a luxury resort, advertised the splendors of its many archaeological sites and the rich cultural history of the indigenous* communities, and built beach resorts at Cancún and Ixtapa. Mexico also joined BELIZE, GUATEMALA, HONDURAS, and EL SALVADOR in exploiting the MAYA ruins for tourism. By 1990, tourism was one of Mexico's main sources of foreign currency.

In the 1950s and 1960s, the Caribbean islands began to develop tourist facilities, which today contribute significantly to the national economy. Countries in South America and Central America started later but have also increased their share of tourism. Environmental tourism attracts many visitors to the rain forests and nature preserves in COSTA RICA, BRAZIL, and ECUADOR. In ARGENTINA and CHILE, the tourism departments advertise skiing during their winter months, which correspond to summer in the Northern Hemisphere. In Guatemala and PANAMA, revenue from tourism is based in part on the region's handicrafts produced by indigenous women.

The rapid growth of tourism has raised several concerns, such as destruction of fragile environments, disruption of local communities, displacement of local businesses by international agencies, and the income inequality between foreign tourists and Latin Americans, prompting some in the industry to reevaluate their policies and practices. These debates aside, tourism remains an important source of revenue for the region.

Toussaint L'Ouverture

Toussaint L'Ouverture

ca. 1743–1803
Haitian slave leader

* **mulatto** person of mixed black and white ancestry
* **guerrilla** member of a fighting force outside the regular army that uses surprise raids to obstruct or harass an enemy or overthrow a government
* **sharecropping** practice by which a rural worker provides labor in exchange for access to the land or a portion of the harvest

Toussaint L'Ouverture, the charismatic leader of the Haitian independence movement, is shown here. The name *L'Ouverture*, which means "the Opening," may have been inspired by his ability to break through enemy lines during battle.

Toussaint L'Ouverture was an important figure in the early stages of the HAITIAN REVOLUTION, which eventually led to Saint Domingue's independence from France. Born François Dominique Toussaint near Cap François (present-day Cap Haitien), HAITI, Toussaint was a slave on a plantation for many years. In 1791, when a slave rebellion erupted in Saint Domingue (present-day Haiti), Toussaint first helped his former master escape and then joined the black slaves in their struggle against the whites and mulattos*. By the end of the revolt, Toussaint had assumed leadership of a group of rebels whom he trained as guerrillas*. In 1793, when France and Spain went to war, Toussaint and his guerrilla forces joined the Spaniards. By 1794, however, Toussaint had defected to the French side, prompted by France's abolition of slavery. Shortly thereafter, the Spanish forces were expelled from the region. Over the next few years, Toussaint became renowned for his military capability and rose from lieutenant governor to dictator of Saint Domingue.

Toussaint devoted his attention to restoring the economy. He retained large plantations, invited former planters to return as managers, and distributed large tracts of land to favorite Haitian leaders. Toussaint freed the slaves but instituted *fermage,* a system of forced labor not unlike sharecropping*. By 1800, Saint Domingue had regained much of its economic prosperity. Toussaint also suppressed VOODOO, established Catholicism as the state religion, and imposed a strict moral code by outlawing divorce and demanding marital fidelity. He treated the region's mulattos with contempt and successfully defeated their forces in the War of the Knives in 1799.

In the late 1700s, Toussaint defeated a British invasion and overthrew Spanish rule in Santo Domingo (the present-day Dominican Republic), becoming commander of the entire island of HISPANIOLA. He maintained good relations with the United States, but his relations with France were his undoing. Although he swore loyalty to France, he removed French officials from power and sent them back to Europe. In 1801, when Toussaint proclaimed a new constitution and appointed himself governor-general for life, Napoleon Bonaparte sent troops to regain control of Saint Domingue. Toussaint held out for a few months, but surrendered in 1802, after he had extracted a promise that France would not restore slavery. He was arrested and taken to France, where he died the following year.

Trade and Commerce

Europe's desire for trade with Asia led to the voyages of Christopher COLUMBUS and Vasco da Gama, which in turn led to the colonization of the Americas and India. Europeans soon realized that these newly discovered lands held possibilities for trade. From colonial times to the present, Latin America's relationship with the rest of the world, along with its economic and social development, has been shaped to a great extent by trade.

Trade is the process by which people or nations exchange goods for other goods or for money. A key feature of trade is commerce, the buying

Trade and Commerce

and selling of goods on a scale large enough to require transportation. Three kinds of trade occurred during the colonial period. They were trade within a colony or country (internal trade), trade within a region (intraregional trade), and trade among different countries or regions (external or foreign trade). Between 1500 and 1800, most colonies engaged in all these types, although the trade with the European nations that ruled them was paramount. Since independence, however, the nations of Latin America have greatly increased intraregional trade with one another while maintaining vital foreign trade with the rest of the world.

Remember: Words in small capital letters have separate entries, and the index at the end of this volume will guide you to more information on many topics.

Colonial Trade and Commerce in Spanish America.

Throughout the colonial period, Spain's attitude toward trade with its American colonies was that it should benefit *Spanish* people: first the monarchy, then manufacturers and merchants living in Spain, and finally the colonists of Spanish descent in the Americas. Over the course of 300 years, Spain used various regulations and practices to carry out this policy.

Spanish rulers had a vision of the ideal economic relationship between their country and its overseas territories. The colonists were expected to pay taxes to the crown and to provide raw materials, such as minerals, wood, leather, and agricultural products. In addition, the colonies were expected to buy goods manufactured in Spain, such as shoes, clothing, glass, furniture, and hardware. In fact, the colonies were intended to be a captive market, because Spain outlawed trade between its colonies and other countries. Still, considerable illegal trade with foreign merchants took place.

See color plate 7, vol. 2.

Although the reality of trade and commerce between Spain and Spanish America did not always match the ideal vision, Spain did its best to control and protect its colonies' trade. The Spanish crown set tariffs* on goods that traveled between Spain and the colonies. It also established monopolies* on some goods, which meant that only authorized agents could trade in those items. The crown even restricted colonial trade to one Spanish port—first Seville, later Cádiz. Only from this port could ships legally depart for or return from the Americas.

* **tariff** tax on imported or exported goods
* **monopoly** exclusive control or domination of a particular type of business

Spain also struggled to stop PIRACY and SMUGGLING, which drained off money that otherwise would have entered the royal treasury. The FLEET SYSTEM of shipping, which organized commercial vessels into convoys protected by warships, was created to thwart pirates and privateers*.

By the mid-1700s, the fleet system was failing, smuggling was widespread, other Spanish ports were demanding a share of the colonial trade, and colonists wanted the right to import and export goods as they pleased. By 1789, the Spanish crown had opened 13 licensed ports to trade with the Americas and made all of Spanish America a free-trade zone. This meant that Spanish and Spanish American ports could trade freely with each other, although not with foreigners.

* **privateer** privately owned ship authorized by the government to attack and capture enemy vessels; also, the ship's master

These changes promoted economic growth in Venezuela, Cuba, and other colonial regions that produced agricultural goods for export. However, the changes were not enough to please many Spanish Americans. They wanted the right to trade freely with the world at large, not just

147

Trade and Commerce

with the Spanish empire. By 1810, the quest for truly free trade had become a major factor in the movement for independence from Spain.

Colonial Trade and Commerce in Brazil.

Portugal, like Spain, viewed commerce with its American colony as a monopoly reserved for the crown and its subjects. Throughout the colonial period, Portugal relied on the products of its overseas empire to provide it with goods to trade with the rest of the world. Brazil's exports of sugar, gold, and agricultural goods helped Portugal pay its bills.

In the mid-1500s, Portugal passed several laws that allowed foreign merchants to trade with Brazil. However, trade had to pass through the hands of Portuguese colonists, and merchants had to pay taxes on imports and exports. During the 1500s and early 1600s, these fees were the crown's principal benefit from colonial trade. The crown's biggest difficulty was controlling the illegal trade that was being conducted in Brazil by the French, Dutch, and English. By the 1700s, Portugal was trying to increase its profits from Brazilian trade by forming companies with monopolies on particular goods or with particular regions. In exchange for these monopolies, companies were required to stop illegal trade and encourage greater production of raw materials in the colony.

Modern Trade and Commerce.

In the years following independence, Latin America's foreign trade has gone through three stages. The first, which lasted from 1820 to 1930, was a period of free trade and prosperity. As the old colonial restrictions disappeared and Latin America grew more politically stable, the region's foreign trade increased. The industrialization of Europe and the United States, along with rising incomes that led to increased demand for goods, created a need for more raw materials for manufacturing. At the same time, new technological inventions, such as the steamship, lowered shipping

The Panama Canal greatly influences trade not just for nations in the Americas but for countries throughout the world. The canal saves ships both time and money by enabling them to make a transoceanic passage through Central America instead of sailing around South America. Each year, numerous cruise ships, such as the one shown here, and around 140 million tons of commercial cargo pass through the 51-mile-long canal.

Trading Companies

All-American Free Trade?

In 1994, the North American Free Trade Agreement (NAFTA) created a free-trade zone composed of Mexico, the United States, and Canada. Under NAFTA, goods can be imported and exported from and to the three countries without tariffs. Some people would like to see NAFTA extended to include all of North and South America in what President George Bush of the United States called a "free trade area of the Americas" (FTAA). An FTAA would permit untaxed trade from Alaska to Tierra del Fuego. However, it would have to overcome many barriers, including the fears of labor unions in the United States that jobs would move from the United States to Latin American countries with lower wages. Some Latin Americans fear that their industries would be hurt in a more open market.

° **cacao** bean from which chocolate is made

costs. As a result, agricultural and mineral products from Latin America could compete in the world marketplace with goods from more industrialized nations. Latin America's foreign trade grew more slowly after 1910 because rich mineral deposits were depleted and the best farmlands were already in use.

The second stage of the region's foreign trade began in 1930 with the worldwide economic slowdown known as the Great Depression. The depression cut the demand for Latin America's exports and stopped the flow of money from the United States and Europe. In the years that followed, Latin American governments worked to replace imported goods with items manufactured internally. To encourage domestic industry, they placed high tariffs on imported goods. As imports decreased, however, so did exports, and Latin America became more economically isolated from the rest of the world.

A third stage of foreign trade began around 1973, when Latin American nations began returning to free-trade policies. Governments lowered tariffs and reduced or eliminated other barriers to trade, such as licensing restrictions and extra taxes. Various combinations of Latin American and Caribbean countries also formed intraregional trade organizations aimed at creating a united economy and promoting trade with one another. Among the first such organizations were the Andean Pact (1969) and the Caribbean Common Market (CARICOM, 1973). However, they made little progress toward free trade.

During the 1990s, Latin American governments continued to encourage more regional free trade. Between 1991 and 1995, Argentina, Brazil, Uruguay, and Paraguay formed a free-trade zone called MERCOSUR. The Andean countries, the Central American and Caribbean countries, Mexico, and Chile have also taken steps toward setting up free-trade areas and common markets. The NORTH AMERICAN FREE TRADE AGREEMENT (NAFTA) of 1994 eliminated tariffs on trade between Canada, the United States, and Mexico.

Latin America's intraregional trade includes a high percentage of manufactured goods. Its external trade, however, still relies on exports of raw materials, such as minerals and agricultural products. The basic exports of the region are petroleum, coffee, copper, sugar, beef, iron ore, cotton, bananas, corn, fishmeal, cacao*, and wool. The United States is the region's biggest trade partner. (*See also* **Economic Development; Slave Trade; Trading Companies**.)

Trading Companies

During the great age of European expansion that began in the late 1400s, the European powers established colonies around the world. Once the colonies were established, their rulers granted permission to merchants and captains to trade with the territories. Both the Spanish and Portuguese crowns gave their support to companies that promised to control and promote trade between the colonies and their parent countries. By the late 1700s, however, the colonies were demanding free trade, or the right to do business with merchants from

Trading Companies

° **monopoly** exclusive control or domination of a particular type of business

° **privateer** privately owned ship authorized by the government to attack and capture enemy vessels; also, the ship's master

other colonies or countries. As a result, the officially authorized trading companies lost their monopoly* on colonial commerce.

Brazilian Companies.
In the 1600s and 1700s, Portugal established four trading companies to control trade with its South American colony, BRAZIL. The largest and longest-lasting was the Brazil Company. Founded in 1649, it protected Brazilian colonial shipping from PIRACY and Dutch privateers*. Portugal modeled the Brazil Company on English and Dutch trading companies.

The Brazil Company was responsible for providing 36 warships to protect merchant fleets during their voyages between Portugal and the Brazilian ports of Rio de Janeiro, Bahia, and Recife. In return, the company was granted a monopoly over the import of wine, wheat flour, olive oil, and cod into Brazil and could sell these goods to colonists at whatever price it wished. The company also collected taxes on the hides, tobacco, sugar, cotton, and other exports it carried from Brazil to Portugal.

Smaller Portuguese ports and merchants criticized the Brazil Company because it excluded them from the colonial trade. The colonists criticized the company for failing to supply enough goods and for charging high prices. In 1663, the crown bought the Brazil Company and incorporated it into the Portuguese government in the form of a royal council. This council continued to provide protection for merchant fleets until 1720.

The other three Portugese-Brazilian trading companies were created to supply African slaves to specific regions in Brazil and to export the goods produced in those regions. They were the Maranhão Company, the Grão Pará and Maranhão Company, and the Pernambuco Company. A revolt by colonists brought about the end of the Maranhão Company. The other two companies, established by the Portuguese secretary of state and foreign affairs Marquês de Pombal, collapsed after his fall from power.

Spanish Companies.
During the 1700s, the Spanish crown also chartered, or permitted, companies to trade with its American colonies. The crown also established companies to control trade between Spain and its overseas possessions in the Americas.

The process of forming a company was similar in most cases. After negotiation between merchants and the crown, the king issued a document called a *cedula real* (royal charter) directing the formation of a trading company. The company's directors then sold shares in the company to raise capital*. Once they had raised enough capital, the chartered company began operations.

One reason the Spanish crown established trading companies, such as the Caracas Company, is that the traditional method of shipping treasure from the Americas to Spain, known as the FLEET SYSTEM, had become inefficient. It failed to provide the colonies with enough supplies, and it did little to control illegal trade, such as SMUGGLING. The crown believed that trading companies would increase the legal trade in colonial crops, such as tobacco, and that authorized trade would replace smuggling.

The Chocolate Trade

In 1728, the Spanish crown founded the Caracas Company to control trade between Spain and Venezuela. At the time, Venezuela was a major producer of cacao, the bean from which chocolate is made. In return for a monopoly on shipping cacao to Spain, the Caracas Company agreed to crack down on the illegal smuggling of goods, to defend the Venezuelan coast, and to provide slaves for the colony. The company remained profitable for 40 years, but it could neither end smuggling nor provide enough slaves and European goods to the local market. In 1784, the Spanish crown closed the company, whose most lasting achievement was to make the port of Caracas the economic center of Venezuela.

° **capital** money invested to start a business or industry

Colonists, on the other hand, objected to the trading companies because they offered fewer goods and higher prices than had been available through unofficial or illegal trade.

Trade between Spain and Spanish America increased under the chartered companies, but few of them were successful on a large scale. Even those that achieved early success fell apart by the late 1700s because of corruption, poor management, and the colonists' desire for free trade. (*See also* **Slave Trade; Trade and Commerce.**)

Transportation and Travel

See *Aviation; Highways and Roads; Railroads.*

Trinidad and Tobago

See map in Caribbean Antilles (vol. I).

The nation of Trinidad and Tobago consists of two tropical islands located in the southern Caribbean Sea about seven miles off the coast of Venezuela. Together Trinidad and Tobago have an area of almost 2,000 square miles (slightly smaller than the state of Delaware). The nation they form is noted for its large population of immigrants from India, who came to the islands as laborers during the 1800s.

Colonial History. Although the islands of Trinidad and Tobago are separated by only about 20 miles, they have very different histories. Christopher Columbus made the first known European landing on Trinidad in 1498, during his third voyage to the Americas. Spanish vessels returned to the island in 1510, seizing Arawak Indians as slaves. In the years that followed, pirates used the island as a base.

The Spanish began permanent colonization of Trinidad in 1592. It was in the late 1700s, however, that a large number of colonists began to settle the island. Spain encouraged the use of slave labor as a means of spurring the colony's economic growth. It also encouraged non-Spanish Catholics to settle in Trinidad, and many French colonists did so. In 1783, the town of Port of Spain became the seat of the colonial government. Today it remains the capital of Trinidad and Tobago.

In 1797, a British fleet appeared off the coast of Trinidad. Rather than fight the British, a Spanish admiral burned his own fleet. After this embarrassing show of cowardice, Trinidad became a possession of Great Britain. For many years it remained an agricultural colony where slaves labored on sugarcane plantations. After slavery was abolished in 1834, the British imported East Indian laborers to work the plantations, laying the basis for Trinidad and Tobago's richly multiethnic society.

Unlike Trinidad, Tobago was never a Spanish colony. Ships from many nations visited the island to obtain fresh water, and for several hundred years, European powers argued over its ownership. Between 1626 and 1802, Tobago changed hands 26 times. After 1802, however, it

Trinitaria, La

remained under British control. In 1888, the British government politically linked the island with Trinidad.

The Modern Nation. In the early 1900s, Great Britain developed Trinidad's petroleum industry. Oil became the island's major export, although few Trinidadian people benefited from its profits.

Trinidad and Tobago received independence from Great Britain in 1962. However, independence did not solve the islands' social and economic problems, which included poverty and a history of racial tension between African and East Indian Trinidadians. In 1970, a black power movement resulted in protests and riots known as the February Revolution, although no real change of government occurred.

The country experienced a short period of prosperity as an oil exporter during the 1970s, but since that time, it has suffered an economic downturn. Its main resources are crude oil, natural gas, and asphalt.

Trinitaria, La

La Trinitaria was a political movement that flourished during the mid-1800s in the present-day DOMINICAN REPUBLIC. In 1822, HAITI invaded Santo Domingo, the settlement that became the Dominican Republic. The goal of La Trinitaria was to end the Haitian occupation and achieve Dominican independence.

Juan Pablo DUARTE and other Dominican independence leaders founded La Trinitaria in 1838. Its members were organized in groups of three. Because it was secret, communication involved codes and passwords, and meetings featured rituals with religious symbolism. Within five years, La Trinitaria had members in most of the major towns and cities in the region.

Because La Trinitaria was successful in building opposition to Haitian occupation, Haiti's leaders repressed the movement. After the Haitian occupation ended in 1844, Dominican leaders exiled La Trinitaria's leaders to keep the movement from gaining power. Still, the ideas and symbols of La Trinitaria inspired future prodemocracy movements in the country.

Triple Alliance

See *War of the Triple Alliance.*

Trujillo Molina, Rafael Leónidas

1891–1961
Dominican dictator

For more than 30 years, Rafael Leónidas Trujillo Molina was the dictator of the DOMINICAN REPUBLIC, one of two countries on the Caribbean island of HISPANIOLA. At the time, his rule was the most totalitarian* that Latin America had known.

Trujillo was born in San Cristóbal and worked as a telegraph operator and security guard. In 1918, he joined the National Guard (later renamed the National Police and then the National Armed Forces), a military organization established by the United States forces that had occupied the country. By 1928, Trujillo had emerged as the commander

° **totalitarian** referring to a government that exercises complete control over individuals, often by force

in chief of the National Armed Forces, and in 1930, he used his power to become president.

Trujillo strengthened his grip on the country by eliminating all political parties, newspapers, radio stations, trade unions, and any other groups that disagreed with him. With the help of his supporters, he bribed, jailed, murdered, or drove away his opponents. In 1937, in an attempt at ethnic cleansing, Trujillo ordered the extermination of all Haitians in the Dominican Republic. About 25,000 Haitians were killed in this massacre.

° **monopoly** exclusive control or domination of a particular type of business

Trujillo modernized the nation with roads, factories, and agricultural machinery, but he did so to benefit his landholdings and monopolies* in the import-export trade. In 1934, Trujillo was reelected president, albeit in a rigged election and, after that term, controlled the nation through puppet presidents. In 1940, he negotiated the Trujillo-Hull Treaty with the United States, ending that country's collection of tariffs* from the Dominican Republic. During the late 1940s, Trujillo tried to improve relations with the United States by portraying himself as an anti-Communist*.

° **tariff** tax on imported or exported goods

° **anti-Communist** person who opposes communism

° **exile** person forced to live away from his or her homeland for a long period of time

By the mid-1950s, however, the opposition to his rule had grown within and outside the Dominican Republic. In 1959, Dominican exiles* invaded the country to oust him but failed. Still, the invasion inspired new anti-Trujillo movements. When Trujillo retaliated with violence, the ORGANIZATION OF AMERICAN STATES and the United States imposed economic sanctions, crippling Dominican trade. Dominicans were further outraged when they learned that Trujillo's agents had raped and murdered three young girls. In 1961, in a desperate attempt to regain power, Trujillo sought the aid of Communist governments in Eastern Europe. The U.S. Central Intelligence Agency responded by supplying weapons to anti-Trujillo activists, who attacked and killed him. (*See also* **Caribbean Antilles; Dictatorships, Military; United States–Latin American Relations.**)

Tupac Amaru

1738–1781
Leader of Peruvian Indian revolt

° **Creole** person of European ancestry born in the Americas

° **mestizo** person of mixed European and Indian ancestry

° **martyr** someone who suffers or dies for the sake of a cause or principle

° **tribute** payment made to a dominant power

In the early 1780s, the Indians of the Peruvian highlands, along with some Creoles* and mestizos*, rose against their Spanish overlords in the Great Andean Rebellion. José Gabriel Condorcanqui, known to his followers as Tupac Amaru II, was the most famous leader, and martyr*, of that revolt.

Born in Tinta, a province of CUZCO in Peru, Tupac Amaru was a descendant of the last Inca emperor of the same name. He was the hereditary CACIQUE, or chief, of many communities. He attended school in Cuzco and married and started a family there. He later worked as a freight carrier between Cuzco and the mining town of Potosí. His travels increased his awareness of growing discontent with colonial rule and of the ways in which the colonial system abused the Indians, such as forcing them to labor in the mines and to pay tribute* to the colonists. In the late 1770s, Tupac Amaru spent several months in Lima, unsuccessfully trying to persuade the colonial authorities to eliminate the labor requirement for his people.

Tupac Catari

> **The Power of the Inca Name**
>
> In 1572, the Spaniards captured the jungle outpost of Vilcabamba, the last Inca capital, and seized Tupac Amaru and his family. Taken to Cuzco, the emperor was executed in front of a huge crowd of Indians, a fate that also befell his descendant more than 200 years later. José Gabriel Condorcanqui has not been the only rebel in Peru to draw on the name of the Inca emperor. In the 1990s, an antigovernment group called the Tupac Amaru Revolutionary Movement emerged in Peru.

Failing in his efforts, Tupac Amaru began to plot a revolt, while tax increases and other government demands continued to spread dissatisfaction among the region's Creoles, mestizos, and Indians. In 1780, he arrested and executed a colonial official in Tinta. He then raised a large rebel army, which contained many of his own relatives, who also served as the revolt's leaders. The same year, the rebel forces defeated the royalists* at Sangarara, but the resulting violence prompted many Creoles and mestizos to withdraw their support.

Nevertheless, in 1781, Tupac Amaru and his army of 40,000 to 60,000 followers laid siege to Cuzco. However, caciques loyal to the Spanish crown prevented the city's fall, and Tupac Amaru withdrew to Tinta in defeat. He was captured by the Spaniards, who took him back to Cuzco. There he was forced to witness the torture and execution of his wife and other family members. He himself was drawn and quartered—pulled apart by four horses.

Ultimately, Tupac Amaru failed because the colonial government had amassed a huge army against him and because he did not have the support of the Creoles and mestizos. Many caciques, comfortable in their relationships with the Spanish, also opposed him. The Great Andean Rebellion continued until 1783 under other leaders, but Tupac Amaru had been the most important because of the respect his Inca heritage commanded. (*See also* **Andes; Cultures, Pre-Columbian; Inca; Peru; Race and Ethnicity; Slavery.**)

* **royalist** supporter of the king or queen, especially in times of civil war or rebellion

Tupac Catari

ca. 1750–1781
Rebel leader in colonial Peru

Tupac Catari led the AYMARA Indians of southern Peru in revolt against Spanish forces. Born Julián Apaza, he took the name Tupac Catari to associate himself with two of Peru's most admired Indian leaders: TUPAC AMARU and Tómas Catari.

Tupac Catari was born in Ayoayo in the province of Sicasica. He worked in the Spanish-controlled mines and traded cloth and coca leaves. He gained the attention of the public in 1781, when an Aymara uprising shook three provinces in Peru. At first authorities erroneously blamed the disturbances on rebel leader Tupac Amaru, who was leading a revolt near Cuzco, but it soon became clear that Tupac Catari had taken command of the Aymara around the city of LA PAZ. Speaking only Aymara and claiming to receive messages from God, Tupac Catari drew on Christian and indigenous* traditions when speaking to his followers. His goals were to drive the Spaniards from Peru and to free the Aymara from Inca domination.

In 1817, Tupac Catari undertook the siege* of La Paz. His army of 10,000 to 40,000 rebels disrupted access to the city and brutally killed anyone who tried to escape. More than 5,000 members of his forces were killed at La Paz, and the city lost two to three times as many, mostly from starvation and disease. The approach of a royal army saved the city and forced Tupac Catari to retreat. The same year, a former comrade betrayed him to the Spaniards, who promptly captured and executed him.

* **indigenous** referring to the original inhabitants of a region

* **siege** prolonged effort by armed troops to force the surrender of a town or fort by surrounding it and cutting it off from aid

Tupi

- **pre-Columbian** before the arrival of Christopher Columbus and other Europeans in the Americas in the 1490s
- **indigenous** referring to the original inhabitants of a region

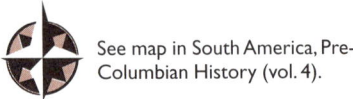
See map in South America, Pre-Columbian History (vol. 4).

- **missionary** person who works to convert nonbelievers to his or her faith

The term *Tupi* refers to one of the main pre-Columbian* language groups of South America and to the Indian societies that traditionally spoke those languages. The Tupi language group had seven distinct branches, of which the Tupi-Guarani was the most widespread. The indigenous* peoples of early colonial BRAZIL, who lived along the coast between the Amazon River and the Río de la Plata, were Tupi speakers.

According to colonial historians, war and politics among the various Tupi-speaking groups highlighted their ethnic differences. Beneath these differences, however, lay a shared culture and way of life. The farming village was the main unit of Tupi social and political organization. During the 1500s, Tupi villages consisted of 100 to more than 1,000 inhabitants, who lived in four to eight large *malocas,* or lodges. These communities moved when their crops failed or game became scarce, and they frequently split to form new communities. Warfare was a central element in Tupi society and history. The goal of war was to capture prisoners, and the victors sacrificed and ate their captives in elaborate ceremonies.

The Portuguese conquest brought disease, slavery, and other profound changes to the Tupi world. Although the Tupi resisted the conquest by joining violent uprisings against European missionaries* and colonists, their population had declined seriously by the mid-1600s, especially in the coastal regions. Today several Tupi societies continue to flourish in central Brazil and in the Amazon basin. (*See also* **Indians**.)

Tupi-Guarani

See *Languages.*

Tuyutí, Battle of

See *War of the Triple Alliance.*

Tzendal Rebellion

- **indigenous** referring to the original inhabitants of a region
- **tribute** payment made to a dominant power
- **cult** system of religious beliefs and rituals not officially approved by mainstream faiths; group following these beliefs

Between 1712 and 1713, three indigenous* groups in the state of CHIAPAS, Mexico, rose in revolt against the Spanish colonists. Known as the Tzendal Rebellion, this uprising was an attempt by the Tzeltal, Chol, and Tzotzil Indians to win their political and religious independence from Spain.

The rebellion, which began simmering in the 1690s, stemmed from the terrible conditions in Chiapas. The Indians there were suffering from diseases and plagues of locusts that destroyed crops. As the population declined, the Spaniards' demands for labor and tribute* increased. The people were discontented not only with their own circumstances but also with their leaders for failing to protect them.

In 1708, the people were further angered when their religious cults* were deemed guilty of heresy* by the Spanish priests. In 1712, the Virgin

155

Ubico y Castañeda, Jorge

* **heresy** religious belief that conflicts with the teachings of the Catholic Church

Mary appeared to a girl in the village of Cancuc, and another new cult emerged. When the authorities tried to destroy it, the village fought back. They were soon joined in their struggle by more than 20 other villages, and the local government troops could no longer control the revolt. Reinforcements arrived from Guatemala and the city of Campeche, and after a series of battles, the Spanish troops captured Cancuc and put down the rebellion.

* **clergy** priests and other church officials qualified to perform church ceremonies

During their brief independence, the Cancuc leaders had tried to set up a new government and establish an Indian clergy*. This show of freedom seriously alarmed the Spanish authorities, who crushed the revolt so firmly that Chiapas was left devastated and in deeper poverty. (*See also* **Indians**.)

Ubico y Castañeda, Jorge

1878–1946
Guatemalan general and president

Jorge Ubico y Castañeda played a key role in Guatemala's government from the 1920s to the 1940s. As military leader, governor, and finally president, he used harsh, dictatorial tactics to bring progress and order to the nation.

Born in Guatemala City and educated in the United States and in Guatemala's military academy, Ubico entered the army in 1897. He then served as the governor of two states, and in 1922, he was appointed the country's minister of war. After he was elected president in 1931, Ubico personally controlled all aspects of the government. He also controlled Guatemala's radio stations and news services, and his security forces kept a watchful eye on the people, ruthlessly eliminating any opposition.

* **subsistence farming** system of farming that provides all or almost all the food needed by the farm family without a surplus for sale

Ubico's most significant accomplishment was the establishment of a network of telegraph lines and roads that helped promote national unity by linking remote regions to the capital. He also brought water and electricity to rural regions and transformed Guatemala City by paving the streets and constructing many government buildings, including the Presidential Palace. Ubico tried to revive agriculture and integrate the Indians into the national economy by drawing them from subsistence farming* to commercial agriculture. His presidency ended in 1944, when he was overthrown by a revolution led by students, junior military officers, and urban middle-class people who felt that his policies favored landowners. Ubico went into exile in the United States, where he died two years later.

Umbanda

Umbanda is a Brazilian religion that combines African, indigenous*, and Roman Catholic elements and traditions. It first emerged in the 1920s and 1930s, and it is practiced today by millions of Brazilians, primarily in urban areas. Umbandist services are aimed at helping people deal with personal problems and illnesses by seeking advice and guidance from the spirits.

° **indigenous** referring to the original inhabitants of a region

° **syncretized** referring to the uniting of beliefs or rituals of different religions

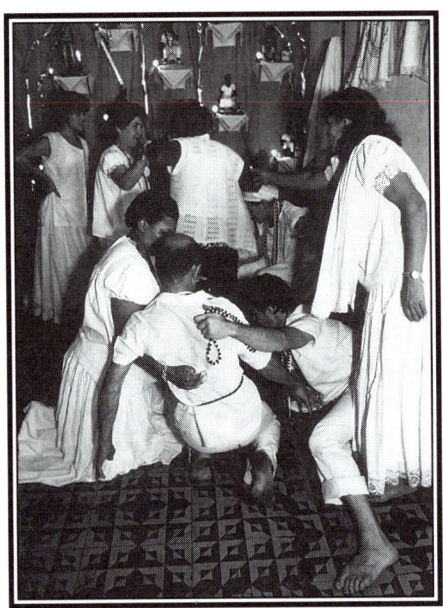

Mediums, such as the one shown here, attempt to make the spirits of the dead enter their bodies during Umbanda ceremonies. As the mediums dance to the rhythms of percussion instruments, they sing praises to important deities and to the spirits of the dead. As the drumming and singing intensify, the possession is believed to occur.

Umbandists generally hold public sessions twice a week at centers in working-class and middle-class neighborhoods. A typical center is divided into two areas. People who have come for spiritual guidance assemble in the rear section of the room (men and women sit separately). The front section is devoted to the rituals. It contains an altar and images of Old Blacks (spirits of African Brazilians), Catholic saints, and Caboclos (spirits of Brazilian Indians).

The service begins with an offering to Exú, an Umbanda deity, so that he will open the path of communication and not disrupt the proceedings. The Umbanda leader, known as Mother or Father, then burns incense to purify the room and may deliver a brief talk. At this time, the mediums assembled in the front of the room begin to dance to the beat of drums. They join the leaders in recognizing important deities and spirits through song. As the drumming and singing become more intense, the mediums enter a trance and become possessed by the spirits of the dead. Worshipers then come forward to ask the spirits for guidance. The guidance given may include practical advice or mystical suggestions, such as burning a candle to influence a particular spirit. Finally, the spirit may turn the individual around several times or cause the medium's hands to pass over the worshiper's body to remove the evil fluids that are believed to cause the person's problems.

Observers who have studied Umbanda claim that it helps individuals cope with the stresses of urban society. Umbanda also serves as a political force, having elected several representatives at the state level. Umbanda centers are further seen as a place for social networking. Because the majority of mediums are women, the practice affords women the chance to serve in positions of authority. Finally, by merging Central African spirits, West African gods and goddesses, Catholic saints, and black and Indian spirits into one syncretized* religion, Umbanda serves as a religion that provides a national identity for many people. (*See also* **Candomblé; Orixás; Religions, African–Latin American.**)

Unión de Armas

° **ducat** gold coin formerly used as currency in some European nations

During the 1600s, the Spanish crown proposed several plans to help pay for its war expenses in Europe. The most ambitious of these plans was the *unión de armas,* which called for each province of the empire to contribute to Spain's military reserve. Because the American colonies could not easily provide manpower to defend Spain, they were required to contribute money—350,000 ducats* each year from Peru and 250,000 from Mexico—for a period of 15 years, beginning in 1627. Colonists in Mexico disapproved of the *unión de armas,* and town councils there debated the issue for five years before they reluctantly approved the plan. In Peru, opposition to the plan was even stronger until there was an acceptable compromise—levying taxes on wine and doubling the sales and fleet taxes. The *unión de armas* raised a substantial amount of money in the colonies, but that amount never approached the 600,000 ducats demanded by the crown.

United Fruit Company

United Fruit Company

° **imperialism** domination of the political, economic, and cultural life of one country or region by another country

The United Fruit Company was one of the first and largest multinational corporations in the Western Hemisphere. Over the years, the company changed its name several times: AMK, United Brands, and since the 1990s, Chiquita, Inc. At its peak, United Fruit exemplified the economic imperialism* of the United States. In fact, Latin Americans called the company *el pulpo* (the octopus) because it touched so many aspects of their lives.

The company was formed by three men: Lorenzo Dow Baker, Andrew W. Preston, and Minor C. Keith. Baker, a ship captain from New England had been supplementing his cargo with Jamaican bananas since 1870. In 1885, he joined Preston, another fruit importer, to form the Boston Fruit Company. The third, and principal founder, Keith, was a railroad developer who had acquired plantations in the region and had built a railroad in Costa Rica as early as 1872. In 1899, the three men joined to form the United Fruit Company to export tropical fruits from Latin America.

By the early 1900s, United Fruit had a fleet of more than 100 ships, owned hundreds of thousands of acres of land in Central America, and was the largest employer in the region. The company also became involved in the politics of the Latin American nations where it owned land. In 1954, for example, United Fruit participated in the overthrow of Guatemalan president Jacobo ARBENZ GUZMÁN, who had enacted a land reform law that impeded the company. Since then, however, United Fruit has lost much of its power and is no longer a major landowner in the region. Instead, the company buys fruit from local growers, and with a more diversified product line, it is no longer dependent on Latin America for its income. (*See also* **Banana Industry**.)

United Nations

° **autonomy** ability to make decisions and take action on one's own

° **sovereignty** independence

The United Nations is a multinational organization that works to promote international cooperation and the peaceful settlement of disputes. During the 1980s and 1990s, the United Nations intervened in several Latin American conflicts. Throughout their membership in the United Nations, Latin American nations have been concerned with protecting the autonomy* of their regional systems and maintaining their sovereignty* as small powers.

Before the formation of the United Nations, the countries of the Americas resolved regional disputes through the Inter-American System, a collection of organizations that promote regional peace and development. When world leaders began to discuss plans for a United Nations, Latin Americans wanted some assurance that the new organization would not replace the old regional system, which had worked well for them in the past.

At the founding conference of the United Nations in 1945, Latin American countries, which had been excluded from the earlier planning discussions, succeeded in retaining their regional systems. Latin American nations also acquired 2 of the 11 seats in the United Nations Security Council, 2 of the 15 seats on the International Court of Justice, and 4 of the 18 seats on the Economic and Social Council. As the membership

in the United Nations grew, Latin America's representation also increased. In 1982, Javier Pérez de Cuéllar of Peru became the first Latin American to be appointed secretary-general, the United Nations' highest office.

In 1984, when a major struggle developed between the United States and Nicaragua's Sandinista government, Nicaragua brought its case before the International Court of Justice of the United Nations. The Sandinistas accused the United States of interfering in Nicaraguan affairs, and in 1986, the court ruled against the United States. Later the presidents of Central America requested that the United Nations oversee the end of fighting in Nicaragua and the national elections that followed.

During the 1990s, the United Nations created observer groups to help end the civil wars in El Salvador and Guatemala and to oversee elections in the region to ensure that they are conducted fairly. United Nations subgroups, such as the Economic Commission for Latin America and the Caribbean, serve the region, as do United Nations relief organizations. In early 1999, for example, the United Nations World Food Program and the United Nations Children's Fund delivered emergency aid to Colombia after two cities there were struck by a devastating earthquake. (*See also* **Inter-American Relations; Pan-American Conferences; Pan-Americanism.**)

United States–Latin American Relations

An imbalance of power has always affected the relationship between the United States and Latin America. The United States, which emerged as a nation at least 50 years before most Latin American colonies achieved their independence, has always been richer and stronger than its southern neighbors. This power imbalance has made the United States the dominant force in regional politics and in the ORGANIZATION OF AMERICAN STATES (OAS). Of all the Latin American nations, Mexico has been most influenced by the policies of the United States because the two nations share a border.

Much of the tension that has troubled United States–Latin American relations has concerned intervention, the act of becoming directly involved in another country's internal affairs. The United States, assuming the job of policing the Americas and sometimes seeming to regard Latin America as its own backyard, has intervened in matters outside its own borders. Because Latin Americans are concerned about protecting their sovereignty*, they have often resisted or resented acts of intervention.

In the past, relations between the United States and Latin America were largely concerned with political or military matters or with economic issues, such as trade agreements. In modern times, the links between the United States and Latin America have become more complex. Social and cultural matters as varied as tourism, immigration, and the spread of American Protestant religions in Latin America are now among the issues shaping the relationship between Latin America and the United States.

* **sovereignty** independence

United States–Latin American Relations

° **annex** to add a territory to an existing state

From 1776 to 1900. In the early 1800s, Spain and the newly formed United States came into conflict over Spanish FLORIDA, which the United States wanted to annex*. The United States government encouraged American citizens to move into Florida, and it eventually acquired that territory in 1819. During the same period, Latin American colonies began fighting for their independence. Officially, the United States remained neutral during the struggle between Spain and its rebellious colonies. However, many people in the United States supported the goals of the rebels, and some revolutionary fighters were able to obtain weapons and support in the United States.

After Mexico gained its independence in 1821, the policy of the United States government was to recognize the new republics of Latin America as members of the community of nations. In 1823, fearing that Spain might try to reconquer its former territories, the United States issued the MONROE DOCTRINE. This doctrine stated that the United States would oppose any European attempt to seize territory in Latin America.

Between 1830 and 1900, the United States had many interests in Latin America. One was promoting commerce; another was creating a sea passage between the Atlantic and Pacific oceans across Central America (this eventually became the PANAMA CANAL). A third interest was annexing Mexican territory. Mexico had lost Texas in the 1830s, and after its defeat in the MEXICAN-AMERICAN WAR in 1848, it accepted the United States annexation of Texas. Mexico ceded California to the United States as well as the present-day southwestern United States. The United States also attempted to buy Cuba from Spain, which controlled this last piece of its once great American empire, but the attempt failed. Some Latin American nations feared that the United States might grow amibitous for further expansion.

Instead of territorial expansion, however, the United States increased its economic influence in the region. United States interests in mining, ranching, and the railroads in Mexico greatly increased after the 1870s. In addition, United States businesses became involved in the Cuban sugar industry. That involvement was one of the reasons the United States entered the SPANISH-AMERICAN WAR in 1898. The United States intervened during the conflict between Spain and Cuba partly to keep the sugar industry from collapsing and partly to fulfill a desire to make Cuba a part of the United States. The United States also feared that a different European power would take control of the weakened island once Spain had been overthrown.

After the victory over Spain, United States power and influence increased in Latin America, especially in the Caribbean. Although the United States did not take possession of Cuba, the Cuban republic owed its independence to the United States. Under the PLATT AMENDMENT, Cuba agreed to accept future United States interventions if they became necessary. United States troops ruled the country from 1906 to 1909 and established naval stations that still exist on the island at Guantánamo Bay.

The 1900s. At the beginning of the 1900s, President Theodore Roosevelt added a twist to the Monroe Doctrine. Called the ROOSEVELT COROLLARY, it claimed that the United States was permitted to intervene in Latin

Controlling Nicaragua

In 1912, President Taft of the United States sent marines to Nicaragua when that country's president, Adolfo Díaz, asked for help in suppressing a rebellion. The troops crushed the revolt, took over Nicaragua's railways, and occupied the main cities. Díaz then signed a treaty that gave the United States control of Nicaragua's financial system and the right to intervene when United States business interests in the country were threatened. Until 1928, when the U.S. Marines finally withdrew from Nicaragua, the nation was essentially a protectorate of the United States, much like Cuba, Panama, and the Dominican Republic.

See color plate 8, vol. 4.

United States–Latin American Relations

This cartoon, created in 1897, shows Uncle Sam waiting patiently for new territories to fall into his possession. When this cartoon was created, the United States was on the brink of war with Spain. After the war had successfully expelled Spain from the "New World," the U.S. military occupied Cuba and annexed Puerto Rico.

* **communism** system in which land, goods, and the means of production are owned by the state or community rather than by individuals

American affairs to prevent European intervention. Roosevelt's insistence that the United States had a right to take action to protect the lives of its citizens and their property was called the Big Stick Policy. A few years later, President William Howard Taft promoted DOLLAR DIPLOMACY, or financial involvement in Latin America as a way to avoid using troops. During his term in office, however, Taft sent troops to Nicaragua.

President Woodrow Wilson condemned both dollar diplomacy and "gunboat diplomacy"—the use of money and the threat of military force to influence Latin America. Yet he became the biggest interventionist of all as he attempted to influence the outcome of the Mexican Revolution and sent troops to occupy Haiti and the Dominican Republic.

By the 1920s, the United States was clearly the dominant economic presence in Latin America. It was also a powerful cultural force. In a trend that continues today, Latin American scholars and writers began expressing their concerns that United States styles, customs, and influences would overwhelm Latin American traditions.

A new era in United States–Latin American relations began in the 1930s, when President Franklin Roosevelt launched his GOOD NEIGHBOR POLICY. The policy was based on nonintervention and noninterference in Latin American affairs. Roosevelt ended the military occupation of Haiti, repealed the Platt Amendment, and signed economic agreements with several Latin American governments.

After WORLD WAR II broke out in Europe in 1939, the United States worked to convince Latin America to support Great Britain and the Allied forces against Germany. The United States also influenced Latin American nations to support the United States war effort. Anti-United States feeling was strong in Latin America, especially in Mexico and Argentina. The United States government established the BRACERO PROGRAM, which brought Mexicans into the United States to replace American farmworkers who had gone overseas to fight. The recognition that the nations of the Americas could present a united front in world affairs led to the formation in 1948 of the OAS.

United States political interests in Latin America during the second half of the 1900s were largely concerned with fighting communism*, which the United States government saw as a serious threat. This policy led to the BAY OF PIGS INVASION of Cuba in 1961; armed interventions in Grenada, Panama, and elsewhere; and support for opposition groups in Chile and Nicaragua. The United States also provided economic and social aid to Latin America through such programs as the ALLIANCE FOR PROGRESS, which helped build roads, dams, and schools.

By the end of the 1900s, United States–Latin American relations were affected by new concerns, including the movement of illegal immigrants into the United States and the damage caused by the drug trade. In Mexico, foreign companies built assembly plants called MAQUILADORAS on the United States–Mexico border to take advantage of the low cost of labor there. The economies of the United States and Latin American continued to become more closely linked through pacts, such as the North American Free Trade Agreement (NAFTA), and plans concerning a possible free-trade agreement for all the nations of the Americas. (*See also* **Communism; Imperialism; Inter-American**

United States–Mexico Border

Relations; North American Free Trade Agreement; Pan-American Conferences; Pan-Americanism; United Nations; United States–Mexico Border.)

United States–Mexico Border

An international border can cause conflict over such issues as territorial claims and smuggling. It can also provide opportunities for migration, trade, and cultural exchange. The United States–Mexico border has done both. As El Norte, the northern part of Mexico, became closely linked through trade and employment with the American Southwest during the second half of the 1900s, the population and economic development of the border areas increased.

By the 1990s, economic developments, such as the NORTH AMERICAN FREE TRADE AGREEMENT (NAFTA), had lowered commercial barriers between Mexico and the United States. Yet even as people and goods traveled between the two countries with increasing ease, controlling illegal border crossings and the smuggling of illegal drugs into the United States remained major challenges for both nations.

Border Conflicts. During the 1800s, border conflicts disrupted relations between the United States and Mexico. The United States was eager to annex* territory that had traditionally been part of Mexico. It acquired TEXAS and then, after the MEXICAN-AMERICAN WAR, gained control of CALIFORNIA and the Southwest. When it came to pinpointing the exact location of the border, however, surveying errors and other disagreements caused frequent disputes.

In 1970, the United States and Mexico signed a treaty aimed at settling all border disputes and reducing the possibility of serious conflict over boundary differences. However, border questions still arise. In 1998, Mexico and the United States began negotiating territorial claims in the western Gulf of Mexico, which may contain valuable petroleum deposits.

* **annex** to add a territory to an existing state

Throughout the 1800s, lawlessness plagued the frontier districts along the border and created tension between the two nations. Raids into Mexican territory by Indians operating from the United States side of the border enraged the Mexican government. Filibusters—adventurers with private armies who left the United States to establish colonies in Mexico—caused much destruction as did retaliatory raids from Mexico. Texans, meanwhile, suffered from cattle rustling and smuggling.

The MEXICAN REVOLUTION, which began in 1910, made the borderlands more unstable and violent than ever. Mexican bandits and revolutionaries raided Texas and NEW MEXICO, raising fears that Mexico would try to recapture its former territories. Several times, the United States sent troops deep into Mexico. For a time it seemed likely that the two nations would go to war, but as the revolution drew to a close, borderland violence declined.

Another troubling issue concerned the right to use the water in the Rio Grande and the Colorado River, which flow through the border

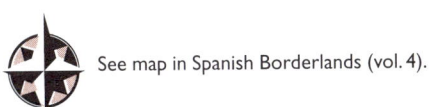
See map in Spanish Borderlands (vol. 4).

region. Mexico and the United States began arguing over water rights in the 1870s, when irrigation systems were developed in the border areas. In 1973, they signed an agreement that settled some long-standing water disputes.

Border Connections. After the mid-1800s, people began moving in larger numbers from the interiors of the United States and Mexico to the borderlands. Old settlements grew and new ones appeared. At the same time, United States companies became deeply involved in mining, ranching, farming, and other industries in El Norte. Although many Mexicans worked in United States–owned businesses, they resented the control that these foreigners had in Mexico. That resentment may have helped ignite the Mexican Revolution.

The borderlands entered a period of great social and economic change after the mid-1900s. The United States government built highways, military bases, and factories throughout the Southwest, sparking an economic boom that also affected El Norte, across the border. By the 1990s, El Norte was one of the most modern and prosperous regions in Mexico. The combined population of the Mexican–United States borderlands had grown from 23.5 million in 1960 to more than 65 million in 1990.

On both sides of the border, manufacturing and high-technology industries are replacing agriculture and mining as major economic activities. Foreign-owned assembly plants called MAQUILADORAS have sprung up on the Mexican side of the border. Some border communities have developed into twin cities that sprawl across the border, with people who commute daily between them. In places such as Tijuana–San Diego, Ciudad Juárez–El Paso, and Matamoros–Brownsville there is a growing sense that the border does not exist and that the United States town is merely the Mexican section of the United States town. (*See also* **Drugs and Drug Trade; Immigration and Emigration; Spanish Borderlands; United States–Latin American Relations.**)

A Restless River

Rivers sometimes change their course in unpredictable ways. When a river is an international boundary, such changes can lead to conflict. In 1864, the Rio Grande near El Paso, Texas, shifted its course southward, and a district called El Chamizal, long part of Mexico, suddenly found itself on the United States side of the river. Both nations claimed El Chamizal. In 1911, the International Boundary Commission ruled to divide the area between the two nations, but the United States refused to accept this ruling. El Chamizal remained a source of tension between the two countries until 1963, when President John F. Kennedy officially accepted the 1911 ruling.

Universities and Colleges

For the Spaniards, an important part of colonizing Latin America was bringing the familiar institutions of Spain to the "New World." The Catholic Church and the military were two of those institutions. The university was a third. Little more than a generation after Christopher Columbus's first voyage to the "New World," the Spaniards founded the first university in the Americas. Spanish America eventually boasted more than 30 universities.

Changes in the Latin American universities during the colonial period reflected changes in European ideas about knowledge and the purpose of education. After independence, the universities of Latin America became a source of national pride to the new republics. The role of universities in society continued to change with the times. By the late 1960s, the universities had become both generators of new social welfare programs and centers of conflict between reformers and repressive governments.

Universities and Colleges

Students Grading Teachers

In both major and minor colonial universities, individuals seeking teaching positions had to compete for them by giving trial lectures. Each candidate, working alone, prepared a lesson and then delivered and defended it in front of the students, who chose the winner. These contests became so disorderly and quarrelsome that around 1675, university authorities changed the system by having experts judge the contests and government officials choose the winners.

The Colonial Period. The first university in the Americas was the University of Saint Thomas Aquinas, founded in Santo Domingo on the island of Hispaniola in 1538 by authorization of the pope. Others soon followed as Spanish colonization spread.

The universities of Spanish America were modeled after the University of Salamanca and the University of Alcalá in Spain. Major Spanish American universities copied the organization of Salamanca, which was larger and more privileged. They were governed by councils called Cloisters, which were made up of teachers and graduates with advanced degrees. Each year the Cloister elected one of its members to serve as the rector, or head, of the university. Another official, called the *maestrescuela,* acted as judge of the university. He administered the special laws that applied to graduates, dealt with disputes or crimes involving students, and granted degrees.

Spanish America's major universities were Santo Domingo (established in 1538), Lima (1551), Mexico (1551), Charcas in Bolivia (1614), Córdoba in Argentina (1621), Guatemala (1676), Havana (1721), Caracas (1723), and Santiago in Chile (1738). Because Lima and Mexico were the most populous and wealthiest colonies, their universities became influential. Others were generally smaller, poorer, and more isolated. Organized on the pattern of the University of Alcalá, they were run by RELIGIOUS ORDERS, usually Jesuits or Dominicans. The Cloister of a minor university had authority over such matters as classroom practices and subject matter. A total of about 150,000 students graduated from the universities of colonial Spanish America. Some 15 to 20 percent of graduates received advanced degrees.

As in Europe, the Latin American universities taught theology*, law, and medicine. During the 1700s, however, they too were influenced by the gradual changes in learning that accompanied the Enlightenment, the intellectual trend in Europe toward reason, progress, and modernity. As a result, mathematics, physics, and geography began to receive greater

* **theology** study of religious faith

The Library of the National Autonomous University of Mexico, shown here, was planned and built by Mexican architect and muralist Juan O'Gorman, who also created the mural on the exterior of the building. The numerous mosaics that comprise O'Gorman's mural are constructed of natural minerals. Other buildings on the university campus are decorated with the artwork of Mexico's artists.

attention. Medical students studied anatomy, chemistry, and biology from up-to-date texts, and training in law began to focus on the state rather than the church.

During the colonial period in Brazil, the University of Coimbra in Portugal served most of the educational needs of the empire. Still, several Jesuit colleges and seminaries were established in Brazil to serve as centers for advanced learning.

Independence and the Modern Period. The social turmoil that swept across Latin America as rebellious colonies overthrew Spanish rule during the late 1700s and early 1800s shook the universities but did not change their basic functions. Following the wars of independence, many universities became "national" rather than "royal and pontifical*" institutions. In addition, some of the new republics built new universities. The University of Buenos Aires in Argentina (1821) was one of the first and most important of the new universities. Some of these new institutions, such as the University of the Republic of Uruguay (1833), served as their countries' only institution of higher education throughout the 1800s.

* **pontifical** having to do with the pope

During the 1800s, political and economic difficulties made operation difficult for both old and new universities. Mexico's Royal and Pontifical University, founded in 1551, closed and reopened several times between 1810 and 1865. Mexico finally reestablished its principal university in 1910 as the National University of Mexico.

After independence in Brazil, technical and vocational institutes satisfied the need for higher education until 1920, when the University of Rio de Janeiro was established. This was considered the first Brazilian university until 1931, when the first Statute of Brazilian Universities was passed, requiring that a university consist of the three faculties of law, medicine, and engineering. In 1934, the University of São Paulo became the first educational institution to fulfill the requirements of the statute.

Remember: Consult the index at the end of this volume to find more information on many topics.

A major role of the new universities was to train professionals in law, medicine, engineering, and the sciences to meet the needs of the new republics. The role of religion in education became a hotly debated issue, but in general the trend was toward nonreligious education controlled by the state. In some countries, such as Chile, the national universities controlled the primary and secondary school systems.

The universities were expected to create a framework for orderly economic and social development in their countries. Often, however, the university served the needs of the small elite class rather than those of the entire nation. In the early 1920s, a set of reforms (known as the Córdoba Reforms because they originated at the University of Córdoba in Argentina) revolutionized universities and their development. The Córdoba Reforms called for political and financial independence for universities, free education, participation of students and graduates in the election of university officials, and new programs that would make the universities agents of social reform. Although few of these proposals were adopted in their entirety, the Córdoba Reforms showed that the universities were becoming centers of political and social activism.

Urban Life

During the 1960s, Latin American universities entered a period of rising enrollments, including greater numbers of women. The 1960s also saw a new emphasis on social action programs, sometimes called extension programs, to fight such problems as illiteracy*, hunger, and infant deaths. No longer content simply to pass along the culture of the elite class, universities tried to promote positive change at all levels of society.

Along with social activism came political unrest among students, especially at the large public universities. A landmark event in university politics occurred in 1968, when police opened fire at a peaceful demonstration led by students in Mexico, leaving hundreds dead. Similar clashes occurred elsewhere in Latin America, especially in nations under military or dictatorial leaders. Repressive governments, viewing universities as places where people question the existing order, have sometimes limited the freedoms and rights of students and teachers. The return to democratic government in most Latin American nations, however, has brought a return to academic freedom. (*See also* **Education**.)

* **illiteracy** inability to read and write

Urban Life

See *Cities and Urbanization*.

Urquiza, Justo José de

1801–1870
Argentine soldier and statesman

* **provincial** having to do with the provinces, outlying districts, administrative divisions, or conquered territories of a country or empire
* **militia** army of citizens who may be called into action in a time of emergency
* **conservative** inclined to maintain existing political and social views, conditions, and institutions
* **confederation** group of states joined together for a purpose; an alliance
* **secede** to withdraw from a political alliance, federation, or union

Justo José de Urquiza was born in Entre Ríos, ARGENTINA, and educated in Buenos Aires. In 1826, he entered politics as a member of the provincial* congress in Entre Ríos. By 1845, he had gained recognition and was named governor of the province. As governor, Urquiza formed a well-equipped militia* and started programs to improve education and the economy.

Using Entre Ríos as a power base, Urquiza formed alliances with many provincial and national leaders. In 1851, he began a campaign against Juan Manuel de ROSAS, the conservative* dictator of Argentina. Urquiza gathered his forces and advanced to Buenos Aires, where he defeated Rosas at the battle of Caseros. The following year, he was named temporary head of Argentina, which was organized as a confederation*. In 1853, Urquiza adopted a new constitution and began working on economic and political reforms. All the provinces approved the constitution except Buenos Aires, which seceded* from the confederation.

In 1854, Urquiza was elected president. However, he was unable to further the region's economy because his government lacked the resources. He also tried to bring Buenos Aires back into the union but failed. In 1859, the congress authorized Urquiza (who returned to his position as governor in 1860) to use military force to subdue the rebellious province. Two years later, Urquiza's forces clashed with the Buenos Aires army, led by Bartolomé MITRE, at Pavón. The battle was indecisive, and Urquiza withdrew from the battlefield, leaving Mitre the victor. Urquiza retired to Entre Ríos but remained active in Argentine politics until 1870, when he was assassinated by political enemies.

Uruguay

° **progressive** inclined to support social improvement and political change by governmental action

° **indigenous** referring to the original inhabitants of a region

° **persecution** harassment of a group of people, usually because of their beliefs, race, or ethnic origin

° **mestizo** person of mixed European and Indian ancestry

Uruguay is the smallest nation in South America except for Suriname. Wedged between Argentina and Brazil, it is bordered by the Atlantic Ocean and the RÍO DE LA PLATA. Uruguay has a mild and temperate climate, and flat or gently rolling grasslands dominate the landscape. Forests are scarce and are generally found in patches along major waterways. The nation's greatest natural resource is its rich agricultural land, most of which is devoted to raising LIVESTOCK. In the early 1900s, Uruguay became one of the most progressive* and prosperous nations in Latin America.

Conquest and Colonization

Before the arrival of Europeans, Uruguay was inhabited by several semi-nomadic Indian tribes, including the Charrúas, Minuanes, Yaros, and Guaranis. The territories of these indigenous* peoples spread beyond present-day Uruguay and into the present-day nations of Argentina and Brazil. During the colonial period, many of these Indian peoples died because of diseases, warfare, and persecution*. Some of those who survived mixed with the colonists, which resulted in a large mestizo* population.

European Conquest and Settlement.
The first Europeans arrived in Uruguay in 1516, when Spanish navigator Juan Díaz de Solís sailed into the Río de la Plata while exploring the Atlantic coast of South America. The Indians killed Solís and chased away his crew. Because the region offered little of value, the Spaniards did not colonize it for the next 100 years. They named the region Banda Oriental, or East Bank, because of its location on the eastern side of the broad Río de la Plata.

In 1624, the Spaniards established their first permanent settlement—Soriano—in the Banda Oriental. In 1680, Portuguese colonists from Brazil established a settlement called Colonia del Sacramento on the shores of the Río de la Plata opposite the Spanish settlement of Buenos Aires in Argentina. The Portuguese hoped to make their settlement a thriving trading center. Spain felt threatened by the Portuguese settlement and by Portugal's interest in the Banda Oriental. In the 1720s, to counter the Portuguese presence in the region, the Spaniards established a fortified settlement named San Felipe de Montevideo on the opposite shore of the Río de la Plata and from there, eventually drove the Portuguese from the region.

Early Spanish Rule.
MONTEVIDEO quickly became the major Spanish port on the Atlantic coast of South America. Settlements spread across the Banda Oriental, and the region was soon divided into large *estancias,* or ranches. Herds of European cattle that had roamed freely in Uruguay since the 1500s, became the basis for a thriving ranching industry.

Throughout the 1700s and 1800s, the dominant figures in rural Uruguay were the *estancieros,* or ranch owners. GAUCHOS, or cowboys, rounded up cattle, and black slaves worked in meat-processing plants.

Uruguay

° **viceroyalty** region governed by a viceroy, a royally appointed official

The port of Montevideo maintained both a legal trade with Spain and its colonies and an illegal trade with Portuguese Brazil.

In 1776, the Banda Oriental became part of the Viceroyalty* of the Río de la Plata. Still, the local government was controlled by wealthy traders and *estancieros*. By 1800, the population of the Banda Oriental had risen to about 30,000, one-third of whom lived in Montevideo. Colonial society in the city was divided on the basis of wealth and social class. Merchants, *estancieros*, and government officials formed an upper class that maintained strong ties to Spain. Traders, storekeepers, soldiers, artisans, and lesser officials—mainly mestizos—comprised the middle class. The black slave population, one-third of the total, comprised the lower class of society.

The interior of the Banda Oriental was mostly rural, and social distinctions tended to be blurred. *Estancieros* made up a wealthy rural elite, while the rest of the population consisted primarily of mestizo and Indian gauchos and laborers. The rough and independent gauchos generally resented the ruling elites in Montevideo, and there were many conflicting loyalties and rivalries between the two groups. These rivalries played an important role in political conflicts throughout the 1800s.

Struggle for Independence

In the early 1800s, Uruguay became involved in the independence movements sweeping through Latin America. Because of its small size and location between Portuguese Brazil and Spanish Argentina, the region also found itself in the middle of a struggle between rival powers.

Moves Toward Independence.
In 1810, a campaign for independence began in the Viceroyalty of Río de la Plata. Because Montevideo had large numbers of Spanish military forces, it remained loyal to Spanish colonial rule. However, in rural areas, the people resented the power of the Spanish officials in Montevideo and consequently supported independence.

The following year, the interior of the Banda Oriental rebelled against Spanish authorities in Montevideo. The revolution was led by military commander José Gervasio ARTIGAS. At first, Artigas and the rural rebels (*orientales*) respected the authority of the revolutionary government in Buenos Aires, known as the Junta* de Mayo, which sought to establish an independent confederation* of provinces. However, political, social, and economic differences soon separated the *orientales* from the *porteños*, or revolutionaries*, in Buenos Aires.

Between 1811 and 1814, Artigas and the *orientales* fought against the Spanish forces. With the assistance of Buenos Aires, they succeeded in occupying Montevideo. Then, in 1814, Artigas broke away from Buenos Aires and began a struggle to win full independence for Uruguay. By 1815, he had defeated the *porteños*, seized Montevideo for the *orientales*, and established his authority in Uruguay.

Struggle with Brazil.
Beginning in 1816, Artigas faced the threat of invasion from Brazil. The Portuguese in Rio de Janeiro wanted to occupy

---

A Unique Experiment in Democracy

In 1952, Uruguayans voted to abolish the office of president and replace it with an executive council known as the National Council of Government. This idea was originally proposed by President José Batlle y Ordóñez in 1913. A unique experiment in democracy, the National Council was composed of nine members. Six of them belonged to the political party that had received the most votes in the election. The remaining three members were from the party receiving the second-largest number of votes. The institution was supposed to minimize political rivalries and result in more efficient government. However, the experiment was short-lived because it failed to live up to expectations. In 1966, Uruguay adopted a constitution that restored the office of the president.

° **junta** small group of people who run a government, usually after seizing power by force

° **confederation** group of states joined together for a purpose; an alliance

° **revolutionary** person engaged in war to bring about change

Uruguay

During the colonial period, the territory of present-day Uruguay was claimed by both the Spanish (in Argentina) and the Portuguese (in Brazil). The Spanish founded the city of Montevideo after the Portuguese built the city of Colonia del Sacramento across the Río de la Plata from Buenos Aires, Argentina. In 1828, Uruguay broke free of both Argentina and Brazil and declared itself an independent republic.

the Banda Oriental, especially because they feared that independence movements in former Spanish lands might spread to Brazil.

In 1820, the Portuguese defeated Artigas and took over the region. Uruguay was under Portuguese control between 1820 and 1822 and then under Brazilian control from 1822 until 1825. The Uruguayan elite supported the Portuguese because they promised to enforce order and restore property that had been confiscated by Artigas during the revolution. In 1821, a group of Uruguayan leaders voted to incorporate the region—then called the Cisplatine Province—into the United Kingdom of Portugal and Brazil.

In time, however, the Uruguayan elite became disillusioned with Brazilian rule, and anti-Portuguese feelings arose. This led to a second revolution in 1825, when 33 *orientales* invaded Uruguay from Argentina in an attempt to win independence from Brazil. This time the *porteños* supported the *orientales* and entered the war on their side. The war with Brazil ended in 1827 with an indecisive victory for the *orientales* at Ituzaingó. Great Britain became involved in the war because it was concerned that Argentina might gain total control over the Río de la Plata and threaten British trade in the region. Britain helped negotiate a treaty that created an independent buffer state between Argentina and Brazil. The Treaty was signed in 1828 and marked the birth of a fully independent Uruguay.

Uruguay

An Era of Conflict and Change

For the next 50 years, Uruguayan politics was dominated by a series of civil wars between rival factions within the country. Out of these struggles emerged the two political parties—Colorados and Blancos—that dominated the nation throughout the 1800s and 1900s.

Political Rivalries.

In 1830, Fructuoso Rivera became the first president of Uruguay. Almost immediately, he faced a challenge from longtime rival Juan Antonio Lavalleja, a rural caudillo* who had been a leader in the Uruguayan struggle for independence from Brazil. When Manuel ORIBE succeeded Rivera to the presidency in 1835, Rivera revolted against Oribe.

It was during the struggle between Oribe and Rivera that the two warring factions gained their identities: *blanco* (white) and *colorado* (red). In 1838, Rivera's Colorados overthrew Oribe's Blancos and occupied Montevideo. The following year, Rivera declared war on the Argentine dictator, Juan Manuel de ROSAS, because he supported Oribe's presidency.

Between 1839 and 1851, Uruguay was engulfed by the GUERRA GRANDE (Great War), a civil war between the Colorados and Blancos. The Colorados had the support of the French, the British, and Rosas's Argentine enemies. Both France and Britain feared that Argentina might try to annex* Uruguay. In 1843, the Blancos, who were supported by Rosas, began a siege* of Montevideo that lasted until 1851. The war ended when Argentine general Justo José de URQUIZA withdrew Argentine support for the Blancos during his successful campaign to overthrow Rosas. Although Oribe was defeated, the peace agreement declared that neither side had won.

After the Guerra Grande, the Colorados and Blancos tried to reconcile their differences. However, the division between them remained strong, and civil conflicts continued to erupt intermittently. Civil strife broke out in 1852, when the Colorados overthrew Blanco president Juan Giró, and again several years later, when a group of Colorados rebelled against the government of Blanco president Gabriel Pereyra.

In 1864, General Venancio Flores, a Colorado, overthrew Blanco president Bernardo Berro and took over the leadership of the country. During Flores's regime*, Uruguay joined forces with Brazil and Argentina against Paraguay in the WAR OF THE TRIPLE ALLIANCE, fought from 1864 to 1870.

The rivalry between the Colorados and Blancos continued to dominate Uruguayan politics for many years. The Colorados generally identified with the city of Montevideo, immigrants, and European culture and ideas. The Blancos, with their roots in the countryside, identified with the agricultural community and the great landowners.

Growing Peace and Prosperity.

Between 1876 and 1890, military governments led by Colorados consolidated power in Uruguay. They gained dominance over rural caudillos, making rural uprisings less frequent. Another factor that contributed to stability and domestic peace

---

* **caudillo** authoritarian leader or dictator, often from the military

* **annex** to add a territory to an existing state

* **siege** prolonged effort by armed troops to force the surrender of a town or fort by surrounding it and cutting it off from aid

* **regime** prevailing political system or rule

was the emergence of nationalist* sentiments. As Uruguayans became more concerned about their own nation, they became less interested in having Argentina or Brazil take sides in their internal disputes.

Domestic peace and strong central government contributed to changes in the population, economy, society, and culture of Uruguay. Between 1830 and 1875, the population grew from 70,000 inhabitants to 450,000. By 1900, the population had reached a million. This dramatic increase resulted from a combination of high birthrates, low death rates, and waves of immigration from Europe. Many of the immigrants who came to Uruguay became pioneers in establishing a modern manufacturing industry.

The emergence of manufacturing was accompanied by changes in the rural economy. Sheep farming was introduced between 1850 and 1870, and by 1884, wool had become the nation's most important export. Sheep farming also became the foundation of a rural middle class because it required less land than cattle ranching, enabling families with modest incomes to participate. However, when landowners began to fence their grasslands for the sheep, they destroyed the livelihood of the gauchos who herded livestock.

Economic developments resulted in changes to the social structure of Uruguay. The divisions between social classes became greater, and the gap between rich and poor increased. Rural gauchos, once respected for their skills and lifestyle, were reduced to domestic labor, smuggling, and cattle stealing. Rural poverty led to migration from the countryside to cities, which contributed to a growing urban lower class.

The nation also experienced many cultural changes. The Catholic Church began to lose its power, and society became more secular*. Education improved throughout the country, resulting in increased literacy*. These changes made Uruguay more "European" than other nations in South America.

* **nationalist** relating to devotion to the nation's interests

* **secular** nonreligious; connected with everyday life
* **literacy** ability to read and write; illiteracy is the inability to read and write

Modern Uruguay

The history of Uruguay since 1900 contrasts remarkably with the preceding period. By the early 1900s, Uruguay had developed a degree of political, social and economic progress that made it one of the most stable, prosperous, and modern nations in Latin America. Stability and prosperity allowed Uruguayans to develop a progressive and democratic society that was also culturally diverse.

An Age of Reform. In 1903, a strong Colorado leader, José BATLLE Y ORDÓÑEZ, was elected president. During his two terms as president, Batlle had a greater influence on Uruguay's development than any other figure in the nation's history.

He initiated a series of far-reaching economic, social, and political reforms. In economic matters, he implemented policies to expand ranching production, reduce the nation's dependency on imports, and decrease the influence of foreign investors. Batlle also improved working conditions by establishing an eight-hour workday and creating generous medical and retirement programs for workers.

Uruguay

In other areas, Batlle expanded education, increased the separation of church and state, abolished capital punishment, gave women the right to initiate divorce proceedings, and protected the rights of children. These reforms placed Uruguay at the forefront of social change in Latin America and created a welfare state that gave Uruguayans tremendous security.

During his second term in office, Batlle took steps to ensure that his reforms could not be easily reversed by a future president or dictator. In 1913, he proposed amendments to the constitution to create a nine-person executive council—a *colegiado*—to replace the president. Although Batlle's idea was rejected, a new constitution adopted in 1918 created the National Council of Administration to share power with the president.

Reaction and Renewed Efforts at Reform.

In 1933, President Gabriel Terra staged a coup* that abolished the National Council of Administration. Assuming dictatorial power, he organized an authoritarian* government based on conservative* ideas. Yet Terra did not reverse the reforms begun by Batlle y Ordóñez. Instead, partly to help counter the effects of a worldwide economic depression*, he enacted new labor laws, increased social benefits, and expanded the government's role in industry.

Uruguay prospered during World War II because of its exports of meat, wool, and leather. Renewed prosperity helped restore the country to democratic rule, and new reforms were enacted in the late 1940s and early 1950s. These reforms included the extension of retirement programs, greater protections for workers, policies to support the development of new industries, and the purchase of the railroads and other British-owned utilities. Reform efforts reached their peak in 1952, when a new constitution was adopted. It replaced the office of president with the National Council of Government.

Reform efforts slowed dramatically in the 1950s, and Uruguay began to face serious economic problems, including high rates of inflation*, poor economic performance, declining exports, and faltering industrial growth. These problems placed a great strain on the nation's social welfare policies. Government attempts to resolve the problems led to growing dissatisfaction among the population.

As the economy worsened, Uruguayans turned to other groups for solutions. In 1958, the Blancos won their first presidential election in 93 years. Their victory was repeated in 1962, but in 1966, when their policies failed to improve conditions, they lost to the Colorados. As the economic crisis deepened, Uruguay faced growing protests and demonstrations by workers and students. The increasing unrest in Uruguay was heightened by the emergence of an urban guerrilla* group called the National Liberation Movement (MLN-T), or Tupamaros. This guerrilla movement, which took its name from Peruvian Indian leader TUPAC AMARU, started in 1963, and the increasingly oppressive policies of the government after 1968 hastened its rise. The Tupamaros sought to bring about a social revolution. During the late 1960s and early 1970s, they resorted to terrorist activities—bombings, kidnappings, and executions—

---

* **coup** sudden, often violent overthrow of a ruler or government

* **authoritarian** referring to leadership with strong, unquestioned powers

* **conservative** inclined to maintain existing political and social views, conditions, and institutions

* **depression** period of little economic activity during which many people become unemployed

* **inflation** sharp increase in prices due to an increase in the amount of money or credit relative to available goods and services

* **guerrilla** referring to a group that uses surprise raids to obstruct or harass an enemy

Uxmal

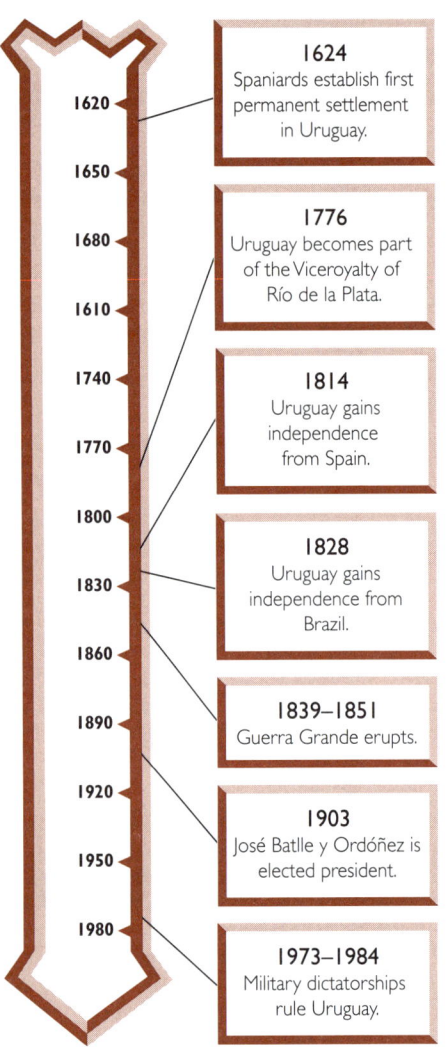

to achieve their goals. The increasingly violent tactics eroded support for the Tupamaros, and the military defeated the rebels in 1972.

Dictatorship and Democracy. The defeat of the Tupamaros by the military marked the start of a serious threat to Uruguay's democratic institutions. By 1972, the military had come to regard all political leaders as corrupt. The following year, they staged a coup and took control of the country.

The military launched a period of brutal repression previously unknown in Uruguay's history. Its leaders dissolved the legislature and silenced the opposition. They imposed censorship, outlawed labor unions, suspended all political activity, and took away people's civil rights. These actions, combined with torture, killings, and disappearances, caused many nations to protest the HUMAN RIGHTS violations there.

In economic matters, the military government encouraged foreign investment and enacted policies to stimulate the growth of industry and agriculture. The economy grew steadily between 1973 and 1980, but then it began to decline once more. As the economic situation worsened, opposition to the military government grew. Finally, in 1984, the military leaders permitted national elections, the first in 13 years.

The election of civilian president Julio María SANGUINETTI in 1984 marked the return of democracy to Uruguay. Sanguinetti attempted to restore national unity by granting amnesty* to many political prisoners and also to military leaders for their role in human rights violations. But Sanguinetti hesitated to make dramatic economic reforms, and the economy remained weak. In 1989, frustrated with the Colorados, Uruguayan's elected Blanco candidate Luis Alberto Lacalle to the presidency. However, Lacalle's government was largely unsuccessful and was accused of corruption. In the 1994 elections, the vote was evenly split among the Colorados, the Blancos, and a third political force—the Encuentro Progresista (EP—Progressive Encounter). The Colorados' Sanguinetti returned to power, but because he did not win a majority, he had to form a coalition government.

Since its restoration in 1984, democracy has remained strong in Uruguay, and the Colorados and Blancos still dominate the political system. The economic situation remains uncertain, however. Since 1990, the government has introduced several reforms, including changes in the social security system and the privatization* of many state-owned enterprises. (*See also* **Immigration and Emigration; Industrialization; Labor and Labor Movements; Meat Industry; Río de la Plata, Viceroyalty of; Southern Cone.**)

* **amnesty** official pardon granted to individuals for past offenses against the government

* **privatization** changing of a business or industry from public to private ownership

U.S. Virgin Islands

See *Virgin Islands of the United States.*

Uxmal

See *Archaeology; Maya.*

Valdivia, Pedro de

ca. 1500–1553
Spanish conquistador

* **encomienda** right granted to a conqueror that enabled him to control the labor of and collect payment from an Indian community
* **royalist** supporter of the king or queen, especially in times of civil war or rebellion

Pedro de Valdivia was an experienced soldier when he came to the Americas in 1535 on an expedition bound for Venezuela. In 1537, he went to help Francisco PIZARRO quell an Indian rebellion in Peru and became Pizarro's trusted assistant. He later helped defeat Diego de ALMAGRO, who had hoped to overthrow Pizarro. As a reward, Pizarro granted Valdivia an *encomienda** in Peru, but Valdivia asked for permission to lead an expedition to Chile. In 1540, he set out with 12 Spaniards, including 1 woman—Inés de SUÁREZ—a few black slaves, and about 1,000 Indians. A year later, he founded the city of SANTIAGO. Valdivia then continued southward, returning to Peru in 1547. There he found himself in the midst of a rebellion led by Pizarro's brother, Gonzalo. Valdivia sided with the royalists* and helped defeat Gonzalo. He later returned to Chile and founded many towns before his death in a battle against the ARAUCANIANS in 1553. (*See also* **Conquistadors; Explorers and Exploration.**)

Valenzuela, Luisa

born 1938
Argentine writer

Luisa Valenzuela is well known for her short stories and novels, which explore politics, sexuality, and the use of language. Born in Buenos Aires, Valenzuela published her first short story at age 17. She began her writing career as a journalist with the prominent newspaper *La Nación*. In 1966, Valenzuela gained recognition as a writer with the publication of a novel, *Hay que sonreír (One Has to Smile),* and a collection of short stories, *Los heréticos* (The Heretics). Three years later, she received a grant to attend an international writer's workshop in the United States, where she wrote *El gato eficaz* (The Efficient Cat), a novel in which she focused on language rather than the characters. In the mid-1970s, Valenzuela began to feel threatened by the military government in Argentina and moved to New York City, where she lived until 1983. Many of her later novels deal with modern Argentina. (*See also* **Literature.**)

Valle, José Cecilio del

1776–1834
Honduran scholar and statesman

* **captaincy-general** area under the control of a captain-general, provincial ruler in colonial Latin America whose main duty was the military defense of that area

José Cecilio del Valle was a prominent Honduran scholar and an authority in economics. He became involved in politics at an early age and was elected president of the short-lived United Provinces of Central America.

Born in HONDURAS, Valle moved with his family to GUATEMALA in 1789. He studied philosophy and law and was admitted to the bar in 1803. Valle served the captaincy-general* of Guatemala for almost 20 years in the hope of obtaining a higher position in Spain. In the years before independence, he reluctantly became a leader of the independence movement, and was largely responsible for writing Guatemala's declaration of independence.

After independence, Valle served in the provisional government that controlled Central America until its annexation* to MEXICO in 1821. He served as the Honduran representative to the Mexican congress and

- **annexation** addition of a territory to an existing state

- **secede** to withdraw from a political alliance, federation, or union

- **plurality** largest number of votes won in an election but less than a majority

quickly rose to become its vice president. During this time, Valle was imprisoned briefly on false charges of conspiracy. After his release, however, he was appointed secretary of foreign and domestic affairs and then secretary of the department of justice and ecclesiastical affairs.

When Central America seceded* from Mexico in 1824, Valle returned to Guatemala and became a member of the provisional government of what later became the United Provinces of Central America. In 1825, Valle won a plurality* in the presidential elections but was prevented from taking office because of a technicality. The congress elected Manuel José ARCE president instead. Valle ran for the presidency again in 1830 but lost to Francisco MORAZÁN. Finally elected president in 1834, Valle became seriously ill and died en route to his inauguration. (*See also* **Central America, United Provinces of.**)

Vallejo, César

1892–1938
Peruvian poet

- **mestizo** person of mixed European and Indian ancestry

- **communism** system in which land, goods, and the means of production are owned by the state or community rather than by individuals

- **socialist** relating to socialism, a system in which the means of production and distribution of goods in a society are owned and controlled by the state

César Vallejo, one of the greatest modern Latin American poets, is famous for his striking originality and for the complexity and power of his works. Many of Vallejo's poems reveal his concern for the suffering of the poor and the oppressed and a nostalgia for his Andean childhood. In addition to poetry, he also wrote dramas, novels, short stories, and articles, which were published in magazines and literary journals.

Vallejo was born to mestizo* parents in Santiago de Chuco, PERU. He began writing poetry in college and published his first book of poems, *Los heraldos negros* (The Dark Messengers), in 1918. The poems deal with themes of personal loss and the inability of individuals to reach their potential because of oppression and injustice.

In the early 1920s, Vallejo was imprisoned for a few months, after being falsely accused of participating in political violence in his hometown. He often referred to this period in his poetry, calling it the "gravest moment" of his life. In 1923, he went to Europe and remained there until his death. In Europe, he became a supporter of communism* and worked with other writers to support the Communist and socialist* cause in the Spanish Civil War.

Some of Vallejo's best-known works include *Trilce*, a collection of dark, tragic poems in which he experimented with language and form, and *Poemas humanos* (Human Poems). The latter was inspired by the Spanish Civil War and expresses the plight of humans in a society filled with evil, alienation, and despair.

Valparaíso

A major port and the second-largest city in CHILE, Valparaíso is located on the Pacific Ocean about 90 miles west of Santiago, the nation's capital. An important industrial center, the picturesque city spreads over steep hills surrounding a wide, well-protected bay. Visited in 1536 by Juan de Saavedra, a captain of conquistador* Diego de ALMAGRO, Valparaíso was not settled permanently until 1544,

Vaqueros

° **conquistador** Spanish explorer and conqueror

° **garrison** military post

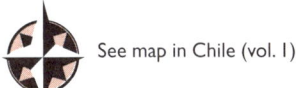
See map in Chile (vol. 1).

when Pedro de VALDIVIA arrived in the region. During the colonial period, the city served as a port for vessels bound for Peru. Although the port was protected by a garrison*, it was attacked by English and Dutch pirates several times in the 1500s and 1600s.

Valparaíso remained relatively obscure until the 1800s, when independence from Spain brought great prosperity to the city. In 1821, Valparaíso served as the point of departure for José de SAN MARTÍN's expedition to liberate Peru. Commercial agents from the United States and Europe chose Valparaíso as the port of entry for trade with Chile and other South American countries on the Pacific coast. This contributed greatly to population growth, and by the late 1800s, Valparaíso was larger than Santiago. Around the early 1900s, following the opening of the Panama Canal, the city became isolated from trading activity between the Atlantic and Pacific oceans and began to decline. Today Valparaíso is a manufacturing and cultural center. The city serves as Chile's navy and marine base and is home to three universities and *El Mercurio,* a newspaper founded in 1827 and possibly the oldest surviving journal in the Spanish language.

Vaqueros

See *Gauchos.*

Varela y Morales, Félix

1788–1853
Cuban priest and patriot

° **nationalism** devotion to the interests and culture of one's country

° **seminary** religious school where priests are trained

Félix Varela y Morales is considered the founding father of Cuban nationalism* and an inspiration for the Cuban independence movement in the early 1800s. He was also an ardent defender of Catholicism.

In 1803, Varela began studying for the priesthood in Havana, CUBA. Ordained in 1811, he wrote philosophical textbooks and gave lectures at the seminary* and soon became one of the leading intellectuals of his time. In 1821, Varela was elected to represent Cuba at the Cortes, or national assembly, in Spain. There he advocated more lenient rule over the colonies and called for the abolition of SLAVERY. However, his views were strongly opposed, and he was forced into exile in the United States. Varela settled in New York City, where he worked as a parish priest. He was well respected and became known for his work with the sick and the poor. In 1837, he was appointed vicar general of New York, the second most important Catholic official in the city and a trusted adviser to American bishops.

Although Varela never returned to Cuba, he always considered it his country. He became the prophet of Cuban independence, publishing pro-independence articles in *El Habanero,* a newspaper he founded in the United States. Varela's writings provided a moral justification for Cubans to rebel against the oppressive Spanish colonial government.

In 1998, Fidel Castro presented a rare, 120-year-old copy of Varela's biography to Pope John Paul II, who was visiting Cuba for the first time. (*See also* **Wars of Independence.**)

Vargas, Getúlio Dornelles

1883–1954
President of Brazil

Getúlio Dornelles Vargas was a prominent figure in Brazilian politics for nearly 25 years. He was revered by those who admired his actions against big businesses and large landowners, but he was criticized by others for his unprincipled, dictatorial leadership.

Vargas was born in São Borja, a small town in the Brazilian state of Rio Grande do Sul. He originally planned to pursue a military career but resigned from the army after five years to study law. While he was in law school, Vargas became involved in politics, when he helped a candidate campaign for state governor. As a reward, he was appointed to the district attorney's office in Pôrto Alegre in 1907. Two years later, he won a seat in the state legislature but was removed from his position in 1912. Vargas was also barred from reelection for five years for criticizing the state governor, Antônio Borges de Medeiros. Nevertheless, Vargas gradually rose to national prominence in the 1920s, a period of protest by young military officers *(tenentes)* against corruption in government. Vargas was elected to Brazil's congress in 1922. He later became Brazil's minister of finance, and in 1928, he was elected governor of Rio Grande do Sul.

As governor, Vargas launched projects to help farmers and businessmen and worked with opposition groups to achieve his goals. Although he was willing to use force to achieve those goals, Vargas preferred nonviolent methods. In 1930, supported by the *tenentes*, he ran for the presidency but was defeated. Later that year, he launched a rebellion and within a few weeks, controlled most of the coastal states. Army leaders in Rio de Janeiro then staged a coup* to halt the war, deposed* President Washington Luis, and installed Vargas as the provisional head of government.

* **coup** sudden, often violent overthrow of a ruler or government
* **depose** to remove from office

To strengthen his power, Vargas suspended the Constitution of 1891, dismissed the congress and all state legislatures, and appointed his supporters to positions in the state and central governments. He thus eliminated any constitutional checks on his power and controlled politics throughout Brazil. He then pursued policies aimed at solving Brazil's social problems and strengthening its economy.

In 1937, supposedly responding to a Communist* threat, Vargas and the military staged a coup that created the Estado Nôvo (New State). Inspired by European dictatorships of the time, the Estado Nôvo was a totalitarian state in which Vargas was the supreme power. His policies continued to focus mainly on the economy and industrialization, but he also enacted social reforms and established a minimum wage for workers. In 1945, he ended some of the restrictive policies of the Estado Nôvo. He abolished CENSORSHIP, released political prisoners, allowed the formation of political parties, and called for new elections. Fearing that Vargas was planning another coup, the army overthrew him in late 1945.

* **Communist** referring to a social system in which land, goods, and the means of production are owned by the state or community rather than by individuals

In 1950, Vargas successfully ran for the presidency, but as a democratically elected president, he was forced to share power with the congress. He was unable to cope with Brazil's growing economic problems and was overwhelmed by charges of corruption. On August 24, 1954, the military demanded his resignation. Getúlio Vargas complied, and later that day, he committed suicide. (*See also* **Dictatorships, Military; Tenentismo.**)

Vargas Llosa, Mario

Vargas Llosa, Mario

born 1936
Peruvian writer

° **exploitation** relationship in which one side benefits at the other's expense

° **socialism** economic or political system based on the idea that the government or groups of workers should own and run the means of production and distribution of goods

° **communism** system in which land, goods, and the means of production are owned by the state or community rather than by individuals

° **ideology** set of concepts or opinions of a person or group

Mario Vargas Llosa is Peru's best-known novelist and one of the creators of the so-called boom in Latin American fiction in the 1960s. A celebrated author, he has written many novels, short stories, plays, and essays. His works often offer sharp and insightful criticisms of corruption, violence, and exploitation* by the government and ruling classes. Vargas Llosa was also briefly involved in politics in the early 1990s.

Born in Arequipa to a middle-class family, Vargas Llosa coped with his parent's separation and his life in a military school as a youth. He wrote about his experiences in military school in his first novel, *La ciudad y los perros (The Time of the Hero),* published in 1963. After its publication, officials at the school burned a thousand copies of the book because of its unflattering descriptions of the school as a symbol of the male dominance and the prejudices and hypocrisy of Peruvian society.

In the 1950s, Vargas Llosa became interested in socialism* and communism* but was soon disillusioned with these ideologies*. Later in that decade, his short stories began appearing in Peruvian journals and newspapers. He won several prizes for his stories, including a trip to France and a scholarship to study at the University of Madrid. In 1959, Vargas Llosa moved to Paris, where he worked in radio and television. He lived in Europe and the United States until 1974, when he returned to Peru.

Two of Vargas Llosa's most important novels—*La casa verde (The Green House)* and *Conversación en la catedral (Conversation in the Cathedral)*—were published in the 1960s. They brought him international fame and several subsequent awards. Many of his novels are experimental works in which he uses shifting points of view, complex plots, jumbled time sequences, slang, and references to popular culture. *La guerra del fin del mundo (The War of the End of the World),* published in 1981, is considered a major contribution to world literature. His later novels include *Elogio de la madrastra (In Praise of the Stepmother)* and *El pez en el agua: Memorias (A Fish in the Water: A Memoir).*

Like many of his contemporaries, Vargas Llosa has made criticism of society and politics an important part of his fiction. His growing interest in politics led him to campaign for the presidency of Peru in 1990, which he lost to Alberto FUJIMORI. Since then, Vargas Llosa has lived in Spain and England. In 1994, he became a Spanish citizen. (*See also* **Literature**.)

Velasco Alvarado, Juan

1910–1977
President of Peru

A radical* military leader, Juan Velasco Alvarado introduced many important reforms in PERU and increased state control over economic, social, and political affairs. His government was unique among modern Latin American military regimes* because it supported reforms at a time when most governments opposed them.

Born to working-class parents in the town of Piura, Velasco joined the Peruvian army in 1929 and gradually rose in rank. In 1959, he was appointed brigadier general and served at the Peruvian embassy in Paris from 1962 to 1963. Five years later, Velasco and 12 other army officers plotted

* **radical** favoring extreme changes or reforms
* **regime** prevailing political system or rule
* **coup** sudden, often violent overthrow of a ruler or government
* **junta** small group of people who run a government, usually after seizing power by force
* **nationalize** to bring land, industries, or public works under state control or ownership
* **Communist** referring to a social system in which land, goods, and the means of production are owned by the state or community rather than by individuals

to overthrow President Fernando Belaúnde Terry of Peru. They devised the Plan Inca, which proposed strategic reforms to modernize the country while at the same time avoiding social uprisings. The coup* occurred in late 1968, and a military junta* with Velasco as president took control of the government.

Velasco immediately launched sweeping changes in Peru's economy and society. His government nationalized* the petroleum, mining, and fishing industries, as well as the agriculture, transportation, and communication sectors. Velasco worked to limit United States influence on the economy and actively defied the United States over many economic and political issues. His government also established relations with major Communist* countries. Although most Peruvians initially supported Velasco, his popularity had declined considerably by 1975. He was overthrown the same year by a military coup and died four years later in Lima.

Venezuela

One of the most prosperous nations in South America, Venezuela is located on the northern coast of the continent. It is bordered by the Caribbean Sea on the north, Colombia on the west, Brazil on the south, and Guyana on the east. Before the 1900s, Venezuela was a relatively poor agricultural society plagued by political instability. During the 1900s, however, wealth from rich oil deposits rapidly transformed the nation into a modern democratic society with a notable degree of political stability.

The Geography of Venezuela

A land of great diversity, Venezuela consists of six geographic regions. The coastal region is a narrow strip of lowland along the Caribbean Sea that stretches from Lake Maracaibo in the west to the delta of the Orinoco River in the east. The Segovia Highlands are located in the western part of Venezuela. This region is a transitional area between the coastal lowlands and the ANDES mountains, which make up a third geographic region.

The fourth geographic region consists of two coastal mountain ranges located behind the central coastal lowlands. Most of Venezuela's population lives in this region. The fifth region is the llanos, a vast low-lying grassland surrounding the Orinoco River and forming the interior heartland of Venezuela. Finally, Guiana Highlands, which lie east of the Orinoco River, is an almost inaccessible and largely unexplored wilderness of dense forests and mountains, which makes up almost half the country.

The differences between these regions made it difficult for Venezuela to develop into a unified nation. For most of the country's history, the coastal ranges have dominated the other regions, and many of Venezuela's most important cities are located there, including the capital of CARACAS.

Venezuela

* **indigenous** referring to the original inhabitants of a region

Conquest and Colonization

Before the arrival of Europeans, a variety of indigenous* peoples inhabited the area that became Venezuela. Among them were the Arawaks and the warlike CARIBS, who lived primarily in the coastal regions. The Indian groups living along the coast and in the major river valleys were nomadic hunters, fishers, and gatherers. Other Indian groups who lived in the Andes and coastal mountain ranges practiced agriculture. Scattered tribes also lived in the dense forests and mountainous areas of Guayana.

European Discovery and Settlement.

Christopher COLUMBUS explored the mouth of the Orinoco River in Venezuela in 1498, during his third voyage to the "New World." The following year, an expedition led by Alonso de Ojeda and Amerigo VESPUCCI explored the Venezuelan coast as far west as Lake Maracaibo. According to historians, Vespucci named the region Venezuela (Little Venice) because he saw Indian villages rising above the water on wooden stilts that reminded him of the Italian city of Venice.

Most of the early exploration of Venezuela resulted from a search for slaves to serve the Spanish settlers in Cuba and Hispaniola. The Spaniards also were attracted to the offshore islands of Cubagua and Margarita, which had rich beds of pearls. The first Spanish settlements in Venezuela were established along the coast at Cumaná in 1520 and Coro in 1527.

Serious exploration of western Venezuela began in 1528, when the king of Spain granted a group of German bankers, the Welsers, the right to exploit that region's resources. Over the next 20 years, the Germans led a number of expeditions, driven partly by their desire to find EL DORADO,

Venezuela is one of the world's leading producers and exporters of petroleum. Many of the nation's richest oil fields lie near or off the coast. As a result, most of Venezuela's major cities are located along the coast, as shown by this map.

Venezuela

the fabled city of gold. The search for gold and other riches proved unsuccessful, and their grant was terminated in 1556.

By 1600, the Spaniards had established more than 20 settlements in the Andes and coastal ranges. To encourage economic development, many of the colonists were granted *encomiendas**. But the settlements were hampered by Indian attacks, especially by the Caribs. By the 1580s, however, many Indians had been killed by European DISEASES and warfare.

* ***encomienda*** right granted to a conqueror that enabled him to control the labor of and collect payment from an Indian community

The Colonial Period.

Because Venezuela had few mineral resources, it was ignored by Spain for many years. By the mid-1700s, it had not yet developed into a unified colony but was a collection of independent regions that were tied to the Viceroyalty of New Granada, colonies in the Caribbean, or Spain. The city of Caracas, for example, interacted more with distant parts of the Spanish empire than with other regions of Venezuela.

By the 1600s, agriculture had become Venezuela's chief economic activity. Rich farmlands in highland valleys and the llanos produced crops for export to British, French, or Dutch traders, such as cacao*, wheat, cotton, and tobacco. The revenue from trade went largely to purchase manufactured goods from Europe and African slaves for PLANTATIONS. Caracas became a major trading center and eventually emerged as the dominant city and region of Venezuela. SMUGGLING was also an important economic activity.

* **cacao** bean from which chocolate is made

Venezuela's success in trade attracted the attention of the crown and led to the formation of the Caracas Company in 1728. The crown gave the company a monopoly* on the cacao trade between Venezuela and Spain. In return, the company agreed to eliminate smuggling, defend the Venezuelan coast, increase cacao production, and provide slaves to the colony. However, the company, which remained in existence until 1784, was only partially successful. Trade expanded and profits increased until the 1760s, but this did not improve the overall economic condition of the colony. The company failed to stop smugglers and was unable to supply the colony with sufficient slaves or European goods. However, it did help centralize the Venezuelan economy around the city of Caracas. This established the city as the economic, political, and cultural center of the colony.

* **monopoly** exclusive control or domination of a particular type of business

In 1776, the Spanish crown created the Intendancy of Venezuela, an administrative unit that placed the colony's provinces under a single financial administrator in Caracas. Political and military authority were centralized in Caracas with the creation of the Captaincy-General* of Venezuela in 1777. The final centralization occurred in 1786 with the creation of the Audiencia* of Caracas. These changes, part of the BOURBON REFORMS, reinforced the dominance of Caracas and helped unify the colony.

* **captaincy-general** area under control of a captain-general, provincial ruler in colonial Latin America whose main duty was the military defense of that area
* **audencia** highest regional court in a Spanish colony; also the district under its jurisdiction

Struggle for Independence

In the early 1800s, Venezuela was at the center of the independence movement that was sweeping Latin America. It produced not only

the first successful revolt against Spanish rule in the Americas but also the leading hero in the entire South American struggle for independence: Simón BOLÍVAR.

First Steps Toward Independence. In 1795, slaves and free laborers in Venezuela seized several plantations before being defeated by Spanish forces. Two years later, royal officials uncovered a plot by Creole* rebels against the government. These failed rebellions marked the beginning of the revolutionary movements that would soon engulf Latin America.

In 1806, revolutionary leader Francisco de MIRANDA made two unsuccessful attempts to liberate Venezuela from Spanish rule. Four years later, in 1810, the CABILDO, or city council, of Caracas overthrew the ruling captain-general and audiencia. The leaders of the council appointed a junta* to govern the colony. In March 1811, the rebels declared their independence from Spain and chose Miranda to be leader in the fight against royalist* forces. However, the royalists proved too strong. Miranda surrendered in 1812 and was imprisoned in Spain.

The struggle for independence fell under the leadership of Simón Bolívar. Despite some successes, Bolívar and his revolutionary forces were defeated repeatedly by the royalists, particularly José Tomás Boves. In 1815, the Spanish crown sent reinforcements to Venezuela, and Bolívar was forced to flee the country.

Continuing the Struggle. The harsh policies of the royalists angered many Venezuelans. Realizing that only independence would maintain their power and status, the Creole elites joined forces with Bolívar and other groups. One of the most important military leaders was José Antonio PÁEZ, a mestizo* from the llanos who organized a cavalry* to fight the Spanish.

In 1819, Venezuela's revolutionary Congress of Angostura called for the creation of the Republic of GRAN COLOMBIA, which would unite Venezuela, New Granada, and Ecuador into a single nation. Bolívar, named provisional president of Gran Colombia, now began a conquest of northern South America. Soon afterward, he freed New Granada. In 1821, his troops fought the decisive battle of Carabobo, which liberated Caracas from Spanish rule. Yet this victory was only the first step toward Venezuelan independence.

Bolívar went on to liberate Ecuador, Bolivia, and Peru, Meanwhile, Gran Colombia was proving to be politically unworkable. The Venezuelans resented being governed by official in far-off Bogotá, in Colombia. In 1829, José Antonio Páez led a successful rebellion to separate from Gran Colombia. This marked Venezuela's emergence as a separate and independent nation.

A Century of Dictators

Between 1830 and 1935, Venezuela was ruled by a series of powerful leaders called CAUDILLOS. Often backed by personal armies, these leaders generally governed for their own personal benefit rather than for the

---

* **Creole** person of European ancestry born in the Americas

* **junta** small group of people who run a government, usually after seizing power by force
* **royalist** supporter of the king or queen, especially in times of civil war or rebellion

* **mestizo** person of mixed European and Indian ancestry
* **cavalry** soldiers who fight on horseback

good of the nation. Yet this period also laid the groundwork for the development of Venezuela's economy and political organization.

Conservative Rule.
In 1830, the revolutionary hero José Antonio Páez became president of Venezuela. Supported by conservative* landowners and merchants, Páez helped unite the nation by limiting the power of regional caudillos. He dominated Venezuelan politics until 1848. When not serving as president, Páez governed indirectly through others.

During the first decade of conservative rule, the Venezuelan economy grew steadily, and the nation prospered from increased production of agricultural exports. Opposition to the conservatives began to develop in 1840, when the economy declined and liberals* demanded political and economic changes. In 1848, the political crisis reached its peak when Páez and his followers tried to overthrow the government. However, they were defeated by President José Tadeo Monagas.

Liberal Rule and Civil War.
Between 1848 to 1858, Venezuela was ruled by Monagas and his brother, José Gregorio Monagas. Supported by the liberals, these dictators enacted a number of reforms, including the abolition of slavery and the extension of voting rights. Meanwhile, however, the Venezuelan economy continued to decline.

In 1857, the Monagas brothers were overthrown by a temporary alliance of conservatives and liberals. The alliance did not last, however, and the overthrow resulted in five years of rebellion and civil war between conservatives and liberals. During this chaotic and bloody conflict, known as the FEDERAL WAR, the government changed hands several times. One of the issues behind the struggle was that of central versus state authority and power. The liberals supported the idea of federalism*, while the conservatives supported a more centralized government.

The liberals won the war, and one of their leaders, General Juan Falcón, became president. The liberal vision of federalism proved to be a disaster. Falcón failed to exert strong leadership, and local caudillos seized control over their regions. Out of the resulting chaos emerged a strong leader, Antonio Leocadio GUZMÁN BLANCO. Supported by both conservatives and liberals, Guzmán Blanco overthrew the government in 1870 and took control of Venezuela.

Progress and Stability.
Between 1870 and 1908, Venezuela experienced considerable economic and political progress under a relatively strong and stable central government. The country began to modernize, and Venezuelans placed a heavy emphasis on the values of hard work and order. The leaders during this period strove to link their country with the economic, social, and intellectual interests of the United States and Europe.

Guzmán Blanco ruled Venezuela with absolute power. He expanded education, reduced the power and influence of the CATHOLIC CHURCH, modernized communications and transportation, encouraged foreign investment, and strengthened the power of the central government.

---

* **conservative** inclined to maintain existing political and social views, conditions, and institutions

* **liberal** person who supports greater participation in government for individuals; one who is not bound by political and social traditions

* **federalism** distribution of power between a central government and the member states

Venezuela

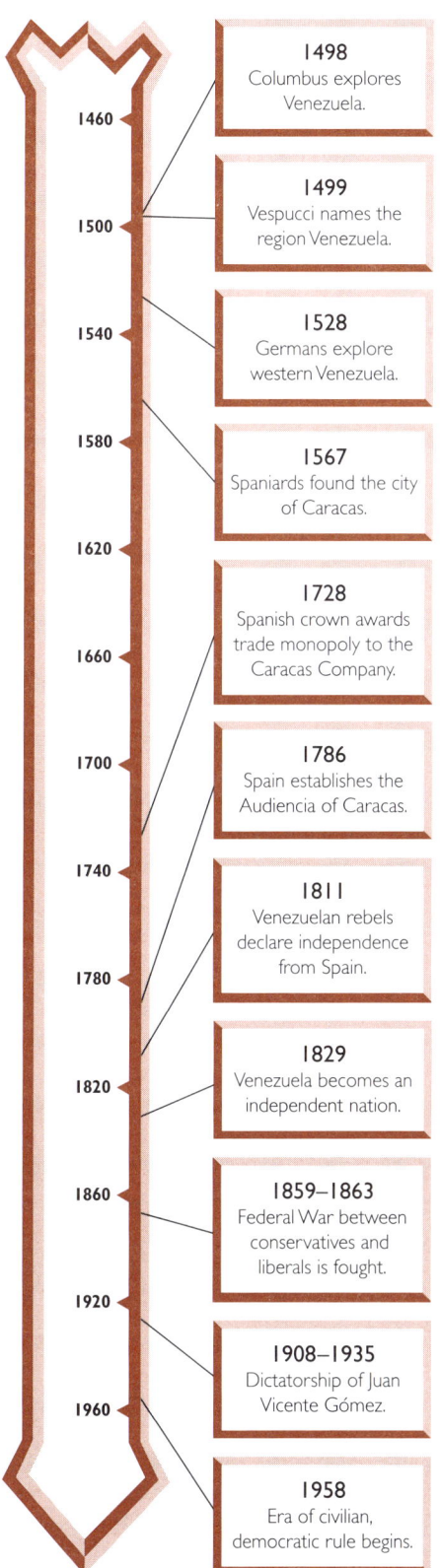

Guzmán Blanco ruled directly, and indirectly through hand-picked successors, until 1888. Despite ruling as a dictator, he did much to improve the nation.

A Shift in Power. The end of the 1800s marked a turning point in the history of Venezuela. In 1899, Cipriano Castro, a caudillo from the Andes region, seized the presidency. For the next 60 years, a series of military dictators from the same region controlled the nation. Because of their origin in the Andes, these rulers became known as the Andinos.

Castro's rule, which lasted from 1899 to 1908, was marked by financial corruption, incompetence, and domestic turmoil. His refusal to repay foreign loans resulted in a British, German, and Italian blockade of the Venezuelan coast. While Castro was traveling in Europe in 1908, a fellow Andino, Juan Vicente GÓMEZ, seized power and took over the presidency.

In the early years of Gómez's rule, European petroleum companies discovered large oil reserves in western Venezuela around Lake Maracaibo. Within a short time, the nation became one of the world's foremost exporters of petroleum. The thriving PETROLEUM INDUSTRY had a dramatic impact on the nation's economy and its future. Today petroleum continues to be the most important industry in the country.

The Gómez Era. A powerful dictator, Gómez controlled Venezuela from 1908 until his death in 1935. During that time, he used the revenues from oil exports to modernize Venezuela and transform it from an agricultural society to a modern export economy.

Gómez also transformed the political process. He manipulated elections, abolished organized political activity, and suppressed all opposition. He maintained his power through the army and a secret police, which used unrestricted force against those considered to be enemies of the state. Thousands of people were tortured, imprisoned, or forced into exile during Gómez's many years in power.

The petroleum industry brought great wealth to Venezuela and to Gómez, who amassed a large personal fortune. Oil revenues were used to construct roads, railroads, and port facilities. The country managed to repay its entire foreign debt and create many high-paying jobs. The petroleum industry also generated a labor movement. In response to growing labor demands, the government eventually approved a number of labor laws. However, they did not take effect until the end of the Gómez era.

Oil generated enormous prosperity for Venezuela, but this wealth was distributed unevenly. A small minority of government officials and upper-class Venezuelans grew enormously rich. Yet the vast majority of the people continued to live in poverty, and the government ignored their basic needs, such as health care, education, and housing. When Gómez died in 1935, many Venezuelans rejoiced at the end of a long and brutal dictatorship. The end of the Gómez regime* also marked the beginning a new period of transition in Venezuela, during which the nation moved steadily toward democracy.

° **regime** prevailing political system or rule

Venezuela

Venezuela Since 1935

The death of Gómez did not mark the immediate end of dictatorship in Venezuela. For the next 23 years the nation struggled to build democratic institutions that would free it from authoritarian rule. In recent years, Venezuela has struggled with growing economic problems.

The Triumph of Democracy.
Between 1935 and 1958, Venezuela alternated between civilian and military rule. Democracy moved forward sporadically during this period, with political reforms supported by some governments and opposed by others. Despite periods of repression, important democratic institutions began to take shape, including the formation of organized political parties and new election systems.

The last leader of this period, Marcos Pérez Jiménez, was a dictator whose policies led to a popular uprising in 1958. His overthrow ended the cycle of authoritarian regimes in Venezuela and ushered in a new political era. From that time until the present, the nation has enjoyed an uninterrupted period of civilian, democratic rule.

Political and Economic Challenges.
Although a military junta took control of the government after Pérez Jiménez, its members agreed to hold presidential elections and support the winner. The new president, Rómulo BETANCOURT, launched programs to modernize agriculture, develop industry, and improve the lives of the people. He enacted AGRARIAN REFORM, adopted new labor laws, restored civil liberties, expanded funding for housing and health care, and provided money for various state-run industries.

Despite the progress made during his rule, Betancourt faced mounting political unrest. Several attempts were made to assassinate him, and various political groups, such as the Armed Forces of National Liberation (FALN), tried to overthrow his government. Betancourt's successors continued to adopt policies aimed at modernizing Venezuela.

Beginning in the 1970s, Venezuela experienced a serious economic decline, caused largely by changing demand for petroleum products and decreasing oil revenues. The economic crisis contributed to rising inflation*, growing foreign debt, unemployment, and other problems.

Since the 1970s, Venezuela's leaders have struggled to solve the economic challenges facing the country. After Carlos Andrés Pérez was elected president in 1973, he nationalized* several foreign-owned industries, including petroleum and steel. During his second administration, Pérez made drastic spending cuts in a number of popular social programs, which led to violent street riots and demonstrations in 1989. Four years later, Perez was forced out of office on charges of corruption. After two acting presidents, Rafael Caldera Rodríguez of the Democratic Convergence was elected to the presidency in 1994. Although Caldera's regime has been criticized as a failure, his supporters believe that he restored stability to Venezuela. In 1999, Caldera was succeeded by Hugo Rafael Chávez Frías of the Movement for the Venezuelan Republic (MVR). Chávez, who won a sweeping victory in the elections, promised

---

Black Gold

Early Spanish explorers and colonists found little gold in Venezuela. However, they noticed pools of thick black liquid in western Venezuela, although they had no idea that this substance—petroleum—would one day be much more valuable than gold. Since the early 1900s, oil has played a major role in Venezuela's economic development. In 1960, the nation became a founding member of the Organization of Petroleum Exporting Countries (OPEC), a multinational organization that coordinates petroleum policies among its members. Venezuela's vast oil reserves and membership in OPEC remain the basis of its declining prosperity.

° **inflation** sharp increase in prices due to an increase in the amount of money or credit relative to available goods and services

° **nationalize** to bring land, industries, or public works under state control or ownership

to end corruption and institute constitutional reform in Venezuela. He also promised to redistribute the nation's oil wealth and to reorganize and reform the political institutions.

During the 1990s, Venezuela continued to struggle with a weakened economy and political turmoil caused by economic problems. Many Venezuelans found themselves worse off than in earlier decades, with as much as 40 percent of the population living in poverty. Despite the economic challenges, Venezuela continues to embrace democracy and reject the authoritarian rule that played so large a role in the nation's history. (*See also* **Cacao Industry; Captaincy System; Federalism; Foreign Investment; Germans in Latin America; Industrialization.**)

Veracruz

The principal seaport of MEXICO, Veracruz is located on the Gulf of Mexico, about 265 miles southeast of Mexico City. Veracruz has been a major trade center since the Spanish conquest of Mexico in the early 1500s. Today the city contains several important industries and is a major tourist resort.

In 1519, Hernán CORTÉS landed an expedition on an island off the Gulf coast of Mexico and established a base there. He then founded a settlement to the north, where ships could anchor easily, and named it Villa Rica de la Vera Cruz (Rich Town of the True Cross). Cortés also formed a local government, making Veracruz the first Spanish town in Mexico. In 1599, the town was relocated to its present site next to the port. Veracruz flourished as the only official gulf port of New Spain*. In fact, the city's trade was the primary source of revenue for the colonial government. However, its wealth also attracted privateers*, prompting the Spaniards to build massive fortifications.

In the 1800s, during the MEXICAN WAR OF INDEPENDENCE, Veracruz was the stronghold of Spanish royalists*. After independence, the city was often the prey of foreign troops because of its wealth. During the MEXICAN REVOLUTION, Veracruz was invaded by United States forces in 1914 and then became the headquarters of General Venustiano CARRANZA. Although weakened by these conflicts, Veracruz always revived. By 1990, the city and its surroundings had developed into a commercial and industrial center with more than a million inhabitants. Despite a hot, humid climate, its slow pace of life and picturesque colonial heritage attract many tourists.

* **New Spain** Spanish colony in Mexico

* **privateer** privately owned ship authorized by a government to attack and capture enemy vessels; also, the ship's master

* **royalist** supporter of the king or queen, especially in times of civil war or rebellion

Vespucci, Amerigo

1454–1512
Italian navigator

Amerigo Vespucci, of Florence, Italy, was one of the early explorers of the "New World." In 1497, he embarked on his first voyage to explore coastal Central America as well as the Gulf and Atlantic coasts of North America. He may have served as navigator on this expedition. The following year, Vespucci joined Alonso de Ojeda on a voyage to South America, where the Italian navigator explored the mouth of the AMAZON RIVER. In 1501, Vespucci entered Portuguese service and sailed southward along the Brazilian coast, becoming the first

Viceroys and Viceroyalties

European to reach the Río de la Plata. He returned to Europe and wrote several letters stating that the lands explored by himself, Columbus, and others were not the Indies but a new continent, which he called Mundus Novus, or "New World." In 1507, German mapmaker Martin Waldseemüller renamed the continent South America in honor of the navigator, and later the name was applied to North America as well.

Viceroys and Viceroyalties

* **provincial** having to do with the provinces, outlying districts, administrative divisions, or conquered territories of a country or empire

During its 300 years of colonial rule in the Americas, Spain governed its colonies through a system that divided the empire into administrative units. The smallest of these units were the local and provincial* governments. Larger administrative units included AUDIENCIAS, or high courts, and captaincies. The largest territorial unit of Spanish administration was the viceroyalty, which was governed by a powerful official called the viceroy.

The Viceroyalties. Among the earliest forms of colonial administration in Spanish America were the audiencias, the first of which—the Audiencia of Santo Domingo—was established in 1511. However, the audiencias failed to provide stable colonial rule. The desire to gain greater control over the colonies led to the creation of the viceroyalties.

The first viceroyalty created in Spanish America was the Viceroyalty of New Spain. Established in 1535, it came to include all of Mexico and extended to the Spanish Borderlands in the north. For governmental purposes, the viceroyalty also included Spanish possessions in the Caribbean, parts of Central America to the north of Panama, parts of Venezuela, and the Philippines. In reality, however, those regions were effectively ruled by their own provincial governors and audiencias.

The next viceroyalty was established in Peru in 1543 and included Panama and all Spanish territory in South America except a coastal strip of Venezuela. As the South American colonies grew, the task of governing them under a single viceroyalty eventually became impossible. As a result, new audiencias were created within South America.

In 1717, Spain created the Viceroyalty of New Granada, with its capital at Santa Fe de Bogotá. After an unsuccessful beginning, it was reestablished in 1739. This viceroyalty was formed, in part, from territory detached from the Viceroyalty of Peru and included present-day Colombia, Venezuela, Ecuador, and Panama, as well as parts of Peru. It was created to increase the economic development of northern South America and to strengthen Spain's military position in that region. In 1777, a number of its eastern provinces were joined with Caracas to form a self-governing military and defensive unit called the Captaincy-General of Venezuela.

Other Viceroys

The title of viceroy was not limited to colonial rulers of Spanish America. In Spain, the governors of *reinos* (kingdoms), such as Aragon and Valencia, were also called viceroys. Beginning in 1720, the Portuguese in Brazil used the term for the official who headed a captaincy. The English also used the title for certain high officials. Starting in the 1300s, the English gave the title to the crown-appointed governors who ruled Ireland. Between the mid-1800s and 1935, the title of viceroy was bestowed on the British governors-general who ruled India.

The last viceroyalty to be created in Spanish America was the Viceroyalty of Río de la Plata. Established in 1776, it was carved largely out of the Viceroyalty of Peru, and its territory included present-day Argentina, Paraguay, Uruguay, and Bolivia. The creation of this viceroyalty was part of the Bourbon Reforms, measures taken by the Spanish monarchy to strengthen Spain's control over its colonies.

Viceroys and Viceroyalties

In 1535, New Spain became the first viceroyalty to be established in Spanish America. Eventually, others were formed, and by 1800, Spanish America was divided into the four viceroyalties shown on this map.

° **bureaucracy** large departmental organization that performs the activities of government

° **secede** to withdraw from a political alliance, federation, or union

The Spanish crown experimented with the administration of the Viceroyalty of Río de la Plata and introduced several measures aimed at improving colonial government. The monarchy was able to do this largely because the region had no established aristocracy or bureaucracy* that might oppose such change.

The Viceroyalty of Río de la Plata was more of a frontier outpost than other parts of Spanish America because of its small population, its lack of the riches of Mexico and Peru, and the strategic importance of the Caribbean region. Generally left on its own, the viceroyalty flourished as a center of trade, with commercial links to foreign ports throughout Europe. Its relative isolation also enabled local officials to exercise greater independent power. When independence movements arose throughout Spanish America in the early 1800s, parts of the Río de la Plata became the first of the territories to secede* effectively.

The Viceroys. The highest officials in Spanish America, the viceroys were appointed by the king of Spain and the COUNCIL OF THE INDIES, the institution responsible for overseeing the affairs of Spain's colonies in the Americas. Many viceroys came from noble Spanish families. Most were born and raised in Spain. As a result, they were generally supposed to be more loyal to Spain and the monarchy than to the colonies and their inhabitants.

As the highest appointed representatives of the Spanish crown, the viceroys symbolized royal power. Therefore, they lived in lavish palaces that resembled the royal court in Spain. The viceroys had extensive powers and broad responsibilities. They served as commanders in chief of the military and as royal patrons* of the church. They were responsible for the economic development of their viceroyalty, and they supervised the settlement of its territory. They also were responsible for collecting tax revenues, using them to pay necessary colonial expenses, and then sending all remaining revenues to the royal treasury in Spain. In addition, they enforced the laws and oversaw the treatment of INDIANS.

* **patron** special guardian, protector, or supporter

Despite such enormous responsibilities, the powers of the viceroys were subject to certain limitations. Other royally appointed colonial officials could sometimes act independently of the viceroys and deal directly with officials in Spain. Moreover, the many rules and regulations issued by the Spanish government often left the viceroys with little freedom to determine their own administrative policies. Their policies and actions were also subject to a periodic review by Spanish officials. Nevertheless, viceroys often decided which of the laws they would enforce.

Viceroys were appointed for a limited period, averaging between six and seven years. This relatively short term helped ensure that they would not gain too much power of their own or become too close to the local population. During the 1700s, the Spanish crown began to choose viceroys who had extensive military backgrounds because of the growing threat from other colonial powers and the need to defend Spanish territory. (*See also* **Captaincy System; Intendancy System; Spain and the Spanish Empire.**)

Vicuña

See *Llama*.

Vieira, Antônio

1608–1697
Portuguese missionary and writer

Antônio Vieira is considered one of the greatest writers in the Portuguese language. His sermons, letters, and other writings provide valuable insights into life in the 1600s. Vieira also played a central role in the political and religious history of Portugal and colonial Brazil.

Born in Lisbon, Portugal, Vieira went to Bahia, Brazil, with his parents while still a child. In 1623, he went to live in the city's Jesuit* college and was ordained as a priest. In 1641, the viceroy* of Bahia sent him to

Villa, Francisco "Pancho"

- **Jesuit** popular name for the Roman Catholic religious order officially known as the Society of Jesus; also, a member of that order
- **viceroy** one who governs a country or province as a monarch's representative; royally appointed official
- **diplomatic** demonstrating tact and skill at conducting negotiations among nations
- **cede** to yield or surrender, usually by treaty
- **mission** settlement started by Catholic priests whose purpose was to convert local people to Christianity

Lisbon, where he became the court preacher and a confidant of the king, who sent him on several diplomatic* missions. However, Vieira angered many with his proposals to limit the power of the INQUISITION and to cede* PERNAMBUCO to the Dutch. He returned to Brazil in 1653 as head of Jesuit missions* in the Amazon region, where he worked to improve relations between the Jesuits and the settlers and led expeditions into the interior. Vieira also tried to curb slavery and protect the Indians from abuse by settlers.

In 1655, Vieira went to Lisbon to present his case against the settlers to the monarchy. He returned to Brazil shortly thereafter and continued his missionary work in the Amazon. In 1663, he was arrested and imprisoned by the Inquisition for criticizing the church in his writings. After his release in 1668, he preached in Rome and later returned to Brazil and spent the rest of his life as an administrator for the Jesuits. Vieira also published several sermons and continued fighting for the rights of Indians until his death. (*See also* **Slavery; Slavery, Abolition of.**)

Villa, Francisco "Pancho"

1878–1923
Mexican revolutionary leader

Francisco "Pancho" Villa was one of the most important and controversial leaders of the MEXICAN REVOLUTION. He helped overthrow the dictatorial regimes* of Porfirio DÍAZ and Victoriano HUERTA, and after the revolution, he engaged in civil war and banditry, primarily in northern Mexico.

Born Doroteo Arango, Villa and his sister were orphaned at an early age. According to legend, he killed a landowner who had raped his sister, and he then took up a life of banditry, changing his name in the process. His exploits as a bandit and cattle rustler brought him much notoriety.

In 1910, Villa joined the revolution led by Francisco MADERO against Mexican dictator Porfirio Díaz. After Díaz was overthrown, Villa retired from fighting and began a meatpacking business. However, he returned to military duty in 1912 to fight against counterrevolutionary forces. His commander, General Victoriano Huerta, ordered Villa executed for disobeying orders. Madero intervened, however, and sent Villa to prison instead. After a few months, Villa escaped and fled to the United States, where he spent a few months in exile. He later returned to Mexico to seek revenge for Madero's assassination by Huerta in 1913.

From late 1913 through 1914, Villa and his forces captured the estates of wealthy landowners and used the revenue to finance an army called the Division of the North. With the goal of overthrowing Huerta's dictatorship, Villa united with Venustiano CARRANZA, a leader of the opposition against Huerta.

The revolutionary forces defeated Huerta in 1914, but rivalry between Villa and Carranza soon led to a break between the two leaders. Forced to flee Mexico City, Villa joined forces with Emiliano ZAPATA, a peasant leader from central Mexico. Villa demanded that Carranza resign as leader of the revolution. When Carranza refused, Villa and Zapata rose up against him.

In a series of brutal battles in 1915, Villa suffered major defeats at the hands of Carranza's forces. The alliance with Zapata faded, and Villa's army fell apart. Villa fled to northern Mexico, where he received strong

Villa and General Pershing

After his defeat by Venustiano Carranza's forces, Villa was driven back into northern Mexico. From there, he supported raids across the border into the United States. In 1916, Villa's men raided Columbus, New Mexico, burning the town and killing 18 people. These acts of banditry may have been a response to official United States recognition of the Carranza government, which angered Villa. President Woodrow Wilson sent General John Pershing into Mexico to capture Villa. However, Villa's knowledge of the mountainous terrain and his support by the local people enabled him to elude Pershing for almost a year before the United States gave up.

In this famous photograph, taken at Sanborn's Restaurant in Mexico City, Francisco "Pancho" Villa (*center*) is seated next to his ally Emiliano Zapata (*on Villa's left*). The personalities of the two men were vastly different. Villa seems comfortable and at ease, while Zapata, unaccustomed to the big city, is watchful and on his guard.

* **regime** prevailing political system or rule
* **guerrilla** referring to a group that uses surprise raids to obstruct or harass an enemy or overthrow a government
* **hacienda** large rural estate, usually devoted to agriculture

support. From this stronghold, he continued guerrilla* activities against the Carranza regime until its overthrow in 1920.

After the ouster of Carranza, Villa was granted amnesty by the acting president of Mexico, Adolfo de la Huerta. He also received a large hacienda* and money for himself and his troops. In 1923, Villa was assassinated at his ranch, perhaps because some of his enemies feared that he might once again rebel against the government.

Villa-Lobos, Heitor

1887–1959
Brazilian composer

Heitor Villa-Lobos, the most famous Latin American composer of the 1900s, was born in Rio de Janeiro, Brazil. He learned to play the cello from his father and was self-taught in musical composition. His works combine the rhythms of Brazilian folk music with elements of Western classical music.

At the age of 18, Villa-Lobos left home and traveled throughout northern and northeastern Brazil, collecting local folk melodies and rhythms, which he incorporated into his compositions. He returned to Rio de Janeiro around 1911 and began to establish himself as a serious musician and composer. By 1915, Villa-Lobos had composed many works and had performed several concerts. Early critics of his work noted his lack of formal training and his disregard for conventional musical styles. Nevertheless, he received support from French composer Darius Milhaud, who encouraged him to pursue his own interests. Between 1923 and 1930, Villa-Lobos gave concerts throughout Europe and was recognized as a talented and original composer. He returned to Brazil and served as organizer and director of a program of music education intended to instill patriotism.

Villa-Lobos wrote between 2,000 and 3,000 works, including operas, ballets, symphonies, and concertos. Despite his worldwide performances,

Violencia, La

Heitor Villa-Lobos, shown here, influenced the development of Brazilian nationalism in music by incorporating national and regional themes in his work. In a series of compositions titled *Chôros*, Villa-Lobos demonstrated the diversity and rhythms in Brazilian folk and popular music.

most of his music is unknown outside Brazil. Among his best-known compositions is a series of vocal and instrumental pieces called *Bachianas Brasileiras,* which reflects the influence of Brazilian folklore and Western classical music. (*See also* **Music and Dance.**)

Violencia, La

Between the mid-1940s and early 1960s, COLOMBIA experienced a period of political upheaval and violence that claimed as many as 250,000 lives. Known as La Violencia (The Violence), it was a struggle for social and economic equality as well as a battle for power between Colombia's two major political parties: the Liberals and the Conservatives.

The background of the La Violencia was the victory of the Liberal Party in the national election of 1930 and its support for various reforms. The Liberals remained dominant until 1946, when the Conservatives returned to power. The Conservative victory triggered an eruption of violence among rural Colombians, who feared an end to reform efforts. However, the violence soon reflected the growing struggle for power between the two parties.

In 1949, Conservative dictator Mariano Ospina Pérez launched vicious attacks against Liberals and their supporters in rural areas. Liberal guerrillas* responded, and the level of violence greatly increased. Uprisings in cities after the assassination of a popular Liberal leader, Jorge Gaitán, in 1948 brought La Violencia to urban areas, although only briefly.

Between 1950 and 1953, most of rural Colombia was engulfed by La Violencia. On the vast eastern plains, or llanos, Liberal resistance to Conservative rule took on a revolutionary character. Throughout much of the

°guerrilla referring to a group that uses surprise raids to obstruct or harass an enemy or overthrow a government

Violencia, La

Although La Violencia occurred primarily in rural Colombia, several urban centers were also struck by violence and destruction. This photograph, taken in 1948, shows the fires, overturned trolleys, and debris that filled the streets after a riot in Bogotá's Bolívar Plaza.

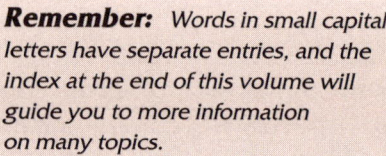

Remember: Words in small capital letters have separate entries, and the index at the end of this volume will guide you to more information on many topics.

country, Conservative and Liberal landholders, sharecroppers, and laborers battled merely because they were members of rival political parties.

The overthrow of the Conservative dictatorship by the military in 1953 slowed La Violencia in some regions, particularly on the llanos. Nevertheless, it continued elsewhere, and the military itself was responsible for vicious acts of violence, including mass executions and aerial bombings of towns.

In 1957, the leaders of the Conservative and Liberal parties reached an agreement, eventually known as the National Front, to share power and work together on certain economic, social, and military strategies. This facilitated the gradual ending of La Violencia in the early 1960s.

La Violencia had enormous consequences for Colombia. In addition to the death toll, vast amounts of property were destroyed. Hundreds of thousands of people fleeing rural violence migrated to Colombia's cities,

Virgin Islands of the United States

° **agribusiness** agriculture as big business, performed by corporations or large-scale investors

stimulating the growth of markets and industrialization. Rural areas also were transformed, as small landowners were displaced by agribusiness* or by urban merchants. Such changes had a profound effect on Colombia's society and economy.

Virgin Islands of the United States

See map in Caribbean Antilles (vol. I).

° **cosmopolitan** having a sophisticated outlook or broad worldview

The Virgin Islands are a string of about 100 small islands located east of Puerto Rico in the Caribbean Sea. The islands are divided politically between the United States and Great Britain. The Virgin Islands of the United States is a self-governing territory administered by the U.S. Department of the Interior. It consists of 3 main islands—St. Thomas, St. Croix, and St. John—and about 50 small islands.

Originally inhabited by Arawak and CARIB Indians, the Virgin Islands were discovered in 1493 by Christopher Columbus, who named them in honor of virgin saints of the Roman Catholic Church. The Spaniards did not colonize the islands because they feared the hostile Caribs. Nevertheless, by 1625 English and French settlers had established farms on St. Croix. In 1672, the Danish West India Company claimed St. Thomas and St. John. In 1733, Denmark bought St. Croix from France and established sugar plantations there. By the early 1800s, the sugar industry had begun to decline, and the islands experienced slave revolts. In 1917, the United States bought the islands from Denmark to protect its trade routes to the Panama Canal.

Of the three islands, St. Thomas is the most commercial and cosmopolitan* and has a large population of United States citizens and immigrants from other Caribbean islands. St. John has a small population and little political influence, and St. Croix is dominated by a small group of wealthy planters. TOURISM is the mainstay of the economy on all three islands. (*See also* **Caribbean Antilles**.)

Volcanoes

° **geological** having to do with the earth's structure and history, especially as recorded in rocks

Volcanoes form an integral part of the landscape in several Latin American countries. Found in Mexico, Central America, the Caribbean Antilles, and nations in the Andean region, they play a significant part in the geological* and human history of the region. Compared with other types of natural disasters, volcanic eruptions are less frequent, result in fewer deaths and injuries, and produce less economic loss. Nevertheless, the resulting mudflows, rock fragments, ash falls, lava flows, and toxic gases, all have devastating consequences for people and societies.

Latin America has many active and dormant (inactive) volcanoes. Among the best-known are Cerro Azul in Chile, Nevado del Ruiz in Colombia, Cotopaxi in Ecuador, Fuego in Guatemala, Pelée on the Caribbean island of Martinique, Popocatépetl and Paricutín in Mexico, Cosigüina (whose 1835 eruption was one of the largest in recorded history) in Nicaragua, and El Misti in Peru. Among the South American nations, Chile has the greatest number of volcanoes, most of which are in the less-populated south. In Central America, Honduras is the only

In 1943, after two weeks of earth tremors, the Paricutín volcano began forming in a cornfield in Mexico. Within weeks, a volcanic cone had developed and erupted, spewing lava, smoke, and ashes that engulfed several towns and villages. This photograph shows the destruction of a church in the nearby village of San Juan Parangaricutiro caused by the eruption.

country without any volcanoes, and Ecuador has some of the largest volcanoes in the world.

The most deadly volcanic eruption in recent times occurred in Colombia in 1985, when mudflows from Nevado del Ruiz destroyed the town of Armero, killing around 25,000 people. Other disastrous eruptions include Peleé, which killed 29,000 people between 1902 and 1905 and El Chinchón (Mexico) in 1982, which resulted in about 2,000 deaths. In 1997, the Soufiere Hills Volcano on the Caribbean island of Montserrat erupted, forcing more 4,000 residents to evacuate. (*See also* **Geography**.)

Voodoo

Voodoo (vodun) is a folk religion that contains elements of both African and Roman Catholic beliefs. Associated largely with HAITI, forms of the religion are found throughout the Caribbean and in the United States. The term *voodoo* comes from *vodun,* a West African word meaning "spirit."

It is believed that voodoo began among African slaves in Haiti between 1750 and 1790. A loosely organized religion, voodoo is based on African beliefs of communication with divine spirits through dances and trances in which participants may become "possessed" by a spirit.

Many of the voodoo spirits, called *loas,* are African gods, but some are also indigenous* to Haiti. They are also associated with Catholic saints and the spirits of ancestors. There are an infinite number of *loas,* both good and evil. They are believed to attach themselves to particular individuals or families, and they require offerings of food and ritual sacrifices of animals.

Voodoo rituals are led by the *houngan* (priest) or *mambo* (priestess). Other participants are the *badjicans* (the priest's assistants), the *serviteurs* (those who become possessed), and the *fidèles* (believers). During rituals,

* **indigenous** referring to the original inhabitants of a region

the *serviteurs* dance, give spiritual advice, perform healing rituals, and display special physical feats while possessed by the *loas*.

Children learn about the *loas* through stories that teach moral lessons. In this way, voodoo helps communicate folk culture as well as social values and traditions from one generation to the next. There are numerous celebrations and annual feasts in honor of the *loas*—the helpers, protectors, and guides of the people. (*See also* **Africans in Latin America; Catholic Church; Religions, African–Latin American; Syncretism.**)

Walcott, Derek

born 1930
West Indian poet and playwright

One of the most distinguished writers of the West Indies, Derek Walcott is best known for his poetry, in which he combines his European and Caribbean backgrounds. In 1992, he won the Nobel Prize for literature, becoming the first writer from the Caribbean islands to win that prestigious award.

Born on the island of Saint Lucia in the Lesser Antilles, Walcott was educated at the University of the West Indies in Jamaica. He began writing poetry at an early age, publishing his first work—*25 Poems*—at the age of 18. In 1953, Walcott moved to Trinidad and in the late 1950s, to New York City, where he founded a theater company, the Trinidad Theatre Workshop. Since then, he has divided his time between Trinidad and the United States.

Walcott gained recognition in 1962 with the publication of *In a Green Night,* a collection of poems that celebrate the natural beauty of the West Indies. In some of his other works, such as *The Castaway, The Gulf, Another Life,* and *Sea Grapes,* Walcott explores the themes of personal isolation and the racial and cultural divide between Europeans and blacks in the Caribbean. Walcott is also an accomplished playwright. In 1971, he won an Obie Award in the United States for his play *Dream on Monkey Mountain.* (*See also* **Literature.**)

Walker, William

1824–1860
American military adventurer

* **filibuster** person who engages in an unauthorized military expedition into a foreign country in order to provoke or support a revolution; a military adventurer

The American filibuster* William Walker was born in Tennessee. After pursuing careers in law and journalism, Walker sought a more adventurous life. In 1853, he headed for MEXICO with a group of followers. His intention was to conquer the Mexican state of Sonora. After capturing the city of La Paz, Walker proclaimed the Republic of Lower California in 1854. Mexican guerrillas* soon forced him to retreat to the United States, however.

Walker next set his sights on CENTRAL AMERICA. In 1855, he and 57 followers, known as the Immortals, set off on a filibustering expedition to NICARAGUA. This time Walker had an invitation from one of the country's political parties. Walker helped the liberals* overthrow the government. Named commander in chief of the Nicaraguan army, he was elected president of the country in 1856.

° **guerrilla** referring to a group that uses surprise raids to obstruct or harass an enemy or overthrow a government

° **liberal** person who supports greater participation in government for individuals; one who is not bound by political and social traditions

Walker dreamed of ruling all of Central America some day. But growing interference by the United States, armed resistance by other Central American states, and opposition from wealthy American industrialists combined to weaken his power. Forced to flee Nicaragua because of growing opposition, he surrendered to the U.S. Navy in 1857.

Walker devoted the rest of his life to other filibustering schemes. In 1860, he led an expedition to HONDURAS, but was forced to surrender to the British navy. Handed over to Honduran authorities, William Walker was executed on September 12, 1860. His invasions of Mexico and Central America caused much death and destruction and led to growing anti-American feelings in the region. (*See also* **Imperialism; United States–Latin American Relations.**)

War of the Mascates

The War of the Mascates was a conflict between native Brazilian planters and Portuguese immigrant merchants that took place between 1709 and 1711. It reflected tensions and resentments between landowning planters and merchants that continued into the 1800s.

In the early 1700s, Portuguese immigrants flooded the interior of BRAZIL, triggering anti-Portuguese feelings in several parts of the colony. One such place was the northeastern state of PERNAMBUCO, where bitter feelings existed between planters who controlled the political life in the capital of Olinda and merchants who lived in the port town of Recife.

The planters referred to the merchants as *mascates,* or peddlers, and considered them their social inferiors. They also blamed the merchants for their financial problems and debts. The merchants and their allies, on the other hand, resented the aristocratic attitude of the planters and their opposition to the incorporation of Recife as an independent town.

These resentments erupted in a series of clashes between the two groups beginning in 1709. The War of the Mascates caused two colonial governors to flee the region. It also led to a long but ineffective siege* of Recife, an uprising by Recife's military forces, a call for regional independence, and severe repression. Although few people were killed in the conflict, the disturbances produced long-lasting antagonisms that came to the surface again in the early 1800s. (*See also* **Class Structure, Colonial and Modern.**)

° **siege** prolonged effort by armed troops to force the surrender of a town or fort by surrounding it and cutting it off from aid

The War of the Pacific was a conflict arising from a long-standing border dispute that pitted CHILE against BOLIVIA and PERU. The war, which began in 1879 and lasted until 1884, resulted in an eventual victory for Chile, which increased in both size and power.

Prelude to War. For years Bolivia and Chile had both claimed portions of the Atacama Desert, a region along the Pacific coast that was rich

197

War of the Pacific

° **nitrate** mineral used in making gunpowder and fertilizer

in mineral resources, such as nitrates*. In 1874, the two countries settled the issue when Chile agreed to give up its claims to the southern portion of the desert in return for Bolivia's promise not to increase taxes on any Chilean company operating in that territory.

The agreement held until late 1878, when Bolivian dictator Hilarión Daza raised the export tax on a Chilean mining company operating in the Atacama. Chile, arguing that Bolivia had broken the 1874 treaty, re-occupied the area it had once claimed. In response, Bolivia declared war on Chile.

Chile did nothing at first. In April 1879, however, Chileans learned that Peru had signed a secret alliance with Bolivia, promising to provide aid if the country went to war with Chile. When Peru acknowledged the treaty and stated that it would honor its promise, Chile declared war on both nations.

Chile's declaration of war seemed foolhardy because its troops were outnumbered two to one by the combined Peruvian and Bolivian forces. Moreover, Peru had a larger naval fleet than Chile. In truth, however, none of the three nations was well prepared for war. Each lacked skilled officers, sufficient weapons, and adequate communication and transportation systems.

Control of the Seas.
The initial actions of the war involved the nations' naval forces. Chile established a blockade* of the Peruvian port of Iquique, believing that this would force the Peruvian fleet to attack. Instead, the Peruvians harassed Chilean merchant ships.

When the Chilean navy sailed north to attack the Peruvian port of Callao, they discovered that the Peruvian navy had gone south to attack

° **blockade** closing off of a port to prevent ships from entering or leaving, thus crippling trade

A Chilean victory in the War of the Pacific seemed unlikely at first because the country's troops were outnumbered by the combined Peruvian and Bolivian forces. Yet Chile was surprisingly successful in that conflict, growing both in power and in size by the war's end. This photograph shows Chilean officers aboard a warship.

War of the Pacific

Chilean naval ships blockading the port of Iquique. During the sea battle, the Peruvians sank the Chilean ship *Esmeralda*. But in the process, one of their armored ships, the *Independencia,* ran aground. The loss of this important ship altered the balance of military power and the course of the war.

The Peruvians continued to attack Chile's coast. The Chileans did little at first but then launched an offensive. In 1879, Chile's two armored ships, the *Blanco Encalada* and the *Cochrane,* won an important victory over the Peruvians, captured their only remaining armored vessel—the *Huascar*—and gained control of the sea-lanes along the Pacific coast.

Fighting Moves to Land.
Chile now had to decide whether to launch a massive attack into the heartland of Peru or just pursue scattered fighting along the edges of their enemies' territory. They decided on the second course of action. In October 1879, Chilean troops attacked enemy fortifications along the coast in the hope of severing military supply lines to the interior. Meanwhile, Peru and Bolivia amassed troops in order to drive the Chileans back to the sea.

The combined Bolivian-Peruvian force launched its attack in November 1879. The Chileans withstood the offensive and forced the enemy to flee into the interior. The Chileans then continued to chip away at enemy territory, gaining control of several cities and provinces. By December 1880, the Chilean army was ready to attack LIMA, the capital of Peru.

The Chileans launched their assault against the Peruvian capital on January 13, 1881. The Peruvians mounted a strong defense, but the Chilean forces proved unstoppable. When an attempt to negotiate the surrender of the Lima failed, the Chileans resumed the attack and easily defeated the remaining defenders. By January 17, the Chileans had conquered Lima.

The War Drags On.
Peace did not follow immediately after the fall of Lima. The Peruvian government refused to cede* other territory to Chile, and remnants of the Peruvian army continued to resist. Faced with the possibility of a lengthy, drawn out war, the Chileans launched expeditions to eliminate further resistance. Unfortunately, the struggle dragged on, consuming increasing amounts of money and lives.

Finally, in 1883, the Chilean army won a decisive victory over the Peruvian resistance fighters. As a result of this victory, Peru agreed to sign the Treaty of Ancón, which ended the war. The treaty ceded the province of Tarapacá to Chile and allowed Chile to occupy Tacna and Arica (the southernmost provinces of Peru) for ten years. When faced with the possibility of invasion, Bolivia accepted an armistice* and gave the Atacama and its outlet to the sea to Chile.

As a result of the war, Chile gained control of valuable nitrates and other mineral resources. It also had increased its size and become the most powerful nation on the Pacific coast of South America. (*See also* **Boundary Disputes; Mining; Nitrate Industry.**)

An Unsettled Question Is Settled

The Treaty of Ancón, which ended the War of the Pacific, gave Chile control of the provinces of Tacna and Arica for ten years. After that, the people of the provinces would decide their future by a vote. However, Chile and Peru could not agree on the terms of this vote, or plebescite, for many years. The dispute over the two provinces became known as the Question of the Pacific. The two sides finally reached an agreement in 1929 with help from the United States. Both agreed that Chile would keep Arica and Peru would regain control of Tacna.

---

* **cede** to yield or surrender, usually by treaty

* **armistice** temporary suspension of fighting by an agreement between the opponents

War of the Peru-Bolivia Confederation

War of the Peru-Bolivia Confederation

* **confederation** group of states joined together for a purpose; an alliance
* **tariff** tax on imported or exported goods
* **diplomat** person authorized by his or her country to conduct international relations

Between 1836 and 1839, CHILE and the newly formed confederation* of PERU and BOLIVIA were engaged in a military struggle known as the War of the Peru-Bolivia Confederation. In 1836, Bolivian leader Andrés de SANTA CRUZ formed a political union with Peru, creating an alliance that was feared by all other South American nations. Chile was especially wary of the confederation because of its strained economic relations with the two countries. Soon after the confederation was formed, Santa Cruz overturned a treaty that had given Chile preferential treatment on tariffs* and imposed new taxes on goods entering Peru through the Chilean port of VALPARAÍSO. Angered by these moves, Chilean leader Diego PORTALES PALAZUELOS ordered his fleet to attack the Peruvian port of Callao, where it seized three Peruvian vessels.

Santa Cruz responded by arresting a Chilean diplomat* but released him almost immediately with an apology. Portales then demanded that Santa Cruz repay the money that Chile had lent to Peru and dissolve the confederation. Santa Cruz refused, and Portales declared war on Bolivia. Chile fared poorly at first. Santa Cruz offered peace and repayment of its debt in exchange for the return of the three ships that Chile had captured and recognition of the confederation. The Chilean government rejected the offer and sent more troops to fight the confederation. In 1839, Chilean forces led by Manuel Bulnes defeated the confederate forces in two decisive battles. Santa Cruz fled and the confederation collapsed, leaving Chile in control of the Pacific coast.

War of the Thousand Days

* **liberal** person who supports greater participation in government for individuals; one who is not bound by political and social traditions
* **conservative** one who is opposed to sudden change, especially in existing political and social institutions
* **guerrilla** referring to a group that uses surprise raids to obstruct or harass an enemy or overthrow a government
* **amnesty** official pardon granted to individuals for past offenses against the government

The War of the Thousand Days occurred in COLOMBIA between 1899 and 1902. A civil war between the country's liberals* and conservatives*, it resulted in the deaths of as many as 100,000 people. In late 1899, the liberals in northeastern Colombia revolted against the conservative government, and the rebellion spread to the rest of the country. Although the liberals won some early victories, the conservatives held the initiative throughout the war. In 1900, government forces defeated the liberals at Palonegro in the largest battle in modern South American history. Over the next two years, the focus shifted to central Colombia, and conventional warfare gave way to guerrilla* warfare. By late 1902, both sides were exhausted, and the war had caused great destruction and resulted in many deaths. The liberals offered a cease-fire in return for amnesty* and political reforms. Shortly after the war, Panama, which had been part of Colombia, separated from the union.

War of the Triple Alliance

The War of the Triple Alliance was a conflict between PARAGUAY and the united forces of ARGENTINA, BRAZIL, and URUGUAY. The causes of the war are still disputed, but most historians believe that it resulted from the efforts of the countries involved to maintain political stability and a balance of power in the region. In the end, the war had a significant impact on those countries, especially Paraguay.

War of the Triple Alliance

Start of the War. The war erupted in 1864, when Brazil invaded Uruguay to ensure that the Colorados (a pro-Brazilian political party) would gain power in that country. Because Paraguay's dictator Francisco Solano López had pledged to defend Uruguay, he closed the Paraguay River to Brazilian ships and seized a Brazilian steamship. He also attacked the Brazilian provinces of Mato Grosso and Rio Grande do Sul. During these attacks on Brazil, Paraguayan troops crossed Argentine territory without permission. This greatly angered Argentina's government. In 1865, Brazil, Argentina, and the newly elected, pro-Brazilian government of Uruguay declared war on Paraguay.

Paraguay had some early victories in the war, but its successes were short-lived. Early in the war, the Brazilian navy severely damaged the Paraguayan fleet in a battle on the Paraná River. At the same time, the invading Paraguayan armies were defeated, and within the next six months, Paraguay's offensive was halted. By 1866, allied ships had blockaded Paraguay, and allied troops had invaded the country. However, Paraguay's troops fought well during the battles of Tuyutí, and the allied forces made little progress during the next 18 months.

Sacrifice at Acosta Ñu

One of the most tragic episodes of the War of the Triple Alliance was the battle of Acosta Ñu in August 1869. The Paraguayan force consisted of 4,500 teenage boys, women, and old men who were ordered to slow down an advancing Brazilian army of 20,000 men. The Paraguayans reportedly wore false beards to make their opponents think they were facing a veteran force. The Paraguayans put up a fierce and bloody resistance, but they were overwhelmed by the Brazilian cavalry. Although the battle failed to stop the Brazilians, it has since become an important symbol of the courage and character of the Paraguayan people.

The Defeat of Paraguay. In January 1868, Brazilian General Luis Alves de LIMA E SILVA took command of the allied forces. The following month, a Brazilian warship sailed up the Paraguay River, defeated the fortified town of Humaitá, and bombarded the Paraguayan capital of Asunción. The fall of Humaitá left Paraguay unable to defend Asunción, so López moved the capital to the town of Piribebuy. Meanwhile, Paraguay lost a series of battles, and the allies seized Asunción. By 1869, allied forces had conquered the new capital at Piribebuy and installed a provisional (temporary) government in Asunción. López continued to fight until 1870, when he was killed by the Brazilian cavalry at Cerro Corá in northeastern Paraguay.

In 1870, the four nations signed a treaty ending the war. The treaty promised elections within three months and guaranteed that the allies would not interfere in Paraguayan politics. The treaty also guaranteed unrestricted use of the Paraguay and Paraná rivers. The last Brazilian troops left Paraguay in 1876, but Argentina continued to oversee a portion of Paraguayan territory until 1878. In that year, United States president Rutherford B. Hayes helped negotiate a settlement that returned control of the territory to Paraguay.

Results of the War. Paraguay paid a high price for its defeat. The war destroyed 50 years of economic development and ended social policies that had helped the poor. In addition, Paraguay lost between 8.7 and 18.5 percent of its population, most of its industry, and nearly 18,000 square miles of valuable territory. Paraguay became economically dependent on Brazil and Argentina and entered a period of political turmoil that brought in 32 presidents between 1870 and 1932.

In Brazil, the war created a new respect for the professional military officers, most of whom came from Brazil's growing middle class. It also delayed consideration of the abolition of slavery. Argentina's ranchers,

Wars of Independence

farmers, and merchants benefited from the Brazilian military's purchases of food and supplies. Argentine President Bartolomé MITRE used the war as an excuse to tighten his control over the interior of his country and increase the power of the central government. In Uruguay, the Colorados stayed in power for the next 96 years.

Wars of Independence

* **Creole** person of European ancestry born in the Americas

By the late 1700s, there were increased complaints in Spanish America against Spanish rule. Colonists expressed their displeasure with restrictions that prohibited them from trading with countries other than Spain. Creoles* resented the fact that the Spanish-born elite held nearly all the top posts in the colonial government. Despite these grievances, however, colonists in Spanish America expressed little interest in outright independence from Spain before the 1800s. In fact, there was generally widespread support for the Spanish monarchy. The situation began to change when France invaded Spain and took control of the Spanish crown in 1808.

Rise of Revolutionary Activity. The political crisis in Spain led to the formation of juntas* throughout the colonies and to struggles for power between *peninsulares** and Creoles. Many of these juntas were headed by Creoles determined to assume greater control over colonial affairs.

* **junta** small group of people who run a government, usually after seizing power by force
* ***peninsular*** Spanish-born Latin American

All the newly formed juntas enacted economic and political reforms aimed at resolving grievances against Spain. Some of the more radical* leaders began to promote the idea of independence. The first Spanish colony to actually declare its separation from Spain was VENEZUELA in 1811.

* **radical** favoring extreme changes or reforms

Not everyone welcomed the creation of revolutionary juntas and the changes they enacted. Loyalist groups, often led by *peninsulares*, resisted any change in the relationship between Spain and the colonies. Some Creoles also distrusted change and feared the possibility of increased power in the hands of Indians and mestizos*. Despite resistence from some colonists, however, the movement toward independence continued to gain strength.

* **mestizo** person of mixed European and Indian ancestry

See color plate 5, vol. 4.

Independence Struggle in South America. The wars that liberated the South American colonies from Spanish rule arose from opposite ends of the continent. The war in the north was led by Simón BOLÍVAR, while the campaign in the south was headed by José de SAN MARTÍN.

The war in the north began in Venezuela in 1812, when Spanish forces launched an offensive against the patriots*. Early in the struggle, Spanish forces crushed the patriots and forced Bolívar into exile. He returned in 1813 and waged a ferocious campaign, which he called a "war to the death." The royalists* fought back equally hard, however, and by the end of 1814, they had chased Bolívar and other patriot leaders into exile once again.

* **patriot** one who favored independence of the colonies in the Americas
* **royalist** supporter of the king or queen, especially in times of civil war or rebellion

Meanwhile, in the southern part of South America, revolutionaries were achieving greater success. In 1816, ARGENTINA formally declared its

Wars of Independence

independence from Spain. Early the next year, a patriot army led by Argentina's José de San Martín crossed the Andes into CHILE, defeated the royalist forces there, and set up a revolutionary government headed by Bernardo O'HIGGINS.

With most of Argentina and Chile in patriot hands, San Martín began preparing for an expedition northward to PERU. After gaining a foothold on the Peruvian coast in 1820, San Martín and his troops marched to LIMA and occupied the capital. He proclaimed Peruvian independence in 1821.

In the north, Bolívar had returned to Venezuela and created patriot strongholds in several regions. He achieved his greatest military triumph in 1819, when his troops marched into the Viceroyalty* of NEW GRANADA and won a crucial victory in the battle of BOYACÁ. Loyalist resistance quickly collapsed in the central core of that colony.

It took three more years to expel royalists from all outlying areas of New Granada. Meanwhile, in 1821, Bolívar and other patriots liberated the remaining areas of Venezuela. Later that same year, they took control of Panama, and in May 1822, patriot forces freed ECUADOR from Spanish rule. In 1822, Bolívar and San Martín met in Ecuador and discussed how to liberate the rest of South America. After this meeting, Bolívar mounted a campaign in Peru that eventually resulted in victory at the battle of Ayacucho on December 9, 1824. Royalist resistance collapsed soon after this battle. The last Spanish fortress in South America, at the Peruvian port of Callao, surrendered to patriot armies in January 1826.

The wars of independence in South America had uneven effects. Some areas were very hard hit, while others went almost untouched. Agriculture, mining, and trade were disrupted in many regions. Overall, the conflict left the newly independent governments with the burden of rebuilding their economies and finding ways to govern effectively.

Mexico, Central America, and the Caribbean.

The first call for independence in Mexico came in 1810, when a Catholic priest, Miguel HIDALGO Y COSTILLA, and a military leader, Ignacio Allende, led an uprising of mestizos and Indians against the colonists. The uprising shocked the ruling classes, especially when the rebels attacked towns in central Mexico.

Hidalgo was captured and executed in 1811, but the movement he started outlived him. The cause was taken up by others, principally another priest named José María MORELOS Y PAVÓN, who was also captured and executed, in 1815. Guerrilla* warfare erupted periodically between 1812 and 1820. Finally, leading Creoles turned against Spanish rule and supported independence. In 1821, they reached an agreement with General Agustín de ITURBIDE, a former royalist commander, that resulted in Mexico's independence.

In CENTRAL AMERICA, several provinces sought to gain independence between 1811 and 1814, but Spanish authorities put down all uprisings. The events in Mexico changed the situation in Central America. News of Mexican independence in 1821 spread rapidly throughout the region, and the Kingdom of GUATEMALA (which included present-day

---

See color plate 5, vol. 3.

* **viceroyalty** region governed by a viceroy, a royally appointed official

The Last Battle

The battle of Ayacucho in 1824 was the final battle in the war to liberate the South American colonies from Spanish rule. The question of independence had divided many colonists, and victory was by no means assured. Although the revolutionaries were outnumbered, they quickly defeated the Spanish forces, killing about 1,400 loyalist soldiers. As a result of this defeat, Spanish forces were forced to withdraw from Peru and Bolivia. Two years later, the last Spanish forces departed South America from the port of Callao near Lima, Peru.

* **guerrilla** referring to a group that uses surprise raids to obstruct or harass an enemy or overthrow a government

Wars of Independence

* **annex** a territory to an existing state

* **federation** political union of separate states with a central government

Guatemala, EL SALVADOR, HONDURAS, NICARAGUA, COSTA RICA, and parts of southern Mexico) declared independence. The following year Agustín de Iturbide proclaimed himself emperor of Mexico and annexed* all of Central America except Panama. When Iturbide was overthrown in 1823, the Central American states declared their independence and formed the United Provinces of Central America. This federation* held together until 1838, when internal conflicts led to the creation of several independent states.

In the CARIBBEAN, HAITI, on the island of Hispaniola, was the first Latin American colony to gain its independence. In 1791, African slaves began to revolt against their French rulers. British and Spanish troops intervened in the struggle but then withdrew. In 1801, TOUSSAINT L'OUVERTURE proclaimed himself governor-general for life. The following year, when France attempted to regain control of the colony, Toussaint was captured and taken to France, where he died in prison. Haitian rebels continued their struggle for freedom from France, and by 1804, Haiti had won its independence. Forty years later, the DOMINICAN REPUBLIC

In 1808, Spain was invaded and conquered by France. As a result, colonists in Spanish America felt emboldened to seek independence. However, Spain was not the only colonial power overthrown in Latin America during the 1800s. Haiti won its independence from France in 1804, and Brazil declared its independence from Portugal in 1822.

Independence in Latin America

Nation	Year
Haiti	1804
Venezuela	1811
Paraguay	1813
Argentina	1816
Chile	1818
Colombia	1819
Dominican Republic	1821
Mexico	1821
Peru	1821
Brazil	1822
Bolivia	1825
Uruguay	1828
Ecuador	1830
Costa Rica	1838
Honduras	1838
Guatemala	1847
Nicaragua	1854
El Salvador	1856
Cuba	1898
Panama (from Colombia)	1903

(also on the island of Hispaniola) gained its independence. CUBA revolted twice—once in 1868 and again in 1895. The second rebellion led to the SPANISH AMERICAN WAR, which pitted the United States against Spain. The United States defeated Spain, enabling Cuba to become a republic in 1902. Spain was forced to cede* its colony of Puerto Rico to the United States. Most of the smaller Caribbean islands remained under British, Dutch, or French rule until the mid-1900s, when many underwent peaceful transfers of power.

* **cede** to yield or surrender, usually by treaty

Portuguese Brazil. Brazil gained its independence with little of the violence that marked the revolutionary struggles in the rest of Latin America. When Napoleon invaded Portugal in 1807, Prince JOÃO VI fled to Brazil and established his 15,000-member court in RIO DE JANEIRO. For more than a decade, the city served as the capital of the Portuguese empire. When João VI returned to Portugal in 1821, his son, Dom Pedro, remained to rule Brazil. Realizing that the region could not return to colonial status, Pedro proclaimed independence in 1822 and became emperor PEDRO I OF BRAZIL. (*See also* **Central America, United Provinces of; Mexican War of Independence.**)

Watermelon Riot

The Watermelon Riot was an anti-American riot that erupted in the city of Colón in present-day PANAMA in 1856. At the time, Panama was part of the nation of NEW GRANADA. In 1846, New Granada granted the United States permission to cross Panama. In return, the United States promised to support the neutrality of the Isthmus* of Panama and maintain uninterrupted transit across it. After the discovery of gold in California in 1849, United States investors built a railroad across Panama and the amount of traffic through the isthmus increased.

* **isthmus** narrow strip of land connecting two larger landmasses

The riot was triggered in the spring of 1856, when a United States citizen refused to pay a street vendor for a slice of watermelon. The argument led to gunfire, and an angry crowd of about 600 Panamanians began attacking United States citizens. The riot resulted in the deaths of 18 North Americans and 3 Panamanians. In response, the United States stationed warships off the coast of Panama. Later that year, 160 U.S. Marines landed at Colón to protect North Americans and preserve order. A commission investigating the incident awarded United States citizens $160,000 in damages for losses resulting from the riot. (*See also* **United States–Latin American Relations.**)

Since World War II, several Latin American nations have developed weapons industries to produce arms for their own countries and to export arms to buyers overseas. The region's leading producers of arms are Argentina, Brazil, and Chile, each of which built up its weapons industry while under military rule. Today these nations produce weapons ranging from handguns and rifles to tanks, combat aircraft, missiles, and submarines.

West Indies

The development of weapons industries in the region resulted from several factors, including the refusal of the United States to sell weapons to some Latin American countries, a desire to be free from dependence on foreigners for arms, and a natural expansion into a profitable industry. Argentina began its arms industry during World War II as a way to reduce its dependence on imported arms. Brazil's industry developed in the late 1970s as a result of disputes with the United States, its own growing industrial base, and an increased demand for weapons by other countries. Chile developed its weapons industry after the United States refused to sell arms to its leader, General Augusto Pinochet, who ruled the country from 1973 to 1990.

The Latin American weapons industry reached its peak during the early 1980s, when the region controlled about 10 percent of the world's arms market. The Middle East was the region's principal buyer, with Iraq alone spending more than $1 billion on Brazilian arms in 1985. In the late 1980s, the industry declined after the cold war ended, Iran and Iraq stopped fighting, and several military dictators were replaced by elected leaders who cut military spending.

West Indies

See *Caribbean Antilles*.

West Indies Federation

See *British West Indies*.

Windward Islands

See *Caribbean Antilles*.

Wine Industry

* **conquistador** Spanish explorer and conqueror
* **secular** nonreligious; connected with everyday life
* **sanctify** to make sacred or holy
* **encomendero** holder of a royal grant that enabled an individual to control the labor of and to collect payment from an Indian community

Wine is an important part of Spanish culture that was brought to Latin America by the early Spanish conquistadors* and settlers. Not only was wine very popular among the wealthy secular* population, but it was also used to sanctify* various religious rituals in the Catholic Church. Vineyards and wineries eventually appeared throughout the region, and today every country in Latin America produces wine.

The Colonial Wine Industry.
Grape cultivation and wine making followed the path of conquest in Latin America. After Hernán CORTÉS defeated the Aztecs in 1521, he ordered his *encomenderos** to plant 1,000 grapevines for every 100 Indians under their care, each year for five years. Wine production in Mexico was centered north of Mexico City, and the first commercial winery in the area began operation around 1623. Grapevines were first brought to missions* in California in 1779,

° **mission** settlement started by Catholic priests whose purpose was to convert local people to Christianity

° **capital** money invested to start a business or industry

° **viticulture** the cultivation of grapes, especially for making wine

and within 50 years, Mission San Gabriel in California was producing 400 to 600 barrels of wine annually.

During the 1540s, Spanish settlers brought grapevines to Peru. In 1548, a member of Pedro de Valdivia's expedition to Chile introduced grapevines to the region, and seven years later the first wine was produced in the country. Grapevines were carried across the Andes into Argentina before 1570, and Catholic missionaries brought grapevines to the more remote regions of South America. On the east coast of South America, the earliest grapevines arrived in Brazil in 1532. By the mid-1500s, vineyards had been established in Paraguay, and in the early 1600s, grape cultivation was introduced into the territory of Rio Grande do Sul (present-day Brazil).

Colonial wine making was so successful that in 1595 Spanish wine makers convinced King PHILIP II to impose limits on its production in the Americas. By the mid-1600s, the establishment of new vineyards was prohibited and existing wine production was taxed. Although these efforts did not significantly hurt wine production in the Americas, other factors did. These factors included small regional markets for wine, limited capital*, outdated technology, and deterioration in the quality of grapevines. When independence from Spain brought an end to colonial trade restrictions, European wines flooded the Latin American market.

In the 1930s, the Chilean government, influenced by prohibitionists, began placing restrictions on wine production. It was not until 1974 that the government stopped regulating the production of wine in Chile. Today Chile is a leading exporter of wine. This photograph shows a vineyard worker manually directing the flow of water to the plants.

Postcolonial Wine Making. By the mid-1800s, local entrepreneurs supplying new capital, new technology, and new varieties of grapevines enabled wine making in the Americas to become a large commercial enterprise. This occurred first in California during the 1830s, but the wine industries in Argentina and Chile soon began to show a profit as well. Winegrowers persuaded their national governments to help modernize their wineries and to bring in new varieties of grapes and the technical expertise to run viticulture* schools. During the 1900s, both Chile and Argentina provided significant government aid to their wine industries.

Since World War II, Latin America's wine industry has grown dramatically. Between 1952 and the mid-1980s, Chile's wine production doubled to 160 million gallons per year. By 1993, Argentina had planted some 500,000 acres of grapevines and is now the world's fourth-largest wine producer. Wines from both countries have earned international recognition for their quality. Mexico and Brazil have also developed successful wine industries, and wine is now popular among all classes in Latin America. (*See also* **Food and Drink**.)

Women

Throughout history, women in Latin America, as elsewhere, usually have had fewer rights and lower social status than men. Class, race, ethnicity, age, and marital status have also been factors in what is expected of women in Latin American society. Despite these limitations, women have made great contributions to the region's culture and society. Today the status of all Latin American women is moving toward equality with men.

Women

Pre-Columbian, Colonial, and Independent Latin America

Before the arrival of Europeans, women played a variety of roles in Indian societies. They were political leaders, priestesses, healers, midwives, farmers, prostitutes, and slaves. In the indigenous* societies that had more contact with Europeans, women's participation in certain activities, such as religion and politics, decreased sharply. This reflected the traditional Iberian* view that such affairs were the proper concern of men. In many communities that had less connection to colonial society, women continued to enjoy an active role in public life.

Colonial Women's Roles.
The accepted roles for women in colonial society were largely defined by the institutions of family, state, and church. Marriage or a religious life as a nun were the only respectable choices for colonial Creole* women. However, these women were often deeply involved in family decisions and business matters. Many upper-class women ran the family estate and tended to the family when the men in the household were too busy, away, or had died. Among the poorer classes, women often contributed as much labor and income to support their families as did men.

The role of either wife or nun was largely applied to European, Creole, and mestizo* women. Female African slaves and their descendants typically fell outside of the concern of larger colonial society. In the Caribbean, female slaves worked alongside men on PLANTATIONS, planting and harvesting sugar, cotton, tobacco, and coffee. In Brazil, many female slaves worked in cities as household servants, street vendors, wet nurses, and prostitutes. African women also played an active role in the religious life of their communities, keeping alive traditional religious and cultural practices. Many of the leaders of AFRICAN–LATIN AMERICAN RELIGIONS, such as CANDOMBLÉ and VOODOO, were female. Their activities deeply influenced the formation of national cultures in Brazil, Colombia, Venezuela, and the Caribbean.

Women and Independence.
Women patriots were vital to the success of independence movements throughout Latin America. Stories of their deeds were used by male politicians to inspire patriotism and by women to argue for full citizenship. Many of the newly independent governments were strongly against church involvement in society and politics. This growing secular* viewpoint led to new ideas about acceptable female roles. These ideas involved attitudes about women working outside the home and about their involvement in politics.

From the 1890s to the 1920s, the newly independent nations struggled to define themselves. Violent conflicts often arose between wealthy conservatives*, who wished to maintain their power, and revolutionaries, who championed the rights of the common people. Women distinguished themselves in numerous ways during these struggles. Women soldiers, known as *mambisas* fought Spanish troops during the long guerrilla* wars in Cuba in the late 1800s. Women

---

* **indigenous** referring to the original inhabitants of a region

* **Iberian** from or related to Spain and Portugal, the countries that occupy Europe's Iberian Peninsula

* **Creole** person of European ancestry born in the Americas

* **mestizo** person of mixed European and Indian ancestry

* **secular** nonreligious; connected with everyday life

* **conservative** one who is opposed to sudden change, especially in existing political and social institutions

* **guerrilla** referring to a group that uses surprise raids to obstruct or harass an enemy or overthrow a government

schoolteachers and factory workers influenced the political movement that led to the MEXICAN REVOLUTION of 1910, while female soldiers known as *soldaderas* fought beside their men. However, not all women supported revolution and the rights of the poor. Many of those belonging to the wealthy ruling classes were just as passionate as men in their support of the established order.

The Early 1900s: Change and Continuity

The early 1900s was a period of great change for women in the areas of work and politics. There was an increase in the number of women in the so-called middle sector of the economy—the skilled factory workers, teachers, and government clerks as opposed to the women who labored as domestics, vendors, laundresses, and prostitutes. At the same time, most Latin American women still lived in the countryside and did not participate in this growth of the female workforce in the cities.

Remember: Consult the index at the end of this volume to find more information on many topics.

Women's Work and Working Women.

Those women who entered the middle sector of the economy received more pay, benefits, and job security than women in the informal sectors of the economy, such as domestic servants, laundresses, and agricultural laborers. Women from immigrant or peasant groups were the primary laborers in the textile and tobacco industries after 1900. Despite their dominance in these industries, they had great difficulty in improving their working conditions. Faced with hostility from their employers, indifference from their male coworkers, and the responsibilities of family life, these women had little time to organize unions.

By 1930, most women still lived in the countryside, unaffected by the appearance of urban women in new fields of work. Rural work remained varied. Women worked in mines; served as agricultural laborers in Peru; worked the sugar, rubber, and banana plantations in Brazil and the Caribbean; and served as domestic servants on ranches, estates, and plantations. In addition to these jobs, rural women had the primary responsibility for family work, such as cooking, cleaning, and child care.

Legal and Civil Changes.

Before 1900, the legal status of women was determined by their relationship to the male head of the household. Complex civil and religious laws regulated marriage, divorce, property ownership, and many other aspects of women's lives. Prior to 1929, no Latin American nation had granted women the right to vote. In most countries in the region, full citizenship was limited to men who owned property.

The long campaign for women's suffrage* had its first success in Ecuador in 1929. Less than a decade later, Brazil, Uruguay, and Cuba also passed laws giving the vote to women. Between 1945 and 1961, the remaining nations of the region allowed women to vote, but many still had requirements limiting the vote to Spanish speakers or those who could read and write. This effectively denied many rural women the vote.

* **suffrage** the right to vote

In Peru, Quechua-speaking Indian men and women were not allowed to vote until 1980.

Women in Modern Latin America

The success of the CUBAN REVOLUTION in 1959 influenced gender relations in Latin America. The ideals of the revolution, such as social equality, were embraced by some young women in the region. Women became active in revolutionary and guerilla movements. Haydée Tamara Bunke Bider, known as Tania, aided Ernesto "Che" GUEVARA's efforts to establish a revolutionary front in Bolivia. She died in 1967 while fighting against Bolivian soldiers and soon became a symbol of courage and freedom for a generation of Latin American women. Women were also active in the Nicaraguan Revolution of 1979 and in the Salvadoran rebel movement.

Political Activism. By the 1970s, the international women's movement had gained influence throughout Latin America, and more women were organizing to demand political and social change. In Cuba, women called for more child care centers and a nonsexist attitude toward child raising. As military dictatorships seized power in the nations of Brazil, Uruguay, Paraguay, Argentina, and Chile, women became active opponents of state-sponsored terrorism. Mass arrests, the disappearance of many young people, and the torture and killing of political opponents led many women to take up nonviolent forms of protest. The most famous of these women were probably *las madres,* a group of seven Argentine mothers whose loved ones had "disappeared" under the military government. In 1977, they staged a silent demonstration in the Plaza de Mayo, the historic central square in Buenos Aires. During the next four years, more than 6,000 other Argentines joined them to protest continued human rights violations by the military regime. When dictatorships in the area crumbled in the mid-1980s, women were successful in making issues such as health care, divorce, and domestic violence a priority for the emerging democratic governments of the region.

Social Change. Several trends in the 1990s indicated dramatic social change in the life of Latin American women. First, the number of women living in cities increased dramatically. No country in the region had more than 20 percent of women living in the countryside. Second, between 1970 and 1990, the number of middle-class women in the labor force increased by more than 80 percent everywhere in Latin America except the Caribbean. Increasing employment outside the home and greater educational opportunities also led to a drop in the birthrate. For example, in 1950, the average Mexican woman had six children in her lifetime; by 1990, the number was three or fewer. The growth of multinational corporations in the region brought more rural women into the workforce as did the MAQUILADORAS (manufacturing plants) on the United States–Mexico border. The tourism industry also hired many women, employing them as hotel clerks, tourist guides, maids,

Unexpected Activism

When Romy Medeiros da Fonseca graduated from law school, she had no idea she would become an activist in the women's rights movement in Brazil. In 1959, while attending a legal conference in Chile with her husband, Romy Medeiros gave an impromptu presentation on the legal status of women in her country. As she discussed the few rights Brazilian women had, she found a new focus for her life. Since that time, Medeiros has helped Brazilian women attain more freedoms. She created the National Day for Women and has helped women gain the right to divorce their spouses. Medeiros is currently serving as the president of the National Council of Brazilian Women.

and cooks. As more and more Latin American women become educated and economically independent, social norms and gender roles will continue to change.

Political Change. Several decades of political activism have resulted in impressive political gains by Latin American women. They have achieved greater rights in marriage and divorce, and more attention has been given to the problem of domestic violence. Since the mid-1980s, women have also been elected to political office in much greater numbers, following the 1979 election of Lidia Gueiler Tejada as president of Bolivia. Much of this is due to the highly visible role played by women protesting the military regimes of the 1970s and 1980s and to their participation in the civil wars that occurred in Central America during that same time. Several of the major parties competing in Mexican elections in the 1990s emphasized their commitment to women's issues. In Venezuela in 1988, 19 women were elected to the House of Deputies and 4 to the Senate. In 1991, Argentine women succeeded in passing a law requiring that one-third of all candidates in national elections be female. In 1990, Violeta Barrios de Chamorro was elected president of Nicaragua.

Modern Latin American women are more educated and active in politics, the economy, and society than ever before. However, political and economic instability and inequality remain a problem in the region, threatening the gains made in recent years. For women in Latin America, the key to holding on to their hard-won victories is healthy democratic government that not only respects the rights of all people but invites the participation of men and women alike in shaping society. (*See also* **Children; Family; Marriage and Divorce; Mestizo; Soldaderas.**)

Work

See *Labor and Labor Movements; Slavery.*

World Wars I and II

Although very few Latin American soldiers fought in either World War I or World War II, both conflicts had a significant impact on Latin America. Both wars interrupted the region's traditional trade relationships with Europe and increased Latin America's economic dependence on the United States. Before World War I, most of the foreign investment in Latin America had come from France and England. By the end of World War II, the United States had emerged as the region's dominant economic partner.

World War I. During the early 1900s, Germany became an important source of foreign capital* for many Latin American nations. At the same time, nations in the region had good relationships with the

* **capital** money invested to start a business or industry

World Wars I and II

United States despite its tendency toward interference in Latin America to promote its interests there. Thus, when the United States declared war on Germany in 1917, Brazil, Cuba, Costa Rica, Guatemala, Haiti, Honduras, Nicaragua, and Panama did so as well. Bolivia, the Dominican Republic, Ecuador, Peru, and Uruguay broke diplomatic relations with Germany. Although Argentina, Chile, and Mexico refused to take such steps, they nevertheless refrained from openly supporting Germany.

The war's most immediate impact on Latin America was the loss of trade with the warring nations in Europe. As a result, Latin American nations turned to the United States as well as to each other to make up for the loss. An increased demand for raw materials to support the war effort, such as nitrates* from Chile, helped some Latin American countries prosper during the conflict. For most of the region, however, the war resulted in economic hardship and an end to a prewar economic boom based on trade with and investment from Europe. In 1919, after the war had ended, 11 Latin American nations attended the multinational conference in Versailles, France. Ten of these nations signed the Treaty of Versailles and became charter members of the League of Nations.

* **nitrate** mineral used in making gunpowder and fertilizer

World War II. In the 1930s, the threat of war in Europe caused the United States to worry about the security of the Western Hemisphere. In 1936, the United States failed to persuade Latin American nations to support an economic embargo* against the warring European powers. Two years later, the United States failed to persuade Latin Americans to join a mutual defense pact that would include all the nations in the hemisphere. Most Latin American nations were more interested in making sure that the United States upheld its GOOD NEIGHBOR POLICY, which sought to reduce United States interference in Latin America.

* **embargo** official order prohibiting the movement of merchant ships in or out of certain ports or countries.

The first collective action by Latin America taken against the Axis powers (Germany, Japan, and Italy) was the 1939 Declaration of Panama. The declaration established a safety zone extending from 300 to 1,000 miles off the coasts of the Western Hemisphere nations, in which no warlike action would be tolerated. After Germany defeated France in 1940, the nations of the Americas met in Havana, Cuba, to declare the European colonies in the hemisphere off-limits to the Axis powers. They also declared that any act of aggression against one nation in the hemisphere would be considered an act of aggression against them all. It was agreed that Latin American armies would not participate in the fighting overseas. The Lend-Lease Act of 1941 provided $400 million in United States military assistance to Latin America. After Japan attacked Pearl Harbor on December 7, 1941, the nations of Central America, as well as Cuba, Haiti and the Dominican Republic, declared war on the Axis powers.

Although the fighting did not directly affect much of Latin America, German submarines patrolling the Caribbean Sea sank ships belonging to the Allied forces (which included the United Kingdom and the United States). Several Latin American nations deported German, Japanese, and Italian nationals to their homelands or to camps in the United States. Latin America's economic losses during this war were

Fighting for Freedom at Home

One important consequence of World War II in Latin America was the emergence of hostile feelings toward dictators in the region. At the time, dictators who were supported by either the United States government or United States business interests ruled many Latin American nations. Allied propaganda stressed that the war was being fought to eliminate tyranny in Asia and Europe. Many Latin Americans questioned why they should suffer under tyranny while others around the world were being liberated. As a result, socialist, Communist, and anti-United States governments gained influence throughout the region after the war ended.

great. The lack of access to European markets and the decreased demand for products—such as coffee, sugar, and tropical fruit—caused severe hardship in the Caribbean and Central America. The need for Bolivian tin, Chilean copper, and Venezuelan petroleum did bring some prosperity to those countries. Because Europe was in ruins when the war ended in 1945, Latin America did not resume its trade with European nations, and United States economic influence in the region increased, particularly in Brazil and Mexico, where the United States built steel mills.

As the end of the war approached, the United States warned Latin American nations that only those who had declared war on the Axis powers would be eligible for membership in the newly formed UNITED NATIONS. This threat caused all the remaining South American nations except Argentina to declare war. In response to Argentina's refusal, the United States froze its gold stocks, restricted its shipping, and refused to recognize the rule of Argentine president Edelmiro Farrell. At a meeting in Mexico City in early 1945, the nations of the hemisphere agreed to a provision stating that under the MONROE DOCTRINE, American republics would be protected against any aggression, even from other countries within the hemisphere. Argentina, satisfied that it would not be punished for its failure to support the Allied cause earlier, finally declared war on the Axis powers in March 1945. (*See also* **Fascism; Germans in Latin America; United States–Latin American Relations; Zimmerman Telegram.**)

Xochimilco

See *Mexico.*

Yanaconas

* **viceroy** one who governs a country or province as a monarch's representative; royally appointed official

* **census** an official count of the population

The term *yanaconas* was used by the Spanish during the colonial era to refer to INDIANS who were separated from their native communities. The term is believed to come from the Inca word *yana,* meaning "a personal servant whose special duties separate him or her from other members of the Indian community." The Spanish first used the word *yanaconas* to refer to Indian servants.

In the 1570s, the viceroy* of Peru, Francisco de TOLEDO Y FIGUEROA, reorganized the colony's Indian communities and made a distinction between *yanaconas de españoles* (servants of Spaniards) and *yanaconas del rey* (servants of the king). Servants of Spaniards owed loyalty to private employers, while servants of the king owed allegiance to the Spanish crown. Toledo conducted a census* of the *yanacona* population, limiting the number of Indians who could claim *yanacona* status. Many Indians sought this status because *yanaconas* paid fewer taxes and were protected from the *mita,* the state's forced labor system. Employers tried to get Indians licensed as *yanaconas* because it gave them total control over the *yanaconas'* labor.

The increasing number of Indians with *yanacona* status weakened the state's labor system. By the 1700s, Indians living apart from their

Yanomami

native communities outnumbered Indians living in those communities. Wealthy Spaniards blocked the efforts of viceroys to force *yanaconas* into the state labor system. When Spanish rule ended in Latin America in the 1800s, the legal definition and regulations regarding *yanaconas* changed, but the word was still applied to Indian laborers. (*See also* **Slavery**.)

Yanomami

* **indigenous** referring to the original inhabitants of a region

* **artifact** in archaeology, a human-made object such as a tool, household utensil, or work of art

The Yanomami are the largest surviving indigenous* group in the South American RAIN FOREST whose way of life has remained relatively unchanged since before the arrival of Europeans. The word *Yanomami* (also written *Yanoama* or *Yanomamö*) means "human being." The Yanomami are skilled farmers who live in communal settlements. Their language and cultural traits separate them from surrounding Indian groups, such as those who speak a CARIB or Arawak language. Although the Yanomami live in the Guiana Highlands on the border between Venezuela and Brazil, very few have adopted the culture of either country.

The Yanomami were first seen by outsiders during the colonial period, when Spanish and Portuguese explorers encountered a few small groups in remote areas of the rain forest. Because of the humid environment in the rain forest, very few Yanomami artifacts* survive for long, and evidence of the tribe's past is extremely rare. Nevertheless, it is likely that the people known today as the Yanomami are the descendants of the people who have been referred to as Waika, Shamatari, Shirishana, or Guajaribo since the 1700s. Although previously characterized as fierce and warlike, recent studies note their gentle, undemanding, cooperative way of life.

Today about 20,000 Yanomami live in an area of some 30,000 square miles (about the size of the state of South Carolina). Since the 1980s, they have suffered from dangerous diseases, primarily malaria, and from intrusions by Brazilian gold prospectors and tin miners. In 1991 and 1992, Brazil and Venezuela each set aside about 22 million acres of Yanomami territory as legally protected areas. (*See also* **Indians**.)

Yerba Maté

See *Food and Drink*.

Yrigoyen, Hipólito

1852–1933
President of Argentina

Hipólito Yrigoyen was one of Argentina's most popular presidents. As leader of the Radical Party, he worked for free elections and the secret ballot in ARGENTINA. During his presidency, Yrigoyen regulated labor conditions and kept his country out of World War I. His second term in office ended when he was overthrown by a military coup*.

The illegitimate son of a blacksmith, Yrigoyen began his public career in 1872 as superintendent of police in a district of Buenos Aires.

* **coup** sudden, often violent overthrow of a ruler or government

However, he lost the job when he was accused of illegally controlling elections. Later he helped establish the short-lived Republican Party that supported the rights of provinces and attacked corrupt politicians. In 1879, Yrigoyen was elected to Congress. One year later, he was appointed to Argentina's National Council for Education, where he served a two-year term before retiring from public service.

In 1890, Yrigoyen became politically active again when he took part in an armed uprising that toppled the Argentine government. He later gained control of the Radical Party, which had taken part in the coup. Although he rarely made public speeches, Yrigoyen gained an enthusiastic following among the people of Argentina, especially the middle class. A skilled negotiator, he preferred to work behind the scenes. In 1912, he helped enact a law that gave the vote to all adult males and provided for a secret ballot. Four years later, Yrigoyen was elected president.

Yrigoyen's presidency was marked by contradictions. Although he claimed to support honest politics, he often used his power to interfere with local elections. While supporting organized labor, he also used force against strikers who demanded more than he was willing to give them. Instead of establishing political programs to benefit his supporters, he rewarded them with free bread, meat, milk, and seed. The focus of the Radical Party thus became Yrigoyen himself, with patronage* and personal loyalty to the president becoming more important than open political participation.

* **patronage** act of guarding, protecting, or supporting a person or institution

Ultimately Yrigoyen's presidency was weakened by his misuse of the military. He used the army for unpopular tasks, such as strikebreaking and interfering in local elections. In 1930, when the Great Depression was causing economic turmoil, Yrigoyen lost his popular support, and the army seized the opportunity to overthrow him. When Yrigoyen died in 1933, he received a magnificent funeral and became a symbol of the hopes of Argentina's middle class.

Yucatán

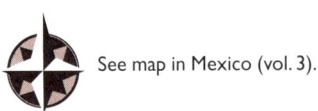

See map in Mexico (vol. 3).

The Yucatán is a peninsula in southeastern MEXICO that also contains the northern parts of BELIZE and GUATEMALA. The region has been inhabited for thousands of years, most notably by the MAYA, who built a civilization in the area sometime after 300 B.C. Europeans arrived in Yucatán shortly after 1500, and less than 50 years later, Spanish CONQUISTADORS had conquered the Maya.

During the early colonial period, Yucatán's economy depended on Maya labor. The Maya produced food and cotton TEXTILES for Spanish colonists. By 1800, the Spaniards had established large estates that produced MAIZE, sugarcane, RICE, and cotton. After Mexico gained independence from Spain in 1821, Yucatán's rulers attempted to declare the peninsula a separate, independent nation. These rulers also took land away from the Maya, who in response rose in rebellion during the CASTE WAR OF YUCATÁN. The war began in 1847 and lasted many years, causing much death and destruction.

During the late 1800s, Yucatán became the wealthiest region in Mexico by exporting sisal* fibers. However, the wealth was controlled

* **sisal** plant whose leaves contain a stiff fiber used for making rope

Zapata, Emiliano

° **exploitation** relationship in which one side benefits at the other's expense

by a few landowners who exploited Maya laborers. Yucatán changed little during the early years of the Mexican Revolution. From 1915 to 1923, governors ended the worst forms of exploitation* and permitted the formation of labor organizations. In the 1930s, President Lázaro Cárdenas in Mexico City took control of Yucatán politics and carried out land reform. Tourism and commerce became the region's most important industries. The Yucatán resorts of Cancún and the island of Cozumel are two of Mexico's most popular tourist destinations.

Zapata, Emiliano

ca. 1879–1919
Mexican revolutionary

° **guerrilla** referring to a group that uses surprise raids to obstruct or harass an enemy or overthrow a government

Emiliano Zapata was one of the most important leaders of the MEXICAN REVOLUTION and is remembered for his fight for land reform and peasants' rights. One of ten children of a peasant family, Zapata was well aware of how the expansion of large agricultural estates, called HACIENDAS, affected the livelihood of peasants. After early brushes with the law, he became a spokesman for local peasants and led his people in their struggle to regain their lands. In 1909, he was elected president of his hometown's village council. The following year, Francisco MADERO began the revolution to overthrow dictator Porfirio DÍAZ, and in March 1911, Zapata formed a guerrilla* army to support Madero. By May, Zapata had captured an important town near Mexico City, which helped bring about the fall of Díaz.

Zapata soon discovered that Madero, a hacienda owner himself, was more interested in political changes than in supporting land reform or helping the peasants. In response, Zapata helped create the Plan of Ayala, which sought to return stolen land to the peasants. Zapata used his army to enforce the plan. When Zapata refused to disarm, Madero sent troops against him commanded by Victoriano HUERTA. Then, in 1913, Huerta assassinated Madero and seized power. Zapata refused to make peace with Huerta, and by 1914, he had gained control of territory around Mexico City and helped force Huerta from power.

Zapata then had to decide which of his two fellow revolutionary leaders—Venustiano CARRANZA or Francisco "Pancho" VILLA—he would support. He sided with Villa, and by the end of the year, their forces had captured Mexico City. During early 1915, Zapata began to implement land reform, but after Villa's troops lost several major battles to Carranza's forces, Zapata's troops were pushed out of Mexico City. By 1916, it was clear that Zapata could not defeat Carranza. Still, he refused to give up and sought new allies for his struggle.

By this time, however, long-standing disputes between members of Zapata's movement caused several prominent leaders to leave the group. Zapata became desperate for new supporters, and he finally invited Jesús Guajardo, a supposedly dissatisfied follower of Carranza, to join him. On April 10, 1919, Zapata and Guajardo planned to meet at Chinameca. When Zapata rode through the gate of the hacienda where the meeting was to occur, Guajardo's troops shot and killed him.

Although Zapata failed in his attempt to bring relief to Mexico's peasants, he became a lasting symbol of their struggle for justice. Some

Viva Zapata!

Zapata's struggle for land reform and peasants' rights is continued today in the claims made by another guerrilla group, the Zapatista Army of National Liberation, or EZLN. The EZLN first gained attention in January 1994, after seizing the town of San Cristóbal de las Casas in the Mexican state of Chiapas. The EZLN demanded the repeal of the North American Free Trade Agreement (NAFTA), and like Zapata, asked for social justice and economic benefits for the people. Although the Mexican government began negotiations with the EZLN in February of that year, the talks broke down and the conflict erupted again in 1995. Despite being reduced in strength by battles with Mexican police and soldiers, the EZLN still wages a guerrilla campaign in Chiapas.

even claim that he is not dead but hiding in the mountains until the people need him again.

Zapotecs

* **indigenous** referring to the original inhabitants of a region

* **Mesoamerica** culture region that includes central and southern Mexico, Guatemala, Belize, El Salvador, and parts of Honduras, Nicaragua, and Costa Rica

* **hieroglyphic** referring to a system of writing that uses pictorial characters, or hieroglyphics

* **artisan** skilled crafts worker

* **pre-Columbian** before the arrival of Christopher Columbus and other Europeans in the Americas in the 1490s

The Zapotecs are a group of indigenous* peoples of southern MEXICO who are related by a language family called Otomanguean. Since about 1500 B.C., they have occupied the area that is the present-day state of Oaxaca. The Zapotecs call themselves *bene zaa*, meaning "the native people" or "the cloud people." However, the term *Zapotec* comes from the word *Tzapotecatl*, which means "people of the *zapote* tree" in Nahuatl, the AZTEC language.

The Zapotec people developed one of the earliest writing systems in Mesoamerica* around 500 B.C. Many hieroglyphic* inscriptions have been found at the ancient Zapotec city of MONTE ALBÁN, which is now an important Mexican archaeological site. From about 100 A.D. to 800 A.D., this city rivaled other important Mesoamerican cities in central Mexico, such as Teotihuacán. Monte Albán fell in about 800, but the Zapotecs continued to maintain a strong and distinct culture in the region. However, invading groups, such as the MIXTECS, and later the Aztecs, reduced the power of Zapotec leaders. During Mexico's colonial period, the Zapotecs were mostly peasants, farmers, and artisans*.

The Zapotec languages, which are unrelated to Mayan or Aztec languages, are among the oldest in Mesoamerica. They are distinct from one another and scholars recognize anywhere from 5 to 45 separate Zapotec languages. Today Zapotec culture is a mixture of modern, colonial, and pre-Columbian* Mexican cultures. Some Zapotec villages specialize in traditional CRAFTS, such as potterymaking and weaving, and their works have become internationally famous. This has renewed interest and pride among the Zapotecs in preserving their unique language and customs. (*See also* **Indians**.)

Zelaya, José Santos

1853–1919
President of Nicaragua

* **liberal** supporting greater participation in government for individuals; not bound by political and social traditions

* **secularize** to convert to nonreligious control

José Santos Zelaya, one of the earliest rulers from the Liberal* Party in Nicaraguan history, took great steps to modernize and secularize* the nation. During his regime*, he oversaw a period of strong economic growth, and NICARAGUA exercised its greatest influence in Central American politics.

Zelaya came to power in 1893 after a revolution overthrew Conservative* president Roberto Sacasa. A political reformer, Zelaya separated church and state, guaranteed secular* education, established a legislature, and abolished the death penalty. Economically, he promoted export agriculture, the development of the country's natural resources, the expansion of the railroad, and the use of steamships on Lakes Managua and Nicaragua. Despite his liberal beliefs, Zelaya manipulated many elections and ruled as a dictator, defeating about 15 attempts to overthrow him.

Zimmerman Telegram

° **regime** prevailing political system or rule

° **conservative** one who is opposed to sudden change, especially in existing political and social institutions

° **secular** nonreligious; connected with everyday life

° **confederation** group of states joined together for a purpose; an alliance

However, Zelaya made his greatest impact in international affairs. In 1895, he supported the creation of the República Mayor, a confederation* that united Nicaragua, EL SALVADOR, and HONDURAS. However, when a coup in El Salvador threatened the union, he refused to use force to keep the union together, and the República Mayor collapsed. Zelaya promoted many peace conferences between states in Central America and began talks that led to the resolution of border disputes with both Honduras and Costa Rica.

Zelaya had more difficulty in maintaining good relations with Great Britain and the United States. During his first year in office, he sent troops to expel the British from the Miskito Coast (located on Nicaragua's Caribbean coast). The British blockaded the coast, but in 1904, they signed a treaty giving Nicaragua full control over the region, which was renamed the Department of Zelaya. The United States supported Zelaya in this dispute but clashed with him over plans for a canal across Central America. The original plan called for the canal to be built through Nicaragua, but Zelaya objected to demands that the canal zone be controlled by the United States. In 1904, construction began on the PANAMA CANAL, but the United States believed Zelaya was trying to convince other nations to build a rival canal in Nicaragua. After two United States mercenaries* were executed in Nicaragua in 1909, the United States supported a rebellion against Zelaya. Realizing he could not defeat forces backed by the United States, Zelaya resigned from office in December 1909. (*See also* **British–Latin American Relations; United States–Latin American Relations.**)

° **mercenary** hired soldier

The Zimmerman Telegram was a message sent by Germany to Mexico during WORLD WAR I, proposing an alliance between the two countries. Sent by German foreign minister Arthur Zimmerman, the telegram promised German support to help Mexico take Texas, New Mexico, and Arizona from the United States. It raised the possibility of asking Japan to join the alliance as well. At the time, the Germans had decided to resume unlimited submarine warfare, a decision they feared might bring the United States into the war against them. The aim of the proposal was to prevent United States forces from fighting in Europe by engaging them in a war with Mexico and Japan.

The telegram was sent in January 1917, but it was intercepted by British intelligence and published in the United States press. The resulting public outrage was a major factor in the United States decision to declare war on Germany on April 6, 1917. The Mexican government rejected the proposal, helping to improve Mexican–United States relations, which had been strained by the United States seizure of Veracruz in 1914 and United States general John Pershing's relentless pursuit of Mexican revolutionary Pancho VILLA. (*See also* **United States–Latin American Relations.**)

Suggested Readings

Atlases and Encyclopedias

Alexander, Robert J., ed. *Biographical Dictionary of Latin American and Caribbean Political Leaders.* Westport, Conn.: Greenwood Press, 1988.

The Atlas of Central America and the Caribbean. New York: Macmillan, 1985.

*Bunson, Margaret. *Encyclopedia of Ancient Mesoamerica.* New York: Facts on File, 1996.

Brawer, Moshe. *Atlas of South America.* New York: Simon and Schuster, 1991.

*Coe, Michael, et al. *Atlas of Ancient America.* New York: Facts on File, 1986.

Collier, Simon, et al., eds. *The Cambridge Encyclopedia of Latin America and the Caribbean.* 2d ed. New York: Cambridge University Press, 1992.

Delpar, Helen, ed. *Encyclopedia of Latin America.* New York: McGraw-Hill, 1974.

Gunson, Phil, et al. *The Dictionary of Contemporary Politics of South America.* New York: Macmillan, 1989.

Martin, Michael Rheta. *An Encyclopedia of Latin American History.* Rev. ed. New York: Abelard-Schuman, 1981.

South America, Central America, and the Caribbean, 1999. 7th ed. London: Europa Publications Limited, 1999.

Tenenbaum, Barbara A., ed. *Encyclopedia of Latin American History and Culture.* New York: Scribners, 1996.

Werner, Michael S., ed. *Encyclopedia of Mexico: History, Society, and Culture.* Chicago: Fitzroy Dearborn Publishers, 1997.

History, General

Bethell, Leslie, ed. *The Cambridge History of Latin America.* 8 vols. New York: Cambridge University Press, 1984–1998.

Burkholder, Mark A. *Colonial Latin America.* 3d ed. New York: Oxford University Press, 1997.

Burns, Bradford E. *Latin America: A Concise Interpretive History.* 5th ed. New York: Prentice Hall, 1990.

Cordingly, David. *Under the Black Flag: The Romance and Reality of Life Among the Pirates.* New York: Harcourt Brace, 1995

Crow, John Armstrong. *The Epic of Latin America.* 4th ed. Berkeley, Calif.: University of California Press, 1992.

Donghi, Tulio Halperín. *The Contemporary History of Latin America.* Translated by John Charles Chasteen. Durham, N.C.: Duke University Press, 1993.

Keen, Benjamin. *A History of Latin America.* 5th ed. Boston: Houghton Mifflin, 1996.

———. *Latin American Civilization, History, and Society, 1492 to the Present.* 6th ed. Boulder, Colo.: Westview Press, 1991.

Kicza, John. *The Indian in Latin American History: Resistance, Resilience, and Acculturation.* Wilmington, Del.: Scholarly Resources, 1999.

Lockhart, James. *Early Latin America: A History of Colonial Spanish America and Brazil.* New York: Cambridge University Press, 1983.

Martin, Luis. *Kingdom of the Sun: A Short History of Peru.* London: Century, 1990.

Meyer, Michael C., William Sherman, and Susan Deeds. *The Course of Mexican History.* New York: Oxford University Press, 1999.

Skidmore, Thomas. *Brazil: Five Centuries of Change.* New York: Oxford University Press, 1999.

Williamson, Edwin. *The Penguin History of Latin America.* New York: Penguin Books, 1992.

Politics and Government

Barbier, Jacques. *Reform and Politics in Bourbon Chile, 1755–1796.* Ottawa: University of Ottawa Press, 1980.

Busey, J. L. *Latin American Political Guide.* 20th ed. Ontario: Juniper Press, 1995.

Dosal, Paul J. *Doing Business with Dictators: A Political History of United Fruit in Guatemala, 1899–1944.* Wilmington, Del.: Scholarly Resources, 1997.

Hughes, Steven W., and Kenneth J. Mijeski. *Politics and Public Policy in Latin America.* Boulder, Colo.: Westview Press, 1985.

Klaiber, Jeffrey. *The Church, Dictatorships, and Democracy in Latin America.* Maryknoll, N.Y.: Orbis Books, 1998.

Peeler, John A. *Building Democracy in Latin America.* Boulder, Colo.: Lynne Rienner Publishers, 1998.

*Asterisk denotes book for young readers.

Suggested Readings

Wiarda, Howard J., and Harvey F. Kline. *Latin American Politics: A World of Possibility.* Belmont, Calif.: Wadsworth Publications, 1995.

Wortman, Miles L. *Government and Society in Central America, 1680–1840.* New York: Columbia University Press, 1982.

Exploration and Discovery

*Bernhard, Brendon. *Pizarro, Orellana, and the Exploration of the Amazon.* New York: Chelsea House, 1991.

Crone, G. R. *The Discovery of America.* New York: Weybright and Talley, 1969.

Goodman, Edward J. *The Explorers of South America.* Norman, Okla.: University of Oklahoma Press, 1992.

Hanson, Earl Parker, ed. *South from the Spanish Main: South America Seen Through the Eyes of Its Discoverers.* New York: Delacorte, 1967.

Machado, Ana Maria. *Exploration into Latin America.* Parsippany, N.J.: New Discovery Books, 1995.

Maslow, Jonathan Evan. *Footsteps in the Jungle: Adventures in the Scientific Exploration of the American Tropics.* Chicago: Ivan R. Dee, 1996.

McLoone, Margo. *Women Explorers in North America and South America.* Mankato, Minn.: Capstone Press, 1997.

Milanich, Jerald T., and Susan Milbrath, eds. *First Encounters: Spanish Exploration in the Caribbean and the United States, 1492–1570.* Gainesville, Fla.: University of Florida Press, 1989.

Morse, Richard M., ed. *The Bandeirantes: The Historical Role of the Brazilian Pathfinders.* New York: Alfred A. Knopf, 1965.

Parry, J. H. *The Discovery of South America.* New York: Taplinger Publishing Company, 1979.

Silverberg, Robert. *The Golden Dream: Seekers of El Dorado.* Athens, Ohio: Ohio University Press, 1996.

Smith, Anthony. *Explorers of the Amazon.* New York: Viking, 1990.

Von Hagen, Victor W. *The Golden Man: A Quest for El Dorado.* Lexington, Mass.: D. C. Heath, 1974.

Conflict and Revolution

*Cheney, Glenn Alan. *Revolution in Central America.* New York: Franklin Watts, 1984.

Cook, Noble David. *Born to Die: Disease and the New World Conquest, 1492–1650.* New York: Cambridge University Press, 1998.

Dunkerley, James. *Rebellion in the Veins: Political Struggle in Bolivia, 1952–1982.* London: Routledge, 1984.

Eisenhower, John S. D. *So Far from God: The U.S. War with Mexico, 1846–1848.* New York: Random House, 1989.

*Gay, Kathlyn, and Martin K. Gay. *Spanish American War.* America at War Series. New York: Twenty-First Century Books, 1995.

Harvey, Neil. *The Chiapas Rebellion: The Struggle for Land and Democracy.* Durham, N.C.: Duke University Press, 1998.

Hemming, John. *Amazon Frontier: The Defeat of the Brazilian Indians.* Cambridge: Harvard University Press, 1987.

———. *The Conquest of the Incas.* New York: Penguin Books, 1983.

Knight, A. *The Mexican Revolution.* 2 vols. New York: Cambridge University Press, 1986.

Las Casas, Bartolomé de. *The Devastation of the Indies: A Brief Account.* Translated by Herma Briffault. Baltimore: Johns Hopkins University Press, 1992.

León-Portilla, Miguel. *The Broken Spears: The Aztec Account of the Conquest of Mexico.* Translated by Lysander Kemp. Boston: Beacon Press, 1962.

Lynch, John. *The Spanish American Revolutions, 1808–1826.* New York: W. W. Norton and Company, 1986.

*Marrin, Albert. *Aztecs and the Spaniards: Cortés and the Conquest of Mexico.* New York: Atheneum, 1986.

Ott, Thomas O. *The Haitian Revolution.* Knoxville: University of Tennessee Press, 1973.

Pérez-Stable, Marifeli. *The Cuban Revolution: Origins, Course, and Legacy.* New York: Oxford University Press, 1998.

Prescott, William H. *History of the Conquest of Mexico.* New York: Modern Library, 1998.

———. *History of the Conquest of Peru.* New York: Modern Library, 1998.

Sater, William F. *Chile and the War of the Pacific.* Lincoln, Neb.: Nebraska Press, 1986.

The Mexican War of Independence. San Diego: Lucent Books, 1997.

Thomas, Hugh. *Conquest: Montezuma, Cortés, and the Fall of Old Mexico.* New York: Simon and Schuster, 1993.

Suggested Readings

Daily Life

Bray, Warwick. *Everyday Life of the Aztecs.* New York: Dorset Press, 1987.

Carrasco, David. *Daily Life of the Aztecs: People of the Sun and Earth.* Westport, Conn.: Greenwood Press, 1998.

Kendall, Ann. *Everyday Life of the Incas.* New York: Dorset Press, 1989.

*Kennett, Frances, and Caroline MacDonald-Haig. *Ethnic Dress.* New York: Facts on File, 1995.

*MacDonald, Fiona. *How Would You Survive As an Aztec?* New York: Franklin Watts, 1997.

Malpass, Michael Andrew. *Daily Life in the Inca Empire.* Westport, Conn.: Greenwood Press, 1996.

Ortiz, Elisabeth L. *The Book of Latin American Cooking.* Hopewell, N.J.: Ecco Press, 1994.

Rojas-Lambardi, Felipe. *The Art of South American Cooking.* New York: HarperCollins, 1991.

Sharer, Robert J. *Daily Life in Maya Civilization.* Westport, Conn.: Greenwood Press, 1996.

Whitlock, Ralph. *Everyday Life of the Maya.* New York: Dorset Press, 1987.

Religion

Baldwin, Neil. *Legends of the Plumed Serpent: Biography of a Mexican God.* New York: Public Affairs, 1998.

Brandon, George. *Santería from Africa to the New World: The Dead Sell Memories.* Bloomington, Ind.: Indiana University Press, 1993.

Carmody, Denise L., and John T. Carmody. *Native American Religions: An Introduction.* New York: Paulist Press, 1993.

Cobo, Bernabé. *Inca Religion and Customs.* Austin, Tex.: University of Texas Press, 1990.

Collins, John J. *Native American Religions: A Geographical Survey.* Lewiston, N.Y.: E. Mellen Press, 1991.

Desmangles, Leslie G. *The Faces of the Gods: Vodou and Roman Catholicism in Haiti.* Chapel Hill, N.C.: University of North Carolina Press, 1992.

Dixon-Kennedy, Mike. *Native American Myth and Legend: An A–Z of People and Places.* New York: Blandford, 1998.

Dussel, Enrique, ed. *The Church in Latin America, 1492–1992.* Maryknoll, N.Y.: Orbis Books, 1992.

Gill, Anthony James. *Rendering unto Caesar: The Catholic Church and the State in Latin America.* Chicago: University of Chicago Press, 1999.

Levine, David H., and Daniel H. Levine. *Religion and Political Conflict in Latin America.* Chapel Hill, N.C.: University of North Carolina Press, 1986.

Marzal, Manuel M., et al. *The Indian Face of God in Latin America.* Translated by Penelope R. Hall. Maryknoll, N.Y.: Orbis Books, 1996.

Matteson Langdon, E. Jean, and Gerhard Baer, eds. *Portals of Power: Shamanism in South America.* Albuquerque: University of New Mexico Press, 1992.

Metraux, Alfred. *Voodoo in Haiti.* New York: Schocken Books, 1989.

Miller, Mary Ellen. *The Gods and Symbols of Ancient Mexico and the Maya: An Illustrated Dictionary of Mesoamerican Religions.* New York: Thames and Hudson, 1993.

Roberts, Timothy R. *Gods of the Maya, Aztecs, and Incas.* New York: Metro Books, 1996.

Taube, Karl. *Aztec and Maya Myths.* Austin, Tex.: University of Texas Press, 1994.

Turner, Harold W. *Latin America.* Boston: G. K. Hall, 1991.

Voeks, Robert A. *Sacred Leaves of Candomblé: African Magic, Medicine, and Religion in Brazil.* Austin, Tex.: University of Texas Press, 1997.

Biography

Adams, Jerome R. *Liberators and Patriots of Latin America: Biographies of Twenty-Three Leaders.* Jefferson, N.C.: McFarland and Company, 1991.

———. *Notable Latin American Women: Twenty-Nine Leaders, Rebels, Poets, Battlers, and Spies, 1500–1900.* Jefferson, N.C.: McFarland and Company, 1995.

Beezley, William H., and Judith Ewell. *The Human Tradition in Modern Latin America.* Wilmington, Del.: Scholarly Resources, 1997.

Brockman, James R. *Romero: A Life.* Maryknoll, N.Y.: Orbis Books, 1990.

Burland, C. A. *Montezuma: Lord of the Aztecs.* New York: Putnam, 1973.

Castañeda, Jorge G. *Compañero: The Life and Death of Che Guevara.* New York: Vintage Books, 1998.

*Condit, Erin, and William Golding. *François and Jean-Claude Duvalier.* New York: Chelsea House, 1989.

Corke, Bettina, ed. *Who's Who in Latin America: Government, Politics, Banking, and Industry.* 4th ed. New York: Norman Ross Publishing, 1997.

Dujovne Ortiz, Alicia. *Eva Perón: A Biography.* Translated by Shawn Fields. Boston: Little Brown, 1997.

Suggested Readings

*Fernandez, José B. *José de San Martín: Latin America's Quiet Hero*. Brookfield, Conn.: Millbrook Press, 1994.

*Goodnough, David. *Simon Bolívar: South American Liberator*. Springfield, N.J.: Enslow Publishers, 1998.

*Gleiter, Jan, et al. *Miguel Hidalgo Y Costilla*. Chatham, N.J.: Raintree/Steck Vaughn, 1989.

*Hoobler, Thomas, and Dorothy Hoobler. *Toussaint L'Ouverture*. New York: Chelsea House, 1989.

*Jacobs, William Jay. *Pizarro, Conqueror of Peru*. New York: Franklin Watts, 1994.

Krauze, Enrique. *Mexico: Biography of Power: A History of Modern Mexico, 1810–1996*. Translated by Hank Heifetz. New York: HarperCollins, 1997.

Macmillan Compendium: Latin American Lives. New York: Macmillan Library Reference, 1998.

*O'Brian, Steven. *Pancho Villa*. New York: Chelsea House, 1999.

Quirk, Robert E. *Fidel Castro*. New York: W. W. Norton Company, 1995.

Tardiff, Joseph C., et al. *Dictionary of Hispanic Biography*. Detroit: Gale Research, 1995.

Literature

Agosin, Marjorie, ed. *A Gabriela Mistral Reader*. Translated by Maria Jacketti. Fredonia, N.Y.: White Pine Press, 1992.

Allende, Isabel. *The House of the Spirits*. Translated by Magda Bojin. New York: Knopf, 1987.

Asturias, Miguel Ángel. *Men of Maize*. Translated by Gerald Martin. Pittsburgh, Pa.: University of Pittsburgh Press, 1994.

Bishop, Elizabeth, and Emanuel Brasil, eds. *An Anthology of Twentieth-Century Brazilian Poetry*. Hanover, N.H.: Wesleyan University Press, 1997.

Fuentes, Carlos. *Terra Nostra*. Translated by Margaret S. Penden. New York: Farrar, Straus and Giroux, 1976.

García Márquez, Gabriel. *One Hundred Years of Solitude*. Translated by Gregory Rabassa. New York: HarperCollins, 1970.

Higman, Perry, trans. *Love Poems: From Spain and Spanish America*. San Francisco: City Lights Books, 1986.

Juana Inés de la Cruz, Sor. *Poems: A Bilingual Anthology*. Translated by Margaret Sayers Peden. Tempe, Ariz.: Bilingual Review Press, 1985.

Levi, Enrique Jaramillo, and Leland H. Chambers, eds. *Contemporary Short Stories from Central America*. Austin, Tex.: University of Texas Press, 1994.

Leonard, Kathy S., and Ana M. Shua, eds. *Cruel Fictions, Cruel Realities: Short Stories by Latin American Women Writers*. Pittsburgh, Pa.: Latin American Literary Review Press, 1997.

Monegal, Emir Rodriguez, ed. *The Borzoi Anthology of Latin American Literature*. 2 vols. New York: Knopf, 1977.

Neruda, Pablo. *Selected Poems*. Edited by Ben Belitt. New York: Grove Press, 1978.

Paz, Octavio. *The Collected Poems of Octavio Paz, 1957–1987*. Translated by Eliot Weinberger. New York: New Directions, 1991.

———. *Labyrinth of Solitude: The Other Mexico, Return to the Labyrinth of Solitude, Mexico and the United States, the Philanthropic Ogre*. (This collection contains several of Paz's works.) Translated by Lysander Kemp. New York: Grove Press, 1989.

Ramirez, Anthony, and Bernard H. Hamel, eds. *The Best of Latin American Short Stories*. Los Angeles: Bilingual Book Press, 1995.

Smith, Verity, ed. *Encyclopedia of Latin American Literature*. Chicago: Fitzroy Dearborn Publishers, 1997.

Solé, Carlos A., ed. *Latin American Writers*. 3 vols. New York: Scribners, 1989.

Vargas Llosa, Mario. *Green House*. Translated by Gregory Rabassa. New York: Harper and Row, 1968.

Walcott, Derek. *Collected Poems, 1948–1984*. New York: Farrar, Straus, and Giroux, 1986.

Art and Architecture

Ades, Dawn. *Art in Latin America: The Modern Era, 1820–1980*. New Haven: Yale University Press, 1989.

Castedo, Leopoldo. *A History of Latin American Art and Architecture from Pre-Columbian Times to the Present*. Edited and Translated by Phyllis Freeman. New York: Praeger, 1969.

Catlin, Stanton L., and Terence Grieder. *The Art of Latin America Since Independence*. Rev. ed. New Haven: Yale University Press, 1966.

Chaplik, Dorothy. *Latin American Art: An Introduction to Works of the Twentieth Century*. Jefferson, N.C.: McFarland and Company, 1989.

Grizzard, M. *Spanish Colonial Art and Architecture of Mexico and the U.S. Southwest*. London: University Press of America, 1987.

Kubler, George. *The Art and Architecture of Ancient America: The Mexican, Maya, and Andean Peoples*. 3d ed. New Haven: Yale University Press, 1992.

Suggested Readings

Lucie-Smith, Edward. *Latin American Art of the Twentieth Century.* New York: Thames and Hudson, 1993.

Miller, Mary Ellen. *The Art of Mesoamerica: From Olmec to Aztec.* New York: Thames and Hudson, 1996.

Oettinger, Marion, Jr. *The Folk Art of Latin America: Visiones del Pueblo.* New York: E. P. Dutton, 1992.

Panyella, August, ed. *Folk Art of the Americas.* New York: Harry N. Abrams, 1973.

Robertson, Donald. *Pre-Columbian Architecture.* London: Studio Vista, 1963.

Rochfort, Desmond. *Mexican Muralists: Orozco, Rivera, Siqueiros.* San Francisco: Chronicle Books, 1998.

Sayer, Chloe, and David Lavender. *Arts and Crafts of Mexico.* San Francisco: Chronicle Books, 1990.

Scott, John F. *Latin American Art: Ancient to Modern.* Gainesville, Fla.: University of Florida Press, 1999.

Segre, Roberto, and Fernando K. Kusnetzoff, eds. *Latin America and Its Architecture.* New York: Holmes and Meier, 1980.

Stevens, Donald F., ed. *Based on a True Story: Latin American History at the Movies.* Wilmington, Del.: Scholarly Resources, 1997.

Traba, Marta. *Art of Latin America, 1900–1980.* Baltimore: Johns Hopkins University Press, 1994.

Films

The following films are available from the Latin American Video Archives: http://www.lavavideo.org

Everyday Art. 1994. A documentary exploring the influence of African and Latino culture on Cuba's musicians, dancers, and other contemporary artists.

The Garifuna Journey. A documentary about the Garifuna, the descendants of Africans and Caribs, who resisted slavery and fought to maintain their homeland on the Caribbean island of St. Vincent.

Slave Ship. 1994. A documentary about a former street child from Rio de Janeiro who helps rescue slum children from their hopeless struggle to survive on the streets by training them in music and dance.

Where Land Is Life. 1989. A documentary exploring the Quechua and Aymara peoples' beliefs about land ownership and their fight to reclaim the land of their ancestors in the Peruvian highlands.

On-line Resources

Latin American Network Information Center, University of Texas. *Contains a multitude of links to web sites about Latin American history, culture, government, education, and recreation.*
http://www.lanic.utexas.edu

Latin American Alliance Network. *Contains information about the latest environmental issues facing Latin America.*
http://www.latinsynergy.org

Information Services Latin America—Current News. *Provides information about current news stories in Latin America.*
http://www.igc.org/isla/current.html

Organization of American States. *Contains information about the Organization of the American States, including news, speeches, events, and history.*
http://www.oas.org/

Pan American Health Organization. *Provides information on medical issues, such as vaccination programs, in the Americas.*
http://www.paho.org/default.htm

Hispanic Reading Room, Library of Congress. *Provides access to the Library of Congress catalog for books on Latin American topics. Also supplies a variety of other links.*
http://lcweb.loc.gov/rr/hispanic/

Latin American Library at Tulane University. *Contains images of architecture, peoples, and ancient books as well as links to other related sites.*
http://www.tulane.edu/~latinlib/lalhome.html

Latin America on the Net. *Contains information about Latin America's geography, culture, politics, and economics as well as links to additional web sites.*
http://www.latinworld.com

Maya Civilization. *Contains information on the Maya, including their history, culture, science, and religion.*
http://www.civilization.ca/membrs/civiliz/maya/mmc01eng.html

Aztec History. *Provides information about the Aztecs, including their religion, medicine, and rulers.*
http://northcoast.com/~spdtom/aztec.html

Suggested Readings

Peace Corps: Inter-America and Caribbean. *Contains stories about daily life in Latin American countries written by Peace Corp volunteers.*
http://www.peacecorps.gov/countries/americas.html

Mexico Web Guide. *Provides information about Mexico's history, leaders, and national documents.*
http://mexico.web.com.mx/fhistoria.html

Latin America Database, University of New Mexico. *Provides news bulletins from Latin America's major new stories.*
http://ladb.unm.edu/

Geography and History. *Provides information about Latin America's geography and history and contains a calendar listing national holidays.*
http://www.interknowledge.com

Gateway to Latin America. *Contains a slide show of images from several countries as well as links to web sites about Latin America.*
http://www.latin-america.com

Archaeology and Anthropology of the Americas. *Provides information on the Maya, Aztec, and Inca civilizations.*
http://www.realtime.net/maya/

Archaeology Resources. *Contains links to web sites about Latin America's ancient civilizations.*
http://archnet.uconn.edu/regions/

Political Database of the Americas. *Contains information on Latin American politics, including information about elections and political parties.*
http://www.georgetown.edu/pdba

U.S. Department of State Report on Trade in Latin America. *Contains economic information about Latin American countries, such as the gross domestic product and the rate of unemployment.*
http://www.state.gov/www/issues/economic/trade_reports

U.S. Interventions in Latin America. *Contains a brief history of United States intervention in Latin America. Includes a time line and the text of the Monroe Doctrine.*
http://www.smplanet.com/imperialism/teddy.html

Economic Commission for Latin America and the Caribbean. *Provides information on Latin American economies, including statistics on foreign investment in Latin America.*
http://www.eclac.org

Photo Credits

Volume 1

Color Plates

for *Art and Architecture* between pages 126 and 127:
1: John Taylor/Art Resource, N.Y.; **2:** Victor Englebert/Photo Researchers, Inc.; **3:** Erich Lessing/Art Resource, N.Y.; **4:** George Holton/Photo Researchers, Inc.; **5:** Christie's Images/SuperStock; **6:** Chip and Rosa Maria Peterson; **7:** Library of Congress; **8:** Peabody Museum, Harvard University; **9:** Werner Forman Archive/David Bernstein Fine Art/Art Resource, N.Y.; **10:** Jack Child; **11:** Michele Burgess/Stock Boston; **12:** Schalkwijk/Art Resource, N.Y.; **13:** The Granger Collection, New York; **14:** Jack Child; **15:** SuperStock

Black-and-White Photographs

3: Latin American Library, Tulane University, New Orleans, La.; **7:** Jim Whitmer/Stock Boston; **19:** Benson Latin American Collection, University of Texas at Austin; **21:** Library of Congress; **23:** Organization of American States; **34:** Tom McHugh/Photo Researchers, Inc.; **37:** Collection of Elyn Kronemeyer; **42:** Kenneth Garrett/National Geographic Image Collection; **45:** Ned Haines/Photo Researchers, Inc.; **53:** Enrique Shore/Woodfin Camp & Associates, Inc.; **58:** UPI/Corbis; **59:** Reuters/Corbis; **60:** John R. Foster/Photo Researchers, Inc.; **63:** Schalkwijk/Art Resource, N.Y.; **70:** Bob Schalkwijk/Fundación Amparo, Museo Amparo, Pueblo; **77:** Andrew Rakoczy/Art Resource, N.Y.; **78:** O. Louis Mazzatenta/National Geographic Image Collection; **84:** Dagmar Fabricius/Stock Boston; **89:** Museo Templo Major; **93:** Lee Boltin; **103:** Organization of American States; **109:** Henry E. Huntington Library and Art Gallery; **112:** Organization of American States; **114:** Houghton Library, Harvard University; **126:** Don Barletti, Photographer, Los Angeles Times; **127:** George Holton/Photo Researchers, Inc.; **143:** Sociedad Fotografica Argentina de Aficiandados—Cristian Favier Dubois; **145:** Latin American Library, Tulane University, New Orleans, La.; **149:** Bodleian Library, Oxford, United Kingdom; **150:** Lee Boltin; **153:** Lester Sloan, The Gamma Liaison Network; **155:** Cynthia Brito/Pulsar Imagens e Editora; **157:** Dale E. Boyer/Photo Researchers, Inc.; **163:** Juca Martins/Pulsar Imagens e Editora; **166:** Public Domain; **171:** Corbis; **187:** Anthro-Photo File; **192:** Tom Dunham; **208:** Gary Payne/Gamma Liaison

Volume 2

Color Plates

for *Daily Life* between pages 128 and 129:
1: Giraudon/Art Resource,N.Y.; **2:** Brazil Slide Series; **3:** SuperStock; **4:** Lisl Steiner/Photo Researchers, Inc.; **5:** Vincent Dewitt/Stock Boston; **6:** Giraudon/Art Resource, N.Y.; **7:** Chip and Rosa Maria Peterson; **8:** The Granger Collection, New York; **9:** Carl Frank/Photo Researchers, Inc.; **10:** Daniele Pellegrini/Photo Researchers, Inc.; **11:** SuperStock; **12:** The World History Slide Collection/Instructional Resources Corporation; **13:** Wesley Bocxe/Photo Researchers, Inc.; **14:** Underwood Photo Archives, San Francisco, Calif./SuperStock; **15:** Vincent Dewitt/Stock Boston

Black-and-White Photographs

19: Harvard College Library, Harvard University; **35:** Victor Englebert/Photo Researchers, Inc.; **45:** Joe Cavaretta/Associated Press; **48:** UPI/Corbis; **54:** Mariano Diaz; **56:** Martin Chambi; **62:** La Fototeca del INAH; **67:** Dr. G. B. Pineider/Biblioteca Medicea Laurenziana; **73:** Larry Luxner; **84:** UPI/Corbis; **85:** Joe Cavaretta/Associated Press; **87:** Victor Englebert; **93:** Peter

Photo Credits

Menzel/Stock Boston; **101:** Wilber E. Garrett/National Geographic Society; **103:** Owen Franken/Stock Boston; **111:** Renee Lynn/Photo Researchers, Inc.; **124:** Tom Dunham; **127:** Sisse Brimberg/National Geographic Image Collection; **130:** Library of Congress; **133:** Tom Dunham; **141:** Houghton Library, Harvard University; **149:** Reuters/Corbis; **150:** Martin Mejia Stringer/Associated Press; **152:** George Holton/Photo Researchers, Inc.; **155:** UPI/Corbis; **158:** Joan Klatchko/Gamma Liaison; **170:** Giraudon/Art Resource, N.Y.; **175:** The Granger Collection, New York; **184:** Latin American Library, Tulane University; **186:** El Ancora Editores; **190:** UPI/Corbis; **196:** Benson Latin American Collection, University of Texas at Austin; **203:** Library of Congress; **209:** Library of Congress; **211:** Library of Congress; **220:** Alicia D'Amico; **223:** Mario Lopez Stringer/Associated Press; **224:** James P. Blair/National Geographic Image Collection

Volume 3

Color Plates

for *People* between pages 152 and 153:
1: The Granger Collection, New York; **2:** The Granger Collection, New York; **3:** Giraudon/Art Resource, N.Y.; **4:** The Granger Collection, New York; **5:** Giraudon/Art Resource, N.Y.; **6:** The Granger Collection, New York; **7:** The Granger Collection, New York; **8:** Schalkwijk/Art Resource, N.Y.; **9:** F. Ancellet/Rapho; **10:** Piko/Sipa Press; **11:** Corbis; **12:** Jon Dimis/Associated Press; **13:** M. Hippenmeyer/Sipa Press; **14:** Corbis; **15:** Corbis

Black-and-White Photographs

2: Harvard College Library, Harvard University; **5:** Private Collection—Fray Martin de Mura's manuscript; **18:** The New York Public Library, Astor, Lenox, and Tilden Foundations; **24:** M. Dwyer/Stock Boston; **30:** Archivo General de la Nación; **35:** Archivo Cenidiap; **49:** Organization of American States; **55:** Helen Hughes; **56:** Library of Congress; **61:** Courtesy of Jolanda Quezada; **66:** Courtesy of Julia Chambi; **72:** Courtesy of Julia Chambi; **75:** Library of Congress; **76:** Library of Congress; **82:** Library of Congress; **85:** UPI/Corbis; **88:** Harth-Terre Collection, Latin American Library, Tulane University; **90:** Brown Brothers; **94:** Justin Kerr; **100:** Harvard College Library, Harvard University; **114:** Amon Carter Museum; **124:** INBA Collection, Museo de Arte Moderno, Mexico; **129:** The Hispanic Society of America; **134:** The Fine Arts Museum of San Francisco, gift of Eleanor Martin; **139:** Hillel Berger/Peabody Museum, Harvard University; **140:** The Granger Collection, New York; **143:** Tom Dunham; **148:** E. Villasana/United Nations High Commissioner for Refugees; **151:** A. R. Williams; **155:** Photo Researchers, Inc.; **178:** AP/Wide World Photos; **188:** Corbis; **203:** Collection of Prince Dom Pedro de Orleans E Braganca, photo by Otto Hees; **204:** AP/Wide World Photos; **208:** Corbis; **220:** CONTACT Press Images; **224:** The Granger Collection, New York

Volume 4

Color Plates

For *Conflict and Revolution* between pages 128 and 129:
1: Private Collection/ET Archive, London/SuperStock; **2:** The Granger Collection, New York; **3:** The World History Slide Collection; **4:** The Granger Collection, New York; **5:** The Granger Collection, New York; **6:** The Granger Collection, New York; **7:** The Granger Collection, New York; **8:** The Granger Collection, New York; **9:** Gamma Liaison; **10:** Owen Franken/Corbis; **11:** Stephanie Maze/Corbis; **12:** Sipa Press; **13:** Rafael Wollman/Liaison; **14:** Alyx Kellington/Liaison; **15:** Associated Press

Black-and-White Photographs

8: J. S. Rangel/Museu Nacional de Belas Artes; **15:** Courtesy of the Royal Library Copenhagen;

Photo Credits

26: Bibliothèque Nationale; **29:** Mathias Oppersdorff/Photo Researchers, Inc.; **31:** Chip and Rosa Maria Peterson; **37:** Karl Weidmann/Photo Researchers, Inc.; **42:** AP/Wide World Photos; **48:** Organization of American States; **52:** Archivo Cenidap; **54:** Henry E. Mattison; **56:** Sotheby's New York; **60:** Courtesy of the John Carter Brown Library at Brown University; **67:** Archivo General de la Nación, Buenos Aires, Argentina; **70:** UPI/Corbis; **75:** Helen Hughes; **83:** Roxana Antacha/Gamma Liaison; **89:** The Granger Collection, New York; **94:** Houghton Library, Harvard University; **98:** Organization of American States; **111:** The Granger Collection, New York; **114:** UPI/Corbis; **116:** Tom Dunham; **125:** Paulo Fridman/Liaison International; **129:** Courtesy of Department of Library Services, American Museum of Natural History; **130:** Art Resource, N.Y.; **136:** Harvard College Library, Harvard University; **146:** Bibliothèque Nationale; **148:** Will and Deni McIntyre/Photo Researchers, Inc.; **157:** Juca Martins/Pulsar Imagens e Editora; **161:** The Granger Collection, New York; **164:** Stock Boston; **191:** The Granger Collection, New York; **192:** Corbis; **193:** UPI/Corbis; **195:** Associated Press Photo; **198:** Photographic Archive, University of Chile; **207:** Chris Sharp/Photo Researchers, Inc.

Index

A

Abakua, 4:41
Abalos, José de, 1:28
Academy of San Carlos, 1:66
Acamapichtli, 1:89
Acapulco, **1:1**
Acaray River, 3:193
Á Carolina (Machado), 3:72
Achiote, 4:112
Aconcagua, Mt., 1:30, 49 *(map)*, 2:165
Acordada, 2:39
Acosta Ñu, battle of (1869), 4:201
Act of Chapultepec (1945), 3:191, 4:50
Adams, John Quincy, 1:1, 2
Adams-Onís Treaty, **1:1–2**, 2:132
Adelantado (captain-general), 2:20
Africa
    Portuguese explorations in, 4:9–10, 11
Africans in Latin America, **1:2–6** *(illus.)*
    Black Caribs, 1:162
    black consciousness, rise of, 4:33
    in Brazil, 1:4–6
    Carnival and, 1:162
    class position of blacks, 1:215
    Dias, military leader in Brazil, 2:60–61
    diseases introduced by, 2:66–67
    in Esmeraldas, 2:112
    folk music and dance of, 3:150
    in Haiti, 2:197–201
    in Hispanic nations, 1:2–4
    maroons, 3:86–87
    mulattos and zambos, 4:32
    musical instruments of, 3:153
    négritude and, 3:157–58
    in Palmares, 3:182
    population and population growth of, 4:5, 6
    religions, 1:155–56 *(illus.)*, 4:39–41
    slavery and, 4:92–95
    slave trade and, 4:90–92
    voodoo and, 4:195–96
    after wars of independence, 4:32–33
    women, 4:208
Agassiz, Jean Louis Rodolphe, 2:117
Agency for International Development (AID), U.S., 1:13, 181
Age of Reason. *See* Enlightenment
Agnese, Batista, 3:82
Agrarian reform, **1:6–8** *(illus.)*, 1:13. *See also* Land, ownership of
    Allende and, 1:20
    in Chiapas, 1:189
    class structure and, 1:213
    Decree 900, 1:38
    land tenure and, 3:45
    in Mexico, 3:122
Agregados, 2:119
Agribusinesses, 1:213
Agricultural revolution, 1:8–10
Agriculture, **1:8–14** *(map)*
    in altiplano, 1:22
    in Amazon region, 1:24
    in Andes, 2:52, 4:102–3
    of Aymara, 1:87

    in Bahia, 1:90, 91
    banana industry, 1:94–96
    cacao industry, 1:147–48
    coffee industry, 2:3–5
    haciendas and, 1:10–11, 2:195–96 *(illus.)*
    irrigation and, 3:23–25
    livestock and, 3:65–66
    maize and, 3:75–76
    as major sector of economy, 2:90
    in Mesoamerica, 2:50, 3:105
    modern commercial, 1:12–14
    in Paraguay, 3:195, 199
    in Peru, 3:216
    plantation system, 1:11–12, 3:226–27
    potato crop, 4:14–15
    pre-Columbian, 1:8–10, 4:102–3
    rice, 4:46–47
    rural labor unions, 3:43–44
    slash-and-burn, 1:10, 2:140–41
    sugar industry, 4:119–21
    technology and, 4:124, 125
    terrace, 1:10, 3:24
    tobacco industry, 4:140–41
    Toltec, 4:142
    traditional Native American foods and, 2:133
    in Venezuela, 4:181
Aguardiente (cane liquor), 4:29–30
Aguirre, Juan Francisco de, 2:115
Agustini, Delmira, **1:14**
Ah Cacau, 4:138
Ahuitzotl (ruler), 1:90
Ah Xupan, 3:96
AIDS, 2:68
Air forces, 1:85–86
Alakaluf Indians, 3:200
Alamo, battle of the (1836), **1:14–15**, 4:132
Alarcón y Mendoza, Juan Ruiz de, 3:60
Alberdi, Juan Bautista, **1:15–16**, 4:5
Alberni, Pedro de, 3:180
Albizu Campos, Pedro, **1:16**
Albuquerque, Matias de, **1:17**, 2:81
Alcalde, **1:17–18**, 1:149, 2:39
Alcalde mayor, 1:18, 2:39
Alcaldes de los crímenes, 1:83
Alcayaga, Lucila Godoy. *See* Mistral, Gabriela
Alcoholic beverages, 2:134
Aldeias, 3:133
Aleijadinho, **1:18–19** *(illus.)*, 1:46–47, 66
Aleman, Arnoldo, 3:166
Alemàn, Miguel, 1:1
Alexander VI, Pope, 2:114
Alfaro, David Siqueiros, 1:63 *(illus.)*, 67
Alfonsín, Raúl, 1:56, 57
Alfonso I of Portugal, 4:9
Alguaciles, 2:39
Alguaciles mayores, 2:39
Alianza Federal de Pueblos Libres, 1:190–91
Allegados, 2:119
Allende, Ignacio, 2:207, 3:112–13, 4:203
Allende, Isabel, **1:19**
Allende Gossens, Salvador, **1:19–20**, 3:50, 4:1

    CIA and coup against, 1:184
    Frei Montalva vs., 2:144
    socialist reforms of, 1:200
    Soviet–Latin American relations and election of, 4:104–5
Alliance for Progress, **1:20–21**, 2:33, 125, 3:21, 175
Almagro, Diego de, **1:21–22** *(illus.)*, 1:115, 194, 2:115, 116 *(map)*
    Alvarado y Mesía and, 1:23
    conquest of Peru and, 3:210
    Pizarro's dispute with, 3:225
Alonso, Marino Roque, 3:196
Alpacas, 1:33, 3:65, 66
Altiplano, **1:22**, 1:49, 87, 113, 2:165, 3:208–9
Altitude, climate and, 1:216
Alvarado y Mesía, Pedro de, **1:22–23** *(illus.)*, 2:27, 103, 2:180, 3:96
Álvarez, Juan, 3:120
Álvarez de Pineda, Alonso, 4:131
Amado, Jorge, **1:23–24**, 3:64
Amaral, Suzana, 1:206
Amazonas, 3:77
Amazon basin, 1:26
Amazonian Indians, 4:38
Amazon region (Amazonia), **1:24–26**
    arrival of Europeans to, 1:25
    of Brazil, 1:128
    characteristics of, 1:24
    development of, 1:25–26
    Indian cultures of, 3:12
    Manaus, main port of, 3:77–78
    missions in, 3:133
    pre-Columbian cultures of, 2:51–52
    pre-Columbian history of, 4:100–101
Amazon River, 1:25, **1:26–27**, 2:165, 3:174
Americana (*confederato* settlement), 2:18
American Convention of Human Rights, 2:218
American Federation of Labor and Congress of Industrial Organizations (AFL-CIO), 3:169
American Popular Revolutionary Alliance (APRA), 3:214
American Revolution, **1:27–29**, 2:131, 152–53
Amparo, writ of, 3:51–52
Amphibians, 1:33–34
Ampuche. *See* Araucanians
Ampudia, Pedro, 3:114
Anaconda, 1:34
Anarchism, **1:29–30**
Anasazi Indians, 1:59, 60 *(illus.)*, 3:159
Anchieta, José de, **1:30**
Ancón, Treaty of (1883), 1:123, 4:199
Andalusian language, 2:20
Andean highlands, irrigation technique in, 3:24
Andean region
    pre-Columbian history of, 4:101–3
    settlement of, 4:102
Andes, **1:30–31**
    altiplano in, 1:22
    ancient highways through, 2:208–9

229

Index

archaeological study in, 1:41–42
   in Bolivia, 1:113
   clothing of, 2:1
   in Ecuador, 2:91
   geography of, 2:164–65
   pre-Columbian cultures in, 2:52–53, 3:11–12
   silver in, 2:169
Andrada, José Bonifácio de, 1:31, 3:202
Andrade, Mário de, **1:32**
Andresote, 4:90
Anglican Church, 4:17
Angola, 4:58, 93
Anguilla. *See* British West Indies; Caribbean Antilles
Animals, **1:32–35** *(illus.)*
   birds, 1:34–35
   diseases introduced by, 2:66
   domesticated, 1:10–11
   fish, amphibians, and reptiles, 1:33–34
   habitats and human influences on, 1:35
   insects and spiders, 1:34
   livestock, 3:65–66
   llama, 3:66 *(illus.)*
   mammals, 1:32–33
   of Pantanal, 3:192
Anteaters, 1:33
Anticlericalism, **1:35–36**, 1:158, 165, 2:40–41, 3:53–54
Antigua, 1:138
Anti-Semitism, 3:31
Antoneli, Juan Bautista, 2:142
Antunes, João, 1:18
Apache, 1:59, 60, 3:161
Apaza, Julián. *See* Tupac Catari
"Apostle of Brazil." *See* Anchieta, José de
Apprenticeships, 2:191
Aquaculture, 2:127
Arabica coffee beans, 2:4
Arab Muslims, 3:27
Arango, Doroteo. *See* Villa, Francisco "Pancho"
Arantes do Nascimento, Edson. *See* Pelé
Araucanians, **1:37–38** *(illus.)*, 1:194, 3:12
Arawak Indians, 1:160, 162, 2:66, 83, 3:12–13, 27, 4:151
Arbenz Guzmán, Jacobo, **1:38–39**, 1:184, 2:183
Arcabucero, 1:65
Arce, Manuel José, **1:39**, 1:181, 2:104, 181
Archaeology, **1:39–43** *(illus.)*. *See also* Architecture
   in Amazonia, 2:52, 4:100–101
   in Amazon region, 1:42–43
   in Andes, 1:41–42
   at Chan Chan, 1:186–87
   at Chavín de Huántar site, 1:188–89
   at Chichén Itzá site, 1:191
   on Chimu culture, 1:203
   at Copán site, 2:23
   at Easter Island, 2:86
   at El Mirador, 2:101–2 *(illus.)*
   on Huari culture, 2:216
   on Inca, 1:39, 41–42, 3:3–6 *(illus.)*, 4:102
   Kotosh, 3:38
   at La Venta, 3:41
   at Machu Picchu, 3:72–73
   on Maya, 1:39, 40–41, 3:94–95
   in Mexico City, 3:123
   on Mixtec culture, 3:138
   on Moche culture, 3:139–40
   at Monte Albán, 3:144

Nasca lines, 3:154–55
   on Olmecs, 3:173
   at Palenque, 3:181
   on pre-Columbian Mesoamerica, 1:39, 40–41, 3:104–8
   at San Agustín, 4:64
   science of, 1:39–40
   at Templo Mayor, 4:127
   at Tikal site, 4:137–38
   timeline of cultures, 1:41
   on Tiwanaku society, 4:140
   on Toltecs, 4:142
Archaic period, 3:105
Archdioceses, 1:172
Architecture, **1:43–48** *(illus.)*
   of Aleijadinho, 1:18–19 *(illus.)*
   in Andean region, 2:52, 53
   of Brasília, 1:127–28
   in Brazil, 1:46–47, 48, 3:167
   at Chavín de Huántar site, 1:189
   colonial, 1:44–47
   French-style, 2:146
   Huari, 2:216
   Inca, 3:4
   Mesoamerican, 3:105
   in Minas Gerais, 3:128
   Moche, 3:139
   modern, 1:47–48
   neoclassical, 1:47
   of Niemeyer Soares Filho, 3:167
   Olmec, 3:173, 174
   pre-Columbian, 1:43–44, 69, 70, 2:52, 53
   in St. Augustine, 4:61
   of San Xavier del Bac, 4:69
   in Spanish America, 1:45–48
Arequipa, Peru, 3:213, 215
Arévalo Bermejo, Juan José, 1:38, 2:31
Argana, Luis Maria, 3:198–99
Argentina, **1:48–58** *(map)*
   Alberdi, founding father of, 1:15–16
   anti-Semitism in, 3:31
   Artigas and independence of Uruguay, 1:72–73
   boundary disputes of, 1:123, 124
   Buenos Aires, capital of, 1:142–44 *(illus.)*
   censorship of journalism in, 3:34
   Christ of the Andes, between Chile and, 1:203–4
   cinema in, 1:206
   colonial period in, 1:49–51
   Córdoba, province in, 2:24–25
   descamisados in, 2:59–60
   Dirty War in, 2:65
   education in, 2:100
   Falklands/Malvinas War and, 2:117
   geography of, 1:49
   Guerra Grande and, 2:186–87
   human rights activism in, 2:220
   immigration to, 2:227
   independence struggle in, 1:51–52, 143, 4:202–3
   meat industry in, 3:97–98
   Menem, president of, 3:102–3
   Middle Easterners in, 3:125
   Mitre, president of, 3:137
   Paraguay's independence from, 3:195–96
   Perón, president of, 1:55–56, 3:206–7
   popular music and dance in, 3:152
   prostitution in, 2:163
   railroads in, 4:36

   Rivadavia, statesman of, 4:51
   Roca, president of, 4:53
   Rosas and national unity, 1:52–54, 4:55–56
   Saavedra Lamas, statesman of, 4:58
   San Martín and liberation of, 4:67
   Sarmiento, president of, 4:79
   Tierra del Fuego and, 4:137
   universal male suffrage in, 4:119
   Urquiza, statesman of, 4:166
   War of the Triple Alliance and, 4:200–202
   wine industry in, 4:207
   World War II and, 4:213
   Yrigoyen, president of, 4:214–15
Argentine Confederation, 1:16, 52
Argüello, Concepción "Concha," 1:153
Arias Foundation, 1:58
Arias Madrid, Harmodio and Arnulfo, 3:185
Arias plan (Esquipulas II), 1:58
Arias Sánchez, Oscar, **1:58** *(illus.)*, 1:182, 2:32, 3:166, 4:70
Aristide, Jean-Bertrand, **1:58–59** *(illus.)*, 1:176, 2:201
Aristide Foundation for Democracy (AFFD), 1:59 *(illus.)*
Aristotle, 2:109
Arizona, **1:59–61** *(illus.)*
Arlt, Roberto, 4:136
Armada del Mar del Sur, 2:128
Armadillos, 1:33, 34 *(illus.)*
Armed forces, **1:61–63**
   air forces, 1:85–86
   in 1800s, 1:61–62
   military dictatorships and, 2:62–63
   militias, 3:126–28
   modern, 1:62–63
   political intervention by, 4:1
   professionalization of, 2:63–64
   soldaderas and, 4:97
   unión de armas to pay for, 4:157
   weapons industry and, 4:205–6
Arms industry. *See* Weapons industry
Army of the Andes, 4:67
Arns, Paulo Evaristo, 2:220
Arrieta, Pedro de, 1:46
Art, colonial to modern, **1:63–69** *(illus.)*. *See also* Architecture
   Aleijadinho, sculptor, 1:18–19 *(illus.)*
   colonial, 1:64–66
   crafts, 2:35–37 *(illus.)*
   cultural nationalism and, 3:157
   Eckhout, painter, 2:86
   in 1800s, 1:66–67
   folk art, 1:68–69
   indigenismo movement in, 4:33
   of Kahlo, 3:36–37
   Modern Art Week, 3:141
   négritude and, 4:33
   of Pérez Esquivel, 3:205
   photography, 3:220–21
   of Portinari, 4:8–9
   Quito School of Art, 4:29
   retablos and ex-votos, 4:46
   of Rivera, 4:51–52
   of San Xavier del Bac, 4:69
Art, pre-Columbian, **1:69–72** *(illus.)*. *See also* Architecture
   archaeology and, 1:42 *(illus.)*
   Chavin, 1:188
   at Chavín de Huántar site, 1:189
   at La Venta, 3:41
   Mesoamerican art, 1:69–70, 3:106, 107

Moche, 3:139–40 *(illus.)*
Nasca and Nasca lines, 3:154–55
Olmec, 3:173–74
Quetzalcoatl in, 4:26
South American art, 1:71–72
Artigas, José Gervasio, **1:72–73**, 3:176, 4:168–69
Aruba, 2:83
Arzú Irigoyen, Alvaro, 2:184
Ashkenazim Jews, 3:30
Asia
   banking crisis in (1997), 1:100
   diseases from, 2:67
   Portugal's last outpost in, 4:10
Asians in Latin America, **1:73–75**, 2:227, 3:26, 4:32
Asiento, **1:75–76**
Astronomy, **1:76–77** *(illus.)*, 1:149–50, 191, 2:23
Asturias, Miguel Ángel, **1:77–78**, 3:64
Asunción, 1:49, 50, **1:78–79** *(illus.)*
Asunción, Treaty of (1991), 3:104
Asylum, **1:79–81**, 3:52, 85–86
Atacama Desert, 4:197–98
Atahualpa, **1:81**, 3:4, 6, 209–10, 225
Athaide, Manoel da Costa, 1:66
Atlases, 3:82. *See also* Maps and mapmaking
Audiencia, 1:18, **1:81–83** *(map)*, 1:125, 4:187
   of Caracas, 4:181
   of Charcas, 1:115
   evolution of, 1:81–82
   of Guatemala, 2:180
   high court of, 2:39
   laws and legal systems and, 3:51
   organization and function of, 1:82–83
   in Peru, 3:210
   of Quito, 2:93, 4:28
   of Santa Fe de Bogotá, 2:9
   of Santo Domingo, 4:76–77
Audiencia de los Confines, 2:180
Augustine, Saint, 2:109
Augustinians, 4:45
Austin, Stephen F., 4:131, 132
Authoritarian rule, roots of, 2:63. *See also* Dictatorships, military
Automobile industry, **1:83–85** *(illus.)*, 3:15, 23
Avalos Corrientes, battle of (1820), 1:73
Avería, 4:123
Aviation, **1:85–86**, 4:77–78
Ávila, Pedro Arias de, **1:86–87**, 1:93, 2:114–15, 3:189
Aviz dynasty, 4:12–13
Axayacatl (ruler), 1:90
Ayacucho, battle of (1824), 1:112, 4:203
Ayala, Eusebio, 1:185, 186
Ayerza, Francisco, 3:220
Ayllus, 1:87
Aylwin Azócar, Patricio, 1:201
Aymara, 1:22, **1:87–88**, 1:114, 4:154
Aymara language, 3:47
Azcona, José, 2:214
Azevedo, Artur, 4:135–36
Aztecs, **1:88–91** *(illus.)*, 2:51
   ancient highways of, 2:208
   art of, 1:70
   astronomy of, 1:76
   cacao seeds in religion of, 1:147
   calendars of, 1:149–50
   chinampas, 1:91
   conquistadors and, 2:20

   Cortés' conquest of, 1:90, 2:20, 26, 3:76–77
   culture and civilization of, 1:90–91
   divinities of, 2:69–70
   expansion of empire, 1:89–90
   hallucinogen use by, 2:77
   history of, 1:88–90
   irrigation and water control system of, 3:23
   literature of, 3:59
   Malinche and conquest of, 3:76–77
   Moctezuma II, ruler of, 3:140–41
   in Postclassic period, 3:107
   religion of, 4:42
   smallpox among, 2:66
   Tenochtitlán, capital of, 4:128–29
   Toltecs and, 4:142
Azul (Darío), 2:57, 3:63

B

Báez, Buenaventura, 2:73–74
Bahamas, 1:138, 3:223
Bahia, **1:91–92**, 1:129
   architecture of, 1:46
   missionary activity in, 3:133
   Sabinada Revolt in, 4:59–60
   Salvador, capital of, 4:63–64
Baja California, **1:91**
Baker, Lorenzo Dow, 4:158
Balaguer, Joaquín, 2:76
Balboa, Vasco Núñez de, 1:87, **1:92–93**, 1:161, 2:114, 3:179, 183
Balboa (unit of currency), 2:6
Balladares, Ernesto Pérez, 3:186
Ball game, pre-Columbian, 1:44, **1:93–94**, 1:191, 3:95, 4:113
Balmaceda Fernández, José Manuel, **1:94**, 1:198
Banana industry, **1:94–96**, 2:30, 96, 135, 148, 214
Banco de Avío, 1:98
Banco de Buenos Aires, 1:98
Banco do Brasil, 1:98
Bandeirantes, 1:130
Bandeiras, **1:96–97**, 2:116–17, 3:127, 129, 4:78
Banderilleros, 1:144
Banditry, **1:97–98**, 4:57
Banking, **1:98–100**, 1:173
Bank of London and South America (Buenos Aires), 1:47
Banzer Suárez, Hugo, 1:119
Baptista, João Gomes, 1:18
Baptista Firueiredo, João, 1:135
Barbados, 1:138
Barbuda, 1:138
Baroque style architecture, 1:45
Barrio Alto in Santiago, 4:75
Barrios, 1:210
Barrios, Gerardo, **1:100**, 1:166, 2:104
Barrios, Justo Rufino, **1:101**, 2:182
Barrios de Chamorro, Violeta, **1:101**, 3:166, 178, 4:211
Barrundia, José Francisco, **1:102**
Barrundia, Juan, 2:181
Barú (volcano), 3:186
Basadre, Jorge, 3:156
Baseball, 1:170, 4:114 *(illus.)*
Bases (Alberdi), 1:15
Basoalto, Neftalí Eliecer Ricardo Reyes. *See* Neruda, Pablo
Bastidas, Rodrigo de, 2:9

Batista y Zaldívar, Fulgencio, **1:102–3**, 2:44–45, 189
   Castro and overthrow of, 1:169, 170, 2:49
Batlle y Ordóñez, José, **1:103–4** *(illus.)*, 4:168, 171–72
Batouala (Maran), 3:157–58
Bautista de Anza, Juan, 3:161
Bay of Pigs Invasion, **1:104**, 1:170, 184, 2:46, 49
Beans, 2:134
Beef, 2:135, 3:97–98
Bejareque, 1:44
Belalcázar, Sebastián de, 1:150, 2:8, 9, 92, 115, 186
Belaúnde Terry, Fernando, 4:179
Belize, **1:104–6**, 1:107
Bello, Andrés, **1:106–7**, 3:61
Belmopan, 1:106, **1:107**
Belo Horizonte, 3:128
Beltrán, Manuela, 2:17
Bemberg, Maria Luisa, 1:206
Benedictines, 4:45
Beringia, 3:10
Berlanga, Thomás de, 2:151
Berni, Antonio, 1:68
Berro, Bernardo, 4:170
Betancourt, Rómulo, **1:107–8**, 2:75, 4:185
Beverages, 2:134–35
Bider, Haydée Tamara Bunke, 4:210
Big Stick Policy, 4:161
Bimetallic system of coinage, 2:6
Bingham, Hiram, 1:41, 3:72, 73
Biodiversity, preservation of, 2:111
Birds, 1:34–35
Birthrate, 4:210–11
Bishop, Maurice, 2:174
Bishops, 1:173–74
Blackbeard (Edward Teach), 3:224
Black Caribs (Garifuna), 1:162
Black consciousness, rise of, 4:33
Black Legend, **1:108–9** *(illus.)*, 3:60
Black nationalist movement in Haiti, 2:84
Blacks. *See* Africans in Latin America
Blaize, Herbert, 2:174
Blanco Party, 4:170
Blanes, Juan Manuel, 1:67
Bogotá, Santa Fe de, 1:48, **1:110–11**, 2:8, 17, 4:193 *(illus.)*
   Audiencia of, 2:9
Boleadoras, 2:158
Bolívar, Simón, **1:111–13** *(illus.)*, 3:184
   anticlericalism and, 1:35
   at Boyacá, battle of, 1:126
   Gran Colombia facilitated by, 2:173
   independence of Bolivia and, 1:117
   Peruvian independence and, 3:212
   Republic of Colombia established by, 2:11
   San Martín and, 4:68
   Santander and, 4:74
   Venezuelan independence struggle and, 4:182
   wars of independence and, 4:202, 203
Bolívar (unit of currency), 2:6
Bolivia, **1:113–20** *(illus.)*
   armed forces in, 1:62
   Aymara in, 1:88
   boundary disputes of, 1:123–24, 198
   Chaco War and, 1:119, 185–86 *(map)*, 3:197
   claims to Chaco, 1:123
   colonial period in, 1:115–16

231

Index

Guevara's guerrilla movement in, 2:189–90 (illus.)
history of, 1:114–20
independence of, 1:116–17
Indian policy in, 3:8–9
Indians of, 1:114–15
issues since independence, 1:117–20
Japanese immigrants in, 1:75
land of, 1:113
La Paz, capital of, 3:40–41
Melgarejo, president of, 3:101–2
Paz Estenssoro, president of, 3:200
Potosí, 4:15–16
revolution of 1952, 3:130
San Martín and liberation of, 4:67
Santa Cruz, president of, 4:73–74
Sucre, president of, 4:118
tin industry in, 3:130, 4:138–39
in War of the Pacific, 4:197–99
War of the Peru-Bolivia Confederation and, 4:200
Bolivian Revolution, 1:119, **1:120–21**
Bolivian social revolution, 1:120
Bomba, 3:151
Bombal, María Luisa, 3:64
Bonaire, 2:83
Bonampak, 1:71
Bonaparte, Joseph, 4:110
Bonny, Anne, 3:223, 224 (illus.)
Bonpländ, Aimé Jacques, 2:110, 221
Bookmaking, pre-Columbian, 3:79–80
Bordaberry, Juan María, 4:72
Borderlands. *See* Spanish Borderlands
Borge, Tomás, 4:69
Borges, Jorge Luis, **1:121–22**, 3:64
Borgia Group, 3:80
Boriquén. *See* Puerto Rico
Bosch, Juan, 2:75
Bossa nova, 3:151–52
Boston Fruit Company, 1:95, 2:148, 4:158. *See also* United Fruit Company
Botero, Fernando, 1:68
Boundary disputes, **1:122–24**
    Brazil and, 1:123–24, 132
    in Central America and Mexico, 1:124
    Chile and, 1:123, 198
    Christ of the Andes and, 1:203–4
    colonial, between Spain and Portugal, 1:130
    colonial legacy and, 1:122–23
    Ecuador–Peru, 2:96–97
    Gadsden Purchase and, 2:151
    Guyana and, 2:193
    military professionalization and, 2:63
    in South America, 1:123–24
    Treaty of Guadalupe Hidalgo and, 2:176–77
    War of the Pacific and, 4:197–99
Bourbon Reforms, **1:124–26**, 1:179, 4:107, 110
    agrarian reforms, 1:6
    on *audiencias,* 1:83
    Charles III and, 1:187
    in Honduras, 2:212
    in Mexico, 3:117–18
    in Peru, 3:212
    Provincias Internas organized as part of, 4:18–19
    in Puerto Rico, 4:23
Bouterse, Desi, 4:122
Boves, José Tomás, 4:182
Bowie, Jim, 1:15

Boxing, 4:115
Boyacá, battle of (1819), **1:126**, 2:11, 4:203
Boyer, Jean-Pierre, 2:80, 199
Bracero program, **1:126** (illus.), 1:190, 3:84, 4:161
Bragança dynasty, 4:13
Braithwaite, Nicholas, 2:174
Brasília, 1:48, **1:127–28** (illus.), 1:134, 3:38, 39, 167
Brazil, **1:128–36** (map)
    African–Latin American religious traditions in, 4:40
    Africans in, 1:4–6, 4:33
    agrarian reform in, 1:7–8
    Albuquerque, governor of, 1:17
    Amazon region of, 1:26
    Amazon River in, 1:26–27
    Andrada, statesman of, 1:31
    architecture in, 1:18–19 (illus.), 46–47, 48, 3:167
    artists of, 4:8–9
    Bahia, state of, 1:91–92
    bandeiras and opening of frontier of, 1:96–97
    boundary disputes of, 1:123–24, 132
    Brasília, capital of, 1:127–28 (illus.)
    Cabral's discovery of, 1:134, 146–47
    Candomblé, social role in, 1:155–56 (illus.)
    captaincy system in, 1:156
    Cardoso, president of, 1:159
    Carnival in, 1:162–63
    Castello Branco, president of, 1:168
    Catholic Church in, 1:174
    cinema in, 1:206
    coffee industry in, 2:4–5
    colonial art in, 1:65
    colonial period, 1:129–31
    Conselheiro, religious leader in, 2:21
    Constitution of 1824, 3:202
    coronel, political boss in, 2:25
    cultural diversity of, 1:128
    Cunha's writing on, 2:53–54
    democracy, return to, 1:134–35
    diamonds in, 2:160
    Dias, black military leader in, 2:60–61
    drought region in, 1:216
    Dutch in, 2:81–82
    education in, 2:99
    ex-Confederates in, 2:18
    explorations of, 2:115–17
    Farroupilha Revolt, 2:120
    federalism in, 2:123
    gold and silver in, 2:169
    history of, 1:129–35
    human rights activism in, 2:221
    independence and empire, 1:131–33, 4:11
    Indian policies in, 3:9
    iron and steel industry in, 3:23
    Jesuits in, 4:44
    João VI ruling from, 3:31
    juntas in, 3:36
    Kubitschek de Oliveira, president of, 3:38–39
    land of, 1:128–29
    laws and legal system in, 3:52–53
    Maurits, governor-general of Dutch, 3:92
    meat industry in, 3:97
    messianism in, 3:109
    Middle Easterners in, 3:125
    Minas Gerais, 3:128
    mining in, 3:128–30

    missions and missionaries in, 3:132–34
    modernist movement in, 3:63
    natural gas in, 2:108
    novelists of, 1:23–24
    Pantanal of, 3:192–93
    Pedro I of, 3:201–2
    Pedro II of, 3:202–3
    Pernambuco in, 3:206
    political parties in, 4:2
    Pombaline reforms in, 4:2–3
    popular music and dance of, 3:151–52
    population and population growth in, 4:6
    Portuguese immigrants in, 2:225–27, 4:12
    Portuguese language of, 3:48
    positivism in, 4:14
    Princess Isabel of, 3:25
    public sector in, 4:20, 21
    quilombos in, 4:27
    railroads in, 4:36
    Republic of United States of Brazil, 1:133–34
    rice industry in, 4:47
    Rio de Janeiro, 4:47–48
    road construction program in, 2:210
    rubber industry in, 4:57
    Sabinada Revolt in, 4:59–60
    Salvador, 4:63–64
    São Paulo, 4:78–79
    senado da câmara in colonial, 4:82–83
    Silva Xavier, independence fighter in, 4:88–89
    slave revolts in, 4:89–90
    slavery in, 4:93–95
    slavery in, abolition of, 4:95–96
    Sousa, governor-general of, 4:99
    spiritism in, 4:112–13
    street children in, 1:193
    tenentismo in, 4:128
    trade and commerce in, 4:148
    trading companies of, 4:150
    Treaty of Madrid and boundary of, 3:73–74
    Tupi of, 4:155
    universities in, 4:165
    Uruguay's struggle with, 4:168–69
    Vargas, president of, 4:177
    War of the Mascates in, 4:197
    War of the Triple Alliance and, 4:200–202
    wars of independence in, 4:205
    whaling industry in, 2:127–28
Brazil Company, 4:150
Brazilwood, 3:69
Brevísima relación de la destrucción de las Indias (Las Casas), 3:49
British abolition movement, 4:95
British Guiana, 2:193
British–Latin American relations, **1:137–38**
    Argentina and, 1:52, 55, 56
    in Belize, 1:105, 106
    Clayton-Bulwer Treaty, 1:215
    Crown Colony system, 1:106
    Falklands/Malvinas War and, 2:117
    foreign investment, 2:139
    Guyana and, 2:193–94
    Zelaya and, 4:218
British West Indies, **1:138–39**, 1:141–42, 3:28–29
Brito, Francisco Javier de, 1:66
Brotherhood of St. Cecilia, 2:154

232

Brotherhoods, **1:139–40**
Bryan, William Jennings, 1:140
Bryan-Chamorro Treaty (1914), **1:140**
Bubonic plague, 2:66, 3:101
Bucaram, Abdalá, 2:97
Buccaneers, **1:140–42**, 2:142, 3:28, 147, 223
Buena Vista, battle of (1847), **1:142**
Buenos Aires, **1:142–44** (illus.), 1:208 (illus.)
    Argentine Confederation and, 1:52, 53–54
    Argentine independence and, 1:51–52
    colonial, 1:50–51
    founding of, 1:49
    independence movement vs. Spanish viceroys in, 1:72–73
    Mitre, governor of province, 3:137
    Pan-American Conference at, 3:190
Bullfighting, **1:144–45** (illus.), 4:114
Bulnes, Manuel, 4:200
Bulwer, Henry L., 1:215
Bunau-Varilla, Philippe, 2:205
Burnham, Forbes, 2:193
Bush, George, 3:169, 4:149
Bustamante, Anastasio, 3:119
Bustamante y Rivero, Luis José, 2:206
Butterflies, 1:34

C

Caaybaté, battle at (1756), 2:179
Caballería, 3:45
Cabeza de Vaca, Alvar Núñez, **1:145–46**, 3:159–60, 4:131
Cabildo, 1:17–18, **1:146**, 1:157, 2:9
Cabot, Sebastian, 1:56, 2:115
Cabral, Pedro Álvares, 1:129, 134, 146–47, 2:114, 4:10
Cabrera, Miguel, 1:65
Cabrillo, Juan Rodríguez, 1:152, 2:115
Cacao industry, **1:147–48**, 2:94, 95, 3:93–94, 4:150, 181
Cáceres, Ramón, 2:74
Cachirí, battle of (1816), 4:74
Cacicazgos, 2:8
Caciques, **1:148–49** (illus.), 1:176, 2:197, 4:153–54
Caciquismo, 1:149
Caddo culture, 4:131
Cahuachi, 3:154
Caiman, 1:34
Calchaqui Indians, 1:50
Caldera Rodríguez, Rafael, 4:185
Calderón, Fernando, 4:135
Calderón Fournier, Rafael Ángel, 2:32
Calderón Guardia, Rafael Ángel, 2:30–31, 125
Calendar rounds, 1:149–50 (illus.)
Calendars, pre-Columbian, 1:76, **1:149–50** (illus.)
Cali, **1:150–51**
Cali cartel, 1:151, 2:79
California, **1:151–54**, 3:114, 4:84
Calleja, Félix, 3:113
Calles, Plutarco Elías, **1:154**, 1:158, 176, 2:40, 3:121, 172
Camargo, Joracy, 4:136
Campesinos, 1:12, 13
Cámpora, Héctor, 1:56
Canada, NAFTA and, 3:168–69
Canals, 1:202, 3:23–24. See also Panama Canal
Candomblé, **1:155–56** (illus.), 4:40
    orixás, gods and goddesses of, 3:176–77

Cantino map of 1502, 3:82
Canto general (Neruda), 3:158
Cantos de la mañana (Agustini), 1:14
Cantos de vida y esperanza (Darío), 2:57
Canudos (religious community), 2:21
Captaincy system, **1:156**, 1:183, 4:181
Capuchins, 4:43
Capybara, 1:33
Carabobo, battle of (1821), 3:180, 4:182
Caracas, **1:157–58** (illus.), 4:181
Caracas Company, 4:90, 150, 181
Caracol, Maya site of, 1:41, 76, 77 (illus.), 105, 191
Caramurus, 3:202
Carbon-14 dating, 2:53
Cardenas, Victor Hugo, 3:8
Cárdenas Del Río, Lázaro, 1:154, **1:158–59**, 3:121–22, 4:216
Cardoso, Fernando Henrique, 1:135, **1:159**
Carías Andino, Tiburcio, 2:64, 214
Caribbean Antilles, 1:138, **1:159–61** (map)
    Dominican Republic, 2:72–76 (illus.)
    Dutch West Indies, 2:83–84, 282
    Haiti, 2:196–201
    Hawkins' trading voyages to, 2:204
    Jamaica, 3:27–29
    Puerto Rico, 4:22–25
    sugar plantations in, 3:227
    tourism to, 4:145
    wars of independence in, 4:204–5
Caribbean region
    geography of, 2:167
    Indian cultures of, 3:12–13
Caribbean Sea, **1:161**
    buccaneers in, 1:140–42
    Cumaná as port for Spanish colonies in, 2:53
    pirate fleets in, 3:223
Caribs, 1:160–61, **1:162**, 2:83, 173–74, 3:13
Carlota. See Maximilian and Carlota
Carmelites, 4:46
Carnival, **1:162–63** (illus.), 2:124, 3:150, 151
Carpentier, Alejo, **1:163–64**
Carranza, Venustiano, **1:164**
    Mexican Revolution and, 3:111, 112, 121
    Obregón and, 3:171
    Villa and, 4:190–91
Carrasquilla, Tomás, 3:62
Carrera, José Miguel, **1:165**, 1:195
Carrera, José Rafael, 1:100, **1:165–66**, 1:181, 184, 2:63, 154, 3:145–46
    guerrilla movement led by, 2:187
    rule in Guatemala, 2:181–82
Carrillo Colina, Braulio, 2:29
Cartagena, **1:166–67** (illus.), 2:11, 77, 142–43
Cartagena Manifesto, 1:111
Cartels, drug, 1:151, 2:79, 80
Carter, Jimmy, 1:182, 3:85
Cartography. See Maps and mapmaking
Casa de Contratación, **1:167**, 3:81
Casa Grande, Arizona, 1:77
Casa poblada, 2:118
Casa Rinconada, 1:77
Casa verde, La (Vargas Llosa), 4:178
Caseros, battle of (1852), 1:52, 4:166
Cassava. See Manioc
Casta paintings, 1:66
Castas, 1:211, 2:38
Castello Branco, Humberto de Alencar, **1:168**

Caste system, 1:211–12. See also Class structure, colonial and modern
Caste War of Yucatán, **1:167–68**, 2:187, 3:96–97, 4:215
Castilla, Ramón, **1:169**, 2:63, 3:213
Castillo de San Marcos, 4:60
Castizos. See Mestizo
Castle and Cooke, 1:96
Castro, Cipriano, 2:170, 4:184
Castro, José Gil de, 1:67
Castro, Julián, 2:122
Castro, Raúl, 2:45, 49
Castro Ruz, Fidel, 1:20, 103, **1:169–71** (illus.), 2:188, 204, 4:137, 176
    Bay of Pigs Invasion and, 1:104
    Catholic Church and, 2:42
    CIA and, 1:184, 2:46
    communism and, 2:16
    counterinsurgency and concern over, 2:33
    Cuban missile crisis and, 2:47–48
    Cuban Revolution and, 2:45, 48–49
    foco model of insurgency, 2:34
    Guevara and, 2:189
    Mariel boatlift and, 3:85–86
    Soviet Union and, 4:104
Cathedral of Córdoba (Argentina), 1:46
Cathedral of Mexico City, 1:45
Catherwood, Frederick, 1:40
Catholic Church, **1:171–76**
    African–Latin American religions and, 4:39
    anticlericalism vs., 1:35–36
    architecture of, 1:45–46
    in Argentina, 1:54, 55, 56
    Black Legend and, 1:109
    brotherhoods, 1:139–40
    Candomblé discouraged by, 1:156
    Carrera and, 1:166
    Christian Base Communities, 1:204
    colonial art and establishment of Christianity, 1:64
    in colonial period, 1:171–73
    Cristero Rebellion and, 2:40–41
    Duvalier and, 2:84 (illus.)
    education and, 2:98
    Enlightenment and, 2:109
    expeditions of conquistadors and, 2:19
    gender roles and, 2:160, 161
    Gutiérrez and, 2:192
    Guzmán Blanco and, 2:194
    human rights activism and, 2:220
    Inquisition and, 3:17–18 (illus.)
    liberalism and reform of, 3:54
    liberation theology and, 3:54–56 (illus.)
    marriage and divorce practices and, 2:162, 3:87
    Maximilian and, 3:92, 93
    missions and missionaries, 3:132–36
    Penitentes and, 3:204–5
    Pombaline reforms and, 4:2
    in Quito, 4:29
    religious festivals of, 2:124–25
    sacred music and, 3:148–49
    Salinas and, 4:62
    in San Juan, Puerto Rico, 4:66
    syncretism and, 4:123
    taxes supporting, 4:123
    Virgin of Guadalupe and, 2:175–76
Cattle and cattle ranching, 3:65–66, 67, 97–98
Caudillismo, 1:176
Caudillos, 1:62, 149, **1:176–77**
    Artigas, 1:72–73

233

Index

    in Dominican Republic, 2:73
    Estrada Cabrera, 2:113
    in Guatemala, 2:182
    Guzmán Blanco, 2:194–95
    liberal, 1:181
    Melgarejo, 3:101–2
    military dictatorships under, 2:63
    in Peru, 3:213
    in Venezuela, 4:182–84
Cauto, Liberato. *See* Molina, Pedro
Cayenne, French Guiana, 2:145
Cayman Islands, 1:138
Ceballos, Gregorio Vázquez, 1:64
Cedras, Raoul, 1:59, 2:201
Censorship, 1:135, **1:177–78**, 1:206, 3:33–34
Central America, **1:178–82** *(map)*
    boundary disputes in, 1:124
    Clayton-Bulwer Treaty, 1:215
    clothing of, 2:1
    coffee industry in, 2:5
    colonial period in, 1:179
    El Salvador, 2:102–6 *(illus.)*
    geography of, 2:167
    Guatemala, 2:180–84 *(illus.)*
    Honduras, 2:211–15
    from independence to 1900s, 1:179–81
    Indian cultures of, 3:10–11
    nations of, 1:178
    Nicaragua, 3:162–67
    wars of independence in, 4:203–4
Central America, United Provinces of, 1:124, 178, 180, **1:183–84**, 3:163, 4:65
    Arce, president of, 1:39
    Barrundia's leadership of, 1:102
    Carrera and end of, 1:165, 166
    Costa Rica and, 2:28, 29
    Delgado and constitution of, 2:59
    formation of, 2:104
    Guatemala and, 2:181
    Guatemala City as capital of, 2:185
    Honduras and, 2:213
    Molina as diplomat for, 3:142
    Morazán, president of, 3:145–46
    San Salvador as capital of, 4:68
    Valle, president of, 4:174–75
Central American Common Market (CACM), 1:181, 182, 2:136
Central American Socialist Party, 3:89
Central Intelligence Agency, **1:184**
    Allende and, 1:20
    in Cuba, 2:46
    in Guatemala, 1:38, 2:183
    in Nicaragua, 3:166, 4:70
Cepeda, battle of (1820), 1:73
Cerro Corá, battle of, 3:67
Cerro Rico, 4:15
Césaire, Aimé, 3:157
Céspedes, Carlos Manuel de, 4:127
Chacabuco, battle of (1817), 1:196
Chacmool statues, 1:70
Chaco (Gran chaco), 1:49, 113, 185, 3:197
Chaco Boreal, 1:185, 3:197
Chaco Indians, 1:50
Chaco War, 1:62, 85, 119, **1:185–86** *(map)*, 3:197, 4:58
Chacras, 1:194, 3:45
Chambi, Martín, 3:221
Chamorro, Emiliano, 3:164–65
Chamorro, Fruto, 3:163
Chamorro Cardenal, Pedro Joaquín, 1:101, 3:166
Chamorro Vargas, Emiliano, 1:140

Chanca, 3:4
Chancay, 2:53
Chan Chan, 1:42, 72, **1:186–87** *(illus.)*, 1:207, 4:103
Chapultepec, Act of (1945), 3:191, 4:50
Charca Indians, 1:114
Charcas, 1:115–16
    Audiencia of, 1:115
Charismatic movement, 1:175
Charles I of Spain, 3:49, 210, 4:106, 109
Charles II, 2:5, 4:109
Charles III, 1:18, 173, **1:187–88**, 2:110, 4:49, 110
Charles IV, 1:125, 4:110
Charles V, 2:27, 167
Charqueadas, 3:97
Charqui (jerky), 3:98
Charreada, 4:114
Charrúa Indians, 2:179
Chávez, César, 1:190, 191
Chávez Frías, Hugo Rafael, 4:185–86
Chavin, 1:41, **1:188**, 3:11
    art of, 1:71
    copper mining by, 2:23
Chavín de Huántar, **1:188–89**, 4:103
Chiapas, **1:189–90**, 3:116
    guerrilla movements in, 2:188–89
    Tzendal Rebellion in, 4:155–56
    Zapatista movement in, 4:62
Chibcha Indians, 1:110, 2:8
Chicanos, **1:190–91**
Chichén Itzá, **1:191**, 3:108
    archaeological study of, 1:41
    Caracol at, 1:41, 76, 77 *(illus.)*, 105, 191
    establishment of, 3:95–96
    pyramid at, 1:45 *(illus.)*
Chichimecs, 3:138–39
Chicle, trade in, 1:105
Chico Mendes Extractive Reserve, 2:111
Chiefdoms in Amazonia, 4:100
Children, **1:192–93** *(illus.)*. *See also* Family
    education of, 2:97–100
    household and, 2:119
Chile, **1:193–201** *(map)*
    Allende, president of, 1:19–20
    armed forces in, 1:61
    Balmaceda Fernández, president of, 1:95
    Bello, intellectual in, 1:107
    boundary disputes of, 1:123, 198
    Carrera and independence of, 1:165
    Christ of the Andes between Argentina and, 1:203–4
    Civil Code of Republic of, 1:106
    climate of, 1:216
    colonial settlement and rule, 1:194–95
    Communist Party in, 2:16
    copper mining in, 2:24
    earthquakes in, 2:85
    Easter Island and, 2:85
    education in, 2:99–100
    emergence of modern, 1:199–201
    Frei Montalva, president of, 2:144
    independence, struggle for, 1:195–96, 4:203
    irrigation technique in, 3:24
    latifundia in, 3:50
    nitrate industry in, 3:167–68
    O'Higgins, freedom fighter in, 3:172–73
    Parliamentary Republic of, 1:198
    Pinochet Ugarte, president of, 3:221–22
    Portales Palazuelos, leader of, 4:7–8
    public sector in, 4:20–21

    railroads in, 4:36
    revolution (1891), 1:61
    San Martín and liberation of, 4:67
    Santiago, capital of, 4:74–76
    Soviet relations with, 4:104–5
    Spanish conquest of, 1:194, 4:117–18
    Tierra del Fuego and, 4:137
    Valparaíso, 4:175–76
    volcanoes in, 4:194
    in War of the Pacific, 4:197–99
    War of the Peru-Bolivia Confederation and, 4:200
    wine industry in, 4:207
Chiles, 1:201–2, 2:135, 4:112
Chili powder, 4:112
Chimor, Kingdom of, 1:202
Chimu, 1:42, **1:202**, 3:6
    art of, 1:72
    Chan Chan, capital of, 1:186–87 *(illus.)*
    Incan conquest of, 1:202, 3:4
Chinampas, 1:10, 91, 3:24
Chincha Islands, 2:178
Chinchorro culture, 1:40, 42, 4:103
Chinese in Latin America, 1:74
Chinos de manila, 1:73
Chiriguanos, 1:118, **1:203**
Cholera, 2:67, 154, 181
Cholos, 3:40
Christian base communities, **1:204**, 3:55
Christ of the Andes, **1:203–4**
Christophe, Henri, **1:204–5**, 2:198, 199, 202
Chrysler Corporation, 1:84
Church. *See* Catholic Church; Protestantism
Church of São Francisco (Salvador), 1:65
CIA. *See* Central Intelligence Agency
Cíbola. *See* Seven Cities of Cíbola
Científicos, 2:61, 4:14
Cigars, 4:141
Cimarrónes. *See* Maroons
Cinema, **1:205–7**, 4:25. *See also* Theater
Cisplatine province, 4:169
Cities and urbanization, **1:207–10** *(illus.)*
    Acapulco, 1:1
    Asunción, 1:78–79
    Aztec, 1:89
    Brasília, 1:127–28 *(illus.)*
    Caracas, 1:158
    changes in class structure and, 1:213, 214
    in Colombia, 2:12–13
    economic development and, 2:89
    European influence on, 1:207–9
    Guatemala City, 2:184–85
    independence and urban life, 1:209
    La Paz, 3:40–41
    Manaus, 3:77–78
    in Mexico, 3:122–23
    Mexico City, 3:123–25
    Montevideo, 3:144–45
    in 1900s, 1:209–10
    Port-au-Prince, 4:7
    in pre-Columbian cultures, 1:207, 2:52
    Recife, 4:38–39
    Rio de Janeiro, 4:47–48
    Salvador, 4:63–64
    Santiago, 4:74–76
    São Paulo, 4:78–79
    street vendors and, 4:115–16
    urban households, 2:119–20
    urban planning, 1:46
    urban society, 1:214
    Valparaíso, 4:175–76
Ciudadelas, 1:187

Civilian air transport, 1:86
Civil law, 3:50
Civil rights, 2:218, 219, 3:54
Clark, George Rogers, 2:152
Classic period, 3:95, 106–7
Class structure, colonial and modern, **1:210–15**
   Caste War of Yucatán and, 1:167–68
   changes in, 1:212–13
   in Chimu society, 1:202
   in Colombia, 2:8, 12
   colonial, 1:179, 211–12
   debt peonage and, 2:58
   domestic labor in, 2:71–72
   economic development and, 2:88, 89
   education and, 2:98
   in El Salvador, 2:105
   in French West Indies, 2:147–48
   in Haiti, 2:197–98
   hidalgo in, 2:206–7
   Inca, 3:4–5
   marriage and divorce and, 3:87, 88
   Mayan, 3:95
   mestizos in, 3:109–10
   in Mexico, 3:117–18
   Moche, 3:139
   other social developments, 1:215
   in Peru, 3:215
   poverty and, 3:7–8
   race and ethnicity and, 4:31–32
   social structure and income inequality, 3:7
   of today, 1:213–14
   in Uruguay, 4:168, 171
   War of the Mascates and, 4:197
Clayton, John M., 1:215
Clayton-Bulwer Treaty (1850), **1:215**, 3:164
Clergy, 1:172, 173
Clericalism, 1:35
Climate and vegetation, **1:216–18**
   in Amazon region, 1:24–26
   in Caribbean, 2:167
   in Central America, 2:167
   in Colombia, 2:7
   disease and, 3:101
   ecosystems and animals, 1:35
   El Niño and, 2:102
   forest, savanna, and desert, 1:217–18
   in Honduras, 2:212
   latitude and altitude, 1:216
   of llanos, 3:67
   in Mexico, 3:116
   in Paraguay, 3:193
   in rain forests, 4:36–38
   seasonal variations, 1:216–17
   soil and, 1:217
   in South America, 2:165–66
   vegetation, 1:217–18
Climate zones, 1:217
Clinton, Bill, 3:169
Clothing, **2:1–2**, 2:3, 9
Coahuila-Tejas, 1:15
Coal resources, 2:108–9
Coard, Bernard, 2:174
Cocaine, 2:78, 79, 3:99
Coca leaves, 3:99
Coche, Treaty of (1863), 2:122
Cochineal industry, **2:3**, 2:181
Cocoms dynasty, 3:96
Code Rurale, 2:199
Codex Vindobonensis, 3:80
Codices, 3:79–80

Coelho, Gonçalo, 2:115
Coffee industry, 1:13, **2:3–5**
   in Colombia, 2:7, 12
   in Costa Rica, 2:29
   in El Salvador, 2:104–5
   in Guatemala City, 2:185
   industrial growth and, 3:15
   plantations, 3:227
   production (1997–1998), 2:4
   railroads and, 4:36
   Rio de Janeiro and, 4:47–48
Coffee (painting), 4:8 *(illus.)*, 9
Cofradía, 1:140
Coins and coinage, **2:5–7**
Colbert, Jean-Baptiste, 2:147
Cold War, 2:46, 47–48, 4:104
Colhua Mexica. *See* Aztecs
Colla Indians, 1:114
Colleges. *See* Universities and colleges
Collor de Mello, Fernando, 1:135
Colombia, **2:7–14** (map)
   banditry in, 1:98
   Bogotá, capital of, 1:110–11
   boundary disputes of, 1:123
   Cali, city in, 1:150–51
   church–state relations in, 1:172
   coal resources in, 2:108–9
   coffee industry in, 2:4, 5
   colonial, 2:8–10
   Comunero Revolt in, 2:17
   disunity and regionalism in, 2:11–12
   drug trade in, 2:79
   emeralds in, 2:159
   federalism in, 2:123
   geography of, 2:7
   independence of, 2:11, 3:153–54
   La Violencia in, 4:192–94
   Nariño, independence leader in, 3:153–54
   Panama as part of, 3:184
   precolonial history, 2:7–8
   San Agustín site in, 4:64
   since 1900, 2:12–14
   social tension and regeneration in, 2:12
   Spanish conquest of, 2:8
   War of the Thousand Days in, 4:200
   wars of independence in, 1:126
Colón, Diego, 4:77
Colón, Watermelon Riot in, 4:205
Colonial period
   architecture of, 1:44–47
   in Argentina, 1:49–51
   in Arizona, 1:60
   art of, 1:64–66
   attitudes toward industrialization in, 3:15
   in Bolivia, 1:115–16
   boundary disputes as legacy of, 1:122–23
   Bourbon Reforms in, 1:124–25
   in Brazil, 1:129–31
   Catholic Church in, 1:171–73
   cities built during, 1:207–9
   in Colombia, 2:8–10
   crime and punishment in, 2:37–40
   in Cuba, 2:42–43
   domestic labor in, 2:71
   in Dutch West Indies, 2:83
   economic development in, 2:86–87
   education in, 2:97–98
   in El Salvador, 2:103–4
   family during, 2:118
   fleet systems in, 2:128–29
   foreign investment in, 2:138–39
   French West Indies in, 2:146–47

   in Grenada, 2:173–74
   in Guatemala, 2:180
   guerrilla movements in, 2:187
   hacienda agriculture of, 1:10–11
   highways during, 2:209–10
   human rights abuses in, 2:219–20
   impact of European colonization on Indians, 3:13
   land ownership in, 3:44–45
   laws and legal systems in, 3:51
   literature of, 3:60
   marriage, sexuality, and patriarchy in, 2:162–63
   medicine in, 3:100
   in Mexico, 3:116–18
   mining in, 3:129–30
   missions and missionaries of, 3:132–36
   in Nicaragua, 3:163–64
   nutrition in, 3:170
   in Paraguay, 3:194–95
   plantation agriculture in, 3:226–27
   public sector roots in, 4:19
   race and ethnicity in, 4:30–32
   science in, 4:80
   Spanish empire, 4:105–7
   sugar plantations in, 4:119–20
   taxes in, 4:123
   in Texas, 4:131
   textile industry in, 4:133
   theater in, 4:135
   trade and commerce in, 4:147–48
   in Trinidad and Tobago, 4:151–52
   universities and colleges during, 4:164–65
   wine industry in, 4:206–7
   women's roles in, 4:208
Colonos (rural workers), 2:58
Colón (unit of currency), 2:6
Colorado Party, 3:198–99, 4:117, 170
Colorado River, water rights and, 4:162–63
Colosio, Luis Donaldo, 3:122, 4:62
Columbus, Bartholomew, 4:76
Columbus, Christopher, 1:138, **2:14–15**
   age of exploration begun by, 2:113, 114
   Caribbean explorations, 1:160
   in Cuba, 2:42
   in Hispaniola, 2:14, 15, 197, 210
   Indians and, use of term, 3:10
   in Jamaica, 3:28
   maps made by, 3:81
   in Puerto Rico, 4:22
   sugarcane introduced by, 1:13, 4:119
   in Trinidad, 4:151
   in Venezuela, 4:180
   Virgin Islands, discovery of, 4:194
Columbus, Diego, 4:22
Comanche, 3:161
Comayagua, 4:126
Comintern, 2:15, 16
Commerce. *See* Trade and commerce
Commercial agriculture, modern, 1:12–14
Commercial holidays, 2:125
Commercial policy. *See* Trade and commerce
Commonwealth, Puerto Rico as, 4:25
Communism, **2:15–17**
   Allende and, 1:20
   Alliance for Progress and, 1:20–21
   armed forces and, 1:62
   Castro and, 1:170–71
   in Central America, 1:182
   counterinsurgency vs., 2:32–34
   in Cuba, 2:45–47
   Cuban Communist Party, 2:44, 47

235

Index

Cuban Revolution and, 2:48–49
  in El Salvador, 2:105, 3:89
  guerrilla movements and, 2:188
  labor movements and, 3:43
  military dictatorships and, 2:64
  in modern Latin America, 2:16–17
  Sendero Luminoso and, 3:214, 4:83–84
  Soviet–Latin American relations and, 4:104–5
  U.S.–Latin American relations and, 4:161
  from World War II to 1980s, 2:16
Communist parties, Soviet–Latin American relations and, 4:104–5. *See also* Communism
Comonfort, Ignacio, 3:120
Compadrazgo (ritual kinship), 2:119
Compañia de Barcelona, 4:23
Company of the Islands of the Americas, 2:147
Complete knockdown kits (CKDs), 1:84
Computers, 4:126
Comte, Auguste, 4:14
Comunero Revolts, 1:78, 2:10, **2:17**
Comunidades Eclesiales de Base. *See* Christian base communities
CONAVIGUA, 1:214
Concepción, Chile, 1:37
Conchabados, 1:51
Concha War, 2:112
Concordat of 1887, 1:172
Condor, 1:35
Condorcanqui, José Gabriel. *See* Tupac Amaru
Confederates in Brazil and Mexico, **2:18**
Conference of Latin American Bishops (CELAM), 1:175, 176
Congress of Indigenous Literature of the Americas, 3:58
Conquistadors, 1:179, **2:18–21** *(illus.)*
  Almagro, 1:21–22 *(illus.)*
  Alvarado y Mesía, 1:22–23 *(illus.)*
  attitudes toward Indians, 4:30–31
  audiencias and limitation of powers of, 1:81
  Balboa, 1:92–93
  bullfighting introduced by, 1:144
  Cabeza de Vaca, 1:145–46
  in Chile, 1:194
  copper mining by, 2:24
  Cortés, 2:26–28
  in Ecuador, 2:92–93
  expeditions of conquest, 2:19–20, 3:209–10, 4:124
  explorations of, 2:114–15
  fate of, 2:20–21
  in Guatemala, 2:180
  Maya and, 3:96, 4:124
  motivations of, 2:18–19
  Narváez, 3:154
  Orellana, 3:174
  Pizarro brothers, 3:225–26
  Soto, 4:98–99
  Valdivia, 4:174
Conselheiro, Antônio, **2:21**, 2:54, 3:109
Conselho da India, 4:10
Conselho Ultramarino, 4:11
Consensual union, 3:87, 88
Conservative parties, 4:1. *See also* Political parties
  in Central America, 1:180–81
  in Guatemala, 2:182
  in Venezuela, 4:183
Constitutional Coalition, 3:111, 121

Constitutional law, 3:50
Consulado, **2:21–22**
Contarini-Roselli map of 1506, 3:82
Contraband, 4:96
Contraceptives, 2:119
Contras, 1:101, 182, **2:22–23**, 3:166, 178, 4:70
Conversos, 3:30, 31
Cook, James, 3:179
Cooperatives, 1:13–14
Copán, 1:41, **2:23**
Copper industry, 1:199, **2:23–24**, 2:24, 3:131
Copper porphyry, 2:24
Corbia, Rómulo, 1:108
Córdoba, 1:49, **2:24–25**
Córdoba, Treaty of (1821), 3:113, 119
Córdoba Reforms, 4:165
Córdoba (unit of currency), 2:6
Corn. *See* Maize
Cornejo, José María, 1:100
Coronado, Francisco Vázquez de, 2:115, 3:160, 4:87
Coronéis, 1:149
Coronel, **2:25**
Correa, Juan, 1:64
Corregidor, 2:39, 3:29–30
Corrida de toros. *See* Bullfighting
Corrido, 3:151
Cortázar, Julio, **2:26**, 3:64
Cortés, Hernán, **2:26–28**
  Alvarado y Mesía and, 1:22
  Aztecs, conquest of, 1:90, 2:20, 26, 3:76–77
  early life and adventures, 2:26–27
  explorations of, 2:115
  Malinche and, 3:76–77
  Moctezuma II and, 3:140, 141
  sugar plantations of, 1:13
  Veracruz founded by, 4:186
  writings of, 3:60
Cortés Castro, León, 2:30
Cosa, Juan de la, 2:8, 114, 3:81–82
Costa, Lúcio, 1:127
Costa e Silva Bridge, 1:127
Costa Rica, **2:28–32**
  Arias Sánchez, president of, 1:58 *(illus.)*
  civil war in, 2:31
  coffee industry in, 2:5
  democracy and reform in, 2:30–31
  Figueres Ferrer, president of, 2:125–26
  geography of, 2:28
  National War in, 2:29–30
  railroad and banana trade in, 2:30
  reforestation in, 2:111 *(illus.)*
  San José, capital of, 4:65–66
  since 1950, 2:31–32
Costumbrismo, 3:108
Costume. *See* Clothing
Council of the Indies, 1:83, **2:32**, 3:117, 4:189
Counterinsurgency, **2:32–34**
  contras, 2:22–23
  guerrilla activity, 2:187
  nationalism and, rise of, 2:33
  during 1960s, 2:33–34
  since 1970, 2:34
Courts, colonial, 2:39–40. *See also* Laws and legal systems
Courts of First Instance, 3:52
Cowboys. *See* Gauchos
Crafts, **2:35–37** *(illus.)*
  folk art, 1:68–69

guilds of artisans, 2:190–91
in Mesoamerica, 2:50
Zapotec, 4:217
Creole(s), 1:179, **2:37**
  on *audiencia*, 1:83
  Chiriguanos and, 1:203
  as class, 1:211
  in colonial Mexico, 3:117, 118
  colonial schools for, 2:98
  Cuban, 2:43
  militias of, 2:63
  in Peru, 3:211
  Salvadoran, 2:104
  wars of independence and, 4:202
Creole languages, 3:48
Crime and punishment, colonial, **2:37–40**, 4:57
Criminal law, 3:50
Cristero Rebellion, 1:154, **2:40–41**, 3:121
Cristiani, Alfredo, 2:81, 106
Cristo Redentor. *See* Christ of the Andes
Crockett, Davy, 1:15
Crónica, 3:60
Crops, 1:9–10, 11. *See also* Agriculture; specific crops
Crown Colony of British Honduras, 1:105
Cruz, Oswaldo, 3:101
Cruzada de los Treinta y Tres, La, 3:176
Cruzob, 1:168
Cuacuauhpitzahuac (ruler), 1:89
Cuauhtemoc (ruler), 1:90
Cuba, **2:41–47** *(illus.)*
  agrarian reform in, 1:8
  American Revolution and, 1:28
  asylum policy, 3:85
  Batista y Zaldívar, president of, 1:102–3
  Bay of Pigs Invasion of, 1:104
  Carpentier, writer in, 1:163–64
  under Castro, 1:169–71 *(illus.)*, 2:45–47
  Catholic Church in, 1:174
  CIA and Operation Zapata in, 1:184
  cinema in, 1:206–7
  colonial, 2:42–43
  Columbus at, 2:14
  Cortés in, 2:26
  Guillén, national poet of, 2:191–92
  Havana, capital of, 2:202–4 *(illus.)*
  heroic women in, 2:161, 4:208
  history of, 2:42–45
  human rights abuses in, 2:220
  independence struggles of, 2:43, 3:87, 89–91, 4:205
  land of, 2:41
  Maceo, liberation army and, 3:70–71
  Mariel boatlift and, 3:85–86
  maroons and war for independence in, 3:87
  Martí y Pérez and independence in, 3:89–91
  Platt Amendment in constitution of, 3:228
  popular music and dance of, 3:151
  prostitution in, 2:163
  refugees from, 2:132
  revolution in, 2:43–45
  Spanish-American War and, 4:110, 111
  sugar industry in, 4:121
  Ten Years' War in, 4:127
  tourism in, 4:145
  U.S. interventions in, 4:160
  USS *Maine* sent to, 3:74–75
  Varela y Morales and nationalism in, 4:176

236

Cuban Missile Crisis, 1:170, 2:46, 47–48, 4:104
Cuban Revolution, 1:14, **2:48–49** (illus.)
   Castro and, 1:169, 170
   communism and, 2:16
   Cuba since, 2:45–47
   events leading to, 2:43–45
   Gómez y Báez in, 2:171–72
   guerrilla warfare in, 2:188
   Guevara and, 2:189
   interference with journalism in, 3:33
   race and, 1:5
   Soviet–Latin American relations and, 4:104
   women and, 4:210
Cubas, Raul, 3:198–99
Cubatão, Brazil, 2:111 (illus.)
Cuicuilco, 1:40
Cuisines, development of, 2:135–36
Cuitlahuac (ruler), 1:90, 2:27
Cultural nationalism, 3:157
Cultural stratigraphy, 1:41
Cultures, pre-Columbian, **2:49–53**
   agriculture in, 1:8–10
   archaeology and study of, 1:40–43
   architecture of, 1:43–44
   Aztec, 1:88–91 (illus.)
   beginnings of, 4:102–3
   Chavin, 1:188
   Chavín de Huántar site, 1:188–89
   cities of, 1:207
   crafts of, 2:35, 36
   death rate in, 4:4, 6
   diseases in, 2:65–66
   divinities in, 2:68–70
   El Mirador, 2:101–2 (illus.)
   Huari, 2:216
   Inca, 3:3–6 (illus.)
   jaguars' symbolic role in, 3:27
   literature of, 3:59–60
   manuscripts and writing of, 3:79–81
   Maya, 3:93–97
   Mayan center at Copán, 2:23
   in Mesoamerica, 2:50–51, 3:104–8
   in Mexico, 3:116
   Mixtecs, 3:138
   Moche, 3:139–40
   Monte Albán, 3:143–44
   musical instruments of, 3:152–53
   Olmecs, 3:173–74
   population of, 4:4
   rise of, 3:10–13
   in South America, 2:51–53
   technology of, 4:124
   Teotihuacán and, 4:129–30
   in Texas, 4:131
   textiles in, 4:133, 134
   Tiwanaku, 4:139–40
   Toltecs, 4:142–43
   women in, 4:208
Cumaná, 2:53
Cundinamarca, state of, 2:11, 3:154
Cunha, Euclides da, 2:53–54
Cupisnique people, 2:52
Curaçao, 2:83
Curanderos, **2:54–55** (illus.), 3:98, 100
Currents, ocean
   climate and, 1:216
   El Niño, 2:102
   Humboldt Current, 2:178, 221
Cuzco, **2:55–56** (illus.)
   Almagro and, 1:21–22 (illus.)
   architecture of, 1:43
   Inca culture and, 3:3, 4
   Inca roads branching out of, 2:208–9
   Temple of the Sun in, 1:76
Cuzco School, 1:65, 3:221

D

Dairy industry, 3:97
Dance, secular art, 3:150. *See also* Music and dance
Dance of the Millions, 4:121
Danish West India Company, 4:194
Danish West Indies. *See* Virgin Islands of the United States
Darién, Balboa as governor of, 1:93
Darío, Rubén, **2:57**, 3:62–63
Darwin, Charles, 1:34, 2:91, 151, 4:81
D'Aubuisson, Roberto, **2:57–58**, 2:80–81, 106
Dávila, Pedrarias. *See* Ávila, Pedro Arias de
Day count, 1:150
Daza, Hilarión, 4:198
Death squads, 2:57, 65, 184, 219
Debt, foreign. *See* Foreign debt
Debt crises, 4:20
   cycles of, 2:137–38
Debt peonage, **2:58–59**, 3:96, 97
Decena Trágica, 3:73
Deciduous forests, 2:140
Declaration of Panama (1939), 4:212
Defense, reforming colonial, 1:125
Defoe, Daniel, 3:224
Deforestation, 1:26, 2:140–41
Delgado, José Matías, **2:59**
Del Rio, Dolores, 1:206
Del Rosario, Andrés López (Andresote), 4:90
Democracy
   in Brazil, 1:135
   in Costa Rica, 2:30–31
   in Uruguay, 4:171–72, 173
   in Venezuela, 4:185
Depression
   from 1907–1909, 3:110
   of 1930s. *See* Great Depression
Déprestre, René, 3:158
Descamisados, **2:59–60**, 3:206, 208
Descartes, René, 2:109
Desert, 1:218
Dessalines, Jean Jacques, **2:60**, 2:198–99, 202, 3:217
Detroit Industry (mural), 4:51
Devil's Island, 2:145
Diamonds, 2:160
Dias, Bartholomeu, 4:10
Dias, Henrique, **2:60–61**
Díaz, Adolfo, 3:164, 4:71, 160
Díaz, Porfirio, **2:61–62** (illus.)
   Mexican Revolution and overthrow of, 3:110–12
   Porfiriato and, 3:120–21
   Rurales and, 4:57
Díaz del Castillo, Bernal, 1:210, 2:19
Díaz de Solís, Juan, 4:49
Dictatorships, military, **2:62–64**
   armed forces and, 1:62
   Castro in Cuba, 1:170–71
   caudillos, 1:176–77
   censorship by, 1:178
   in Central America, 1:180
   in Chile, 1:200–201
   in Dominican Republic, 2:73–75
   in 1800s, 2:63
   in El Salvador, 2:105–6
   Gómez, in Venezuela, 2:170–71
   in Guatemala, 2:182
   human rights abuses and, 2:219
   league of dictators, 2:64
   nationalist challenges to, 2:33
   in Peru, 3:214
   Pinochet Ugarte, in Chile, 3:221–22
   Porfiriato in Mexico, 3:120–21
   Rosas, in Argentina, 4:55–56
   Santa Anna, in Mexico, 4:72–73
   Stroessner, of Paraguay, 4:117
   Trujillo Molina, in Dominican Republic, 4:152–53
   in Uruguay, 4:173
   Vargas, in Brazil, 4:177
Diet. *See* Food and drink; Nutrition
Diezmo, 4:123
Dioceses, 1:172
Diphtheria, 2:66
Diplomatic asylum, 1:79
Dirty War (1974–1983), **2:65**
Disarmament in Latin America, 2:156–57
Diseases, **2:65–68** (illus.)
   African and Asian diseases, 2:66–67
   climate and, 3:101
   fight against, 2:67–68
   in Guayaquil, 2:186
   Inca and epidemic, 3:5–6
   Indians of Peru, 3:211
   Maya destroyed by, 3:96
   medicine and, 3:100, 101
   poor diet and, 3:171
   population in Spanish America and, 4:4–5
   in pre-Columbian period, 2:65–66
   slave trade and, 4:91–92
   Spanish arrival and spread of, 2:66
Divinities, **2:68–70**
   jaguars, symbolic role of, 3:27
   Quetzalcoatl, 4:26–27
   South American, 4:42
Divorce, 3:88
Dollar Diplomacy, **2:70–71**, 4:161
Domesticated plants and animals, 1:9–11
Domestic labor/service, 2:71–72, 4:85
Dominica, 1:139
Dominican Republic, **2:72–76** (illus.)
   colonial period, 2:72
   dictators, era of, 2:73–75
   Duarte, independence leader, 2:80
   establishment of, 2:199
   Haitian rule of, 2:73
   indpendence to 1930, 2:73–75
   La Trinitaria, political movement in, 4:152
   popular music and dance of, 3:151–52
   recent history, 2:75–76
   Santo Domingo, capital of, 4:76
   Trujillo, era of, 2:74–75
   Trujillo Molina, dictator of, 4:152–53
   U.S. intervention in, 2:74
Dominicans (Dominican order), 1:172, 2:98, 4:43–44
   Rosa de Lima, 4:55, 56 (illus.)
Don and *doña* (titles), 2:206–7
Donoso, José, 3:65
Dowry, 3:87
Drake, Francis, 1:137, 152, 167, **2:77**, 2:142, 204, 4:76
Drama. *See* Theater
Dresden Codex, 1:76
Dress. *See* Clothing

Index

Dreyfus, Alfred, 2:145
Drought region, 1:216
Drug cartels, 1:151, 2:79, 80
Drugs and drug trade, **2:77–80**
    in Bolivia, 1:120
    Cali cartel, 1:151, 2:79
    in Colombia, 2:13–14
    during and after colonial period, 2:78
    drug trade, 2:78–79
    economics and politics of, 2:79–80
    across U.S.–Mexico border, 4:162
    use of drugs, 2:77–78
    wealth from, 1:214
Duarte, Juan Pablo, 2:73, **2:80**, 4:152
Duarte Fuentes, José Napoleón, **2:80–81**, 2:106
Durán, Diego, 4:44
Dutch in Latin America, **2:81–82**
    Albuquerque's defense of Brazil against, 1:17
    Eckhout as official artist in Dutch Brazil, 2:86
    in Guyana, 2:193
    Maurits, in Dutch Brazil, 3:92
    in Portuguese empire, 4:11
    Sá e Benevides' success in Angola vs., 4:58
    in Suriname, 4:121, 122
Dutch West India Company, 1:17, 2:81
Dutch West Indies, 1:160, 2:82, **2:83–84**
Duvalier family, 1:58, **2:84** *(illus.)*, 2:200–201
    François (Papa Doc), 2:84, 200, 4:7, 143
    Jean-Claude, 2:84, 200–201, 4:143
    Port-au-Prince under, 4:7
    Tonton Macoutes and, 4:143
Dyewoods, 3:69

E

Earthquakes, **2:85** *(illus.)*, 2:166
    in Guatemala City, 2:185
    in Lima, 3:56
    in Managua, 3:77
    in Mexico City, 3:125
    in Nicaragua, 3:165
    in San Salvador, 4:68
Earth Summits (1992, 1997), 2:111
Easter Island, **2:85–86**
Ecclesiastical courts, 2:39
Echagüe, Pedro, 4:135
Echenique, José Rufino, 1:169
Echeverría, Esteban, 3:62
Eckhout, Albert, 1:64, **2:86**, 2:117
Ecology. *See* Environmental movements
Economic Commission for Latin America and the Caribbean (ECLAC), 2:90
Economic development, **2:86–91** *(illus.)*
    Alliance for Progress and, 1:20–21
    in Argentina, 1:50–51, 54, 55, 57, 4:53
    banana industry and, 1:94–96
    in Brazil, 1:135
    in Central America, 1:181–82
    changes in class structure and, 1:212–13
    in Chile, 1:197–98, 199
    in Colombia, 2:8–9
    in colonial times to 1900s, 2:86–88
    consulados and, 2:22
    counterinsurgency and, 2:33
    in Cuba, 2:47
    Dollar Diplomacy and, 2:71
    in Dominican Republic, 2:76
    in El Salvador, 2:106
    environmental movement and, 2:111
    foreign debt and, 2:137–38
    foreign investment and, 2:138–40
    guano industry in Peru and, 2:178
    in Guatemala, 2:183
    in Honduras, 2:212
    industrialization and, 3:14–17
    iron and steel industry and, 3:22–23
    literacy and, 3:58
    major sectors of economy, 2:90–91
    Mercosur and, 3:103–4
    in Mexico, 3:122
    Mexico City and, 3:124–25
    in Panama, 3:184–85
    in Paraguay, 3:195, 199
    in Peru, 3:215–16
    Pombaline reforms and, 4:3
    public sector and, 4:19–21
    social structure and income inequality, 3:7
    trade and commerce and, 4:147–48
    U.S. rule in Puerto Rico and, 4:24
    urbanization and, 1:209
    in Uruguay, 4:171
    in Venezuela, 2:171, 4:185–86
Economic nationalism, 3:157
Ecosystems, 1:35
Ecuador, **2:91–97** *(illus.)*
    banana industry in, 2:148
    Bolívar and liberation of, 1:112
    boundary disputes of, 1:123, 124, 2:96–97
    cacao production in, 1:147
    colonial history of, 2:92–93
    earthquakes in, 2:85 *(illus.)*
    Esmeraldas, 2:112
    Galápagos Islands and, 2:151
    García Moreno, president of, 2:156
    Guayaquil, largest city in, 2:185–86
    independence struggle in, 4:203
    Indian policies in, 3:9
    map of, 2:94 *(map)*
    Quito, capital of, 4:28–29
    Quito Revolt of 1765, 4:29–30
Ecue-Yamba-o! (Carpentier), 1:163
Education, **2:97–100**
    in Argentina, 1:54
    art, 1:66, 68
    in Brazil, 1:130
    Catholic Church and, 1:172
    colonial, 2:97–98
    in Cuba, 2:46–47
    literacy and, 3:58–59
    medical, 3:101
    music, 3:148–49
    positivism and reform of, 4:14
    Sarmiento and, 4:79
    science, 4:80–81
    since independence, 2:98–100
    universities and colleges, 4:163–66
Edwards, Haden, 4:131
Ehecatl Quetzalcoatl, cult of, 4:26
Einstein, Albert, 4:81
Eisenhower, Dwight D., 1:104
Ejercicios de la Encarnación (Juana Inés de la Cruz), 3:34
Ejidos, 3:45
El Ávila (mountain), 1:157
Elcano, Juan Sebastian de, 3:74
El Chamizal, 1:124, 4:163
El Chinchón, eruption of, 4:195
El Dorado, 1:25, **2:100–101**, 2:116 *(map)*, 169, 170 *(illus.)*
Elections, OAS observation of, 3:21
Electoral courts, 3:52
Electronic media, 1:178, 4:34–35
El Inca. *See* Garcilaso de la Vega, El Inca
El Lanzón, 1:189
El Mirador, **2:101–2** *(illus.)*
El Niño, 1:216, **2:102**
El Norte, 4:162, 163
El Pardo, Treaty of (1761), 3:74
El Salvador, **2:102–6** *(illus.)*
    agrarian reform in, 1:8
    Barrios, president of, 1:100
    Catholic Church in, 1:176
    coffee industry in, 2:5
    colonial period in, 2:103–4
    d'Aubuisson, political leader in, 2:57–58
    Delgado, independence leader of, 2:59
    Duarte Fuentes, president of, 2:80–81
    earthquakes in, 2:85 *(illus.)*
    Football War between Honduras and, 2:106, 136
    guerrilla movements in, 2:188
    human rights abuses in, 2:219
    independence of, 2:104
    land of, 2:102–3
    Martí, communist leader in, 3:89
    Matanza (1932), 3:91
    modern history of, 2:104–5
    from 1950s to present, 2:105–6
    refugees from, 1:80
    Romero, archbishop of, 4:54–55
    San Salvador, capital of, 4:68
    Soviet relations with, 4:104
El Zonda (newspaper), 4:79
Emeralds, 2:159–60
Emigration. *See* Immigration and emigration
Emiliano Zapata Liberation Army, 3:169
Employment. *See* Labor and labor movements
Encephalitis, 2:66
Encomenderos, 1:18
Encomienda, **2:107**, 2:118
    agriculture on, 1:11
    cacao industry and, 1:147
    in Colombia, 2:8
    debt peonage and, 2:58
    Guaranis and, 2:179
    imperialism and, 3:2
    Mixtó War vs. system of, 3:138–39
    in Paraguay, 3:195
    as reward for conquistadors, 2:20
    in Spanish Borderlands, 4:108
Endangered species, 1:35
Energy and energy resources, **2:107–9**
    ethanol production, 4:125–26
    Iguaçú Falls and, 2:224 *(illus.)*
    petroleum industry, 3:217–18
England. *See* British–Latin American relations
English buccaneers, 1:141–42
English language, 3:47
Enlightenment, 1:111, **2:109–10**
    anticlericalism and, 1:35, 36
    education and, 2:98
    liberalism and, 3:53
    literature and, 3:60–61
Entrudo, 1:163
Environmental movements, **2:110–11** *(illus.)*
    in Brazil, 1:136
    for forests, 2:140, 141–42, 4:38
    Indians and, 3:9
    nitrate mining and, 3:168
    to protect Pantanal, 3:192, 193

Environmental tourism, 4:145
Epic poems, 3:60
Ercilla y Zúñiga, Alonso de, **2:112**, 3:60
Esmeraldas, **2:112**, 3:86
Espinosa, Alonso, 4:69
Espinoza, Juan de Salazar, 1:78
Esquipulas II (Arias plan), 1:58
Esquival, Juan de, 3:28
Esquivel, Manuel, 1:106
Estado Nôvo, 4:177
Estancia, 2:195, 3:45, 65
Estanciero, 2:195, 4:55, 56, 167–68
Estanqueros, 4:7
Estigarribia, José, 1:185, 186
Estrada, Juan, 3:164
Estrada Cabrera, Manuel, 1:77, **2:113**, 2:183
Estuary, Río de la Plata, 4:48–49
Ethanol production, 4:125–26
Ethnic cleansing, 4:153
European Age of Discovery. *See* Explorers and exploration
Evangelicals, 4:17
Evita. *See* Perón, María Eva Duarte
Explorers and exploration, **2:113–17** *(map)*
 of Brazil, 2:115–17
 Cabeza de Vaca and, 1:145–46
 Cabral, 1:146–47
 Columbus, 2:14–15
 conquistadors, 2:18–21 *(illus.)*
 first explorations, 2:114
 Henry the Navigator, 2:206
 Kino, 3:38
 Magellan, 3:74
 maps and mapmaking and, 3:81–84
 in Mississippi Valley, 3:136
 Narváez, 3:154
 Orellana, 3:174
 Pizarro brothers and, 3:225–26
 Portuguese, 4:9–10
 scientific information gathered by, 4:80
 Soto, 4:98–99
 of Spanish America, 2:114–15
 Valdivia, 4:174
 in Venezuela, 4:180–81
 Vespucci, 4:186–87
Export-led industrialization, 3:15–16
Exports, economic development dependent on primary, 2:88
External (diplomatic) asylum, 1:79
External trade, 4:147
Extinct animals, 1:32
Extractive reserves, 2:111
Ex-votos, 1:65, 4:46

F

Fábricas, 3:97
Factory system, 4:134
Falcón, Juan, 4:183
Falklands/Malvinas War, 1:56, 86, 124, **2:117**
Family, **2:118–20**. *See also* Marriage and divorce
 children in, 1:192–93 *(illus.)*
 colonial, 2:118
 gender roles and sexuality, 2:160–64
 households and, 2:119–20
 kinship and, 2:118–19
 marriage and divorce, 3:87–88
 women and, 4:208, 209, 210
Family size, 2:119

Farabundo Martí Liberation Front (FMLN), 1:184, 2:106, 3:89, 4:104
Farfán, Agustín, 4:45
Farming. *See* Agriculture
Farragut, Jorge, 1:28
Farrell Edelmiro, 4:213
Farroupilha Revolt (1835–1845), **2:120**
Fascism, **2:121–22**
Faustin I, Emperor, 4:99
Favelas, 1:5
Fazendas, 3:45. *See also* Hacienda; Land, ownership of
February Revolution, 4:152
Federação Brasileira pelo Progresso Feminino, 3:70
Federación Latinoamericana de Asociaciones de Familiares de Detenidos-Desaparecidos (FEDEFAM), 2:221
Federal courts, 3:52
Federalism, **2:122–23**
 Alberdi and, 1:15–16
 in Argentina, 1:52–53
 Farroupilha Revolt and, 2:120
 Federal War and, 2:122
 United Provinces of Central America and, 1:183–84
 in Venezuela, 4:183
Federal War (1859–1863), **2:122**, 3:180–81, 4:183
Federation of New Granadan Provinces, 2:11
Federmann, Nicholas, 2:8
Fedon, Julien, 2:173
Feijóo y Montenegro, Benito Jerónimo, 2:110
Félix, Maria, 1:206
Feminism. *See* Women
Feminismo, 2:161
Ferdinand II of Aragon, 2:14, 4:105, 109
Ferdinand VI, 4:110
Ferdinand VII, 2:11, 3:113, 118, 4:110
Fermage, 4:146
Fernández Hidalgo, Gutierre, 3:149
Fernández Reyna, Leonel, 2:76
Ferreira, Benigno, 3:197
Fertilizer, guano as, 2:177–78
Festivals. *See* Fiestas
Fiestas, **2:123–26** *(illus.)*
 Carnival in Brazil, 1:162–63 *(illus.)*
Figueres Ferrer, José, 2:31, **2:125–26**
Filibusters and filibustering, 1:215, 3:1, 2 *(illus.)*, 4:162, 196–97
Film. *See* Cinema
Financieras, 1:99
Finlay, Carlos Juan, 2:66, 4:81
Firewood, energy from, 2:109
Fiscal, 1:82
Fish, 1:33–34
Fisheries, 2:126
Fishing and whaling industries, **2:126–28** *(illus.)*, 2:192
Fleet systems, colonial, **2:128–29**, 2:142, 3:219, 4:147, 150
Flight, Santos-Dumont as pioneer of, 4:77–78. *See also* Aviation
Florentine Codex, 3:80
Flores, Juan José, **2:129**
Flores, Venancio, 4:170
Florida, **2:129–32** *(illus.)*
 cession to U.S., 1:1
 colonial, 2:129, 130–31
 east and west, 2:131–32

 exploration of, 1:145–46, 2:114, 3:154, 4:98–99
 Jesuits in, 4:44
 Latin American links to, 2:132
 Menéndez de Avilés as governor of, 3:103
 St. Augustine, capital of, 4:60–61
 U.S.–Latin American relations over, 4:160
Flota, 2:128
Folk art, 1:68–69, 2:35
Folk healers, 2:54–55
Folk medicine, 3:101
Folk music and dance, 3:150–51
Fonseca, Carlos, 4:69
Food and drink, **2:132–36** *(illus.)*
 agriculture and, 1:8–14 *(map)*
 beef, 3:97–98
 beverages, 2:134–35
 cacao, 1:147
 chiles, 1:201–2
 coffee, 2:3–5
 cuisines, development of, 2:135–36
 fiesta, 2:124
 fruit industry, 2:148
 maize, 3:75–76
 manioc, 3:78–79
 nutrition and, 3:170–71
 potato, 4:14–15
 rice, 4:46–47
 spices and herbs, 4:111–12
 traditional Native American, 2:133–35
 wine industry, 4:206–7
Football War, 1:181, 2:106, **2:136**, 2:214, 3:175
Foraker Act (1900), **2:136–37**, 4:24
Ford Motor Company, 1:84
Foreign debt, 1:99–100, **2:137–38**, 2:213, 3:17
Foreign investment, **2:138–40**
 banana industry and, 1:95–96
 in Cali, 1:151
 in Colombia, 2:13
 in Costa Rica, 2:29
 Dollar Diplomacy and, 2:70–71
 economic development and, 2:87, 88
 in Mexico, 2:62
 postwar industrialization and, 3:16
 in Venezuela, Gómez and, 2:171
Foreign trade, 4:147
 stages of, 4:148–49
Forests, 1:217–18, **2:140–42** *(illus.)*
 in Colombia, 2:7
 destruction of, 2:110
 lumber industry and, 3:69
 rain, 4:36–38
Formative period. *See* Preclassic period
Formentor Prize, 1:122
Fortress church, 1:46
Forts and fortifications, **2:142–43**
 architecture of, 1:45
 at Humaitá, 2:218
 Portuguese, 2:143
 presidios, 4:16
 Spanish, 2:142–43
France, American Revolution and, 1:27. *See also* French in Latin America
Francia, José Gaspar Rodríguez de, 2:63, **2:143–44**, 3:196
Franciscans, 1:203, 3:135, 149, 161, 4:43, 84
Franco, Hernando, 3:149
Franco, Itamar, 1:135, 159

Index

Franco, Rafael, 1:186
Fredonia, Republic of, 4:131
Free blacks, 4:93
Freebooters. *See* Buccaneers
Freedom fighters, 1:111–12
Freedom of press, 1:177–78, 3:33–34
Free Trade Area of the Americas, 3:104, 4:149
Free-trade policies, 4:149
Free trade zone, NAFTA and, 3:168–69
Frei Montalva, Eduardo, 1:200, **2:144**, 3:50
French and Indian War. *See* Seven Years' War
French Guiana, **2:144–45**
French in Latin America, **2:145–46**
    Argentina and, 1:52
    in Haiti, 2:196, 197–98
    Maximilian and Carlota and, 3:92–93
    in New Mexico, 3:160
French language, 3:47
French West Indies, 1:141–42, 160, **2:146–48**
Frondizi, Arturo, 1:56
Frontier presidios, 4:16
Fruit industry, **2:148**
    banana industry, 1:94–96
Fruits, 2:134
FSLN. *See* Sandinistas
Fuca, Juan de, 3:179
Fuentes, Carlos, **2:149** *(illus.)*, 3:64–65
Fuentes y Guzmán, Francisco Antonio de, 1:40
Fueros. *See* Laws and legal systems
Fuerza Aérea Mexicana, 1:85
Fujimori, Alberto Keinya, **2:149–50** *(illus.)*, 3:57, 4:32
    Sendero Luminoso and, 3:214–15

G

Gachupines. See Peninsulares
Gadsden, James, 2:151
Gadsden Purchase, 1:61, **2:151**, 3:120, 4:109
Gairy, Eric, 2:173–74
Gaitán, Jorge Eliécer, 1:110, 4:192
Galápagos Islands, 2:91, **2:151–52** *(illus.)*
Galeones, 2:128
Galibi. *See* Caribs
Galíndez, Jesús de, 2:75
Gallegos, Rómulo, 1:108
Galleon trade, 1:1, 3:78
Gallinazo culture, 4:103
Galtieri, Leopoldo, 1:56
Galván, Ignacio Rodríguez, 4:135
Gálvez, Bernardo de, 1:28, 2:131, **2:152–53**
Gálvez, José de, 1:125, 2:152, **2:153**
    Provincias Internas proposed by, 4:18
    reforms in Mexico, 3:117–18
    Spanish colonization of California and, 1:152
Gálvez, Mariano, 1:165, **2:154**, 2:181
Gama, Vasco da, 4:10
Games. *See* Sports and recreation
Gamio, Manuel, 1:40
Ganja, 2:78
Gante, Pedro de, 3:148
Garay, Juan de, 1:49, 143, 3:144
Garcés, Francisco, 4:69
García, Calixto, 2:171
García, José Maurício Nunes, **2:154–55**
García, Miguel, 1:98
García de Palacios, Don Diego, 2:23

García Márquez, Gabriel, **2:155–56** *(illus.)*, 3:65
García Moreno, Gabriel, 2:95, **2:156**
García Pérez, Alan, 3:214
García Robles, Alfonso, **2:156–57**
Garcilaso de la Vega, El Inca, **2:157**, 2:169, 3:60
Garifuna (Black Caribs), 1:162
Gasca, Pedro de la, 3:226
Gatun Lock, 3:188 *(illus.)*
Gauchesca literature, 3:62
Gauchos, 2:1, **2:157–59** *(illus.)*, 3:65, 91, 4:167, 168
Gays. *See* Homosexuality
Gazetas, 3:32–34
Geisel, Ernesto, 1:135
Gems and gemstones, **2:159–60**. *See also* Mining
Gender roles and sexuality, **2:160–64**. *See also* Family; Marriage and divorce; Women
General Agreement on Tariffs and Trade (GATT), 3:122
General History of the Robberies and Murders of the Most Notorious Pyrates (Defoe), 3:224
General Motors Corporation, 1:84
"Generation of 1837," 1:15
Geoglyphs, 3:155
Geography, **2:164–67**
    altiplano, 1:22
    of Amazon region, 1:24–26
    of Andes, 1:30–31, 2:164–65
    of Argentina, 1:49
    of Baja California, 1:91
    of Bolivia, 1:113
    of Brazil, 1:128–29
    of Caribbean Antilles, 1:159–61 *(map)*, 2:167
    of Central America, 1:179, 2:167
    of Chile, 1:193–94
    of Colombia, 2:7
    colonial justice and, 2:38
    of Costa Rica, 2:28
    of Cuba, 2:41
    of Dutch West Indies, 2:83
    of Ecuador, 2:91–92
    of El Salvador, 2:102–3
    of Guyana, 2:193
    of Honduras, 2:211–12
    Lake Titicaca, 4:139
    llanos, 3:67
    of Mexico, 2:166–67, 3:115–16
    of Mexico City, 3:123
    of Nicaragua, 3:162–63
    of pampas, 3:183
    of Panama, 3:186
    of Pantanal, 3:192–93
    of Paraguay, 3:193
    of Patagonia, 3:200
    of Peru, 3:208–9
    rain forests, 4:36–38
    Río de la Plata estuary, 4:48–49
    rivers and river valleys, 2:165
    Sierra Madre, 4:88
    of South America, 2:164–66
    volcanoes, 4:194–95
Geothermal energy, 2:109
Germans in Latin America, **2:167–68**, 4:180–81, 213
Gibbs, Charles, 3:224
Gilbert, Pedro, 3:224

Giró, Juan, 4:170
Gisbert, Teresa, 1:68
Glaciers, 2:165, 3:10
Glyptodons, 1:32
Godoy, Manuel de, 4:110
Gods. *See* Divinities
Gold and silver, **2:168–70** *(illus.)*
    in altiplano, 1:22
    bandeiras looking for, 1:96
    in Brazil, 2:169
    Cartagena and shipment of, 1:167
    coins and coinage, 2:5–7
    in Colombia, 2:8–9
    conquistadors' wealth from, 2:20
    in Cuba, 2:42
    in French Guiana, 2:145
    in Mexico, 3:117
    mining, 3:128–31
    in Peru, 3:212
    Potosí, 4:15–16
    silver mining in Bolivia, 1:115–16
    since independence, 2:169–70
Golden Law, 4:95
Gómez, Juan Vicente, 1:107, 176, **2:170–71**, 4:184
Gómez Farías, Valentín, 3:119, 4:72–73
Gómez Pedraza, Manuel, 3:119
Gómez y Báez, Máximo, **2:171–72**, 4:127
Gonçalves Dias, Antônio, 3:62
González Camarena, Jorge, 4:31 *(illus.)*
Good Neighbor Policy, **2:172**, 3:192, 4:71, 161, 212
Goodyear, Charles, 1:25
Goribar, Nicolás Javier de, 1:64
Gorostieta, Enrique, 2:41
Gorostiza, Carlos, 4:136
Goulart, João, 1:134–35
Gourde (unit of currency), 2:6
Government. *See also* Dictatorships, military; Political parties; *specific countries*
    Bourbon Reforms and colonial, 1:124–25
    colonial, in Argentina, 1:49–50
    local. *See* Alcalde; *Cabildo*; *Senado da Câmara*
    in Mexico City, 3:125
Government activism, 4:20
Governors, in Argentina, 1:50
Grains, 2:134
Grancia, José Gaspar, 1:176
Gran Colombia, 1:110, 112, 113, 2:11, **2:172–73**
    Ecuador and, 2:95
    Guayaquil incorporated into, 2:186
    Nariño as provisional vice president of, 3:154
    Panama as part of, 3:184
    Sucre and, 4:118
    Venezuela and, 4:182
    Viceroyalty of New Granada as, 3:159
Grande, Rutilio, 4:54
Grant, Ulysses, 2:74
Grão Pará and Maranhão Company, 4:150
Grasslands, 1:218
Grau San Martín, Ramón, 1:102, 2:44
Great Andean Rebellion, 3:212, 4:153–54
Great Depression, 1:213
    in Brazil, 1:133–34
    British–Latin American ties and, 1:138
    economic nationalism and, 3:157
    economy during, 2:183
    foreign trade and, 4:149
    labor movements and, 3:43

nitrate industry and, 3:168
    as turning point in economic development, 2:88
Greater Antilles, 1:160
Great Western Railway Company, 1:97
Greenhouse gases, 2:111
Gremio strikes in Chile, 1:20
Grenada, 1:139, **2:173–74**
Grenadines, 1:139
Grijalva, Juan de, 1:22, 2:26
Gringo, **2:174–75**
Grito de Lares, 4:23
Guadalajara, battle at (1811), 2:207
Guadalupe, Virgin of, 1:46, **2:175–76** (illus.)
Guadalupe Hidalgo, Treaty of (1848), 1:124, 2:151, **2:176–77**, 3:114 (illus.), 115
    Arizona and, 1:60–61
    California ceded to U.S., 1:153
    Texas and, 4:132
Guadeloupe, 2:146, 147, 148
Guajardo, Jesús, 4:216
Guaman Poma de Ayala, Felipe, 2:177
Guano industry, 2:85, **2:177–78**, 3:56, 131, 213
Guarani language, 3:199
Guaranis, 1:78, **2:179–80**
    in Brazil, 1:129
    Chiriguanos, descendants of, 1:203
    enslavement by *bandeiras*, 1:96
    heritage of, 3:199
    impact of European colonization on, 3:13
    Jesuit Republic and, 3:133, 134
    in Paraguay, 3:194–95
Guarani (unit of currency), 2:6–7
Guarani War (1753), **2:178–79**, 2:180, 3:134
Guardia Gutiérrez, Tomás, 2:29
Guatemala, **2:180–84** (illus.)
    Alvarado y Mesía as governor of, 1:23
    Arbenz Guzmán, president of, 1:38–39
    banditry in, 1:98
    Barrundia and liberal doctrine in, 1:102
    Carrera, president of, 1:165–66
    CIA Operation Success in, 1:184
    clothing in, 2:1
    coffee industry in, 2:5
    in colonial period, 2:180
    currency of, 2:6
    earthquakes in, 2:85 (illus.)
    El Mirador, Mayan ruin in, 2:101–2 (illus.)
    Estrada Cabrera, president of, 2:113
    guerrilla movements in, 2:187, 188
    human rights abuses in, 2:219
    from independence to 1850, 2:180–82
    K'iche' Indians in, 3:37
    in late 1800s, 2:182
    Menchú Tum, political activist in, 3:102
    in 1900s, 2:183–84
    refugees from, 1:80
    Republic of, 1:165
    Tikal in, 4:137–38
    Ubico y Castañeda, president of, 4:156
Guatemala, Kingdom of, 1:179, 180, 183
    El Salvador as part of, 2:103–4
    Honduras as part of, 2:212–13
    wars for independence and, 4:203–4
Guatemala City, 1:183, **2:184–85**
Guatemalan Revolution (1944), 2:183
Guayana, 4:179
Guayaquil, **2:185–86**
Gueiler Tejada, Lidia, 1:119
Guerra de Castas. *See* Caste War of Yucatán

Guerra Grande, **2:186–87**, 3:176, 4:170
Guerrero, Vicente, 3:113, 119
Guerrilla movements, **2:187–89**
    in Central America, 1:182
    contras, 2:22–23
    counterinsurgency and, 2:34
    in Guatemala, 2:181, 184
    militias and, 3:127
    modern, 2:188–89
    in Peru, 3:9
    Sendero Luminoso, 4:83–84
    in Uruguay, 4:172–73
Guevara, Ernesto "Che," 1:170, 2:34, 48 (illus.), 49, 188, **2:189–90** (illus.)
Guiana, French. *See* French Guiana
Guilds, 2:21, **2:190–91**
Guillén, Nicolás, **2:191–92**
Guinea pigs, 1:33
Guitar, 3:153
Gulf of Mexico, **2:192**
Gunboat diplomacy, 4:161
Gutiérrez, Gustavo, **2:192**, 3:55
Gutiérrez, José Angel, 1:191
Gutiérrez, Rodrigo, 1:66
Guyana, 1:123, **2:193–94**, 3:26
Guzmán, Abimael, 3:214, 215
Guzmán Blanco, Antonio Leocadio, 1:157, **2:194–95**, 4:183–84
Guzmán Fernández, Antonio, 2:76
Guzmán Reynoso, Abimael, 4:83, 84

H

Habitats, animal, 1:35
Hacendados, 2:196
Hacienda, 1:151, 194, **2:195–96** (illus.), 3:45
    colonial hacienda agriculture, 1:10–11
    debt peonage and, 2:58
Haiti, **2:196–201**
    Aristide, president of, 1:58–59 (illus.)
    black nationalist movement in, 2:84
    "boat people" from, 2:200
    Dessalines, emperor of, 2:60
    Dominican Republic seized by, 2:73
    Duvalier family in, 2:84 (illus.), 200–201
    European discovery and settlement, 2:197
    French colonization of, 2:196, 197–98
    in 1900s, 2:200–201
    Port-au-Prince, capital of, 4:7
    refugees from, 1:80
    revolution and independence, 2:147, 198–200, 4:204
    Tonton Macoutes in, 4:143
    voodoo in, 4:40, 195–96
Haitian Revolution, 1:204–5, 2:198–99, **2:201–2**, 4:146
Hallucinogens, 2:77–78
Hammocks, 2:36
Harpy eagle, 1:35
Hatun runa, 3:5
Havana, 2:42, 142–43, **2:202–4** (illus.), 3:190
Hawkins, John, 1:137, 167, 2:142, **2:204**
Hay, John, 2:205
Haya de la Torre, Víctor Raúl, **2:205–6**, 3:52
Hay-Bunau-Varilla Treaty (1903), 2:205, 3:184, 187, 188
Hayes, Rutherford B., 4:201
Hay-Paunce-Fote Treaty, 1:215
Healers, 2:54–55, 3:98–9
Healey, Giles, 1:71
Hembrismo, 2:161

Henriques, Alfonso, 4:9
Henry the Navigator, Prince, **2:206**, 3:81, 4:9
Herbalists, 2:54–55
Herbs, 4:111–12
Heresy, 4:43
Hernández, José, 3:62, 91
Hernández, Maximiliano, 2:64
Heureaux, Ulises, 2:74
Heyn, Piet, 2:129
Hidalgo, 2:18, **2:206–7**
Hidalgo y Costilla, Miguel, 1:173, **2:207–8**, 3:112–13, 118, 4:203
Hieroglyphic writing, 3:174
Highways and roads, **2:208–10** (illus.)
    in Amazon region, 1:25, 26
    ancient, 2:208–9
    colonial, 2:209–10
    destruction of forests and, 2:140–41
    in Guatemala, 4:156
    Inca, 3:4, 179
    modern, 2:210
    to Montevideo, 3:145
    in Peru, 3:216
Hispaniola, 2:14, 15, 197, **2:210–11** (illus.), 4:92. *See also* Dominican Republic; Haiti
Hispanismo movement, 3:3
HIV, 2:68
Hohokam people, 1:59
Holguín, Melchor Pérez, 1:64–65
Holidays. *See* Fiestas
Homosexuality, 2:40, 162–64
Honduras, **2:211–15**
    colonial history of, 2:212–13
    Football War between El Salvador and, 2:106, 136
    land of, 2:211–12
    modern, 2:215
    Mosquito Indians of, 3:147–48
    since independence, 2:213–14
    Tegucigalpa, capital of, 4:126–27
    Valle, statesman of, 4:174–75
    Walker's adventures in, 4:197
Honor, Spanish concept of, 2:19
Honório de Macedo, Silvino, 2:143
Horse, gauchos' culture centered around, 2:158
Households, 2:119–20
House of Trade. *See* Casa de Contratación
Housing in Mexico City, 3:124
Houssay, Bernardo A., **2:215–16**, 3:101, 4:81
Houston, Sam, 4:65, 132
Huaorani Indians, 3:9
Huari, 2:53, **2:216**, 3:6, 4:103
    art of, 1:71–72
    quipu developed by, 4:27–28
    Tiwanaku culture and, 4:140
Huascar, 1:81, 3:6, 209, 210
Huaso, costume of Chilean, 2:1
Huayna Capac, 1:81, 3:5, 6
Huerta, Adolfo de la, 1:154, 4:191
Huerta, Dolores, 1:191
Huerta, Victoriano, **2:217**, 4:57
    Carranza and opposition to, 1:164
    Mexican Revolution and, 3:111, 112, 121
    Villa and, 4:190
    Zapata and, 4:216
Huichols, **2:217–18**
Huidobro, Vicente, 3:63
Hull-Alfaro Treaty (1936), 3:185
Humaitá, **2:218**

Index

Human rights, **2:218–21** (illus.)
    abuses, 2:219–20
    activism, 2:220–21
    Catholic Church and, 1:175
    in Central America, 1:182
    current status of Indians and, 3:14
    in El Salvador, 2:57, 106
    Romero, advocate of, 4:54–55
    in Uruguay, 4:173
Human sacrifice, 2:69, 4:42
Humboldt, Alexander von, 1:25, 2:110, **2:221**, 3:83
Humboldt Current, 2:178, 221
Hunac Ceel, 3:96
Hunger, 3:170
Hurricanes, 1:106, **2:222–23** (illus.), 4:81
    Mitch, 2:215, 223, 3:166–67
Hydropower, 2:108, 109, 224, 3:193

I

Ibáñez del Campo, Carlos, 1:199
Ibarbourou, Juana de, **2:223**
Ideographic writing, 3:80
Iguaçú Falls, 1:49 (map), **2:224** (illus.)
Illegal immigrants, 2:228
Illegitimate children, 1:192
Illia, Arturo, 1:56
Illiteracy, 3:58
Immigration and emigration, 2:225–28
    Asian, 1:73–75
    to Buenos Aires, 1:143–44
    from Cuba, 2:46
    Florida and, 2:132
    intendancy system and, 3:19
    of Jews, 3:30–31 (illus.)
    to Latin America, 2:225–27
    within and from Latin America, 2:227–28
    of Middle Easterners, 3:125–26
    population and population growth and, 4:5, 6
    of Portuguese, 4:12
    race and ethnicity in Latin America and, 4:33
    refugees, 1:80–81
    to São Paulo, 4:78–79
    across U.S.–Mexico border, 4:162
Imperialism, **3:1–3** (illus.)
    anticlericalism and, 1:35–36
    British–Latin American relations and, 1:138
    Clayton-Bulwer Treaty and, 1:215
    modern, 3:2–3
    National War and, 3:155–56
    relationship of states, 3:1–2
    Roosevelt Corollary and, 4:55
    Spanish, 4:105–7
    Spanish–American War and, 4:110–11
    U.S.–Latin American relations and, 4:159–62
Import substitution, 2:89, 3:16
Impressionism, 1:67
In a Green Night (Walcott), 4:196
Inca, 2:53, **3:3–6** (illus.), 3:12
    ancient highways of, 2:208
    Araucanians resistance to, 1:37
    archaeological study of, 1:41–42
    art of, 1:72
    astronomy of, 1:76
    Atahualpa, ruler of, 1:81
    Aymara and, 1:88
    in Bolivia, 1:115
    calendars of, 1:150
    Cuzco founded by, 2:55
    defeat of Chimu by, 1:202, 3:4
    divinities of, 2:70
    hallucinogen use by, 2:77–78
    Huari civilization and, 2:216
    literary tradition of, 3:59–60
    llama raised by, 3:66
    Machu Picchu, 3:72–73
    messianic movements of, 3:109
    origins of, 3:3–4
    Pachacuti, emperor of, 3:179
    Pizarro brothers and, 3:225–26
    quipu used by, 4:27–28
    religion of, 2:70, 4:42
    smallpox among, 2:66
    society and religion of, 3:4–5
    Spanish conquest and, 1:21–22 (illus.), 3:5–6, 209–10
Incidents of Travel in Central America, Chiapas, and Yucatán (Stephens), 3:181
Income distribution, **3:6–8**, 3:45
Inconfidência Mineira, 1:130, 4:88–89
Independence day celebrations, 2:124
Independence movements. *See* Wars of independence; *individual countries*
Independent newspapers, 3:33
Indian policy, **3:8–9**, 3:14, 48–49
Indians, **3:10–14**
    of Amazon region, 1:25
    Araucanians, 1:37–38 (illus.)
    of Arizona, 1:59
    attitutes toward, in colonial period, 4:30–31
    Aymara, 1:87–88
    of Bolivia, 1:114–15
    of Brazil, 1:129, 4:6
    Cabeza de Vaca and, 1:146
    caciques (leaders), 1:148–49 (illus.)
    of Caribbean Antilles, 1:160
    Caribs, 1:162
    in caste system, 1:211–12, 214
    of Central America, 1:179
    of Chiapas, 1:189–90
    of Chile, 1:194
    class position of, 1:215
    clothing of, 2:1, 2
    of Colombia, 2:7–8
    conquistadors and, 2:20
    cultures, rise of, 3:10–13
    current status of, 3:13–14
    of El Salvador, 2:103, 105
    encomienda and, 2:107
    European colonization and, impact of, 3:13
    folk music and dance of, 3:150
    gender relations among, 2:161
    Guarani, 2:179–80
    guerrilla-style revolts, 2:187
    of Haiti, 2:197
    healing plants of, 3:99
    Huichols, 2:217–18
    human rights abuses toward, 2:219
    indigenismo movement, **3:14**
    indigenous languages of, 3:46–47
    Inquisition and, 3:17
    K'iche', 3:37
    Kuna, 3:39–40
    of Louisiana, Spanish policies toward, 3:68
    mapmaking by, 3:81
    mestizos and, 3:109–10
    migration to Americas, 3:10
    mining by, 3:129, 130
    missions and, 3:132–36
    Mosquito, 3:147–48 (illus.)
    musical instruments of, 3:152
    nutrition of, 3:170
    of Paraguay, 3:194–95
    of Peru, 3:215
    Pombaline reforms and, 4:3
    population of, 4:4–5, 6
    Pueblo, 1:59, 3:159, 161, 4:21–22
    in rain forest, 4:38
    religions of, 4:41–42
    ritual kinship among, 2:119
    Selk'nams, 4:82
    Seminoles, 2:131
    in slavery, 1:25, 4:3, 92, 94–95
    status under law, 2:38
    of Suriname, 4:121
    textile industry and, 4:133
    Treaty of Madrid and, 3:74
    Tupi, 4:155
    Tzendal Rebellion of, 4:155–56
    of Uruguay, 4:167
    yanaconas, 4:213–14
    Yanomami, 4:214
    zambos, 4:32
    Zapotecs, 4:217
Indigenismo, 1:109, 2:56, **3:14**, 3:213, 221, 4:33
Indigenous languages, 3:46–47
Indigo plantations, 2:103, 104
Industrialization, **3:14–17**
    building national economies and, 2:88–89
    changes in class structure and, 1:213
    colonial attitudes toward, 3:15
    export-led, 3:15–16
    import substitution and, 3:16
    industrial boom and bust, 3:16–17
    labor movements and, 3:43
    maquiladoras and, 3:84–85
    organized through household, 2:119
    postwar, 3:16
    trade and commerce and, 4:148–49
Industry(ies)
    automobile, 1:83–85 (illus.)
    banana, 1:94–96
    cacao, 1:147–48
    cities in 1900s and rise of, 1:209–10
    cochineal, 2:3
    coffee, 2:3–5
    copper, 2:23–24
    fishing and whaling, 2:126–28 (illus.)
    fruit, 2:148
    guano, 2:177–78
    iron and steel, 3:22–23
    lumber, 3:69
    as major sector of economy, 2:90–91
    meat, 3:97–98
    nitrate, 3:167–68
    petroleum, 3:217–18
    rice, 4:46–47
    rubber, 4:56–57
    service, 4:85–87
    sugar, 4:119–21
    technological advances, 4:125–26
    textile, 4:133–34
    tin, 4:138–39
    tobacco, 4:140–41 (illus.)
    weapons, 4:205–6
    wine, 4:206–7 (illus.)

Influenza, 2:66
Informal economy, 4:116
Inquietud del rosal, La (Storni), 4:115
Inquilinos, 1:194
Inquisition, Holy Office of the, **3:17–18** (illus.)
  Black Legend and, 1:109
  Cartagena as center for, 1:167
  Jewish settlers escaping, 3:30
  Protestants and, 4:17
Insects and spiders, 1:34
"Institutional" military governments, 1:62
Intendancy system, 1:125, **3:19**
  American Revolution and, 1:28
  cabildo under, 1:146
  Charles III and, 1:187
  in Chile, 1:195
  Intendancy of Venezuela, 4:181
  in Mexico, Gálvez and, 2:153
  Viceroyalty of Río de la Plata, 4:49–50
Inter-American Commission of Human Rights, 2:220
Inter-American Development Bank, 3:21, 22
Inter-American Foundation (IAF), 3:21–22
Inter-American relations, **3:19–22**
  in Central America, 1:180, 181
  current issues in, 3:21–22
  Good Neighbor Policy, 2:172
  origins of Inter-American System, 3:20–21
  postwar issues in, 3:20–21
  Rio Treaty and, 4:50
  United Nations and, 4:159
Inter-American Treaty of Reciprocal Assistance. *See* Rio Treaty (1947)
Intermarriage, 1:4, 211, 2:162, 3:194
Internal asylum, 1:79
Internal Provinces. *See* Provincias Internas
Internal trade, 4:147
International Border Commission, 1:124
International Conferences of American States, 3:20–21, 175, 192
International Military Education and Training Program, 1:62
"International" music, 3:150
Inti (unit of currency), 2:7
Intraregional trade, 4:147
Investment bonds, 2:139. *See also* Foreign investment
Iquique, port of, 4:198, 199
Irala, Domingo de, 1:49
Iron and steel industry, **3:22–23**
Irrigation, uses of, 1:10, **3:23–25**, 3:139, 4:102, 143
Isabel, Princess, 1:133, **3:25**, 3:203, 4:95
Isabella I of Castile, 2:14, 4:105, 109
Islam, **3:25–26**
Issei, 1:75
Isthmus of Panama, road across, 2:209
Itaipú dam and hydroelectric plant, 2:108, 224, 3:193, 198
Iturbide, Agustín de, 2:181, **3:26–27**
  Mexican War of Independence and, 3:113, 119, 4:203, 204
  Santa Anna and, 4:72
Itzás, 3:96
Itzcoatl (ruler), 1:89

J

Jades, Olmec, 3:173–74
Jagan, Cheddi, 2:193
Jaguar, **3:27**

Jai alai, 4:114
Jamaica, 1:137, 139, 2:85, **3:27–29**, 3:147
Japanese in Latin America, 1:74–75, 2:227
Jaramillo, Juan, 3:77
Jefe político, **3:29–30**
Jefferson, Thomas, 2:43
Jesuits, 1:173, 2:98, 4:44–45
  Anchieta, 1:30
  in Argentina, 1:50
  in Asunción, 1:78
  in Brazil, 1:130
  in California, 1:152
  cattle ranching among, 3:97
  Comunero Revolt vs., 2:17
  education and, 1:172
  expulsion by Charles III, 1:187
  missionary efforts, 3:133–34, 135, 4:190
  music education and, 3:148–49
  Pombaline reforms and, 4:2
Jewels. *See* Gems and gemstones
Jewish Colonization Association (JCA), 3:31
Jews in Latin America, 2:81, **3:30–31** (illus.), 3:126
João I of Portugal, 4:12
João II of Portugal, 2:14, 4:10, 12–13
João III of Portugal, 1:156, 4:13
João IV of Portugal, 1:17, 4:13
João V of Portugal, 4:13
João VI of Portugal, 1:131, 2:154, **3:31–32**, 4:13, 206
John I, king of Portugal, 2:206
John Paul II, Pope, 1:176, 2:42, 45, 4:62, 176
Johnson, Lyndon, 1:21
Jones Act (1917), 2:137, 4:24
Jorge Blanco, Salvador, 2:76
José I of Portugal, 4:13
Journalism, **3:32–34**
  censorship of, 1:177–78
Journeymen, 2:191
Juan Diego, 2:175–76
Juana Inés de la Cruz, Sor, **3:34–35**, 3:60, 4:135, 136
Juárez, Benito, 2:138, **3:35–36** (illus.)
  Díaz and, 2:61
  education reforms under, 2:98
  Maximilian and, 3:92
  presidency, 3:120
  Reform Laws of, 1:36
  Rurales founded by, 4:57
Juárez, Luis, 1:64
Juárez Law, 3:120
Juderias, Julián, 1:108
Judges on *audiencia*, 1:82–83
Judicial systems. *See* Laws and legal systems
Junín, battle of (1824), 1:111, 112
Junta, 1:111, **3:36**
Junta de Mayo, 4:168
Jury Tribunals, 3:52
Justice. *See* Crime and punishment, colonial; Laws and legal systems
Justo, José Agustín, 1:54–55, 4:58

K

Kahlo, Frida, **3:36–37**, 3:157, 4:52
Kardec, Allan, 4:112
Keith, Minor Cooper, 2:30, 4:158
Kennedy, John F., 1:20, 2:125, 3:175, 4:163
  Bay of Pigs Invasion and, 1:104
  CIA and, 1:184
  counterinsurgency policy, 2:32–34
  Cuban missile crisis and, 2:47–48

Khrushchev, Nikita, 2:47–48
K'iche', **3:37**, 3:96
Kidd, William, 3:223
Kino, Eusebio Francisco, 1:52, 59, 2:115, **3:37–38**, 3:84, 4:68–69
Kinship, 2:118–19
Kirchhoff, Paul, 3:104, 105
Korner, Emil, 1:62
Kotosh, **3:38**
Kubitschek de Oliveira, Juscelino, 1:127, 134, **3:38–39**
Kukulcan. *See* Quetzalcoatl
Kuna, 2:36, **3:39–40**
Kundt, Hans, 1:62, 186
Kurakas (chiefs), 1:87

L

La Angostura, battle of. *See* Buena Vista, battle of (1847)
Labor and labor movements, **3:41–44**
  anarchism and, 1:29–30
  in Argentina, 1:51, 3:207
  bracero program, 1:126 (illus.)
  changes in class structure and, 1:212
  changing trends in, 3:43
  Chicanos and, 1:191
  in Colombia, 2:13
  descamisados in Argentina, 2:59–60
  domestic labor, 2:71–72
  in El Salvador, 2:105
  emergence of labor organizations, 3:42–43
  in Grenada, 2:173–74
  growth of, 3:43
  maquiladoras system and, 3:84–85
  in Peru, 3:213
  railroads and, 4:36
  street vendors and, 4:115–16
  in Venezuela, 4:184
  yanaconas, 4:213–14
Labor courts, 3:52
Lacalle, Luis Alberto, 4:173
Lacandon forest, 4:37
Lafayette, Marquis de, 1:27
La Florida. *See* Florida
La Guyane. *See* French Guiana
Lake Pitiantutua, battle of (1932), 1:185
La Mesilla, Treaty of (1854), 1:61
Land, ownership of, 1:13, **3:44–45**. *See also* Agrarian reform
  colonial families and, 2:118
  economic development and, 2:90
  haciendas and, 2:195–96 (illus.)
  latifundia, 3:49–50
  of pampas, 3:183
Land Law of 1850 (Brazil), 3:45
Languages, **3:46–48**
  Andalusian, 2:20
  European, 3:47–48
  Inca, 3:5
  indigenous, 3:46–47
  Mayan, 3:94, 96
  missionaries' efforts to learn Indian, 3:135
  of Peru, 3:215
  Tupi, 4:155
  Zapotec, 4:217
La Paz, 1:115, **3:40–41**, 4:154
La Plata, appointment of archbishop to, 1:116
La Raza Unida, 1:191

243

Index

Larreta, Enrique, 3:63
Las Casas, Bartolomé de, 1:108, 2:219, **3:48–49** *(illus.)*, 3:60
Las Encantadas. *See* Galápagos Islands
Las madres, 4:210
Las Piedras, battle at (1811), 1:72
Lathrap, Donald, 1:40, 42
Latifundia, 1:6, 12, 2:118, 3:45, **3:49–50**
Latin America, **3:50**
Latitude, climate and, 1:216
Latorre, Lorenzo, 1:103
Lavalle, Juan, 4:56
Lavalleja, Juan Antonio, 4:170
La Venta, **3:41**
Law of the Free Womb (1871), 3:25
Laws and legal systems, **3:50–53**
   anticlerical laws, 1:36
   audiencia, 1:81–83 *(map)*
   Barrundia and, 1:102
   of Brazil, 3:52–53
   cabildo and enforcement of, 1:146
   Code Rurale in Haiti, 2:199
   colonial courts, 2:39–40
   colonial crime and punishment, 2:37–40
   Enlightenment and, 2:110
   labor laws, 3:42–43
   Pombaline reforms and, 4:3
   slaves' rights, 4:93
   Spanish American, 3:51–52
   women, legal status of, 4:209–10
League of United Latin-American Citizens (LULAC), 1:190
Leeward Islands, 1:160
Legitimate children, 1:192
Leguía, Augusto, 3:213–14
Leloir, Luis F., **3:53**, 3:101, 4:81
Leme do Prado, Sebastino, 2:160
Lempira (unit of currency), 2:7
Lend-Lease Act (1941), 4:212
Leñero, Vicente, 3:64
León de la Barra, Francisco, 3:111
Lerdo de Tejada, Sebastián, 2:61–62, 3:120
Lerdo Law, 3:120
Lesbians. *See* Homosexuality
Lesseps, Ferdinand Marie de, 3:87, 184
Lesser Antilles, 1:160
Letter of marque, 3:223
Liberalism, **3:53–54**
   anticlericalism and, 1:36
   in Brazil, Cardoso and, 1:159
   Catholic Church and struggle with, 1:174
   in Chile, 1:197–98
   principles of, 3:54
   public sector and, 4:19–20
Liberal parties, 4:1
   in Central America, 1:180–81
   in Colombia, 2:13
   in El Salvador, 2:104–5
   in Guatemala, 2:182
   in Honduras, 2:213–14
   Protestantism and, 4:18
   in Venezuela, 4:183
Liberation theology, 1:36, 175, 176, **3:54–56** *(illus.)*
   Christian Base Communities, 1:204
   in El Salvador, 2:106
   Gutiérrez, founder of, 2:192
   Jesuits and, 4:45
   Romero and, 4:54
Lillo, Baldomero, 3:62
Lima, 2:22, **3:56–57** *(illus.)*, 3:213, 215

Lima e Silva, Luís Alves de, 2:120, **3:57**, 4:201
Línea Aérea Nacional (LAN), 1:86
Line of demarcation. *See* Tordesillas, Treaty of (1493)
Linnaeus, Carl, 4:80
Linné, Carl von, 1:96
Lisbôa, Antônio Francisco. *See* Aleijadinho
Lisbôa, Manuel Francisco, 1:18, 19
Lisbon, Portugal, 4:11
Lispector, Clarice, **3:57–58**
Literacy, **3:58–59**
   education and, 2:97–100
Literature, **3:59–65** *(illus.). See also* Journalism; Poetry
   of Allende, 1:19
   of Amado, 1:23–24
   of Andrade, 1:32
   of Asturias, 1:77–78
   Baroque, 3:60
   Bello and postcolonial, 1:106
   Black Legend, 1:108–9 *(illus.)*
   of Borges, 1:121–22
   of Carpentier, 1:163–64
   colonial, 3:60
   of Cortázar, **2:26**
   of Cunha, 2:53–54
   Enlightenment and neoclassicism, 3:60–61
   of Fuentes, 2:149 *(illus.)*
   of García Márquez, 2:155–56 *(illus.)*
   of Garcilaso de la Vega, 2:157
   gauchos in, 2:159
   of Guaman Poma de Ayala, 2:197
   of Ibarbourou, 2:23
   of Las Casas, historian, 3:48–49
   of Lispector, 3:57–58
   of Machado de Assis, 3:71–72
   of Martí y Pérez, 3:90
   Modern Art Week, 3:141
   modernism, 3:62–63
   of Ocampo, 3:172
   of Paz, 3:200–201
   of Piñon, 3:222
   pre-Columbian, 3:59–60, 79, 80–81
   pre-modern, 3:59–62
   of Puig, 4:25
   of Quiroga, 4:28
   realism and naturalism, 3:62
   regional novel and short story, 3:63–64
   of Roa Bastos, 4:52
   Romanticism, 3:61–62
   of Sábato, 4:59
   since 1945, 3:64–65
   theater and, 4:135–37
   ultraísmo, 1:121–22
   of Valenzuela, 4:174
   vanguardism, 3:63
   of Vargas Llosa, 4:178
Litopterns, 1:32
Livestock, 1:10–11, **3:65–66**, 3:216. *See also* Meat industry
Llama, 1:33, 3:65, **3:66** *(illus.)*
Llaneros, 3:67
Llanos, 1:113, **3:67**, 4:179
Locke, John, 2:109
Long Count (calendar), 1:150
Longhorns, 3:65
Loores de Nuestra Señora (Ibarbourou), 2:223
López, Carlos Antonio, 3:196
López, Francisco Solano, 1:78 *(illus.)*, 2:63, **3:67**, 3:196, 4:201

López de Legazpi, Miguel, 3:219
López, José Portillo, 1:99–100
López Tijerina, Reies, 1:190
Lord Shield Pacal, 3:181
Losada, Diego de, 1:157
Los desaparecidos (the "disappeared" ones), 1:53 *(illus.)*, 56, 57, 2:219, 4:59
Los Niños Héroes (The Boy Heroes), 3:114
Los Treinta Años, 3:164
Louisiana, **3:68**
Louisiana Purchase, 3:68
Loyola, Saint Ignatius, 4:44–45
Lugones, Leopoldo, 3:63
Lumber industry, 2:7, 215, **3:69**, 4:38
Lupaqa Indians, 1:114
Lutz, Bertha Maria Julia, **3:70**
Lynch, Elisa, 3:67

M

Macao, 3:182, 4:10
Macchi, Gonzalez, 3:199
Maceo, Antonio, 2:43, 171, **3:70–71**, 4:127, 128
MacGregor, Gregory, 2:132
Machado, Gerardo, 1:30, 102, 2:44
Machado de Assis, Joaquim Maria, **3:71–72**
Machismo, 1:176, 2:161, 163
Machu Picchu, 1:41, 72, **3:72–73** *(illus.)*
Maciel, Antônio Vicente Mendes. *See* Conselheiro, Antônio
McKinley, William, 3:75
Macú of Brazil, 3:12
Madero, Francisco Indalecio, 1:164, 2:62, 217, **3:73**, 4:57
   Mexican Revolution and, 3:110, 111, 121
   Villa and, 4:190
   Zapata and, 4:216
Madrid, Treaty of (1674), 3:28, 147
Madrid, Treaty of (1750), **3:73–74**, 3:134, 4:65
Madriz, José, 3:164
Maestrescuela, 4:164
Magazines. *See* Journalism
Magellan, Ferdinand, **3:74**, 3:144, 219
Mahogany, 1:105, 3:69
Maine, USS, **3:74–75** *(illus.)*, 4:110
Maipú, battle of (1818), 1:196
Maize, 1:9–10, 2:133–34, 134, **3:75–76** *(illus.)*
Malaria, 2:66
Malinche, 2:27, **3:76–77**
Malinchismo, 3:77
Mambisas, 4:208
Mammals, 1:32–33
Managua, **3:77**, 3:164
Manaus, 3:77–78
Manco Capac, 3:3
Manco Inca, 3:210, 225
Mangroves, 4:37
Manila Galleon, 1:1, 73, 74, **3:78**, 3:219
Manioc, 2:134, **3:78–79**
Manley, Michael, 3:29
Manuel I, King, 1:134, 147, 4:13
Manufacturing. *See* Industrialization; *individual industries*
Manufacturing productivity, innovations in, 4:126
Manumission, 4:93
Manuscripts and writing, pre-Columbian, **3:79–81**
   archaeological findings, 1:30, 40

bookmaking, 3:79–80
K'iche', 3:37
Mixtec, 3:138
Olmec, 3:174
writing and literature, 3:79, 80–81
Zapotec writing system, 4:217
Mao Zedong, 2:16, 3:214
Maps and mapmaking, **3:81–84** *(map)*
   early Spanish and Portuguese, 3:81–82
   explorations and, 2:113, 115, 116–17
   of 1500s and 1600s, 3:82–83
   by Kino, 3:38
   Native American, 3:81
   from 1700 to present, 3:83
   of Spanish Borderlands, 3:83–84
Maquiladoras, **3:84–85**, 4:161, 162, 163
Marajoara culture, 1:129, 2:52
Maran, René, 3:157–58
Maranhão, slavery in, 4:94
Maranhão Company, 4:150
Marañón. *See* Amazon River
Maravedí (imaginary monetary unit of account), 2:6
Marcos de Niza, Fray, 3:160
Marianismo, 2:161
Mariel boatlift, 2:46, **3:85–86** *(illus.)*
Marijuana, 2:78, 79
Marín, Luis Muñoz, 1:16
Marine mammals, 1:33
Market at Tlatelalco (mural), 4:52 *(illus.)*
Maroons, 2:187, 197, 3:28, **3:86–87**, 3:182, 4:89
Marqués, René, 3:64
Marranos, 3:30, 31
Marriage and divorce, 2:162, **3:87–88** *(illus.)*
   intermarriage, 1:4, 211, 2:162, 3:194
Marsupials, 1:33
Martí, Agustín Farabundo, 1:184, 2:105, **3:89**, 3:91
Martínez, Hernández, 3:91
Martínez, Tomás Eloy, 3:208
Martínez de Irala, Domingo, 1:146, 2:179, 3:195
Martín Fierro (Hernández) 3:62, **3:91**
Martinique, 2:146, 147, 148
Martí y Pérez, José Julián, 1:170, 2:43, 161, 171, 188, **3:89–91** *(illus.)*, 4:110
   modernism of, 3:62, 63
Marxism, 3:55
Mascates, 4:197
Masferrer, Alberto, 2:105
Masters (guild rank), 2:191
Matadors, 1:144–45
Matanza (1932), 1:8, 2:105, 3:89, **3:91**
Maté. *See* Food and drink
Maternidad, 2:161
Matrilineal society, Kuna as, 3:39
Matto de Turner, Clorinda, 3:62
Maurits, Johan, **3:92**
Maximilian and Carlota, 2:146, 3:35, **3:92–93**, 3:120
Maxtla (ruler), 1:89
Maya, 1:179, 2:50, 51, **3:93–97** *(illus.)*, 3:106
   archaeological study of, 1:40–41
   art of, 1:70
   astronomy of, 1:76
   in Belize, 1:105
   calendars of, 1:149–50 *(illus.)*
   Caste War of Yucatán and, 1:168
   in Chiapas region, 1:189
   Chichén Itzá, 1:191
   from conquest to present, 3:96–97

Copán site, 2:23
divinities of, 2:68–69
Dresden Codex of, 1:76
El Mirador built by, 2:101–2 *(illus.)*
of Guatemala, 2:184 *(illus.)*
in Honduras, 2:212
K'iche' Indians, 3:37
literature of, 3:59
manuscripts and writing, 3:79, 80–81
Palenque, major center of, 3:181
pre-Columbian history of, 3:95–96
Tayasal settlement, 4:124
territory and origins of, 3:93–95
theater of, 4:135
Tikal, 4:137–38
in Yucatán, 4:215
Mayapán, 3:96, 108
Mayombe, 4:41
Mayorazgo, 3:45
Mayorga, Silvio, 4:69
Measles, 2:66
Meat industry, 1:49, 50, 54, **3:97–98**
Medeiros da Fonseca, Romy, 4:210
Medellín cartel, 2:79
Medellín Conference (1968), 1:175
Media, public access to, 1:177–78
Medical schools, 3:101
Medicine, **3:99–101** *(illus.)*
   curanderos and, 2:54–55 *(illus.)*
   diseases and access to, 2:68
   healing plants and modern, 3:99
   science research and, 4:81
   spiritism and, 4:113
Medina, Bartolomé de, 4:125
Megatheria, 1:32
Meiggs, Henry, 4:36
Melgarejo, Mariano, **3:101–2**
Menchú Tum, Rigoberta, **3:102**
Mendes Filho, Francisco Alves, 2:140
Mendoza, Alonso de, 3:40
Mendoza, Antonio de, 3:160
Mendoza, Pedro de, 1:49, 142
Menem, Carlos Saúl, 1:57, 3:102–3, 126
Menéndez de Avilés, Pedro, 2:115, 130, **3:103**, 4:60
Mennonites in Paraguay, 2:225
Mercator, Gerard, 3:83
Mercedarian order, 4:45
Mercenaries, 1:62
Mercosur, 2:89–90, **3:103–4**, 3:198, 4:149
Merengue, 3:151
Mérida, Carlos, 1:68
Mesa Central, 2:166, 3:115
Mesa del Norte, 3:115
Mescaline, 2:78
Mesoamerica: pre-Columbian history, 2:50–51, **3:104–8** *(map)*
   archaeology of, 1:40–41
   Archaic period, 3:105
   architecture of, 1:44
   cacao's importance in, 1:147
   calendars in, 1:149–50 *(illus.)*
   cities, 1:207
   Classic period, 3:106–7
   defining, 3:104–5
   Mayan history, 3:93, 95–96
   Postclassic period, 3:107–8
   Preclassic period, 3:105–6
   religions, 4:41–42
Mesoamerican art, 1:69–70
Messianic movements, **3:108–9**
Mestizo, 1:211, **3:109–10**, 3:117, 4:31

changes in class structure and opportunities for, 1:212–13
Díaz and, 2:61, 62
of La Paz, 3:40
of Peru, 3:215
Metalworking, 1:70, 71, 72
Meteorology, 2:222
Methodists, 4:17
Metropoles, 3:1
Mexica. *See* Aztecs
Mexican Americans. *See* Chicanos
Mexican-American War, 1:124, **3:113–15** *(illus.)*, 3:120, 4:160
   Arizona and, 1:60–61
   Borderlands ceded to U.S. in, 4:109
   Buena Vista, battle of, 1:142
   California ceded to U.S., 1:153
   roots of, 3:113–14
   Texas and, 4:132
   Treaty of Guadalupe Hidalgo ending, 2:176–77
Mexican Plateau, 2:166, 3:115
Mexican Revolution, **3:110–12**, 3:121, 4:162
   agrarian reform and, 1:7
   bandits during, 1:97
   Calles and, 1:154
   Cárdenas Del Rio in, 1:158
   Carranza and Constitutionalist forces during, 1:164
   Hidalgo y Costilla and, 2:207–8
   Huerta and, 2:217
   interference with journalism in, 3:33
   Madero and, 3:73
   Veracruz during, 4:186
   Villa, leader in, 4:190–91
   women in, 4:209
   Zapata, leader in, 4:216–17
Mexican War of Independence (1808–1821), **3:112–13**, 3:118–19, 4:203
   California and, 1:153
   Morelos y Pavón and, 3:146–47
   Ortiz de Domínguez and, 3:178–79
   Santa Anna and, 4:72
   Texas and, 4:131
   Veracruz during, 4:186
Mexico, **3:115–23** *(map)*
   Acapulco, 1:1
   banking in, 1:99–100
   boundary disputes in, 1:124
   bracero program, 1:126 *(illus.)*
   censorship of journalism in, 3:34
   Chiapas, 1:189–90
   Chinese immigrants in, 1:74
   cinema in, 1:206
   clothing of, 2:1
   colonial society in, 3:117–18
   conquest and colonial beginnings, 3:116–17
   copper mining in, 2:24
   Cristero Rebellion, 2:40–41
   cultural nationalism in, 3:157
   debt crisis (1995), 2:138
   Díaz, president of, 2:61–62 *(illus.)*, 3:120–21
   Dominicans in, 4:44
   drug trade and, 2:79, 80
   education in, 2:98
   ex-Confederates in, 2:18
   federalism in, 2:123
   financial crisis (1994), 1:100
   Gadsden Purchase from, 2:151

245

Index

Gálvez' (José) reforms in, 2:153
geography of, 2:166–67
highways in, 2:209
human rights abuses in, 2:220
immigration to U.S. from, 2:226, 227–28
independent, 3:118–19
Indian cultures of, 3:10–11
Indian policies in, 3:9
Institutional Revolutionary Party in, 4:1
iron and steel industry in, 3:23
Jesuits in, 4:44
Juárez, president of, 3:35–36 (illus.), 120
labor and the state in, 3:43
Lacandon forest in, 4:37
land and resources of, 3:115–16
latifundia in, 3:49–50
Manila galleons and trade in, 3:78
Maximilian and Carlota as rulers of, 2:146, 3:92–93
Mexican Revolution, 3:121
modern architecture of, 1:48
NAFTA and, 3:168–69
Pastry War in, 2:146
petroleum industry in, 3:217–18
postindependence presidents, 3:119–20
Rurales in, 4:57
Santa Anna, president of, 4:72–73
Sierra Madre in, 4:88
silver in, 2:169
Soviet relations with, 4:104
textile industry in, 3:15, 4:133–34
tourism in, 4:145
United Provinces of Central America and, 1:183
U.S.–Mexico border, 4:162–63
universities in, 4:165
Veracruz, 4:186
Virgin of Guadalupe, patron saint of, 2:175–76
War of the Reform (1856), 2:61
wars of independence in, 4:203
writ of amparo in, 3:52
Yucatán peninsula, 4:215–16
Mexico City, 1:208, **3:123–25** (illus.)
built on ruins of Tenochtitlán, 4:129
capture during Mexican-American War, 3:114 (illus.), 115
consulados in, 2:22
economy and government of, 3:124–25
geography and early history of, 3:123–24
neoclassical architecture of, 1:47
population growth and development since 1900, 3:124
Middle Easterners in Latin America, 3:26, **3:125–26**
Milhaud, Darius, 4:191
Militant messianism, 3:108
Military, the. See Armed forces
Military Assistance Program, U.S., 1:62
Military courts, 2:39, 3:52
Military dictatorships. See Dictatorships, military
Military regimes, Catholic Church and, 1:175–76
Militias, 2:63, **3:126–28**
Mill, James, 1:29
Milpa (slash and burn) agriculture, 1:10, 2:140–41
Minas Gerais, **3:128**
architecture of, 1:46–47
gold rush in, 2:169
mining in, 3:128, 129

missionary activity in, 3:133
work of Aleijadinho in, 1:18
Mineral resources. See Mining
Minifundia, 1:6, 3:45
Mining, **3:128–31** (illus.)
in altiplano, 1:22
in Bolivia, 1:115–16
in Brazil, 3:128–30
changes in class structure and, 1:212
in Chile, 1:199
coins and coinage, 2:5–7
in Colombia, 2:7, 8–9
copper, 2:23–24
for gems and gemstones, 2:159–60
for gold and silver, 2:169–70, 4:15–16
highways and roads for, 2:209–10
as major sector of economy, 2:90
in Mexico, 3:117
in Minas Gerais, 3:128, 129
for nitrates, 3:167–68
in Patagonia, 3:200
in Peru, 3:215–16
photography of, 3:220 (illus.)
in Potosí, 4:15–16
in Sierra Madre, 4:88
slavery in, 4:94
in Spanish America, 3:130–31
technological advances in, 4:124–25
for tin, 4:138–39
War of the Pacific and, 4:198, 199
Mints, founding of, 2:5
Miralles, Juan de, 1:28
Miranda, Francisco de, **3:131–32**, 3:172, 4:182
Misericórdians, 4:45
Miskito Indians. See Mosquito Indians
Missions and missionaries, **3:132–36** (illus.)
Anchieta, 1:30
architecture of, 1:45–46
in Arizona, 1:59, 60
bandeiras and, 1:96
in California, 1:152, 4:84
of Catholic Church, 1:171, 172
to Chiriguanos, 1:203
in colonial Brazil, 1:30, 3:132–34
in colonial Spanish America, 3:134–36
Conselheiro, 2:21
education and, 2:98
in Florida, 2:130–31
Guaranis and, 2:179–80
Kino, 3:37–38
Las Casas, 3:48–49
in Mexico, 3:117
in New Mexico, 3:161
in Paraguay, 3:195
in Philippines, 3:219
Protestant, 4:17–18
Pueblo Rebellion in New Mexico and, 4:21–22
sacred music used by, 3:148–49
San Xavier del Bac, 4:68–69
of Serra, 4:84
in Spanish Borderlands, 4:108
Treaty of Madrid and, 3:74
of Vieira, 4:189–90
Mississippi Valley, 3:68, **3:136**
Mistral, Gabriela, **3:136–37**
Mita system, 1:115–16, 118
Mitch, hurricane, 2:215, 223, 3:166–67
Mitchell, Keith, 2:174
Mitre, Bartolomé, 1:16, 53, **3:137**, 4:166, 202

Mixtecs, 2:51, 160, 3:80, 108, **3:138**
Mixtón War (1541–1542), **3:138–39**
Moai (stone statues), 2:85
Mobile, battle of (1780), 1:28
Mocambos, 4:27
Moche, 1:42, 71, 2:52, 3:11–12, **3:139–40** (illus.)
Mocobi Indians, 1:50
Moctezuma I, 1:89
Moctezuma II, 1:90, 2:27, **3:140–41** (illus.), 4:27
Modern Art Week, 1:133, **3:141**
Modernism
in architecture, 1:47–48
in art, 1:67
in literature, 3:62–63
Modernismo (literary movement), 1:32, 2:57
Modernization. See also Industrialization
anticlericalism and, 1:35
in Argentina, 1:54
Catholic Church and, 1:175
nutrition and, 3:171
Mogollon people, 1:59
Molasses, 4:120
Molina, Arturo, 2:80
Molina, Pedro, **3:141–42**
Monagas, José Gregorio, 4:183
Monagas, José Tadeo, 3:180, 4:183
Monarchs. See also Portugal and the Portuguese Empire; Spain and the Spanish Empire
Portuguese, 4:12–13
Spanish, 4:109–10
Moncada, José María, 3:165, 4:71
Monkeys, 1:33
Monoculture, 1:12–13, 3:226. See also Plantations
Monopolies, 1:125, 2:22
Monroe, James, 3:142
Monroe Doctrine, 2:70, 74, **3:142–43**, 4:160
British–Latin American relations and, 1:137
as example of imperialism, 3:1
Roosevelt Corollary to, 4:55
Montaña, 3:209, 216
Montane forests, 4:37
Monte Albán, **3:143–44** (illus.)
Monte Caseros, battle of (1852), 4:56
Monte de las Cruces, battle of (1810), 3:113
Montejo, Francisco de, 3:96
Montemayor, Carlos, 3:58
Monte Pascoal, 1:147
Montevideo, **3:144–45**, 3:190, 4:167, 168
Montezuma. See Moctezuma II
Montezuma Castle, 1:60 (illus.)
Montserrat, 1:138, 139, 161
Moors, 1:144, 2:19, 4:107
Mopans, 3:96
Morais, Prudente José de, 1:133
Morant Bay Rebellion (1865), 3:28
Morazán, Francisco, 1:39, 165, 181, 183–84, 2:181, 213, **3:145–46**
Morelos y Pavón, José María, 1:173, **3:146–47**
Mexican War for Independence and, 3:113, 118–19, 4:203
Moreno, Gabriel García, 2:129
Morgan, Henry, 1:141, **3:147**
Morínigo, Higínio, 3:197
Morro Castle, 2:203
Mosques, 3:27

246

Mosquito Coast, 2:212, 3:147
Mosquito Indians, **3:147–48** (illus.)
Mosquito population control program, 2:66, 67
Mothers of the Disappeared, 2:220 (illus.)
Mothers of the Plaza de Mayo, 2:65
Motor vehicles. *See* Automobile industry
Mountains. *See* Andes; Sierra Madre
Muisca people, 2:100–101
Mulattos, 1:4, 211, 4:32
   changes in class structure and opportunities for, 1:212–13
   in Haiti, 2:60, 198, 199–200
   Haitian Revolution and, 2:201–2
Mules, 3:66
Multinational corporations, 2:139–40
Mummies, 1:40, 42, 4:103
Murillo, Bartolomé, 1:65
Mushroom cults, 2:78
Musical instruments, **3:152–53**
Music and dance, **3:148–52** (illus.)
   art, 3:148–50
   folk and popular, 3:150–52
   García, composer, 2:154–55
   Modern Art Week, 3:141
   Villa-Lobos, composer, 4:191–92
Muslims. *See* Islam

N

NAFTA. *See* North American Free Trade Agreement (NAFTA)
Nahuatl language, 3:46, 4:142
Nahuatl literature, 3:80
Nanny (maroon woman), 3:86
Napoleon Bonaparte, 1:51, 4:146
   invasion of Portugal, 1:131
   invasion of Spain, 1:111, 117, 195, 4:110
   troops in Hispaniola, 2:198
Napoleon III of France, 3:92, 120
Nariño, Antonio, 2:10, 11, **3:153–54**
Narváez, Pánfilo de, 1:145–46, 2:42, 3:141, **3:154**
Nasca and Nasca lines, 1:71, 3:11–12, **3:154–55**
National Coffee Growers Federation (Colombia), 2:4, 5
National Confederation of Guatemalan Campesinos (CNCG), 1:38
Nationalism, **3:156–57**
   armed forces and, 1:62
   British–Latin American relations and, 1:138
   in Cuba, Martí y Pérez and, 3:90–91
   cultural and economic, 3:157
   fascism and, 2:121
   modern architecture and, 1:47–48
   in Panama, 3:185
   in Peru, Haya de la Torre and, 2:205–6
   rise of, 2:33
   roots of, 3:156–57
Nationalization of industry, 4:20
   of mines, 3:131
   in Peru, 4:179
   of petroleum industry, 3:218
   postwar industrialization and, 3:16
   of railroads, 4:36
National Republican Alliance (ARENA), 2:57, 106
National War, 2:29, **3:155–56**
Native Americans. *See* Indians
"Nativist" movements, 3:157

Natterer, Johann, 2:117
Natural gas, 2:108
Naturalism in literature, 3:62
Naturalist expeditions, paintings of, 1:67
Natural resources. *See also* Forests; Mining
   of Ecuador, 2:92
   energy, 2:107–9
   of Mexico, 3:116
   of Paraguay, 3:193
   petroleum, 3:217–18
Navajo, 1:59
Nazi Germany, 2:168, 3:197
Neenguirú, Nicolís, 2:179
Negrista poetry, 3:181
Négritude, **3:157–58**, 4:33
Nemontemi, 1:150
Neoclassicism
   in architecture, 1:47
   in art, 1:66–67
   in literature, 3:60–61
Neotropical plant realm, 2:140
Neruda, Pablo, 3:63, **3:158–59**
Netherlands, United Provinces of, 2:81
Netherlands Antilles, 2:83
Nevado del Ruiz, eruption of, 4:195
Nevis, 1:138, 139
New Christians, 2:81
New Granada, Viceroyalty of, 2:9–10, **3:159**, 3:216, 4:187
   capital of, 1:110
   independence struggle in, 4:203
   Panama as part of, 3:183
   revolts against, 2:11
   Watermelon Riot in, 4:205
New Jewel Movement, 2:174
New Mexico, **3:159–62** (map)
   early history and European exploration, 3:159–60
   modern, 3:161–62
   Oñate, founder and governor of, 3:174
   Penitentes in, 3:204–5
   Pueblo Rebellion in, 3:161, 4:21–22
   Spanish and Mexican rule in, 3:161
   Spanish settlement of, 3:160–61
New Orleans, 3:68
New Spain, Viceroyalty of, 1:179, **3:162**, 4:187
   art in, 1:64
   Cortés as conqueror and governor of, 2:27–28
   crackdown on colonial crime in, 2:39
   Mexico as center of, 3:116–17
   Philippines and, 3:219
Newspapers, 1:178, 3:32–34
New Toledo, 1:21
New World, exploration of, 2:114
Nezahualcoyotl (ruler), 1:89, 3:80
Nezahualpilli (ruler), 1:90
Nicaragua, **3:162–67**
   agrarian reform in, 1:7 (illus.), 8
   Arias plan and, 1:58
   Bryan-Chamorro Treaty and, 1:140
   Catholic Church in, 1:176
   CIA in, 1:184
   colonialism and independence of, 3:163–64
   contras in, 2:22–23
   earthquakes in, 2:85 (illus.)
   geography and population of, 3:162–63
   guerrilla movements in, 2:188
   Managua, capital of, 3:77
   modern, 3:166–67

   Mosquito Indians of, 3:147–48
   National War and, 3:155–56
   refugees from, 1:80
   Sandinistas of, 3:166, 4:69–70
   Sandino as hero of, 4:71–72
   Somoza dynasty, 3:165–66
   Soviet relations with, 4:104
   United Nations and, 4:159
   U.S. intervention in, 3:164–645, 4:160
   Walker's adventures in, 4:196–97
Nicaragua, Lake, 1:33–34, 3:163, 164
Nicaragua wood, 3:69
Niemeyer Soares Filho, Oscar, 1:48, 127, **3:167**
Nikkei, 1:75
Niña (ship), 2:14
Nisei, 1:75
Nitrate industry, 2:178, 3:131, **3:167–68**
   Chilean, 1:198
   in Peru, 3:213
   War of the Pacific and, 4:198, 199
Nixon, Richard, 1:20
Niza, Marcos de, 4:87
Nobel Prize recipients
   Arias Sánchez, 1:58 (illus.), 2:32
   Asturias, for literature, 1:78
   García Márquez, for literature, 2:155
   García Robles, 2:157
   Houssay, for medicine, 2:216
   Leloir, for chemistry, 3:53
   Menchú Tum, 3:102
   Mistral, for literature, 3:136
   Paz, for literature, 3:200–201
   Saavedra Lamas, 4:58
   Walcott, for literature, 4:196
Noche triste, 2:27
Nonacademic practitioners, 3:100
Nonformal education, 2:100
Noriega, Manuel, 2:79, 3:185–86
North, Oliver, 2:22
North American Free Trade Agreement (NAFTA), 2:90, **3:168–69**, 4:149
   auto industry and, 1:85
   foreign investments and, 2:140
   maquiladoras and, 3:84
   Mexico and, 3:122
   Salinas and, 4:62
   Texas and, 4:132
Novaro, Maria, 1:206
"Novel of the Northeast," 1:23
Novels. *See* Literature
Nuclear Arms Treaty of Tlatelolco (1967), 2:156
Nuclear Nonproliferation Treaty (1968), 2:156
Nuevo cine (new film) style, 1:206
Nuns, 2:161, 3:34–35
Nutrition, **3:170–71**
   food and drink, 2:132–36 (illus.)

O

Oaxaca, Monte Albán in, 3:143–44
Oaxaca Valley, 3:116
Obrajes (textile mills), 2:93
Obregón Salido, Álvaro, 1:154, 164, **3:171–72**
   Mexican Revolution and, 3:111, 112, 121
Obsidian, 3:93
Ocampo, Sebastián de, 2:192
Ocampo, Victoria, **3:172**
Occidente region in Ecuador, 2:94

247

Index

Ocean currents. *See* Currents, ocean
Ocean fishing rights, 2:126
O'Donojú, Juan, 3:113, 119
O'Gorman, Juan, 4:164
O'Higgins, Bernardo, **3:172–73**, 4:203
    Carrera vs., 1:165
    Chilean independence movement and, 1:195, 196
    San Martín and, 4:67
Oidores, 1:82
Oil. *See* Petroleum industry
Oil crisis of 1973, debt crisis and, 2:138
Ojeda, Alonso de, 2:8, 83, 4:180, 186
Olid, Cristóbal de, 2:27
Olmecs, 2:50, 3:11, **3:173–74**
    archaeological study of, 1:40
    art of, 1:69–70
    La Venta, 3:41
    in Maya territory, 3:94–95
    as Preclassic society, 3:106
    religions of, 4:41–42
Olmedo, Bartolomé de, 3:134
Onas. *See* Selk'nams
Oñate, Juan de, 2:115, 3:160–61, **3:174**
Onganía, Juan Carlos, 1:56, 2:25
Onís y Gonzáles, Luis de, 1:1
Opera, 3:149
Opium, 2:78
Oreamuno, Ricardo Jiménez, 2:29
Orellana, Francisco de, 2:116 *(map),* 186, **3:174**
Organization of American States, 2:75, 3:20, **3:175–76**, 3:192
    current issues for, 3:21
    Pan-American Conference of 1948 and, 3:191
    Unit for the Promotion of Democracy, 3:21
Organization of Central American States (ODECA), 1:181
Organization of Petroleum Exporting Countries (OPEC), 4:185
Oribe, Manuel, 2:186, **3:176**, 4:170
Oriente region in Ecuador, 2:91, 94
Orinoco River, 2:165
Orio, Baltasar de Echave, 1:64
Orixás, **3:176–77**. *See also* Candomblé
Orozco, José Clemente, 1:67
Orozco, Pascual, 3:73, 111
Ortega Saavedra, Daniel, 3:166, **3:177–78** *(illus.),* 4:69, 70
Ortelius, Abraham, 3:82
Ortiz de Domínguez, Josefa, **3:178–79**
Oruro Revolt (1739), 1:117
Ospina Pérez, Mariano, 4:192
Otomanguean language family, 4:217
Ouro Prêto, 3:128
Outlaw bandits, 1:97
Oviedo, Lino, 3:198
Oviedo y Valdés, Gonzalo Fernández, 3:225

P

Pachacamac (god), 3:56
    temple to, 2:216
Pachacuti, 3:4, **3:179**
Pachacuti, Juan Santacruz, 3:60
Pacheco, María Luisa, 1:68
Pacific Northwest, **3:179–80**
Padrón real, 3:81
Páez, José Antonio, 1:112, **3:180–81**, 4:182, 183

Painting. *See* Art, colonial to modern; Art, pre-Columbian
Palenque, **3:181**
Palés Matos, Luis, **3:181**
Palestinians, immigration of, 3:125, 126
Palma, Arturo Alessandri, 1:199
Palmares, **3:182**, 4:90
Palo, 4:41
Pampa de Nasca, 3:155
Pampas, 1:49, **3:183**
    Araucanian expansion into, 1:37, 38
    cattle ranching in, 3:97–98
    climate of, 1:216
    gauchos of, 2:158
    Indians driven from, 1:52
Panama, **3:183–87**
    Ávila, governor of, 1:86–87
    canal politics and independence, 3:184–85
    cultural geography of, 3:186–87
    history of, 3:183–86
    modern, 3:186–87
    Noriega's regime, 3:185–86
    Panama City, capital of, 3:189–90
    Pan-American Conference at, 3:190
    as part of Colombia, 3:184
    under Spanish control, 3:183
    Torrijos Herrera, revolutionary leader in, 4:144
    Watermelon Riot in, 4:205
Panama Canal, 3:164, **3:187–89** *(illus.),* 4:160, 218
    Bryan-Chamorro Treaty and, 1:140
    canal operations, 3:188–89
    Canal Zone, 2:205, 3:186, 189
    economic development of Panama and, 3:184–85
    El Niño's effect on, 2:102
    growth of Cali with opening of, 1:151
    Hay-Bunau-Varilla Treaty and, 2:205
    modern imperialism and, 3:3
    Torrijos-Carter Treaty and, 4:144
    trade and commerce through, 4:148 *(illus.)*
    yellow fever and, 2:66
Panama City, 1:87, 3:186, **3:189–90**
Pan American Airways, 1:86
Pan-American Conferences, 3:20, **3:190–91**, 3:192
Pan-American Highway, 2:209 *(illus.),* 210, 4:68, 75, 126
Pan-Americanism, **3:191–92**
    Inter-American relations and, 3:19–22
    Monroe Doctrine and, 3:143
    Organization of American States and, 3:175–76
    photography and, 3:221
Pan-American Union (PAU), 3:20, 175, 192
Pantanal, **3:192–93**
Pantheon of Heroes (Asunción), 1:78 *(illus.)*
Paracas culture, art of, 1:71
Paraguay, **3:193–99** *(map)*
    architecture of, 1:46
    Asunción, capital of, 1:78–79
    Chaco War between Bolivia and, 1:119, 185–86 *(map),* 3:197
    claims to Chaco, 1:123
    clothing in, 2:2
    colonial period in, 3:194–95
    under the Colorados, 3:198–99
    Comunero Revolt in, 2:17
    economy of, 3:195, 197, 199
    Guaranis of, 2:179–80

    immigration to, 2:227
    independence of, 3:195–96
    Japanese immigrants in, 1:75
    land and resources of, 3:193
    Mennonites in, 2:225
    people of, 3:199
    War of the Triple Alliance and, 3:196, 4:200–202
Paraguay: Image of Your Desolate Country (painting), 1:67
Paraguay River, 2:165, 218, 3:193
Páramo, 1:218
Paraná, Argentina, 1:53
Paraná Indians, 1:56
Paraná River, 2:108, 165, 3:193
Pardon, colonial, 2:40
Pardos. See Mulattos
Paricutin volcano, 4:195 *(illus.)*
Paris, Treaty of (1898), 4:111
Partisan press, 1:178
Pasteur, Louis, 4:81
Pastry War (1838), 2:146, 3:119
Patagonia, 1:49, **3:200**
Patent, 3:223
Patria potestad, 2:161
Patriarchal family, 2:118
Patria vieja, 1:195
Payaguá, 2:179
Payró, Roberto, 3:62
Paz, Ireneo, 3:200
Paz, Octavio, 3:64, **3:200–201**
Paz Estenssoro, Víctor, 1:119–20, 121, **3:201**
Paz García, Policarpo, 2:214
Peace activist, 3:205
Peasant uprisings, 3:43
Pedro I of Brazil, 1:31, 131, 3:31, **3:201–2**, 4:13, 206
Pedro II of Brazil, 1:131–32, 3:57, **3:202–3** *(illus.),* 4:13
Pelé, **3:203–4** *(illus.)*
Pelée, Mount, 2:147, 4:195
Pellagra, 3:76
PEMEX, 1:158, 3:218
Peñaranda, Enrique, 1:186
Peninsulares, 1:179, 195, 211, 2:225
    on *audiencia,* 1:83
    in colonial Mexico, 3:117, 118
    tension between Creoles and, 2:37
    wars of independence and, 4:202
Penitentes, **3:204–5**
Penn, William, 3:28
Pensacola, battle of (1781), 1:28
Pentecostal groups, 4:18
Peons, 1:11, 12, 2:58
Peralta Barnueva y Rocha, Pedro de, 2:110
Percussion instruments, 3:153
Pereyra, Gabriel, 4:170
Pérez, Carlos Andrés, 4:185
Pérez de Cuéllar, Javier, 4:159
Pérez Esquivel, Adolfo, 3:205
Pérez Jiménez, Marcos, 4:185
Pernambucan Revolution (1817), 3:206
Pernambuco, 1:129, 156, **3:206**
    Dutch attacks on, 2:81–82
    missionary activity in, 3:133
    Recife, capital of, 4:38–39
Pernambuco Company, 4:150
Perón, Juan Domingo, 1:177, **3:206–7**
    Borges and opposition to, 1:122
    Córdoba and overthrow of, 2:25
    descamisados, supporters of, 2:59–60
    Dirty War and, 2:65

presidency of, 1:55–56
return of, 1:56
wife of, 3:207–8
Perón, María Eva Duarte, 1:55, 56, 2:60, **3:207–8** *(illus.)*
Pershing, John, 3:112, 4:190, 218
Personalism, 1:62, 2:92
Personal services, 4:86
Perto do coração selvagem (Lispector), 3:58
Peru, **3:208–16** *(map)*
    archaeological studies in, 1:41–42, 3:38
    armed forces in, 1:62
    Asians in, 1:74, 75
    Bolívar and liberation of, 1:111, 112
    boundary disputes of, 1:123, 124
    Chavin culture of, 1:188
    clothing in, 2:2
    colonial, 3:210–12
    copper mining in, 2:24
    Cuzco, 2:55–56 *(illus.)*
    Dominicans in, 4:44
    economy and development of, 3:215–16
    Ecuador's war with, 2:96
    Fujimori, president of, 2:149–50 *(illus.)*
    Garcilaso, historian of, 2:157
    guano industry in, 2:177–78
    guerrilla movements in, 2:188
    Haya de la Torre, political leader of, 2:205–6
    history of, 3:209–15
    Huari civilization in, 2:216
    independence struggle in, 4:203
    Indian cultures of, 3:11–12
    Indian policies in, 3:9
    iron and steel industry in, 3:23
    irrigation technique in, 3:24
    Kotosh site in, 3:38
    land of, 3:208–9
    Lima, capital of, 3:56–57 *(illus.)*
    Machu Picchu in, 3:72–73
    Moche of, 3:139–40
    Nasca and Nasca lines in, 3:154–55
    in 1900s, 3:213–15
    people of modern, 3:215
    Pizarro (Francisco) and conquest of, 3:225
    railroads in, 4:36
    roads in, 2:209–10
    San Martín and liberation of, 4:67
    Sendero Luminoso in, 4:83–84
    silver in, 2:169
    Spanish conquest of, 3:209–10
    Toledo y Figueroa, viceroy of, 4:141–42
    Tupac Amaru and Great Andean Rebellion in, 4:153–54
    Tupac Catari and Aymara uprising in, 4:154
    in War of the Pacific, 4:197–99
    War of the Peru-Bolivia Confederation and, 4:200
    wine industry in, 4:207
    as young republic, 3:212–13
Peru, Viceroyalty of, 1:195, 3:183, 210–11, **3:216–17**, 4:187
    viceroys of, 1:115, 4:141–42
Peru-Bolivia Confederation, 4:74
Peso de oro, 2:5
Pesos, 2:5–6
Pétion, Alexandre Sabès, 2:60, 199, 202, **3:217**
Petroleum industry, 3:131, **3:217–18**
    in Dutch West Indies, 2:83
      economic development and, 2:87

    in Ecuador, 2:96
    energy from, 2:107–8
    Gulf of Mexico as source for, 2:192
    in Mexico, Cárdenas Del Río and, 1:158
    in Peru, 3:216
    in Trinidad and Tobago, 4:152
    in Venezuela, 4:158, 184
Philip II of Spain, 1:173, **3:218–19**, 4:11, 13, 106, 109
Philip III of Spain, 1:49, 4:109
Philip IV of Spain, 2:60, 4:109
Philip V of Spain, 1:125, 2:32, 4:107, 110
Philippines, 3:78, **3:219–20**, 4:110
Phonetic writing, 3:80
Photography, **3:220–21** *(illus.)*, 4:61–62
Physicians, 3:100
Picadors, 1:144
Pichincha, battle of (1822), 2:95
Pictographic writing, 3:59, 80
Pidgin dialects, 3:48
Pimería Alta, 1:60, 3:38
Pinckney's Treaty (1795), 3:68
Pinochet Ugarte, Augusto, 1:177, 2:16, 64, 144, **3:221–22**, 4:1, 206
    military dictatorship of, 1:200–201
    nitrate industry and, 3:168
Piñón, Nélida, **3:222**
Pinta (ship), 2:14
Pipil Indians, 2:103, 104, 3:91, 107
Piracy, **3:222–24** *(illus.)*
    Brazil Company and protection from, 4:150
    buccaneers and, 1:141
Pius XI, Pope, 1:174
Pius XII, Pope, 1:175, 2:176
Pizarro brothers, **3:225–26**
    Almagro and, 1:21, 22
    in Bolivia, 1:115
    conquest of Peru and Inca, 1:81, 3:4, 6, 209–10
    Francisco, 1:21, 22, 81, 2:20, 115, 116 *(map)*, 3:4, 6, 209–10, 225
    Gonzalo, 1:22, 3:174, 225–26, 4:174
    Hernando, 1:22, 2:216, 3:225, 226
Plan of Ayala, 4:216
Plan of Iguala, 3:113, 119
Plantations, 1:11–12, 212, **3:226–27**
    banana, 1:95
    in British West Indies, 1:138–39
    Chinese laborers on, 1:74
    colonial, 3:226–27
    debt peonage and, 2:58
    in El Salvador, 2:104–5
    of ex-Confederates, 2:18
    in Jamaica, 3:28
    modern, 3:227
    slavery and, 4:93
    sugar, 1:11–12, 3:226–27, 4:119–20
Platt, Orville H., 3:228
Platt Amendment, 2:43, 44, **3:228**, 4:160, 161
Playwrights, 4:135–37
Plaza, 1:46
Plaza de Mayo (Buenos Aires), 1:143 *(illus.)*
Plaza Gutiérrez, Leonidas, 2:112
Plena, 3:151
Poetry, 3:60, 62, 64
    of Agustini, 1:14
    of Darío, 2:57
    of Ercilla y Zúñiga, 2:112
    of Guillén, 2:191
    of Ibarbourou, 2:23

    of Juana Inés de la Cruz, 3:34–35
    of Machado de Assis, 3:71
    of Martí y Pérez, 3:90
    of Mistral, 3:136–37
    negrista, 3:181
    of Neruda, 3:158–59
    of Palés Matos, 3:181
    of Paz, 3:200–201
    of Storni, 4:115
    of Vallejo, 4:175
    of Walcott, 4:196
Political activism of women, 4:210
Political bandits, 1:98
Political parties, **4:1–2**
    in Argentina, 1:54
    in Bolivia, 1:119, 120–21
    in Central America, 1:180–81
    in Colombia, La Violencia between, 4:192–94
    communist, 2:15–17, 3:89, 4:104–5
    in El Salvador, 3:89
    in Jamaica, 3:29
    newspapers linked to, 3:33
    in Paraguay, 3:197, 4:117
    in Peru, Haya de la Torre and, 2:205–6
    in Suriname, 4:122
    in Uruguay, 1:103, 2:187, 3:176, 4:170–71, 173
    in Venezuela, 4:185
Political philosophy
    communism, 2:15–17
    liberalism, 3:53–54
Political propaganda in newspapers, 3:32–33
Political rights, 2:218, 219
Politics
    anarchism, 1:29–30
    in colonial Colombia, 2:9–10
    women in, 4:211
Polk, James, 3:114
Pollution, 2:110, 3:218
    in Mexico City, 3:124, 125
Polygamy, 2:162
Pombal, Antônio Francisco, 1:66
Pombal, Marquês de, 1:173, 4:2, 13
Pombaline Reforms, 1:28, **4:2–3**, 4:11, 13
Ponce de León, Juan, 2:114, 130, 4:66
Popé, 4:21
Popocatépetl (volcano), 3:123
Popol Vuh, 3:59, 80–81
Popular music and dance, 3:151–52
Popular Revolutionary Alliance of America (APRA), 2:205
Population and population growth, **4:3–6** *(map)*
    Afro–Latin American, 1:2–3
    in Brazil, 4:6
    immigration and, 2:225
    in Mexico City, 3:124
    in Nicaragua, 3:163
    in Peru, 3:215
    in São Paulo, 4:78–79
    in Spanish America, 4:4–6
    urban life and, 1:209
Populism, 2:121
Porfiriato, 2:62
Portales Palazuelos, Diego José Pedro Víctor, 1:196, **4:7–8**, 4:200
Port-au-Prince, **4:7**
Portinari, Cândido Torquato, 1:67, **4:8–9** *(illus.)*
Port of Spain, Trinidad and Tobago, 4:151
Portraits, 1:66–67

Index

Portugal, Marcos, 2:154
Portugal and the Portuguese Empire, **4:9–11**
    Brazil and, 1:129–31
    Cabral, explorer for, 1:146–47
    captaincy system of, 1:156
    Dias and campaign against Dutch, 2:60–61
    diseases introduced by, 2:66
    Dutch in Brazil and, 2:60–61, 81–82
    explorations and, 2:114, 115–17
    fortifications of, 2:143
    gold and silver, wealth from, 2:169
    Henry the Navigator, 2:206
    João VI, 3:31–32
    missionaries in, 3:132–34
    monarchs of, 4:12–13
    Pombaline Reforms in, 4:2–3
    Sá e Benevides, administrator, 4:58
    slave trade and, 4:91
    Treaty of San Ildefonso and, 4:64–65
Portuguese in Latin America, 2:225–27, **4:12**
Portuguese Inquisition, 3:17
Portuguese language, 3:47–48
Portuguese monarchs, 1:130, 131, **4:12–13**
Posdata (Paz), 3:201
Positivism, 2:113, **4:14**, 4:81
Postclassic period, 3:95–96, 107–8
Postwar industrialization, 3:16
Potato, 2:134, **4:14–15** *(illus.)*
Potosí, 1:114 *(illus.)*, 115, 208, **4:15–16**
    mining in, 3:129 *(illus.)*, 130, 211
Pottery. *See also* Archaeology; Art, pre-Columbian
    in Amazonia, 2:52, 4:100
    dating of oldest, 2:53
    Huari, 2:216
    at Kotosh site, 3:38
Poverty, 3:7–8. *See also* Class structure, colonial and modern
    children in, 1:193
    defining, 3:7
    disease and, 2:68
    urban, 1:214
Preclassic period, 3:94–95, 105–6
Pre-Columbian art. *See* Art, pre-Columbian
Pre-Columbian cultures. *See* Cultures, pre-Columbian
Pregnancy and birth. *See* Women
Prejudice, Afro-Latinos and racial, 1:3–4
Presbyterians, 4:17
Presencia de la América Latina (mural), 4:31
Presidios, 1:125, **4:16**
    in California, 1:152
    in New Spain, 3:162
    in Spanish Borderlands, 4:108
Prestes, Júlio, 1:133–34
Prestes, Luís Carlos, 4:128
Prestes Column, 4:128
Preston, Andrew W., 4:158
Préval, René Garcia, 1:59
Price, George, 1:106
Printing presses, early, 3:32
Prio Socorrás, Carlos, 2:44
Prison. *See* Crime and punishment, colonial
Privateers, 2:77, 3:223, 224. *See also* Buccaneers
Private fiestas, 2:124
Privatization of industry, 2:89, 3:23, 218
Production techniques, technological advances in, 4:124–25
Professional sports, 4:114–15
Property. *See* Land, ownership of

Prostitution, 2:162–64
Protestantism, 1:176, **4:17–18**, 4:39
Protest of Baraguá, 3:70, 4:128
Protocol of Bueno Aires, 3:175
Protocol of Cartagena de Indias, 3:175
Protocol of Managua, 3:175
Provincias Internas, 1:59–61, 2:153, **4:18–19**, 4:108
Psilocybin, 2:78
Public access to media, 1:177–78
Public health, 3:100
Public sector, **4:19–21**
Puebla, battle of (1862), 2:61
Pueblo Indians, 1:59, 152, 189, 3:159, 161, 4:21–22
Pueblo Rebellion, 3:161, **4:21–22**
Puerto Rican National Party, 1:16
Puerto Rico, **4:22–25**
    Albizu Campos, independence activist in, 1:16
    Foraker Act and civilian government in, 2:136–37
    Operation Bootstrap in, 4:24
    popular music and dance of, 3:151–52
    San Juan, capital of, 4:66
    Spanish rule in, 4:22–23
    U.S. rule in, 4:24–25
Puig, Manuel, 3:65, **4:25**
Pulque, 2:134, 135
Puna, 1:218
Punishment of crime, 2:40
Putun Maya, 3:95–96
Pyramids, 1:44, 45 *(illus.)*, 70, 191, 2:101, 4:129 *(illus.)*, 130 *(illus.)*. *See also* Archaeology

Q

Quadros, Jânio, 1:134
Quebracho tree, 3:69
Quechua (language), 3:5, 47
Queirós, Eusébio de, 4:91
Queirós Law, 4:91
Quesada, Gonzalo Jiménez de, 2:8, 9
Quetzal bird, 1:34
Quetzalcoatl, 1:34, 89, 2:69–70, 3:107, **4:26–27** *(illus.)*
Quetzalcoatl (ruler), 1:90, 4:142
Quetzal (currency), 2:6
Quilombo, 3:86, 182, **4:27**, 4:90
Quincha vaults, 1:44
Quinine, 3:99
Quinto ("king's fifth"), 4:123
Quipu, **4:27–28**
Quiroga, Horatio, **4:28**
Quiroga, Rodrigo de, 4:118
Quiterños, 2:93, 94, 95
Quito, 2:92–93, **4:28–29** *(illus.)*. *See also* Ecuador
Quito Revolt of 1765, 2:95, **4:29–30**
Quivira (mythical city), 3:174

R

Rabinal Achí, 4:135
Race and ethnicity, **4:30–33** *(illus.)*
    Africans in Latin America, 1:2–6 *(illus.)*
    in Brazil, 1:136
    Chicanos, 1:190–91
    in colonial Latin America, 4:30–32
    Creoles, 2:37
    in Guyana, 2:193

    in Honduras, 2:215
    independence and change, 4:32–33
    mestizo, 3:109–10
    in modern Latin America, 4:33
    in Panama, 3:186
    population in Brazil and, 4:6
    population in Spanish America and, 4:5
Racially mixed groups, 1:211. *See also* Mestizo; Mulattos; *Zambos*
Racism, 1:3–4, 5, 2:75
Rackham, "Calico Jack," 3:223
Radio and television, **4:34–35**
Ragamuffin War. *See* Farroupilha Revolt (1835–1845)
Railroads, **4:35–36**
    in Argentina, 1:54
    in Costa Rica, 2:30
    foreign investment for, 2:139
    industrial growth and, 3:15
    in Mexico, 3:120–21
    in Panama, 3:184
    textile industry and, 4:134
Rainfall, 2:166
Rain forests, 1:217, 2:140, **4:36–38** *(illus.)*
    Amazon, 1:24
    of Colombia, 2:7
    of Suriname, 4:121
    Yanomami living in, 4:214
Raleigh, Walter, 2:101
Ramírez, Francisco, 1:73
Ramírez Duran, Oscar, 4:84
Ranches and ranching, 1:50, 54, 2:195, 3:65–66, 67, 97–98. *See also* Hacienda; Land, ownership of; Livestock
Ranqueles Indians, 4:53
Rapa Nui. *See* Easter Island
Rape, 2:39
Rapôso Tavares, Antônio, 2:117
Rationalism, 1:48
Read, Mary, 3:223, 224 *(illus.)*
Reagan, Ronald, 1:182, 2:57, 174, 3:166, 4:70
Real acuerdo, 1:83
Realism in literature, 3:62
Real (unit of currency), 2:6
Recife, **4:38–39**
Recôncavo, 4:63
Recreation. *See* Sports and recreation
Reducciones, 1:115, 3:133, **4:44–45**
Reed, Walter, 2:66
Refugees, 1:80–81, 2:46, 132, 3:85–86. *See also* Asylum
Regalism, 1:35–36
Regeneration (Colombia), 2:12
Regional banks, 1:99
Regional free trade, 4:149
Regional novel and short story, 3:63–64
Regional trade associations, 2:89–90
Reina, Carlos Roberto, 2:214
Religions, African–Latin American, **4:39–41**. *See also* Santería
    Candomblé, 1:155–56 *(illus.)*
    Islam, 3:25–26
    orixás worship, 3:176–77
    spiritism and, 4:112–13
    tobacco used in, 4:140
    Umbanda, 4:156–57
    voodoo, 4:195–96
    women in, 4:208
Religions, Indian, **4:41–42** *(illus.)*
    Cabeza de Vaco and, 1:146

craft work reflecting blend of Christian and, 2:36
cult of Chavin, 1:188
divinities of, 2:68–70
drugs as part of, 2:77
Inca, 3:5
messianic movements, 3:108–9
pre-Columbian calendars and, 1:150
spiritism and, 4:112–13
syncretism and, 4:122–23
Tzendal Rebellion and, 4:155–56
Religious festivals, 2:124–25
Religious groups. See Catholic Church; Islam; Jews in Latin America; Protestantism; Religions, African–Latin American; Religions, Indian
Religious orders, **4:43–46**. See also Dominicans (Dominican order); Franciscans; Jesuits
  of Catholic Church, 1:172
  in Códoba, 2:24–25
  education and, 2:98
  missions and missionaries of, 3:132–36
  universities run by, 4:164
Remittances, 4:20
Rendón, Francisco, 1:28
Reptiles, 1:33–34
República Mayor, 4:218
Research
  medical, 3:101, 4:81
  nutrition, 3:171
  scientific, 4:80–81
  technological, 4:125
Reservoir-canal system, 3:23
Retablos and ex-votos, 1:65, **4:46**
Reyna Barrios, José, 2:113
Rezanov, Nikolai, 1:153
Rice, 2:135
Rice industry, **4:46–47**
Riché, Jean-Baptiste, 4:99
Ricketts, Juan Landázuri, 1:175
Rigaud, André, 2:202
Riggs, Francis, 1:16
Rights
  human. See Human rights
  of slaves, 4:93
Ring of Fire, 2:166
Rio de Janeiro, **4:47–48** (illus.)
  Carnival in, 1:163
  gold rush in, 2:169
  Pan-American Conference at, 3:191
  samba schools of, 3:150
Río de la Plata, 1:49, 51, **4:48–49**
  confederation of, 1:72
  gauchos of, 2:157–58
  Treaty of Madrid and boundary of, 3:73–74
  United Provinces of, 4:51
  Viceroyalty of, 3:195, 216, **4:49–50**, 4:168–69, 187–88
Rio Grande, 2:176, **4:50**, 4:162–63
Rio Grande do Sul, 2:120
Rio Protocol (1942), 2:96
Rio Treaty (1947), 3:20, 175, 191, 192, 4:50
Ritual kinship (compadrazgo), 2:119
Rivadavia, Bernardino, 1:52, **4:51**
Rivera, Diego, 1:67, 3:157, **4:51–52** (illus.)
  Kahlo, wife of, 3:36–37
Rivera, Fructuoso, 2:120, 186–87, 3:176, 4:170
Rivers and river valleys, 2:165
Roa Bastos, Augusto, 3:64, **4:52–53**
Roads. See Highways and roads

Robusta coffee beans, 2:4
Roca, Julio Argentino, **4:53**
Rocafuerte, Vicente, 2:95
Roca-Runciman Pact (1933), 1:55
Rockefeller Foundation, 4:81
Rock salt, 4:63
Rodents, 1:33
Rodeo, 4:114
Rodó, José Enrique, 3:63
Rodón, Pancho, 1:68
Rodríguez, Andrés, 3:198, 4:117
Rodríguez, Hortalez and Company, 1:27
Rodríguez, Martin, 1:52
Rodríguez, Melitono, 3:220
Rodríguez de Toro, María Teresa, 1:111
Rodríguez Zeledón, José, 2:30
Rogers, Woodes, 3:224
Rojas Paúl, Pablo, 2:195
Roldós Aguilera, Jaime, 2:96
Roman Catholic Church. See Catholic Church
Romanticism, 3:61–62
Romero, Oscar Arnulfo, 1:176, 2:57, 106, **4:54–55** (illus.), 4:68
Rondon, Cândido Mariano da Silva, 2:115
Roosevelt, Franklin D., 2:172, 3:190, 4:71, 98 (illus.), 145, 161
Roosevelt, Theodore, 2:70, 3:143, 4:55, 160
Roosevelt Corollary, 2:70, 74, 3:143, **4:55**, 4:160–61
Rosa de Lima, Santa, 4:55, 56 (illus.)
Rosas, Juan Manuel de, 1:15, 2:186, 187, **4:55–56**, 4:79, 135
  national unity and, 1:52
  Oribe and, 3:176
  Urquiza's campaign vs., 4:166
Rousseau, Jean Jacques, 2:109
Royal patronage, clergy and, 1:172, 173, 174
Royal Protomedicato, 3:100
Rubber industry, 1:25, 118–19, 3:78, **4:56–57**
Rubens, Peter Paul, 1:65
Ruíz de Alarcón, Juan, 4:135
Rumba, 3:151
Rurales, 2:39, 3:120, **4:57**
Rural labor unions, 3:43–44
Rural society, 1:214
Russians in Pacific Northwest, 3:179, 180
Ryswick, Treaty of (1697), 2:197

S

Saavedra, Juan de, 4:175
Saavedra Lamas, Carlos, **4:58**
Saba, 2:83
Sábato, Ernesto, **4:59**
Sabinada Revolt, 4:59–60, 63
Sabino Álvares da Rocha Vieira, Francisco, 4:59
Sacasa, Juan Bautista, 3:165, 4:71, 97
Sacasa, Roberto, 4:217
Sacred music, 3:148–49
Sacrifice, human, 2:69, 4:42
Sacsahuaman, 1:41, 2:55, 3:4
Sá e Benavides, Salvador Correia de, **4:58**
Sáenz Peña Law (1912), 4:119
Sahagún, Bernardino de, 2:78, 3:80, 4:127
Sainete criollo (Creole farce), 4:136
Saint, first American, 4:55, 56 (illus.)
St. Augustine, **4:60–61** (illus.)
St. Barthélemy (St. Barts Gustavia), 2:147
St. Christopher (St. Kitts), 1:138, 139, 2:147

St. Croix, 4:194
St. Domingue, 2:72, 146, 147, 197–98. See also Haiti
St. Eustatius, 2:83
St. John, 4:194
St. Kitts. See St. Christopher (St. Kitts)
St. Lucia, 1:139
St. Martin, 2:83
Saints' days, 2:125
St. Thomas, 4:194
St. Vincent, 1:139
Sajama, Mt., 1:113
Salamanca, Daniel, 1:185, 186
Salesians, 4:45–46
Sales taxes, 4:123
Salgado, Sebastião, 3:220 (illus.), 221, **4:61–62**
Salinas de Gortari, Carlos, 1:100, 2:111, 3:122, 169, **4:62**
Salitreros, 3:168
Salsa (dance), 3:151
Salsa (sauce), 2:134
Salt trade, **4:63**
Salvador, 4:59, **4:63–64**, 4:99
Samaniego, Manuel de, 1:65
Samba, 3:150, 151
San Agustín, **4:64**
San Antonio de Valero mission, 1:15
San Blas Islands, **3:39–40**
San Carlos Borromeo mission, 4:84
San Carlos Canal, 3:173
Sánchez, Miguel, 2:176
Sánchez Cerro, Luis, 2:205–6
San Diego de Alcalá mission, 1:152
Sandinistas, 1:7 (illus.), 182, **4:69–70** (illus.)
  Barrios de Chamorro and, 1:101
  communism and, 2:16
  contras vs., 2:22–23
  control of Nicaragua, 3:166
  Mosquito Indians and, 3:147–48
  opposition to Somozas, 3:165–66
  Ortega Saavedra, leader of, 3:177–78
  Sandino as inspiration for, 4:71–72
  Soviet relations with, 4:104
Sandino, Augusto César, 3:165, 4:69, **4:71–72**, 4:97
San Francisco Xavier, University of, 1:116
Sanguinetti, Julio María, **4:72**, 4:173
San Ildefonso, Treaty of (1777), 1:123, 3:74, 4:49, **4:64–65**
Sanín, Noemi, 2:9
San Jacinto, battle of (1836), **4:65**, 4:132
San José, Costa Rica, 2:28–29, **4:65–66**
San Juan, Puerto Rico, 4:22, 23, **4:66**
San Luis Obispo de Tolosa, mission of, 3:134 (illus.)
San Martín, José Francisco de, 1:165, 196, **4:66–68** (illus.)
  Bolívar and, 1:112
  independence struggle and, 3:212, 4:203
  O'Higgins and, 3:173
San Román, Miguel de, 1:169
San Salvador, 2:14, **4:68**
San Sebastiá de Urabá, 2:8
Sansei, 1:75
Santa Anna, Antonio López de, **4:72–73**
  at Alamo, battle of the, 1:14, 15
  at Buena Vista, battle of, 1:142
  Mexican-American War and, 3:114, 115
  presidency of, 3:119, 120
  at San Jacinto, battle of, 4:65
  Texas Revolution and, 4:131–32

251

Index

Santa Casa da Misericórdia, 4:45
Santa Cruz, Andrés de, 1:117, 118, **4:73–74**, 4:200
Santa Cruz, Foraleza de, 2:143
Santa Cruz de la Sierra, Bolivia, 1:115
Santa Fe Trail, 3:161
Santa María, Domingo, 1:94
Santamaría, Juan, 2:29
Santa Maria (ship), 2:14
Santana, Pedro, 2:73–74, 80
Santander, Francisco de Paulo, 1:112, 113, 126, **4:74**
Santería, 1:155, 4:40–41
Santiago, 1:194, **4:74–76** *(illus.)*
Santiago, Miguel de, 1:64
Santiago de Guatemala, 1:179
Santidade (holiness) movement, 3:109
Santo Domingo, 2:72, 76, 210, 211 *(illus.)*, **4:76**
  Audiencia of, 1:82, **4:76–77**
  Drake's attack on, 2:77
Santos, Máximo, 1:103
Santos-Dumont, Alberto, **4:77–78**
Santo Tomás, Domingo de, 4:44
San Xavier del Bac, 1:60, **4:68–69**
São Francisco river, 2:165
São Paulo, 2:4, 3:141, 4:48, **4:78–79**, 4:94
São Vicente, 1:156
Sarmiento, Domingo Faustino, 1:53, 2:100, 3:62, **4:79**
Savanna region, 1:216, 218, 2:165
Savoy, Gene, 3:214
Schools. *See* Education
Science, **4:80–81**
  Andrada and, 1:31
  of archaeology, 1:39–40
  of astronomy, 1:76–77 *(illus.)*
  expeditions in Amazon region for, 1:25
  exploration of Brazil for, 2:117
  Houssay and, 2:215–16
  Humboldt and, 2:221
  Leloir and, 3:53
  technology and, 4:124–26
Scott, Winfield, 3:115
Sculpture. *See* Art, colonial to modern; Art, pre-Columbian
Sea salt, 4:63
Seasonal climate variations, 1:216–17
Second Vatican Council, 1:175, 3:55
Secular art and music, 3:149–50
Secular clergy, 1:172, 173
Secular schooling, 2:98
Sédar Senghor, Léopold, 3:158
Segovia Highlands, 4:179
Selk'nams, **4:82**
Selva, 1:24
Semana Trágica, 3:30 *(illus.)*, 31
Seminoles, 2:131
Senado da Câmara, **4:82–83**
Sendero Luminoso, 2:16, 79, 150, 188, 3:214–15, **4:83–84** *(illus.)*
Sepé Tiarayú, 2:179
Sephardim Jews, 3:30
Serra, Junípero, 1:28, 3:134 *(illus.)*, **4:84**
Serranía del Darién, 3:186
Serranía de Tabasará, 3:186
Sertão, 1:129, 3:206
Service for Peace and Justice (SerPAJ), 3:205
Service industry, 2:83, **4:85–87**. *See also* Banking; Education; Medicine; Trade and commerce
Sesmarias, 1:7, 3:2, 44

Seven Cities of Cíbola, 3:160, **4:87**
Seven Years' War, **4:87**
Seville-Cádiz trade monopoly, 2:22
Sexuality. *See* Gender roles and sexuality
Shamanism, 1:146, 2:55, 3:27, 4:42
Sheep ranching, 3:66
Shining Path. *See* Sendero Luminoso
Ships and shipping. *See* Fleet systems, colonial; Manila Galleon
Short story. *See* Literature
Sierra
  in Ecuador, 2:91–92
  in Peru, 3:209
Sierra Madre, **4:88**
Sierra Madre de Chiapas, 4:88
Sierra Madre del Sur, 3:116, 4:88
Sierra Madre de Ozxaca, 4:88
Sierra Madre Occidental, 2:166, 3:115, 4:88
Sierra Madre Oriental, 2:166, 3:115, 4:88
Sierra Maestra, 2:41
Siesta, 4:85
Sigüenza y Góngora, Carlos de, 1:40, 2:110
Silent film, 1:205
Silva, Bento Gonçalves da, 2:120
Silva, Bérnardo Pires da, 1:66
Silva Xavier, Joaquim José da, **4:88–89**
Silver. *See* Gold and silver
Silver peso, 2:5
Silvino, Antônio, 1:97
Sipán, Moche tombs at, 1:42
Siqueiros, David Alfaro, 1:63 *(illus.)*, 67
Sixtus IV, Pope, 3:17
Skin color, Afro-Brazilians and, 1:5–6
"Slash and burn" agriculture, 1:10, 2:140–41
Slave revolts, 2:147, 201, **4:89–90** *(illus.)*
Slavery, **4:92–95** *(illus.)*
  Africans in Latin America and, 1:2–6 *(illus.)*
  in Argentina, 1:50, 51
  artistic traditions introduced by slaves, 1:68
  bandeiras and, 1:96–97
  Black Caribs, 1:162
  in Brazil, 1:130, 132–33, 4:93–95
  in British West Indies, 1:138–39
  Cali and, 1:150–51
  in Caribbean Antilles, 1:161
  caste system and, 1:212
  colonial justice for black slaves, 2:38–39
  debt peonage as type of, 2:58–59
  diseases introduced from Africa, 2:66–67
  in French West Indies, 2:147
  in Grenada, 2:173
  in Haiti, 2:197–98
  Indian, 1:25, 4:3, 92, 94–95
  interracial sexual relations and, 2:162
  in Jamaica, 3:28
  maroons, escapees from, 3:86–87
  mining and, 3:129, 130
  mulattos and zambos and, 4:32
  plantation agriculture and, 3:226–27
  population of slaves, 4:5, 6
  runaways in *quilombos*, 4:27
  in Spanish America, 4:92–93
  women in, 4:208
Slavery, abolition of, 4:32, 95–96
  abolition of slave trade and, 4:92
  by Isabel, in Brazil, 3:25, 203
  in Jamaica, 3:28
  in Peru, 1:169
  Pombaline reforms and, 4:2
  São Paulo as abolitionist center, 4:78

Ten Years' War and, 4:127–28
Vieira's efforts for, 4:190
Slave trade, **4:90–92**
  asiento and, 1:75–76
  Brazilian trading companies and, 4:150
  Cartagena as stopover port for, 1:167
  in Cuba, 2:42–43
  development of, 4:91
  Esmeraldas and, 2:112
  laws against, 2:38
  plantation system and, 1:12
  Portuguese and, 4:10
  traders, 4:90–91
  triangular trade and, 4:120
Smallpox, 1:90, 2:66, 67 *(illus.)*
Smuggling, 1:76, **4:96–97**, 4:109, 147, 181
Soccer, 4:114
Social activism at universities, 4:166
Social bandits, 1:97
Social Catholicism, 1:36
Social Indicators of Development, 3:7
Socialism in Chile, 1:200. *See also* Communism
Social realism, 1:67–68
Social structure. *See* Class structure, colonial and modern; Race and ethnicity
Sociedad Colombo-Alemana de Transportes Aéreos, 1:86
Sociedad de Beneficiencia in Argentina, 1:193
Socioeconomic rights, 2:218, 219
Soil, 1:217
Soldaderas, **4:97**, 4:209
Solimoes. *See* Amazon River
Solís, Juan Díaz de, 4:167
Solórzano, Carlos, 3:165
Somoza family, 2:64, 3:165–66, **4:97–98** *(illus.)*
  Anastasio Somoza Debayle (Tachito), 1:182, 2:22, 3:165–66, 4:69–70, 98
  Anastasio Somoza García, 3:165, 4:71, 97, 98 *(illus.)*
  Luis Somoza Debayle, 3:165, 4:97–89, 97–98
  Sandinistas and overthrow of,, 1:101, 3:177, 4:69–70
Sonora, Mexican state of, 1:60
Soroeta, Ignacio de, 2:17
Soto, Hernando de, 3:136, **4:98–99**, 4:116
Soto Alfaro, Bernardo, 2:30
Soufière Volcano, eruption of, 4:195
Soulouque, Faustin Élie, 2:200, **4:99**
Sound film, 1:205–6
Sousa, Martim Afonso de, 4:78
Sousa, Tomé de, 1:129, 156, 3:132, **4:99**
South America
  boundary disputes in, 1:123–24
  geography of, 2:164–66
  Indian religions in, 4:42
  pre-Columbian cultures in, 2:51–53, 3:11–12
  Suriname, 4:121–22
  Tierra del Fuego, 4:137
  Uruguay, 4:167–73
  wars of independence in, 4:202–3
  wine industry in, 4:207
South America, pre-Columbian history, 3:38, **4:100–103** *(map)*
South American art, 1:71–72
Southern Cone, **4:103–4**
Southern oscillation, 2:102
Soviet–Latin American relations, **4:104–5**

252

Castro and, 1:170–71
communism and, 2:16–17
Cuba and, 2:46
Cuban missile crisis and, 2:47–48
Havana and, 2:204
in Nicaragua, 3:166
Spain and the Spanish Empire, **4:104–7** *(map)*
  Africans in, 1:2–4
  American Revolution and, 1:27–28
  in Argentina, 1:49–51
  asiento and slavery in, 1:75–76
  audiencias introduced by, 1:81–82
  Black Legend and negative image of, 1:108–9 *(illus.)*
  Bourbon Reforms in, 1:124–26
  Cabeza de Vaca and, 1:145–46
  cabildo in, 1:146
  in California, 1:152–53
  in Central America, 1:179
  Charles III and, 1:187–88
  in Chile, 1:194–96
  in Colombia, 2:8
  conquest of Aymara, 1:88
  conquistadors and, 2:18–21 *(illus.)*
  Cortés and, 2:27–28
  Council of the Indies and, 2:32
  in Cuba, 2:41–43
  decline of, 4:106–7
  diseases introduced by, 2:66
  in Dominican Republic, 2:72
  Dutch in Brazil and, 2:81–82
  end of empire, 4:107
  expansion of, 4:105–6
  explorations and, 2:114–15
  in Florida, 2:130–32
  forts and fortifications in, 2:142–43
  Gálvez (José), statesman of, 2:153
  gold and silver, wealth from, 2:169
  "golden ages" of, 4:107
  in Guatemala, 2:180–81
  Havana as stronghold of, 2:203
  intendancy system in, 3:19
  in Louisiana, 3:68
  Menéndez de Avilés, naval officer in, 3:103
  Mexican War of Independence and, 3:112–13
  militias in, 3:127–28
  in New Granada, Viceroyalty of, 3:159
  in New Mexico, 3:160–61
  in New Spain, Viceroyalty of, 3:162
  in Pacific Northwest, 3:179–80
  in Panama, 3:183
  in Peru, 3:209–12
  Philip II of, 3:218–19
  in Philippines, 3:219–20
  Pizarro brothers and, 3:225–26
  Provincias Internas in, 4:18–19
  in Puerto Rico, 4:22–23
  in Río de la Plata, Viceroyalty of, 4:49–50
  trading companies of, 4:150–51
  Treaty of San Ildefonso and, 4:64–65
  unification of Spain and, 4:105
  in Uruguay, 4:167–68
  viceroys and viceroyalties, 4:187–89
Spaniards, social class of, 1:211
Spanish America
  abolition of slavery in, 4:95
  architecture in, 1:45–46, 47–48
  explorations of, 2:114–15
  laws and legal system in, 3:51–52

  militias in colonial, 3:127–28
  mining in, 3:130–31
  missions and missionaries in, 3:134–36
  population and population growth in, 4:4–6
  slave revolts in, 4:89
  slavery in, 4:92–93
  trade and commerce in, 4:147–48
  universities of, 4:164–65
Spanish-American War, **4:110–11** *(illus.)*, 4:160
  Cuban independence and, 2:43
  end of Spanish empire and, 4:107
  San Juan during, 4:66
  U.S. in Puerto Rico and, 4:24
  USS *Maine* and start of, 3:75
Spanish Armada, 2:77
Spanish Borderlands, 3:83–84, 136, 160–61, **4:107–9** *(map)*
Spanish Constitution of 1812, 3:54
Spanish emigrants, 2:225
Spanish Inquisition, 3:17
Spanish language, 3:47–48
Spanish Main. *See* Caribbean Sea
Spanish monarchs, **4:109–10**
  empire of, 4:105–7
Special Inter-American Conference on the Problems of War and Peace, 3:20
Specialized farm, 2:195
Spices and herbs, **4:111–12**
Spiritism, 1:155–56, 4:40–41, **4:112–13**
Sports and recreation, **4:113–15** *(illus.)*
  bullfighting, 1:144–45 *(illus.)*
  European, 4:113–14
  Native American, 4:113
  Pelé, soccer player, 3:203–4
  pre-Columbian ball game, 1:93–94
  today, 4:114–15
Squier, Ephraim George, 2:215
Standard Fruit, 1:96
Standard Oil Company of the United States, 2:82
State banks, 1:99
State courts, 3:52
State-run corporations, 4:20
Steam engine, invention of, 4:125
Steelmaking. *See* Iron and steel industry
Stelae, 1:70
Stephens, John Lloyd, 1:40, 3:181
Steuben, Baron von, 1:27
Stock markets, 1:99, 100
Stonework, 1:44
Storni, Alfonsina, **4:115**v
Stratigraphy, cultural, 1:41
Street children, 1:193, 2:100
Street vendors, **4:115–16** *(illus.)*
Strikes, labor, 1:29, 30, 3:42
Stroessner, Alfredo, 1:176, 3:198, **4:117**
Suárez, Inés de, **4:117–18**
Suburbs, 1:210
Sucre Alcalá, Antonio José de, 1:112, 118, 2:95, 3:212, 4:73, **4:118**
Sucre (unit of currency), 2:6
Suffrage movement, 2:164, 3:70, **4:118–19**, 4:209–10
Suffrage, universal male, 4:118–19
Sugarcane, 2:135
Sugar industry, **4:119–21**
  in British West Indies, 1:138–39
  in Cuba, 2:42–43
  explorers and introduction of, 1:13
  in French West Indies, 2:147

  in Grenada, 2:173
  plantations and, 1:11–12, 3:226–27, 4:119–20
  slavery and, 1:212, 4:93
  in Suriname, 4:122
  technological advances in, 4:125
Suriname, 1:123, 2:82, 3:26, **4:121–22**
Surrealism, 1:68
Sweden, control of St. Barts by, 2:147
Syncretism, 1:156, 2:68, 4:40, 112, **4:122–23**
Syndicalism, 1:29, 30
Szyzlo, Fernando de, 1:68

T

Taft, William Howard, 2:70, 4:161
Tahuantinsuyu (Inca empire), 3:4, 209
Taino Indians, 2:210, 222, 4:22, 23
Taironas Indians, 2:7
Tajumulco, 2:185
Taki Onkoy (dancing sickness) movement, 3:109
Tango, 3:151 *(illus.),* 152
Tapajós, culture of, 3:12
Taperinha, dating of pottery from, 2:53
Tariffs, NAFTA and, 3:169
Taxes and taxation, 1:21, 3:5, 16, 19, **4:123–24**
Tayasal, **4:124**
Taycanamu (ruler), 1:202
Taylor, Zachary, 1:142, 3:114
Tea, 2:135
Teach, Edward (Blackbeard), 3:224
Teatro de coringa, 4:137
Technical training, 2:98
Technology, **4:124–26** *(illus.)*
  crafts and, 2:36
  radio and television, 4:34–35
  Rivera's belief in power of, 4:51
  science and, 4:80–81
  in sugar industry, 4:121
Tegucigalpa, **4:126–27**
Tehuantepec, Isthmus of, 3:116
Teixeira Albernas II, João, 3:83
Teixera, Pedro, 2:116
Tejada, Lidia Gueiler, 4:211
Television, 1:178, 4:34–35
Teller Amendment, 4:110
Temperate climates, 2:165–66
Temperature. *See* Climate and vegetation
Temple of the Inscriptions, 3:181
Templo Mayor, 3:122, 123, **4:127**
Tenatiuh. *See* Alvarado y Mesía, Pedro de
Tenentismo, 1:133, **4:128**, 4:177
Tennis, 4:114–15
Tenochca. *See* Aztecs
Tenochtitlán, 1:76, 88–90, 2:51, **4:128–29** *(illus.)*
  Cortés' siege of, 2:27, 3:141
  founding of, 1:88–89
  in Postclassic period, 3:107
  Templo Mayor, ceremonial center at, 4:127
  as Venice of the Americas, 1:210
Ten Years' War, 2:43, 48, 3:70, 4:127–28
Teotihuacán, 1:40, 207, 2:51, **4:129–30** *(illus.)*
  art of, 1:70
  in Classic period, 3:107
  grid arrangement of, 1:44
  in Preclassic period, 3:106

253

Index

Tepanecas, 1:89
Te-Pito-o-te-Henua. *See* Easter Island
Terra, Gabriel, 4:172
Terrace agriculture, 1:10, 3:24
Terrorism in Peru, 2:150
Texas, 1:1, 3:113–14, 4:65, **4:130–32** *(illus.)*
Texas Revolution, 1:14–15, 4:131–32
Textiles and textile industry, **4:133–34**
   clothing, 2:1–2
   cochineal for dyes, 2:3
   in Colombia, 2:9
   colonial, 3:15
   in Ecuador, 2:93, 94, 4:29
   weaving crafts, 2:36
Tezozomoc (ruler), 1:89
Theater, 3:64, **4:135–37** *(illus.)*, 4:196
Thousand Days, War of the. *See* War of the Thousand Days
Tierra caliente, 1:217
Tierra del Fuego, 1:49, 4:82, **4:137**
Tierra fria, 1:217
Tierra helada, 1:217, 218
Tierra nevada, 1:217
Tierra templada, 1:217
Tijuana, 1:91
Tikal, 1:40, 41, 207, **4:137–38**
Timber industry. *See* Lumber industry
Timerman, Jacobo, 3:33
Tin industry, 1:118, 3:130, 4:16, **4:138–39**
Tinoco Granados, Federico, 2:30
Tiradentes. *See* Silva Xavier, Joaquim José da
Tithe, conflicts among clergy over, 1:173
Titicaca, Lake, 1:113, 2:165, **4:139**
Tiwanaku, 1:71–72, 114, 2:53, 4:103, **4:139–40**
Tizoc (ruler), 1:90
Tlaloc (god), 2:69–70
Tlapacoya, 3:105
Tlatelolco, city of, 1:89–90
Tlaxcala, 2:27
Tobacco industry, 3:99, **4:140–41** *(illus.)*
Tobago. *See* Trinidad and Tobago
Toledo y Figueroa, Francisco de, 1:203, 3:210, **4:141–42**, 4:213
Tollán, 3:107
Toltecs, 1:40, 191, 2:51, 3:107, **4:142–43**
Tonton Macoutes, 1:59, 2:84, 200, **4:143**
Topa Inca, 3:4
Topiltzín Quetzalcoatl of Tollán, 4:26
Tordesillas, Treaty of (1493), 1:25, 129, 2:114, 3:51, **4:143–44**
Toro, David, 1:186
Torrejón y Velasco, Tomás de, 3:149
Torrijos-Carter Treaty (1977), 4:144
Torrijos Herrera, Omar, 3:185, **4:144**
Tortillas, 2:133
Tortuga Island, 1:141, 142
Totonacs, 2:51
Totora, rafts from, 2:36
Tourism, **4:145**
   crafts and, 2:37
   Cuzco as center of, 2:56
   in French West Indies, 2:148
   on Galápagos Islands, 2:152
   in Havana, 2:203
   in Honduras, 2:215
   as service industry, 4:86–87
Toussaint l'Ouverture, 1:204, 3:217, **4:146** *(illus.)*, 4:204
   Haitian Revolution and, 2:198, 201–2
Town councils, 4:82–83
Trade and commerce, **4:146–49** *(illus.)*
   Argentina and, 1:55
   auto industry and, 1:84–85
   Belize and, 1:105
   Bourbon Reforms and, 1:125
   British–Latin American relations and, 1:137–38
   Cali and, 1:151
   Casa de Contratación, 1:167
   Charles III and, 1:188
   Chile and, 1:197
   Colombia and, 2:9
   colonial, 1:125, 4:147–48
   colonial fleet systems and, 2:128–29
   consulados and, 2:21–22
   drug trade, 2:78–79
   foreign investment and, 2:138–40
   guano industry in Peru and, 2:178
   Hawkins and, 2:204
   highways and roads for, 2:209–10
   Manila Galleon, 3:78
   Mercosur and, 3:103–4
   in Mesoamerica, 2:50
   modern, 4:148–49
   NAFTA and, 3:168–69
   Panama Canal and, 3:189
   regional trade associations, 2:89–90
   salt trade, 4:63
   slave trade, 4:90–92
   smuggling and, 4:96–97
   Spanish Borderlands and, 4:108–9
   sugar industry and triangular trade, 4:120–21
   Venezuela and, 4:181
   World War I and, 4:212
   World War II and, 4:213
Trading companies, 4:2, **4:149–51**
Traditional healing, 3:98
Transamazon Highway, 2:210
Transcontinental Treaty. *See* Adams-Onís Treaty
Transpantaneira, 3:193
Transportation and travel
   aviation, 1:85–86
   highways and roads and, 2:208–10 *(illus.)*
   in Peru, 3:216
   railroads, 4:35–36
   as service industry, 4:86
   slavery and, 4:93–94
Tratado de Cesión. *See* Adams-Onís Treaty
Triangular trade, 4:120–21
Tribute, collection of, 1:169. *See also* Encomienda
Trilce (Vallejo), 4:175
Trinidad and Tobago, 1:139, 2:15, 3:23, **4:151–52**
Trinidad Theatre Workshop, 4:196
Trinitaria, La, **4:152**
Triple Alliance. *See* War of the Triple Alliance
Tropical climate, 2:165
Tropical Trading and Transport Company, 1:95, 2:148
Trotskyists, 2:16
Trujillo-Hull Treaty (1940), 4:153
Trujillo Molina, Rafael Leónidas, 2:74–75, 4:76, **4:152–53**
Truth commissions, 2:221
Tsunamis, 2:222
Tule. *See* Kuna
Tulum, 3:108
Tupac Amaru, 1:117, 3:211, 4:142, **4:153–54**
Tupac Amaru Revolutionary Movement (MRTA), 2:150, 3:57, 215
Tupac Catari, 1:117, 3:40, **4:154**
Tupamaro, 4:172
Tupi, 3:128, **4:155**
Tupi-Guarani language, 3:47, 4:155
Tupinambá, 1:129, 3:12
Turquino (mountain), 2:41
Turquoise, 2:160
Tuyuc, Rosalina, 1:214
Tuyutí, battle of (1866), 4:201
TV Globo, 4:34
Twenty-Sixth of July Movement, 2:49
Twin cities on U.S.–Mexico border, 4:162, 163
Typhus, 2:66
Tzeltal Indians, 3:109
Tzendal Rebellion, **4:155–56**

U

Ubico y Castañeda, Jorge, 1:38, 2:64, 183, **4:156**
Uhle, Max, 1:40
Ulama (ball game), 1:93
Ulate Blanco, Otilio, 2:31, 125
Ultraísmo, 1:121–22
Umbanda, 2:55, 4:40, **4:156–57** *(illus.)*
Unemployment, street vending and, 4:116
Union activities, 3:42, 43–44. *See also* Labor and labor movements
Unión de armas, 4:157
Union of Indigenous Nations (UNI), 3:14
United Brands, 1:96
United Farm Workers, 1:191
United Fruit Company, 1:38, 95, 96, 2:148, 183, **4:158**
United Nations, 1:59, **4:158–59**, 4:213
   Economic Commission for Latin America (ECLA), 2:90
United States, immigration to, 2:226, 227–28
U.S. Immigration and Naturalization Service (INS), 2:228
United States–Latin American relations, **4:159–62** *(illus.)*
   Allende and, 1:19–20
   Alliance for Progress and, 1:20–21
   in Arizona, 1:60–61
   Bay of Pigs Invasion and, 1:104
   bracero program and, 1:126 *(illus.)*
   in California, 1:153–54
   in Central America, 1:181, 182
   in Chile, 1:200
   CIA and, 1:184
   Clayton-Bulwer Treaty and, 1:215
   in Colombia, 2:13
   contras, U.S. support for, 2:22–23
   counterinsurgency policy, 2:32–34
   in Cuba, 2:43–46
   Cuban missile crisis and, 2:47–48
   Dollar Diplomacy and, 2:70–71
   in Dominican Republic, 2:74, 75
   drug trade and, 2:78–79
   filibustering and, 3:1
   foreign investments and, 2:139
   Gadsden Purchase and, 2:151
   Good Neighbor Policy and, 2:172
   in Grenada, 2:174
   in Haiti, 2:200, 201
   Hay-Bunau-Varilla Treaty and, 2:205
   in Honduras, 2:214

imperialism and, 3:1, 2–3
Inter-American relations and, 3:19–22
Mexican-American War and, 3:113–15
Mexican Revolution and, 3:111, 112
Monroe Doctrine and, 3:142–43
NAFTA and, 3:168–69
in New Mexico, 3:161–62
in Nicaragua, 3:164–65, 166
in 1900s, 4:160–61
in Panama, 3:184–86
Panama Canal and, 3:187–89
Pan-American Conferences and, 3:190–91
in Puerto Rico, 4:24–25
Roosevelt Corollary and, 4:55
Sandinistas and, 4:70
from 1776 to 1900, 4:160
Soviet–Latin American relations and, 4:104
Spanish-American War and, 4:110–11
in Texas, 4:130–32
Torrijos Herrara of Panama and, 4:144
Treaty of Guadalupe Hidalgo and, 2:176–77
U.S. interventions, 4:159
U.S. military assistance programs, 1:62
USS *Maine* and, 3:74–75
Watermelon Riot and, 4:205
in World Wars I and II, 4:211–13
Zimmerman Telegram to Mexico and, 4:218
United States–Mexico border, **4:162–63**
Adams-Onís Treaty and, 1:1–2
Baja California and, 1:91
border connections, 4:163
California and, 1:153
conflicts over, 4:162–63
Gadsden Purchase and, 2:151
maquiladoras on, 3:84–85
migration over, 2:226, 227–28
New Mexico and, 3:159–62
resolution of dispute over, 1:124
Rio Grande as, 4:50
Texas and, 4:130–32
Treaty of Guadalupe Hidalgo and, 2:176–77
U.S. National Drug Control Strategy, 2:79
U.S. Virgin Islands. *See* Virgin Islands of the United States
Universal History of Infamy (Borges), 1:122
Universities and colleges, 2:98, 110, 4:78, 80–81, **4:163–66** *(illus.)*
Unzaga, Luis De, 2:152
Upper classes, 1:214
Urbanization. *See* Cities and urbanization
Urban life. *See* Cities and urbanization
Urban planning, 1:46. *See also* Cities and urbanization
of ancient cities, 1:44
of Brasília, 1:127–28 *(illus.)*
in Caracas, lack of, 1:158
Spanish guidelines for, 1:209
Urban society, 1:214
Urdaneta, Andrés de, 4:45
Uriburu, José, 1:54
Urquiza, Justo José de, 1:52–53, 2:187, 4:56, **4:166**, 4:170
Urubu *(quilombo)*, 4:90
Uruguay, **4:167–73** *(map)*
Artigas, independence leader in, 1:72–73
Batlle y Ordóñez, president of, 1:103–4 *(illus.)*

climate of, 1:217
clothing in, 2:2
conflict and change, era of, 4:170–71
conquest and colonization, 4:167–68
Guerra Grande in, 2:186–87
immigration to, 2:227
modern, 4:171–73
Montevideo, capital of, 3:144–45
Soviet relations with, 4:104
struggle for independence, 4:168–69
War of the Triple Alliance and, 4:200–202
Uruguay River, 2:165
Uspallata Pass, 1:203
Uxmal, 3:95

V

Vague year, 1:150
Valcárcel, Luis, 1:41
Valdéz, Juan (fictitious character), 2:4
Valdivia, Pedro de, 1:37, 194, 2:115, 4:74, 75 *(illus.)*, 117, **4:174**
Valdivia culture, 2:52
Valenzuela, Luisa, **4:174**
Valle, José Cecilio del, 2:213, **4:174–75**
Vallejo, César, 4:175
Valley of Mexico, 2:208
Valparaíso, **4:175–76**
Vanguardism, 3:63
Vanilla, 4:112
Vaqueiros, 3:97
Vaquerías, 1:50
Vaqueros, 2:159
Varela y Morales, Félix, 4:176
Vargas, Getúlio Dornelles, 1:133–34, 2:64, 3:39, 4:128, **4:177**
Vargas, Max T., 3:221
Vargas Llosa, Mario, 3:65, **4:178**
Várzeas (igapós), 1:24, 25, 27, 3:12
Vasconcelos, José, 3:110, 157
Vásquez, Horacio, 2:74
Vatican Council II, 1:175
Vázquez, Pedro Ramírez, 1:46
Vegetables, 2:134
Vegetation. *See* Climate and vegetation
Vela Mena, Augusto, 3:58
Velasco, José María, 1:67
Velasco Alvarado, Juan, 3:214, **4:178–79**
Velasco Ibarra, José María, 2:92, 96
Velázquez, Diego de, 2:26, 27, 202
Velderrain, Fray Juan Bautista, 4:69
Velloso, José Mariano da Conceição, 2:117
Venables, Oliver Robert, 3:28
Venezuela, **4:179–86** *(map)*
Bolívar and liberation of, 1:111–12
boundary disputes of, 1:123
cacao production in, 1:147
Caracas, capital of, 1:157–58 *(illus.)*
colonial period in, 4:181
conquest of, 4:180–81
Cumaná, settlement of, 2:53
dictators, century of, 4:182–84
Dominican Republic and, 2:75
earthquakes in, 2:85 *(illus.)*
Federal War and, 2:122
geography of, 4:179
German settlers in, 2:168
Guzmán Blanco, president of, 2:194–95
independence struggle in, 4:181–82, 202
Miranda, revolutionary leader of, 3:131–32

Portuguese immigrants in, 4:12
since 1935, 4:185–86
slave rebellion in, 4:90
Veracruz, 2:142–43, **4:186**
Vera Cruz, Alonzo de la, 4:45
Vespucci, Amerigo, 1:91, 2:83, 114, 116 *(map)*, 3:83, 4:180, **4:186–87**
Viale, Pedro Blanes, 1:67
Vicente, Gil, 3:60
Viceroys and viceroyalties, **4:187–89** *(map)*
division into intendancies, 3:19
New Granada, 3:159
New Spain, 3:162
Peru, 3:216–17
Río de la Plata, 4:49–50
Toledo y Figueroa, 4:141–42
Victoria, Guadalupe, 3:113, 119
Vicuñas, 1:33
Vieira, Antônio, 3:60, **4:189–90**
Vilanova, María Cristina, 1:38
Vilar, Manuel, 1:66
Vilcabamba, lost Inca city of, 3:214
Villa, Francisco "Pancho," 3:111, 112, 121, **4:190–91** *(illus.)*, 4:216
Villa-Lobos, Heitor, 3:150, **4:191–92**
Villalpando, Cristóbal de, 1:64
Villarroel, Gualberto, 1:119
Viñes y Martorell, Benito, 4:81
Violencia, La, 1:98, 2:13, **4:192–94** *(illus.)*
Viracocha, 3:3, 4
Virgin Islands of the United States, 1:138, 160, **4:194**
Virgin of Guadalupe. *See* Guadalupe, Virgin of
Visconti, Elyseu d'Angelo, 1:67
Visitas, 2:153
"Visiting" relationship, 3:88
Volcanic belt, 2:167
Volcanoes, 2:166, 3:123, **4:194–95** *(illus.)*
Voltaire, 2:109
Voodoo, 4:40, 99, **4:195–96**
Voting rights, 4:118–19
Vulcanization, 1:25, 4:57

W

Walcott, Derek, **4:196**
Waldseemüller, Martin, 3:83, 4:187
Walker, William, 1:100, 166, 2:29, 3:2 *(illus.)*, 163–64, **4:196–97**
War of Restoration (1863), 2:74
War of the Knives (1799), 2:198, 201–2, 4:146
War of the League (1835), 2:28
War of the Mascates, **4:197**
War of the Pacific, 1:118, 123, 198, 3:213, **4:197–99** *(illus.)*
War of the Peru-Bolivia Confederation, 4:8, **4:200**
War of the Reform, 2:61, 3:35
War of the Spanish Succession, 2:131, 4:107
War of the Supremes (1839), 2:12
War of the Thousand Days, 2:12, **4:200**
War of the Triple Alliance, **4:200–202**
Asunción during, 1:78
Brazil and, 1:132
Humaitá as defense in, 2:218
Lima e Silva in, 3:57
López in, 3:67
Mitre in, 3:137
Paraguay and, 3:196

Index

Wars of independence, **4:**202–5
  American Revolution and, 1:27–29
  in Argentina, 1:51–52
  Bolívar and, 1:111–13 *(illus.)*
  in Bolivia, 1:118
  Boyacáa, battle of, 1:126
  in Brazil, 4:205
  in Caribbean, 4:204–5
  Catholic Church and, 1:173
  in Central America, 4:203–4
  in Chile, 1:195–96
  coins and coinage and, 2:6
  in Cuba, 3:70–71, 4:176
  Enlightenment and, 2:110
  Franciscans after, 4:43
  French influence on, 2:146
  gender and sexuality since, 2:163–64
  Germans and, 2:168
  Gran Colombia and, 2:172–73
  Haitian Revolution, 2:201–2
  immigration after, 2:227
  Indians' and blacks' status after, 4:32–33
  latifundia and, 3:50
  in Mexico, 4:203
  Miranda and, in Venezuela, 3:131–32
  Nariñ and, in Colombia, 3:153–54
  nationalism and, 3:156
  privateers and, 3:224
  rise of revolutionary activity, 4:202
  road development and, 2:210
  San Martín, leader during, 4:66–68
  Santander in, 4:74
  in South America, 4:202–3
  Ten Years' War and, 4:127–28
  theater and, 4:135–36
  universities following, 4:165
  in Uruguay, 1:72–73, 4:168–69
  Varela y Morales and Cuban, 4:176
  in Venezuela, 3:131–32, 4:181–82
  women and, 2:161, 4:208–9
Washington, George, 1:28
Washington Office on Latin America (WOLA), 2:220
Wasmosy, Juan Carlos, 3:198
Watermelon Riot, **4:**205
Water rights, U.S.–Mexico conflicts over, 4:162–63
Water Witch, USS, 3:196
Weapons industry, 4:205–6
Weaving, 2:36
Welfare of children, 1:193
Welles, Sumner, 2:172
Welsers, 4:180
West Africa, slaves from, 4:91, 93
West Africans, Islamic, 3:26
West Florida, 2:131–32
West-India Atlas, 1:161

West Indies. *See* Caribbean Antilles
West Indies Federation, 1:139, 3:29
Wetlands, 3:192–93
Whaling, 2:127–28
Wheat, 2:135
Wildlife. *See* Animals
Willemstad, Curaçao, 2:83
Wilson, Woodrow, 2:217, 3:111, 4:161, 190
Wind instruments, 3:152
Windward Islands, 1:160
Wine industry, **4:**206–7 *(illus.)*
Wixarika or Wixarite. *See* Huichols
Women, **4:**207–11. *See also specific women*
  in cinema, 1:206
  clothing of, 2:1, 2
  in Colombia, 2:9
  colonial, 4:208
  colonial justice system and, 2:39
  crimes against, 2:38
  in domestic labor/service, 2:71–72, 4:85
  in early 1900s, 4:209–10
  families headed by, 2:120
  gender roles and sexuality, 2:160–64
  household and, 2:119
  legal and civil changes for, 4:209–10
  Lutz and women's rights, 3:70
  marianismo and, 2:161
  in maroon society, 3:86
  marriage and divorce, 3:87, 88
  modern, 4:210–11
  pirates of Caribbean, 3:223, 224 *(illus.)*
  political activism and, 4:210
  pre-Columbian, 4:208
  in prostitution, 2:162–63
  social and economic role of, 1:215
  social and political change and, 4:210–11
  soldaderas, 4:97
  suffrage movement and, 4:119
  in universities, 4:166
  in wars of independence, 2:161, 4:208–9
  working, 4:209, 210–11
Women's movement, 4:210
Woolen textiles, 4:133
Work and workers. *See* Debt peonage; Labor and labor movements; Slavery
Working classes, 1:214
Working women, 4:209, 210–11
World Bank, 1:38, 3:7, 8
World Wars I and II, **4:**211–13
  air forces during, 1:85–86
  anti-German feelings during, 2:168
  Argentina and, 1:55
  banking business and, 1:99
  bracero program during, 1:126 *(illus.)*
  Brazil and, 1:134
  British–Latin American ties and, 1:138
  class structure changes after, 1:213

  communism before World War II, 2:15–16
  Good Neighbor Policy and, 2:172
  labor unrest and, 3:43
  U.S.–Latin American relations during, 4:161
  Uruguay during, 4:172
  Zimmerman Telegram and, 4:218
Writing, pre-Columbian, 3:80. *See also* Literature
Writ of amparo, 3:51–52

X

Xochimilco. *See* Mexico

Y

Yanaconas, **4:**213–14
Yáñez Pinzón, Vicente, 2:114, 4:121
Yanomami, **4:**214
Yawalapiti Indians of Brazil, 4:42 *(illus.)*
Yaws, 2:66
Yellow fever, 2:66, 131, 3:101, 4:81
Yrigoyen, Hipólito, 1:54, 3:206, 4:119, **4:**214–15
Yuca. *See* Manioc
Yucatán, **4:**215–16
  Belize, 1:104–6
  Caste War of Yucatán, 1:167–68
  Chichén Itzá on, 1:191
  Cortés' voyage to, 2:26–27
Yungas, 1:113
Yupanqui, Tito, 1:116

Z

Zambos, 4:32
Zanjón, Pact of (1878), 4:127
Zapata, Emiliano, 3:73, 111, 121, 4:190, 191 *(illus.)*, **4:**216–17
Zapatista Army of National Liberation (EZLN), 1:190, 4:62, 216
Zapatistas, messianic beliefs of, 3:108
Zapotecs, 2:51, 3:106, **4:**217
  archaeological study of, 1:40
  fiesta process, 2:124 *(illus.)*
  Mixtecs and, 3:138
  Monte Albán, capital of, 3:143–44
Zebu cattle, 3:65
Zedillo, Ernesto, 1:190, 3:122
Zeferina, 4:90
Zelaya, José Santos, 1:140, 3:164, **4:**217–18
Zimmerman Telegram, 1:164, **4:**218
Zumbi, 3:182
Zurbarán, Francisco de, 1:65